Repression, Resistance, and Democratic Transition in Central America

Central America

MEXICO

BELIZE
• Belmopan

GUATEMALA

Guatemala •

HONDURAS

• Tegucigalpa

EL SALVADOR
• San Salvador

NICARAGUA

Gulf of Fonseca

Managua •

CARIBBEAN SEA

• Corn Islands

PACIFIC OCEAN

COSTA RICA

• San José

PANAMÁ

• Panamá City

COLOMBIA

REPRESSION, RESISTANCE, AND DEMOCRATIC TRANSITION IN CENTRAL AMERICA

Edited by **THOMAS W. WALKER** and **ARIEL C. ARMONY**

A Scholarly Resources Inc. Imprint
Wilmington, Delaware

Scholarly Resources Inc.
104 Greenhill Avenue
Wilmington, DE 19805-1897
www.scholarly.com

Cover: The drawing on the paperback cover was created especially for this book by Leoncio Sáenz of Managua, Nicaragua. During the Sandinista revolution, Sáenz was a frequent artistic contributor to *Nicaráuac, Pensamiento Propio*, and other Nicaraguan publications. In addition, his works were hung in President Daniel Ortega's outer office and exhibited around the world.

Library of Congress Cataloging-in-Publication Data

Repression, resistance, and democratic transition in Central America / edited by Thomas W. Walker and Ariel C. Armony.
    p. cm. — (Latin American silhouettes)
   Includes index.
   ISBN 0-8420-2766-1 (cloth : alk. paper) — ISBN 0-8420-2768-8 (paper : alk. paper)
   1. Democracy—Central America. 2. Democratization—Central America. 3. Central America—Politics and government—1979–
I. Walker, Thomas W. II. Armony, Ariel C. III. Series.

JL1416.R47 2000
320.9728—dc21   00-029163

In memory of our dear friend

Ricardo Chavarría (1944–1999)

Christian and Sandinista, in the uncorrupted,

original sense of both words

About the Editors

THOMAS W. WALKER is professor of political science and director of Latin American Studies at Ohio University, Athens, Ohio. He is the author of *The Christian Democratic Movement in Nicaragua* (1970) and *Nicaragua: The Land of Sandino* (3d ed., 1991); the coauthor, with John A. Booth, of *Understanding Central America* (3d ed., 1999); and the editor/coauthor of six other books, including *Reagan versus the Sandinistas: The Undeclared War on Nicaragua* (which appeared on *Choice* magazine's 1987 list of Outstanding Academic Books) and *Nicaragua without Illusions: Regime Transition and Structural Adjustment in the 1990s* (1997).

Walker began his field research in Nicaragua in 1967. In 1982 he was part of the Central American Task Force of the United Presbyterian Church's Council on Church and Society. In 1984 he was founding co-chair of the Latin American Studies Association's (LASA) Task Force on Scholarly Relations with Nicaragua, and in 1984 and 1990 he was a member of LASA delegations observing Nicaragua's national elections. He observed Nicaragua's 1996 elections as part of a Hemispheric Initiatives/Washington Office on Latin America team. Walker holds a B.A. from Brown University and an M.A. and Ph.D. from the University of New Mexico.

ARIEL C. ARMONY is assistant professor of government at Colby College. He is the author of *Argentina, the United States, and the Anti-Communist Crusade in Central America, 1977–1984* (1997), also published in Argentina as *La Argentina, los Estados Unidos y la crusada anticomunista en América Central, 1977–1984* (1999).

Armony has received fellowships from the Woodrow Wilson Center, the Inter-American Foundation, and the Aspen Institute. His current research focuses on civil society and democratization, and he is in the final stages of producing a book tentatively titled *Social Capital and Democracy: Argentina in Comparative Perspective*. Armony holds a B.A. (*Licenciatura*) from the Universidad de Buenos Aires, Master's degrees from Ohio University and the University of Pittsburgh, and a Ph.D. from the University of Pittsburgh.

Acknowledgments

The editors wish to thank the Latin American Studies Association for scheduling back-to-back panels on our topic at its Twenty-first International Congress in Chicago in September 1998. These afforded most of the authors the opportunity to expose their preliminary findings to useful scholarly criticism and feedback. In addition, Thomas Walker wishes to express his gratitude to the Department of Political Science and the Latin American Studies Program at Ohio University for the support they gave in the form of travel funds, supplies, and so forth. Ariel Armony wishes to thank Dinorah Azpuru, Richard Stahler-Sholk, and Kurt Weyland for their feedback as well as Luisa Godoy, Gillian Morejon, and Mark Paustenbach for their research support.

Contents

Introduction
Concepts, Issues, and Background

Thomas W. Walker and Ariel C. Armony

For Central America the last third of the twentieth century was a time of dramatic change in which most of the countries there went from dictatorship to formal, political democracy. Especially during the late 1970s and 1980s, events in Central America were the focal point of U.S. cold war obsession and, for a while, the lead international story in the U.S. media. However, the Central American experience during this period is also important for the unusual set of cases of democratic transition it gave us. Unlike South America and many other parts of the world, where the rebirth of democracy in the 1980s and early 1990s was relatively sudden and peaceful, the process of democratic transition in most Central American countries was made possible only through violent conflict—costing over 350,000 lives[1]—that either toppled the dictatorships or forced them to negotiate transition to a more democratic system. The purpose of this book is to discuss Central American transitions to democracy and to see what these cases—especially the unusual ones—add to our understanding of democratization in the late twentieth century.

Defining Democracy

We have chosen to resist the temptation to adopt a single definition of democracy. This decision was based on the belief that to have done so would have straitjacketed the contributors, thus limiting the analytical and empirical richness of this project. Given the unique, conceptually rich features that Central America offers for the study of democratization, subsuming democracy under one definition would yield a reductionist framework, and most likely, we would have ended up adding another "adjective" to this already elusive concept when trying to describe these regimes.[2] For the purposes of conceptual precision, however, many of the authors in this volume make explicit their particular definition of democracy. A brief discussion of major theories of democracy will help the reader to situate the definitions used in the various chapters. (The notions of transition to democracy and democratic consolidation are discussed later in this introduction.)

As of this writing, the study of democratic transition in Latin America has drawn its conceptual apparatus largely from mainstream theories of democracy. Following the Schumpeterian tradition, many contemporary democratic theorists stress elections as a defining attribute of democracy.[3] These scholars endorse a minimalist definition, which considers the process of selecting elites through electoral competition to be at the heart of this type of political regime. This procedural definition of democracy has been widely used to study the so-called third wave of democratization, the global process of regime change that began in the mid 1970s, dramatically expanding the number of electoral democracies in the world.[4] When assessing whether a regime has become a democracy, these theorists use electoral competition as the measure.

This definition appears to be very useful because it allows scholars to treat democracy as a simple concept. Applied to Central America it seems to offer a parsimonious measure to identify the presence or absence of democratic rule. However, as several of the following chapters show, this emphasis on elections falls short of addressing the complexity of regime change in this region. An obvious illustration is the 1985 elections in Guatemala. While procedurally correct and undoubtedly useful in Guatemala's institutional development, these elections took place against a background of extreme repression and produced a civilian "government" that was essentially powerless relative to that country's entrenched military. Thus it is dubious that the country, as many U.S. apologists claimed at the time, had suddenly become a democracy simply as a result of holding those elections—however clean. Indeed, the simple equating of elections and democracy can often miss important issues such as those of the military veto, impunity for state agents, or a weak or largely inexistent rule of law.[5]

An alternative definition focuses on popular participation in decision-making processes.[6] Theorists concerned with participation argue that it is not the selection of leaders that defines democracy (that is, the rules and procedures governing electoral competition) but the range of values and mechanisms that allows for meaningful participation in the process of governance.[7] When contrasted with the restrictive version of democracy advanced by elite theories, participatory notions seem at first to provide a much more accurate framework for the study of democratization in Central America because they incorporate broader questions of citizenship, rights, and responsiveness. However, these theories, too, present problems for the study of existing democracies because, for instance, they tend to conceive of popular participation in ideal terms.[8]

Among numerous variations on the elite and participatory theories, as well as other attempts to advance original conceptualizations of democracy, two approaches deserve mention. One views democracy in procedural terms but incorporates a central condition that must be met by any polity to be considered democratic: "the extent to which the rule of law is effective across various kinds of issues, regions, and social actors, or equivalently, the extent to which full citizenship, civil and political, has been achieved by the entire adult population."[9] Different from this focus on the legal and institutional framework of democracy, another approach considers democracy as a regime that produces, through elections, governments that are endowed with the capacity to act, that is, to initiate and sustain policies. Therefore, what defines democracy according to this perspective is not the circulation of elites but the extent to which elected elites have latitude for decision making, which should be based on an institutionalized set of practices that link state and society.[10]

We prefer a conceptualization of democracy that goes beyond elections. Even though the implementation of free and fair electoral competition in Central America in the late 1980s or early 1990s was a significant contribution to democratization, analysis based exclusively on elections—as espoused by elite democratic theorists—fails to adequately critique the real nature of democracy in the region. Indeed, in some cases, political experience in Central America in this period clearly showed that "elections, in and of themselves, do not insure democracy."[11] This point is amply illustrated throughout this book.

The Birth of Democracy

It is also important to note that the processes by which democratic forms came into being in several Central American countries—notably Nicaragua, El Salvador, Guatemala, and Panama—might have implications for deepening democracy and that these implications might be different from those of other transitions that took place in other ways. For example, as a result of the Sandinista revolution, Nicaragua experienced, first, a transition to a form of popular democracy that emphasized direct participation through mass organizations (1979–1984) and, then, in 1984, another transition to a more traditional form of electoral democracy.[12] The Nicaraguan case thus challenges the conceptual models centered on "elite-dominated" transitions because its was "a transition from authoritarian rule by way of armed struggle . . . where the accommodation of elite interests [did] not take precedence over the goal of social and economic democracy."[13] In addition, Nicaragua's "second" transition toward electoral democracy—which eventually led to the defeat of the Sandinistas and the peaceful transfer of power to the opposition in 1990—was mainly a response to U.S. aggression and economic crisis rather than a move toward the deepening of democratic rule (or democratic consolidation).[14] Therefore, Nicaragua offers a case of "two transitions" that does not fit neatly within the traditional paradigm.[15]

The cases analyzed in this volume raise questions about the behavior and values of elites and masses in the transition to and in the deepening of democracy. On one hand, we have to look at elite actors (government and opposition) and their role in democratization processes. The cases of El Salvador and Guatemala, for instance, are important in understanding how stalemate in a civil war leads to a democratic transition.[16] Was democracy a second-best compromise for actors who were not, in principle, committed to this kind of regime (at least in terms of pluralism)?[17] On the other hand, it is necessary to consider the role of mobilization "from below" in the transitions to democracy. Were the transitions in the 1990s a result of over four decades of reformist mass mobilization (forcefully resisted by the United States and right-wing domestic elites)?[18] Significantly, several of the chapters in this book place emphasis on the role of popular participation in Central America's democratization processes, a major element that has not been sufficiently studied by most of the transitions literature, which has focused on pacts and bargaining among elites.

The cases of Nicaragua, El Salvador, and Guatemala show that (1) political violence played a central role in the transition of these countries to democracy, (2) these conflicts shaped the democratic transitions, and (3) the particular nature of these transitions affected the institutionalization of democratic practices. This last point is linked, in turn, to the previous problem of defining democracy. Did these transitions produce systems of rule based on mass citizenship? Or did they result in "hybrid" regimes primarily defined by "procedurally correct elections"?[19]

In all the cases studied in this volume, external actors, particularly the United States (Chapter 7) and the Organization of American States and United Nations (Chapter 8) had a significant impact on democratization processes. Whereas U.S. involvement in civil wars was critical in Nicaragua, El Salvador, and Guatemala, the United States exerted strong political influence in Honduras, a vulnerable country that it used as a military base for the Contra war on Nicaragua.[20] The anti-Sandinista war also led to increasing U.S. involvement in Costa Rican affairs.[21] And the United States imposed electoral democracy in Panama through military force in 1989.

One of the major topics addressed in this book is the relationship between neoliberalism and democracy. "Neoliberalism" (Chapter 10) is the label often given to the economic policies that were widespread in Latin America in the late twentieth century. Having an almost religious faith in the virtues of the free market, neoliberals advocated the privatization of government enterprises, the creation of sound currencies through balanced budgets and the reduction of government expenditures, and promotion of international trade through the abolition of tariffs and other barriers. Critics of neoliberalism, however, noted that the implementation of these policies tended to exacerbate problems of poverty and income inequality (Chapter 10) much in the way late-nineteenth- and early-twentieth- century "liberalism" (discussed later in this introduction) had done. Throughout this book, attention is given to the question of whether market-oriented reform diminishes the quality of democracy. Interestingly, at the close of the twentieth century, this question was highly significant for Costa Rica's older democracy as well as for the newly democratic regimes in Central America. Also, a concern with neoliberal reform brings us back to the problem of democratization in revolutionary settings. The question of democracy in Central America in the 1990s was intimately connected to the persistent, structural problem of social and economic inequality. Indeed, it seemed probable that, if this problem were not addressed, the "underlying causes of these revolutions . . . could resurface to undermine the stability of even elected governments."[22] Economics, therefore, was critical to democratization in this region at the end of the 1990s.

Finally, even though we use the concept of "transition" to refer to the end of authoritarian rule and the establishing of political democracy, we acknowledge that this concept is highly problematic because it presupposes "two polar regime types of authoritarianism and democracy."[23] Indeed, as of this writing, in most of Central America, democratic institutions (for instance, national and local authorities selected through free and fair elections) coexisted with authoritarian behavior of state agents, a largely ineffective and biased justice system, and a system of interest intermediation giving precedence to informal connections (mainly corruption) over institutional rules.[24] Similarly, the notion of democratic consolidation is questionable because (1) it circumscribes political processes to predetermined patterns of change, (2) it defines democracy negatively, that is, not for its positive traits but for what it lacks, and (3) it implies a teleological course often modeled on the paradigmatic case of established industrial democracies.[25]

In general, we prefer to use the concept of "democratization," understood in the broader sense of a *process* of constituting a democratic regime. This concept emphasizes the sustainability of democratic institutions, unrestricted electoral participation, inclusion of previously marginalized social groups, expansion of elite and mass consensus around competitive politics, and the effective implementation of the rule of law.[26] Our stress on the notion of process is important because, as this was being written, Central America had experienced limited changes in the direction of democratization beyond the implementation of competitive elections.

An important feature of this book is the belief that processes of democratization cannot be properly understood without attention to nation-specific political development. This is why the country chapters in this volume (Chapters 1–6) introduce major themes in the social, political, and economic history of these nations. Too much of the literature on democracy in Latin America has a strong ahistorical bent. We believe that a historically framed analysis of political change in Central America in the late twentieth century, placed in a global and regional context (discussed in Part II, "Forces"), can contribute to our understanding of the complex phenomenon of democracy in these countries.

Defining Central America

Before moving into the main body of this book, it is also important to define what we mean by "Central America." The most widely accepted definition of Central America would be that it is comprised of six countries: Belize, Guatemala, El Salvador, Honduras, Nicaragua, and Costa Rica. However, readers of this book will immediately notice that we have taken the liberty of dropping Belize and including Panama. Our reasons, quite simply, are pragmatic: Belize is an English-speaking microstate that shares practically none of the social and political experiences held in common by the other five countries. Further, having peacefully received its independence from Great Britain in 1981, it is less relevant for our focus on democratic transitions. Panama, on the other hand, though part of the South American country of Colombia until the United States helped it become "independent" in 1903, is, nevertheless, located on the Isthmus of Central America and is sometimes lumped with Central America. This gives us a tenuous excuse to include it in our book—something we were anxious to do in the first place because it offers an interesting and unusual case of democratic transition. Thus, in this volume, the composition of "Central America" is, at least to some degree, a matter of expediency rather than of definitional purity.

The Early History of Central America

This brings us to the final subject that needs to be examined before we enter the main body of the book: the early history of Central America. Again we run into the matter of Panama versus the other five. Whereas its five neighbors to the north share a common history from the conquest to the formation of individual states in 1838 and while each of them has a long national history, Panama is both separate from that common experience and lacking in a long national history.

Panama

The most striking characteristic of Panama always has been its geographic position. Throughout the colonial period and in the nineteenth century as an isolated part of Colombia, Panama was of importance as a convenient site for overland transit between the Caribbean and the Pacific. During the colonial period, a small economic elite, dependent on international trade within the Spanish Empire, dominated Panama's tiny population. In the nineteenth century the California Gold Rush accentuated the importance of the province of Panama in transisthmian transit. Given these economic interests and the lack of good, tillable land, and, hence, a landed elite, Panama tended to side with the Liberal cause (see below) in Colombia's nineteenth-century conflicts between Liberals and Conservatives. Accordingly, when Colombia's late nineteenth-century civil wars debilitated the Liberals, the small Panamanian elite—which already felt isolated from Bogotá geographically—pushed for independence. In 1903, after failing to obtain a treaty from Colombia for a U.S. canal through the province of Panama, the United States—previously opposed to Panamanian separation—not only encouraged independence but actively guaranteed it by sending naval forces into the region to block the landing of Colombian military units sent to put down the rebels. As a result, Panama's elite won independence and the United States got its canal.

Not surprisingly, the history of Panama—first as an isolated province of Colombia and then as a virtual protectorate of the United States—features concerns with national identity that persisted throughout its short national period. As Steve Ropp argues in Chapter 6, these concerns affected politics and challenged the emergence of democracy—beyond elections—throughout the twentieth century.

The Original Five

Panama's five neighbors to the north shared a common history from the time of the Spanish Conquest through the first third of the nineteenth century—first, under a central Spanish Imperial administration, then, as part of Mexico (1822–23) and, finally, as the United Provinces of Central America (1823–1838). To some extent, this experience forged a common identity—even a sort of Central American nationalism.[27] However, very early on, variations within that common experience molded social and political differences that would be passed down to the late twentieth century—differences that would account for the violent explosions in Guatemala, El Salvador, and Nicaragua, on one hand, and the relative stability of Honduras and Costa Rica, on the other.

The Common History of the Original Five

The first important and formative difference within the common experience was the manner in which the future countries were conquered and colonized. Whereas the areas that are today Guatemala, El Salvador, Honduras, and Nicaragua were colonized within the first two decades after the Spanish first penetrated the region in 1522, Costa Rica was not conquered until the 1560s. Though the indigenous population resisted everywhere, they were more quickly subdued and controlled in the northern countries. The vast majority of the original inhabitants of those countries died off through contact with European diseases or by being exported into slavery,[28] and the surviving demoralized minority soon succumbed to Spanish domination. In Costa Rica, however, local indigenous populations resisted the Conquest and in the end were either killed outright or driven out of the fertile central highlands where the Spaniards wished to settle. In the long run, this meant that the Spaniards in Costa Rica had no racially distinct underclass to use as virtual slaves as did the elites in the colonies to the north. Accordingly, from the start, Costa Rica had a relatively more egalitarian society—albeit not for the best of reasons—while Guatemala, El Salvador, and Nicaragua quickly developed very divided societies in which a tiny Spanish elite ruled over a much larger nonwhite underclass.

Honduras, an economic backwater from the conquest through much of the twentieth century, escaped developing a tradition of extreme class exploitation simply because it never attracted or developed the type of self-confident, powerful elite that quickly came to dominate its three neighbors. Thus, paradoxically, the poorest of the Central American republics would have a relatively less repressive political system, less violence, and, hence, more stability than its immediate neighbors.

Another important result of the Conquest and colonial period was the externalization of the economy. Before the arrival of the Spaniards, the millions of indigenous peoples living in the area had engaged in labor-intensive farming. The common people grew corn, beans, squash, and peppers on land consigned to them by their local chiefs or caciques. Though they had to pay part of their crop in tribute to the chief, they were able to use the rest for consumption in their homes or for barter within the region. However, after the depopulation caused by the conquest, most of the farmland reverted to jungle and the economy became externally oriented. Using the surviving native peoples to do the labor, the Spaniards now produced cattle products (hides, tallow, and dried beef), gold, silver, timber, and dyes for export. Especially in Guatemala, El Salvador, and Nicaragua, this type of exploitative economy concentrated riches in the hands of the tiny European population. Down through the centuries the economies of Central America would be typified by production for export and neglect of the internal consumption needs of the majority.

Independence came to Central America in a relatively bloodless fashion. When Mexico declared independence in 1821, Central America did so, too. From 1822 to 1823 it was actually part of Mexico. In 1823, however, all of the former Central American colonies, except Chiapas, split from that larger state to form the United Provinces of Central America. That union dissolved in 1838, thus producing the five Spanish-speaking states we know today.

Probably the most important feature of the national period from 1838 into the first half of the twentieth century was the emergence and eventual resolution of a dispute between two major elite factions, the Conservatives and the Liberals. Before independence and for a while afterward, Conservatives espoused authoritarian, centralized government, centrally regulated economies, and a continuation of the special privileges enjoyed by the Catholic Church. Liberals, on the other hand, advocated decentralized government, limited representative democracy, the separation of church and state, and free trade and the abolition of most economic regulation. (It is very important that readers familiar with U.S. politics not confuse the way "liberal" is used in the United States with its very different—in some senses, opposite—usage in Latin America. Especially, as regards economic policy, Latin American Liberals were—and are—more like U.S. "conservatives.")

Throughout most of the nineteenth century, Conservatives battled Liberals for control of the state. During the first few decades, the Conservatives generally retained power. Then, starting early in the second half of the century, Liberals eventually replaced them. The triumph of the Liberals—or of their ideas[29]—was a disaster for the average citizen of the region. Anxious to "modernize" their economies and take personal advantage of new international demand for products such as coffee and bananas, the ruling elites implemented the so-called Liberal reforms. Under these, ownership of land was recognized by the state only if it was individually held and certified in a legal deed. In practice, this meant that indigenous communal holdings, as well as the land held by peasants through common law but without formal deed, was suddenly property of the state that could be sold to modern agricultural entrepreneurs. Thus, in one fell swoop, most peasants—indigenous and mestizo[30] alike—found themselves uprooted from the land they had cultivated for generations. To make matters worse, the Liberal reforms also had a "modernizing" bias that, while outlawing the cultivation of the peasant staple crop plantain,[31] provided a cash incentive for the planting of each coffee tree. And, as if that were not enough, there were new vagrancy laws that effectively forced the recently uprooted—and therefore "vagrant"—peasants to take employment on the new agro-export plantations. There they were quickly enslaved through a system of debt peonage involving payment in script that could be spent only at company stores but was rarely sufficient to keep the worker from going into debt. Thus, the implementation of the Liberal reforms, especially in Guatemala, El Salvador, and Nicaragua, simply accentuated already extreme social disparities.

The Individual Histories

A perusal of the individual histories of the five original Central American countries in their first hundred odd years of independence yields a dramatic contrast between Honduras and Costa Rica, on one hand, and Guatemala, El Salvador, and Nicaragua, on the other. The former were far more stable and respectful of human rights than were the latter.

Honduras

Honduras, as noted above, seems paradoxically to have been blessed by its lack of natural resources. Unlike neighboring countries, Honduras did not develop a coffee industry until after the Second World War. Banana cultivation, which emerged late in the nineteenth century, was foreign run. Thus the native economic elite was sufficiently weak that it appears to have been forced to be more respectful of the rights of the poor than was true elsewhere. Honduran governments, though normally not democratic, tended to allow greater civil rights than was true just across the border. Gradually, the strongest labor movement in the region emerged and, on various occasions, the government sided with the unions against foreign employers.

In addition, the Honduran party system did not really develop until well into the twentieth century. There were no nineteenth-century "Liberal reforms." Early plantation agriculture (bananas) occurred in basically unoccupied territory. Since peasants seeking land could find it in abundance elsewhere, there were no significant land problems. Finally, with little need to repress the poor majority, the Honduran army remained weak until well into the twentieth century.

Much of this began to change after the 1950s. Obsessed with cold war phantoms, the United States, from the Kennedy administration onward, began promoting a rapid buildup in the Honduran military. At the same time, the cultivation of coffee and other export products put new pressure on the land. But even these changes did not drastically alter a political tradition that, though not very democratic, made the Honduran system stand out as much more accommodative and nonconfrontational than that of its three closest neighbors.

Costa Rica

The other country with a relatively nonviolent tradition is Costa Rica. Though most of its governments during the first century of independence were not democratic, the seeds of democracy were already being sowed. Immediately after independence, dictator Braulio Carillo (1835–1842) significantly increased the number of small farmers by distributing municipal lands to inhabitants. Then, contrary to trends elsewhere, where large landholders were encouraged to grow coffee, he promoted the cultivation of coffee by small farmers. Later in the century, Liberal dictator Tomás Guardia (1870–1882) confiscated the properties of some large landholders and exiled a number of their leaders. Guardia and some of his successors also promoted public education. The result of all this is that Costa Rica entered the twentieth century as the only majority literate society in Central America and the only one with a large and robust class of small farmers.

With this large class of educated freeholders, Costa Rica gradually began to develop democracy. At the end of the century angry citizens forced the military to respect an opposition electoral victory it was inclined at first to overturn. In the decade from 1905 through 1914, Presidents Cleto González Víquez and Ricardo Jiménez Oreamuno established direct popular elections, expanded suffrage, and allowed free and open campaigning. Though dictatorship and military rule would recur in the first several decades of the twentieth century, the forces of democracy were growing, thus setting the stage for the 1948 transition to democracy described in Chapter 5.

Nevertheless, Costa Rica and Honduras were exceptions to the regional pattern. In Guatemala, El Salvador, and Nicaragua, extraordinarily unequal class structures and traditions of powerful, arbitrary, socially irresponsible elites were inherited from the conquest and colonial period and accentuated by the Liberal reforms and even more socially irresponsible dictatorships during the first century after independence.

Guatemala

In Guatemala the Liberals, who took control in 1871, dominated the country, with minor exceptions and with no democracy, until the 1940s. Almost immediately, the Liberal reforms opened indigenous and Church communal lands to the "modern" cultivation of coffee by large landholders and forced the poor, indigenous majority into virtual slave labor. At the end of the century, the United Fruit Company took over an incipient national banana industry and built a transportation infrastructure that served its interests. In the first decades of the new century, banana and coffee production inexorably expanded, thus dispossessing more and more poor farmers and turning them into debt peons. This whole process was overseen by Liberal strongmen such as the brutal Manuel Estrada Cabrera (1898–1920) (immortalized in Nobel laureate Miguel Angel Asturias's chilling novel *El Señor Presidente*) and, finally, Jorge Ubico (1931–1944). The latter modernized his country's vagrancy laws so that the government could force the poor to work a few days a year for the state. In the 1940s, as fascism was being defeated in Europe, labor and the middle class took the initiative to call for the birth of political democracy in their own country and the military, rather than confront the protestors, chose to support that call. Ubico was ousted and elections were called in 1944. Thus began the process of reform, repression, resistance, and democratic transition described in Chapter 1.

El Salvador

El Salvador experienced an equally grim first century of independence. There, the Liberals were in control throughout the entire period except for brief interludes when Conservative dictators were imposed by neighboring Guatemala. The Liberal reforms, which came early and incrementally to El Salvador, were in full force by the latter half of the century, thus opening land and providing labor for the burgeoning coffee industry. The process continued well into the twentieth century. Indeed, one newspaper editor wrote in 1929 that "the conquest of territory by the coffee industry is alarming. It . . . is now descending into the valleys displacing maize, rice and beans. It is extended like the conquistador, spreading hunger and misery, reducing former proprietors to the worst conditions."[32] As a result of this process, the country developed a small, extremely wealthy elite commonly dubbed the "Fourteen Families," who ruled for their own benefit over a vast impoverished underclass. When the Great Depression hit in the 1930s and workers were forced to absorb much of the resultant economic hardship, peasant uprisings led by charismatic Marxist Agustín Farabundo Martí broke out. These were brutally suppressed in the bloody massacre of 1931–32, which took over thirty thousand lives. From then until the 1980s guerrilla insurgency of the Farabundo Martí Front for National Liberation (Chapter 2), El Salvador would experience direct military rule cycling over and over from brutally repressive to apparently moderate regimes.

Nicaragua

The first century of the national period was equally disastrous for most Nicaraguans. However, in Nicaragua, domestic problems were dramatically compounded by foreign interventions. In the 1850s an American soldier of fortune, William Walker, who had been invited by the Liberals to help them defeat the Conservatives, soon betrayed his Nicaraguan hosts and declared himself to be president, slavery to be legal once again, and English to be the official language. Though Walker was soon defeated and executed, the Liberals were so tainted by their association with him that they could not return to power until 1893. Even so (showing that history is not always as neat as we intellectuals might wish), the Conservative elite implemented the Liberal reforms in the 1870s. Under the presidency of Pedro Joaquín Chamorro, communal and untitled peasant lands were declared open, "vagrancy" was made illegal, and the cultivation of plantain was outlawed.[33] Many of the displaced poor subsequently rose up in the war of the Comuneros of 1881. But, after massacring over five thousand indigenous people, the government restored order and coffee was free to expand as it had elsewhere. Thus the Liberal return to power did not change much—at least not in the eyes of the poor. The Liberal reforms were reinforced, agro-export received even greater emphasis, and a modern infrastructure was built.

Interestingly, however, when the nationalist Liberal dictator José Santos Zelaya first refused the United States concessionary transisthmian canal rights in the late nineteenth century but later began canal negotiations with

European and Japanese interests, Washington moved against the upstart leader. In 1909 a Conservative rebellion was encouraged and then (as in Panama in 1903), when the government tried to put down the rebellion, Washington moved a naval force into the area to impose its will. The resultant Conservative government was able to hold power on its own only until 1912, at which point a nearly successful Liberal insurgency triggered a direct U.S. military intervention that, with one brief interlude in the mid 1920s, would last until the end of 1932. During the second half of this twenty-year period, the U.S. Marines and their surrogate "Nicaraguan National Guard" would fight a long and, ultimately, unsuccessful counterinsurgency campaign against the "Crazy Little Army" of nationalist guerrilla leader Augusto César Sandino. Though the marines were forced to leave in the 1930s, the first Nicaraguan commander of the national guard, Anastasio Somoza García, soon used that position to found a dynastic dictatorship that, with the intermittent backing of Washington, would exploit and agonize the Nicaraguan people until it was destroyed by the Sandinista revolution in 1979 (Chapter 4).

Overview

Thus, while one set of historical developments made violent revolution virtually inevitable in Guatemala, El Salvador, and Nicaragua, others would allow less violent transition in Costa Rica and Honduras. The focus of the chapters that follow is on the dramatic change that took place in Central America in the second half of the twentieth century. The first six chapters examine the recent background to and nature of the democratic transitions in the five historically Central American countries as well as the newcomer, Panama. Then, the five subsequent chapters examine the forces involved in this process of change. The conclusion reflects on the significance and uniqueness of the Central American experience.

The chapters in Part I, on countries, expose five distinct types of transition, most of them involving violence. The first and so far most successful is that of Costa Rica described in Chapter 5. There, a short period of civil war in 1948 installed a democratic system and welfare state, the roots of which had been growing for some time. Another model (described in Chapter 4) is that of Nicaragua, which passed from dictatorship to a period of revolutionary government during which both participatory and formal electoral democracy were implemented. Even after the revolution was voted out of office, the legacies of both participatory and formal democracy would remain strong. A third model is that seen in both Guatemala (Chapter 1) and El Salvador (Chapter 2), where entrenched, U.S.-backed dictatorships were challenged by insurgent groups and ultimately forced to negotiate a transition to formal democracy and greater respect for civil rights. In those countries too, organs of civil society developed during the struggle against the dictatorships would retain an important role in postwar political systems. A fourth mode of transition, described in Chapter 6, occurred in Panama, where electoral democracy was imposed through foreign military intervention. The fifth model is that of Honduras (Chapter 3), which seemed to follow extra-regional pressures and regional trends as it went from relatively mild dicta-torship prior to the 1980s to a very repressive military regime behind a facade of civilian government in the early 1980s, to gradually less repres-sive rule later in the decade to a tentative transition to civilian democratic rule in the 1990s. In all, late-twentieth-century Central America, with its five distinct models, is a remarkably rich laboratory for the study of demo-cratic transition and ongoing democratization.

The chapters in Part II focus on different forces involved in the Central American drama of the late twentieth century. First, Chapters 7 and 8 look at external actors affecting the region. Chapter 7 examines the role of other states—especially, but not exclusively, the United States—while Chapter 8 focuses on the United Nations and the Organization of American States, notably their important role in promoting and consolidating peace. Next, Chapter 9 describes the rich and varied ways in which politics and religion interacted during this period to cause dramatic changes in both. Chapter 10 then analyzes the nature of neoliberal economics in Central America and raises concerns about its compatibility with democratization. Finally, Chap-ter 11 delves into the rich subject of civil society and its role in the process of democratization in the region.

Notes

1. As the chapters in Part I document, over 200,000 died in Guatemala, 75,000 in El Salvador, around 80,000 (in two conflicts) in Nicaragua, and hundreds in Honduras.

2. See David Collier and Steven Levitsky, "Democracy with Adjectives: Con-ceptual Innovation in Comparative Research," *World Politics* 49, no. 3 (April 1997): 430–51. For a useful analysis of the concept of democracy, see Philippe C. Schmitter and Terry Lynn Karl, "What Democracy Is . . . and Is Not," *Journal of Democracy* 2, no. 2 (Summer 1991): 75–88.

3. Joseph A. Schumpeter, *Capitalism, Socialism, and Democracy* (New York: Harper, 1942). See Robert A. Dahl, *Polyarchy: Participation and Opposition* (New Haven: Yale University Press, 1971).

4. Samuel P. Huntington, *The Third Wave: Democratization in the Late Twenti-eth Century* (Norman: University of Oklahoma Press, 1991).

5. For a concise discussion of elite theories of democracy in the Latin Ameri-can context, see, for instance, John A. Booth, "Introduction. Elections and Democ-racy in Central America: A Framework for Analysis," in Mitchell A. Seligson and John A. Booth, eds., *Elections and Democracy in Central America, Revisited* (Chapel Hill: University of North Carolina Press, 1995), 3–4; William I. Robinson, *Promot-ing Polyarchy: Globalization, US Intervention*, and Hegemony (Cambridge, En-gland: Cambridge University Press, 1996), 49–52; Carlos M. Vilas, "Participation,

Inequality, and the Whereabouts of Democracy," in Douglas A. Chalmers et al., eds., *The New Politics of Inequality in Latin America: Rethinking Participation and Representation* (New York: Oxford University Press, 1997), 8–13; Kurt von Mettenheim and James Malloy, "Introduction" and "Conclusion," in Kurt von Mettenheim and James Malloy, eds., *Deepening Democracy in Latin America* (Pittsburgh: University of Pittsburgh Press, 1998), 5–7, 173–74.

6. See Carol Pateman, *Participation and Democratic Theory* (Cambridge, England: Cambridge University Press, 1970).

7. For a brief discussion of participatory theories of democracy in the Latin American setting, see, for example, Booth, "Introduction," 5–7; von Mettenheim and Malloy, "Conclusion," 173–74. See also Vilas, "Participation, Inequality, and the Whereabouts of Democracy," 19–21.

8. von Mettenheim and Malloy, "Introduction," 2.

9. Guillermo O'Donnell, "Polyarchies and the (Un)Rule of Law in Latin America: A Partial Conclusion," in Juan E. Méndez, Guillermo O'Donnell, and Paulo Sérgio Pinheiro, eds., *The (Un)Rule of Law and the Underprivileged in Latin America* (South Bend, IN: University of Notre Dame Press, 1999), 307.

10. von Mettenheim and Malloy, "Introduction," 3, 6, 11; and "Conclusion," 181.

11. Richard Stahler-Sholk, "El Salvador's Negotiated Transition: From Low-Intensity Conflict to Low-Intensity Democracy," *Journal of Interamerican Studies and World Affairs* 36, no. 4 (Winter 1994): 43.

12. Philip J. Williams, "Dual Transitions from Authoritarian Rule: Popular and Electoral Democracy in Nicaragua," *Comparative Politics* 26, no. 2 (January 1994): 169–85.

13. Ibid., 171.

14. See Guillermo O'Donnell, "Transitions, Continuities, and Paradoxes," in Scott Mainwaring, Guillermo O'Donnell, and J. Samuel Valenzuela, eds., *Issues in Democratic Consolidation: The New South American Democracies in Comparative Perspective* (South Bend, IN: University of Notre Dame Press, 1992), 17–56.

15. The literature on transitions to democracy in Latin America is vast. Two of the most widely cited works are Guillermo O'Donnell, Philippe C. Schmitter, and Laurence Whitehead, eds., *Transitions from Authoritarian Rule: Prospects for Democracy*, 4 vols. (Baltimore: Johns Hopkins University Press, 1986); and James M. Malloy and Mitchell A. Seligson, eds., *Authoritarians and Democrats: Regime Transition in Latin America* (Pittsburgh: University of Pittsburgh Press, 1987).

16. See the case studies on El Salvador and Guatemala in Cynthia J. Arnson, ed., *Comparative Peace Processes in Latin America* (Washington, DC, and Stanford: Woodrow Wilson Center Press and Stanford University Press, 1999).

17. See Dankwart A. Rustow, "Transitions to Democracy," *Comparative Politics* 2 (April 1970): 337–63; Scott Mainwaring, "Transitions to Democracy and Democratic Consolidation: Theoretical and Comparative Issues," in Mainwaring, O'Donnell, and Valenzuela, *Issues in Democratic Consolidation*, 308–12.

18. William A. Barnes, "Incomplete Democracy in Central America: Polarization and Voter Turnout in Nicaragua and El Salvador," *Journal of Interamerican Studies and World Affairs* 40, no. 3 (Fall 1998): 66–67.

19. Ibid., 65. See Terry Lynn Karl, "The Hybrid Regimes of Central America," *Journal of Democracy* 6, no. 3 (July 1995): 72–86.

20. See Donald E. Schulz and Deborah Sundloff Schulz, *The United States, Honduras, and the Crisis in Central America* (Boulder, CO: Westview Press, 1994).

21. See Martha Honey, *Hostile Acts: U.S. Policy in Costa Rica in the 1980s* (Gainesville: University Press of Florida, 1994).

22. Stahler-Sholk, "El Salvador's Negotiated Transition," 44.

23. Mainwaring, "Transitions to Democracy and Democratic Consolidation," 296; quotation from von Mettenheim and Malloy, "Conclusion," 175.

24. Vilas, "Participation, Inequality, and the Whereabouts of Democracy," 9–19. See also Guillermo O'Donnell, "On the State, Democratization, and Some Conceptual Problems: A Latin American View with Glances at Some Postcommunist Countries," *World Development* 21, no. 8 (August 1993): 1355–69; Kurt Weyland, "The Politics of Corruption in Latin America," *Journal of Democracy* 9, no. 2 (April 1998): 108–21.

25. von Mettenheim and Malloy, "Conclusion," 175; Guillermo O'Donnell, "Illusions about Consolidation," *Journal of Democracy* 7, no. 2 (April 1996): 39; Collier and Levitsky, "Democracy with Adjectives," 430–31, 443. On democratic consolidation, see, for instance, Juan J. Linz and Alfred Stepan, *Problems of Democratic Transition and Consolidation: Southern Europe, South America, and Post-Communist Europe* (Baltimore: Johns Hopkins University Press, 1996); Larry Diamond, Marc F. Plattner, Yun-han Chu, and Hung-mao Tien, eds., *Consolidating the Third Wave Democracies* (Baltimore: Johns Hopkins University Press, 1997).

26. Karen L. Remmer, "Democratization in Latin America," in Robert O. Slater, Barry M. Schutz, and Steven R. Dorr, eds., *Global Transformation and the Third World* (Boulder, CO: Lynne Rienner, 1993), 92–95; O'Donnell, "Polyarchies and the (Un)Rule of Law in Latin America," 303–26; Barnes, "Incomplete Democracy in Central America," 63–68.

27. See "The Common History" in John A. Booth and Thomas W. Walker, *Understanding Central America* (Boulder, CO: Westview Press, 1999), 20–24. For instance, even during the tensions of the 1980s, all automobile license plates in the region listed the name of the country at the top, as well as "América Central" at the bottom.

28. For a sense of how the conquest affected Nicaragua, for example, see Thomas W. Walker, *Nicaragua: The Land of Sandino* (Boulder, CO: Westview Press, 1991), 10–11.

29. Later in this chapter we show that, although Liberals did not actually come to power in Nicaragua until the 1890s, the "Liberal reforms" sweeping the region were so persuasive and advantageous to the elites—regardless of party—that they were actually implemented there under Conservative regimes before the formal change in party rule.

30. "Mestizo," which formally means people of mixed Indian and European blood, is used in Latin America as a cultural term to cover not only people of mixed blood but also indigenous peoples who have adopted the mainstream language and culture.

31. A member of the banana family, plantain is a starchy staple that—fried or boiled—is basic to the diet of many poor Latin Americans.

32. As quoted in Tommie Sue Montgomery, *Revolution in El Salvador: Origins and Evolution* (Boulder, CO: Westview Press, 1982), 46. See also the second edition of this book (1995).

33. For details about this period in Nicaragua, see Walker, "The Early History," in *Nicaragua*, 9–23.

I

The Countries

1

Guatemala
Intervention, Repression, Revolt, and Negotiated Transition

Susanne Jonas and Thomas W. Walker

In the second half of the twentieth century, Guatemala experienced a unique dynamic of structural problems that gave rise to popular and revolutionary movements. These, in turn, provoked responses by repressive forces that blocked rebels and reformists in pursuit of their goals. In the long run, however, counterinsurgent forces proved unable to address the sources of revolt, to triumph definitively over them, or to control the social forces unleashed by chronic crisis. This dynamic was expressed in Guatemala's thirty-six-year civil war, the longest and bloodiest in the hemisphere, leaving over two hundred thousand civilians dead or "disappeared," primarily among the highlands Maya population.[1] It was a "cold war civil war" that was ideologically, politically, and militarily part of the U.S. confrontation with the Soviet Union and Third World communist forces (real or labeled as such).[2] However, in the 1990s, with the cold war over and the political-military stalemate showing no signs of breaking, Guatemalan elites—with U.S. backing—finally agreed to a negotiated settlement. Though it was far too early at the time of this writing to be certain, this prolonged process of repression, revolt and mobilization, and negotiation seemed to have opened up a democratic transition.

Looking back, the Revolution of 1944–1954 (see below) and its overthrow created the conditions for the civil war's first phase: the armed insurgency during the early 1960s (inspired also by the Cuban Revolution), and

Much of the material in this chapter was adapted from chapters in Susanne Jonas, *Of Centaurs and Doves: Guatemala's Peace Process* (Boulder, CO: Westview Press, 2000).

the ferocious response of 1966–1968, when, under U.S. tutelage, Guatemala's army was shaped into the first counterinsurgency army of Latin America. The second phase of the war reached genocidal proportions in the early 1980s and consolidated the counterinsurgency state.

As a consequence of the war, electoral politics came to have very little meaning in the normal sense. All political arrangements from 1954 until the mid 1990s were dominated by the coalition between the army and economic elites; they were based on an explicit rejection of reformist options and political exclusion of large sectors of the population. Even the return of elected civilian government in the late 1980s did not signify a return to democracy in any real sense, nor did it address any of the glaring social-economic disparities. Hence, the popular and indigenous majorities of the population were not able to seek redress of grievances through electoral means. Instead, they pressured through extraparliamentary (mainly unarmed) organizations that the army and government deemed "subversive" and subjected to levels of repression unmatched anywhere in Latin America.

The vicious cycle of war and exclusionary politics continued for several decades. While the army twice dealt the revolutionary movement nearly fatal blows (in 1966–1968 and in 1981–1983), it was unable to prevent guerrilla resurgence in the late 1980s. Like its historic enemy, the counterinsurgency army, the insurgent movement had to learn through bitter mistakes and several times was reborn from its own ashes. At the same time, the revolutionary movement underwent profound crises and redefinitions of strategy, leading to its subsequent initiatives for a negotiated end to the war.

Antecedents: U.S. Intervention and Its Aftermath

Under the weight of the economic and social crises caused by the world depression of the 1930s, Guatemala's neocolonial order cracked in 1944, when a broad middle- and working-class coalition overthrew military dictator Jorge Ubico. Thus was initiated the Revolution of 1944–1954, the only genuinely democratic experience in Guatemala's entire history. (For a listing of Guatemalan administrations, by type, see table). The governments of Juan José Arévalo (1945–1950) and Jacobo Arbenz (1951–1954) guaranteed basic democratic liberties (including free elections), abolished forced labor (which had been nearly universal for the indigenous majority of the population), granted minimum wages and basic rights for workers and peasants, and increased social welfare and equality. In addition, the Revolution modernized Guatemalan capitalism, undertaking agricultural diversification and industrialization programs, fomenting national enterprises, and regulating foreign investment to serve national priorities. Most significant was Arbenz's far-reaching (but capitalist) agrarian reform of 1952, which distributed land to over one hundred thousand peasant families.

Guatemalan Presidents since 1931

Term	Name	Type
1931–1944	Jorge Ubico	Liberal dictator
1945–1950	Juan José Arévalo	Democratic
1951–1954	Jacobo Arbenz	Democratic
1954–1957	Col. Carlos Castillo Armas	Military dictator
1957–1963	Gen. Miguel Ydígoras Fuentes	Military dictator
1963–1966	Col. Enrique Peralta Azurdia	Military dictator
1966–1970	Julio César Méndez Montenegro	Nominal civilian
1970–1974	Col. Carlos Arana Osorio	Military ruler
1974–1978	Gen. Eugenio Kjell Laugerud García	Military dictator
1978–1982	Gen. Romeo Lucas García	Military dictator
1982–83	Gen. Efraín Ríos Montt	Military dictator
1983–1985	Gen. Oscar Humberto Mejía Victores	Military transition[a]
1986–1990	Vinicio Cerezo Arévalo	Transition civilian[b]
1991–1993	Jorge Serrano Elías	Transition civilian[b]
1993–1996	Ramiro de León Carpio	Transition civilian[b]
1996–2000	Alvaro Arzú	Civilian

[a]Though a dictatorship, this regime oversaw a reasonably clean election in 1985 and transition to formal civilian rule.
[b]Though formally civilian, these presidents were eclipsed by or shared power with a very powerful military establishment.

Coming on top of other nationalistic moves by Arbenz, the expropriation of unused land belonging to the U.S.-based United Fruit Company (the largest landowner in Guatemala) prompted an angry response from the U.S. government. Charging that Guatemala was serving as a "beachhead for Soviet expansion" in the Western hemisphere, the CIA organized the overthrow of the Arbenz government in June 1954 and installed in its place a pro–United States counterrevolutionary regime.[3] This regime immediately reversed the democratic and progressive legislation of the Revolution, including the land reform, and unleashed widespread repression. The legacy of the Revolution and its violent termination was to compound the social polarization already characteristic of Guatemala, throwing the country into permanent crisis.

Nevertheless, even under the post-1954 counterrevolutionary order, history could not be "reversed," since the same underlying structural dynamics and contradictions that had caused the Revolution continued to develop. The Guatemalan economy, like that of all Central America, enjoyed a thirty-year period (1950–1980) of growth based on the expansion and diversification of agricultural exports to the world market and a minimal industrialization during the 1960s and 1970s, carried out mainly by foreign capital. But even export-led growth generated turmoil because of the extreme inequities in resource and income distribution. To take the most telling indicator for Guatemala, 2 percent of the population continued to control

67 percent of the arable land.[4] In the 1970s the diversification of exports brought significant new expropriations (from peasants) and concentrations of land. The main beneficiaries were army generals using their control over the state apparatus to accumulate personal wealth. Thus, impoverishment stemming from land concentration intensified geometrically, as Guatemala became virtually the only country in Latin America not to have carried out even a minimal land reform.

At the social level, the diversification of the productive structure significantly modified Guatemala's traditional class structure and reshaped the ruling coalition (between the army and economic elites). Among other things, diversification of the ruling class meant incorporation of the upper ranks of military officers and a redefinition of the alliance between the army and the bourgeoisie. But rather than "opening up" the class structure, these modifications only accentuated its overall polarization. At the bottom pole of Guatemalan society, meanwhile, industrialization and agricultural diversification did not significantly expand the proletariat as a fully employed labor force. Rather, the countryside saw the growth of a semiproletariat: land-starved peasants from the highlands were forced to work on the southern coast as seasonal migrant laborers during part of the year. In the cities, migrants from rural areas swelled the ranks of an underemployed informal proletariat. As a consequence, the "development" of the 1960s and 1970s actually left a decreasing proportion of the economically active population fully employed on a permanent basis. These tendencies were compounded during the 1980s.

Since 60 percent of the population is indigenous, class divisions in Guatemala became much more explosive through their intersection with ethnic divisions. For centuries the indigenous population was subjected to one or another form of forced labor. The state, and in particular the army, defined for themselves the vocation of disciplining, controlling, and repressing the indigenous majority of the population. In a situation approaching defacto apartheid, issues of ethnic identity and democratic rights for the indigenous majority became central. The combination of class with ethnic tensions accounted for the revolutionary upsurge of the early 1980s and remained a source of social unrest. Late twentieth-century crises also laid the objective foundations for a new protagonism of women, which was just beginning to find specific forms of organized expression in the 1990s.

The profound societal changes produced new generations of social movements after 1954 (labor, peasant, indigenous, community)—first in the 1960s, then in the late 1970s and (after they were destroyed in the early 1980s) again in the second half of the 1980s. In the absence of any serious attempt to use the benefits of growth during the 1960s and 1970s to redistribute wealth to the poor and indigenous populations, these movements continually exerted new pressures upon the state and the established social order. These pressures were contained by a level of repression at times unmatched anywhere else in Latin America. One generation after another of movement leaders and activists, as well as centrist political opposition leaders, was eliminated by the army and illegal paramilitary forces. Although it severely restricted their functioning, even the systematic repression failed to stop the continual reemergence of popular movements in one or another form.

These massive social conflicts defined Guatemalan politics during the latter half of the century. Within an overall framework of direct military rule, there were moments of nominal civilian government: 1966–1970 and 1986 onward, but, even then, the army dominated politics from behind the scenes. Largely as a legacy of the experience of the Revolution of 1944–1954 and its violent overthrow, military predominance faced constant challenges. In fact, the illegitimacy of the ruling coalition and the refusal to permit even moderate reformist options created the conditions for the growth of a revolutionary guerrilla movement. Quite literally, there was no alternative "within the system."

The Early Period of Insurgency

The first wave of guerrilla insurgency, during the 1960s, was centered in the eastern region, where the peasants were Ladino rather than Indian. Although small and without a base among the indigenous population, the insurgency was contained only after a major counterinsurgency effort, organized, financed, and run directly by the United States along the lines of its operations in Vietnam.[5] This was a turning point in Guatemala, with U.S. military advisors playing a decisive role in "professionalizing" the Guatemalan military—transforming that army (previously "weakened" by nationalist tendencies and inefficiency) into a modern, disciplined, brutal counterinsurgency army that subsequently came to dominate the state directly. The counterinsurgency state was institutionalized after 1970, when the head of the 1966–1968 campaign, Colonel Carlos Arana Osorio (the "butcher of Zacapa") used that victory to win the 1970 presidential election. Since the goal of this first "dirty war" had been to eradicate the civilian support base of the guerrillas, it cost the lives of over eight thousand civilians. It was also within this context that such artifacts of counterinsurgency war as semi-official death squads (based in the security forces) and "disappearances" of civilian opposition figures were introduced to Latin America. From that point, Guatemala would have more than forty thousand civilian disappearances, accounting for over 40 percent of the total for all Latin America.

In no way prepared for the army counteroffensive and having made serious mistakes in their own organizing strategies, the insurgents suffered a temporary defeat in 1968. However, they were able to reorganize and reinitiate their struggle in the early 1970s, this time in the western Maya highlands, and with the now-mobilized indigenous communities becoming central participants. The active involvement of up to half a million Mayas in the uprising of the late 1970s and early 1980s was without precedent in Guatemala, indeed in the hemisphere. Coming in the wake of the 1979 Sandinista victory in Nicaragua and the outbreak of civil war in El Salvador, this remarkable "awakening" in the Maya highlands provoked a revolutionary crisis, threatening the army's century-old domination over rural Guatemala.

Insurgency and Counterinsurgency in the 1970s and Beyond

The structural transformations of the 1960s to the 1980s changed the class definition of Guatemala's indigenous populations and, in profoundly affecting their self-conceptions and identities as indigenous, became the basis for the vast Maya uprising in the late 1970s and early 1980s. Economic growth followed by economic crisis broke down the objective barriers that had kept the Mayan communities relatively isolated in the highlands. This cycle was greatly intensified by the economic and political crises of the 1970s and 1980s, when growing numbers of indigenous peasants were forced to migrate to the southern coast as seasonal laborers, and to Guatemala City. These changes and displacements brought them into increased contact with the Ladino, Spanish-speaking world. However, rather than "ladinizing" or acculturating them, this experience reinforced their struggle to preserve their indigenous identity, although in new forms—as Guatemalan scholar Ricardo Falla put it, to discover "new ways of being indigenous."[6] This explains why Guatemala's Mayan population became one of the powerful social forces driving the insurgency of the 1970s and 1980s.

In the countryside the crisis in subsistence agriculture, compounded by a massive earthquake in 1976, uprooted thousands of Indian peasants, causing them to redefine themselves in both class and cultural terms. As producers, they were being semiproletarianized as a seasonal migrant labor force on the plantations of the southern coast, meanwhile often losing even the tiny subsistence plots of land they had traditionally held in the highlands. They were radicalized by their experience both of being evicted from their own lands and of becoming a migrant semiproletariat.

Even the more developmentalist influences were contradictory, in that they raised hopes and expectations in the 1960s, only to dash them in the 1970s. The clearest examples of this dynamic were those peasants who received land from the government's colonization programs in the 1960s, only to have it taken away again in the 1970s, as the powerful army officers grabbed profitable lands in colonization areas.

Other factors radicalized the highland Mayas. Increased cultural contact with Ladino society had the effect of reinforcing their determination to defend their ethnic identity. Contact with new reformist parties, such as Christian Democrats, raised and then dashed expectations. Meanwhile, indigenous organizations were defined by the government as "subversive" and excluded from "normal" political expression. By the late 1970s increased army repression against indigenous communities—rather than terrorizing the Indians into passivity—actually stimulated them to take up arms as the only available means of self-defense. Finally, there was the emergence of Catholic grassroots organizations—Christian base communities—and the gradual emergence of the "Church of the Poor." (See Chapter 9.) These, too, contributed to the radicalization of the indigenous highlands.

All of these strands were woven together by 1976–1978 in the emergence of the Peasant Unity Committee (Comité de Unidad Campesina, CUC) as a national peasant organization, including both peasants and agricultural workers, both Indians and poor Ladinos, but led primarily by Indians—by definition a "subversive" organization from the viewpoint of the ruling coalition. CUC came into the limelight after a major massacre at Panzós, Alta Verapaz, in 1978, and the 1980 massacre at the Spanish embassy, in which Guatemalan security forces burned alive thirty-nine indigenous protesters. In February 1980, CUC staged a massive strike of workers on the southern coast sugar and cotton plantations. From the viewpoint of landowners and the army, this strike was their worst nightmare come true.

Meanwhile, in the wake of their 1968 defeat the insurgents, recognizing the failures of the fundamentaly militaristic strategy of the 1960s and the need for a solid mass base centered on the indigenous population, had undergone an important reevaluation of strategy as well as an organizational recomposition. By the time of their resurgence in the early 1970s, the three major organizations had generally come to understand some of these errors. Two of them, the Guerrilla Army of the Poor (Ejército Guerrillero de los Pobres, EGP) and the Organization of the People in Arms (Organización del Pueblo en Armas, ORPA), actually spent several years being educated by the indigenous population while organizing a political support base in the highlands (and other areas) before renewing armed actions later in the 1970s.

The guerrilla military offensive reached its height in 1980–81, gaining six to eight thousand armed fighters and two hundred fifty thousand to five hundred thousand active collaborators and supporters, and operating in most parts of the country. In the context of the Sandinista triumph in Nicaragua and the outbreak of civil war in El Salvador (both in 1979), the new wave of armed struggle in Guatemala was taken very seriously by the ruling coalition as heralding a possible seizure of power by the insurgents. In early 1982, the various guerrilla organizations united in the Guatemalan National Revolutionary Unity (Unidad Revolucionaria Nacional Guatemalteca, URNG), overcoming years of sectarian divisions.

Even as unity was proclaimed, however, and even as the revolutionary movement achieved its maximal expression during 1980 and 1981, a change in the balance of forces between the insurgents and the army began during the second half of 1981, when the army initiated a massive counteroffensive. By spring of 1982 the revolutionary movement had taken very serious losses to its infrastructure in the city, where security forces had already in 1978–1980 decapitated the unions and other popular movements and political opposition forces. In the highlands, the army unleashed a virtual holocaust upon the indigenous communities. Blinded by its own triumphalism, the URNG had, in fact, lost the initiative and some of its fundamental weaknesses came to the surface. As a result of the URNG's weaknesses and of major changes within the ruling coalition, the army gained the upper hand and dealt decisive blows to the insurgents. On the defensive for the next several years, the URNG did not recover a capacity to take new initiatives until the late 1980s.

A major reason for this second defeat of the guerrillas and the suffering inflicted on its supporters among the population was the failure to have anticipated the extent of the counteroffensive unleashed by the Guatemalan security forces; hence, tens of thousands of highland Mayas were left unprepared to defend themselves. The statistics are staggering: from mid 1981 to 1983 alone, 440 villages were entirely destroyed; up to 150,000 civilians were killed or "disappeared" and over 1 million became displaced persons (1 million were internal refugees and up to 200,000 were refugees in Mexico). Accompanying these massive population displacements was the deliberate destruction of huge areas of the highlands by the burning of forests and other such acts, causing irreversible environmental devastation. The aim of the attacks was not only to eliminate the guerrillas' popular support base but also to destroy the culture, identity, and communal structures of the indigenous populations.

The army carried out its goals in two stages. Between 1981 and 1983 it concentrated on scorched-earth warfare; after 1983 it imposed coercive institutions throughout the countryside, designed to consolidate military control over the population. Among these institutions were mandatory paramilitary "civilian self-defense patrols" (Patrullas de Autodefensa Civil, PACs) that at one point involved one quarter of the adult population; "development poles," rural forced-resettlement camps where every aspect of people's lives was subject to direct army control; and militarization of the entire administrative apparatus of the country. The new Constitution of 1985, designed to provide the juridical framework for subsequent civilian governments, at the same time legalized the counterinsurgency institutions.

The Recomposition of the Counterinsurgency State and the Return to Civilian Rule

Thus, insurgency in Guatemala during the 1960s generated a counterinsurgent response by the United States and the Guatemalan ruling coalition that was institutionalized in state power after 1970. During the late 1970s the ability of the military regimes to govern Guatemala deteriorated seriously, as a consequence of weakened internal cohesion within the ruling coalition and the lack of any consensual basis or societal legitimacy. The clearest examples are the openly fraudulent elections of 1974, 1978, and 1982. By 1982 the deterioration was serious enough to spark recognition of the need for a change in the nature of military rule, to recover some modicum of legitimacy, at least among the ruling sectors, and to end Guatemala's international isolation as a pariah state and hence its restricted access to international financial assistance.

The change or "recomposition" is generally seen as beginning with the coup of March 1982 (following the third successive electoral fraud), which brought to power the regime of General Efraín Ríos Montt. The Ríos Montt government (March 1982–August 1983), however, presided over the bloodiest era, characterized by the majority of the massacres and illegal secret tribunals. It was only after this most brutal phase of the counterinsurgency war had accomplished its goals under Ríos Montt that army leaders and their civilian allies, now under the military government of General Oscar Mejía Victores, took concrete steps toward a return to civilian rule. They recognized that a facade of constitutional democracy was needed to overcome the contradictions of direct military dictatorship. This understanding was the background for the political process of 1983–1985, during which a Constituent Assembly was elected to write a new constitution containing basic guarantees of citizens' rights, at least on paper, and presidential elections were held in late 1985.

The 1985 presidential election, although free of fraud, was severely restricted and unrepresentative of large sectors of the population, because only rightist and centrist parties that had reached agreement with the military were allowed to participate.[7] In addition, there were no real choices on substantive issues. Nevertheless, the election did permit nonmilitary candidates for the first time in fifteen years. The impressive victory of Christian Democrat Vinicio Cerezo, the most progressive of the candidates, was greeted with high hopes for a real change from the many years of military dictatorship.

Despite these hopes and a significant popular mandate, however, Cerezo chose not to fully use the space that he had—not to wage the struggle that would have been needed to achieve a real transfer of power from the military to civilians. His government did very little to control the army or address the country's underlying social and economic problems. Instead, he accepted the army's priority of defeating popular and revolutionary forces and thus significantly limited the possibility for genuinely pluralistic politics or an end to the civil war. In this regard the Cerezo years (1986–1990) turned out to be not so much a "transition to democracy" as a necessary period of adjustment after Guatemala's multiple crises and loss of international credibility. The government evolved into a civilian version of the counterinsurgency state, in some respects a continuation of what had been imposed in the late 1960s.

A second nonfraudulent election, held in 1990, was viewed as significant insofar as it established the continuity of formal civilian rule. Nevertheless, abstention was extremely high, with only 30 percent of eligible voters participating. And, once again, no real opposition parties were permitted.[8] By 1990, however, new currents were emerging from Guatemalan civil society outside the electoral process that did begin to undermine the foundations of the counterinsurgency state. Among the major expressions of these currents was an emerging national consensus brought together primarily by top Church officials, for an end to the civil war. Virtually all political sectors began to recognize that Guatemala could not be truly democratized until the civil war was ended through political negotiations (rather than a military victory by either side), until the country was demilitarized, and until the underlying structural inequalities and ethnic discrimination were acknowledged and addressed.

The Popular Bloc in the 1980s

Structural social crisis—ironically, a product of macroeconomic growth during the 1970s—was compounded during the 1980s, when the international capitalist crisis hit Central America as severely as had the depression of the 1930s. Among its principal manifestations were rising prices for all industrial imports (largely a consequence of the "oil shocks") and falling prices for Central American exports. These crises left the Guatemalan economy suffering negative growth rates during the 1980s while both unemployment and inflation soared to unprecedented levels. As a result, purchasing power in 1989 was 22 percent of what it had been in 1972; and the overall poverty levels of 1980 rose dramatically during the second half of the decade.[9]

Guatemala's central social characteristic during the 1980s and into the 1990s remained increasing concentration of wealth amid pervasive poverty. While all Central American countries shared this characteristic, Guatemalan poverty was particularly extreme, on several counts. First, the inequality of resource and income distribution was greater in Guatemala than in any other Central American country, and no measures had been taken since the overthrow of Arbenz to alleviate it. Second, Guatemala stood out for the number of social indicators on which it ranked worst in the region (illiteracy, physical quality of life, infant mortality). Third, all statistics for the indigenous population were far worse than the national average. As elsewhere, there also had been a marked feminization of poverty.

These characteristics of extreme underdevelopment and inequality were not new to Guatemala, but they worsened dramatically, even at the macroeconomic level, during the 1980s under the impact of the international economic crisis of the 1980s. Guatemala lost over fifteen years' growth during the 1980s, reversing the growth pattern of the previous thirty years. After the mid 1980s the government began to implement more aggressive austerity policies, culminating in the neoliberal structural adjustment "shock measures" of the late 1980s and early 1990s (Chapter 10) that only further aggravated the grave social crisis. And informalization of the urban proletariat (as people earned enough for only a hand-to-mouth existence at jobs, for example as street vendors, not even counted in employment statistics) left only slightly over one-third of the workforce fully and permanently employed.

This last indicator was among the important modifications in Guatemala's class structure during the 1980s, which left close to 90 percent of the population living below the official poverty line by the end of the decade (up from 79 percent in 1980); nearly three-fourths of the population lived in extreme poverty, unable to afford a basic minimum diet.[10]

During the late 1980s the impact of the economic and social crisis in regenerating social ferment among the poor proved greater than the ability of the counterinsurgency state to repress such ferment. Despite the reescalation of repression against labor and other popular movements, the constitution of this huge majority of the population, united by being poor, led to a slow rebuilding and reemergence of popular movements after the disasters of the early 1980s and a stream of austerity protests, beginning in 1985 and continuing with surprising vigor.

Guatemala's new popular movements grew out of the country's multiple crises, including the many crises of uprooted populations, as well as the austerity measures. The war alone left over 10 percent of the population displaced. War, economic crisis, and natural disaster during the 1980s brought significant migration to the capital, causing its population to double. Increasingly, the urban poor were indigenous people and more than half of the households were headed by women. A significant number of the new urban poor (between a quarter million and half a million people) lived in the city's massive shantytowns in precarious squatter settlements. The absence of basic social services (running water, sewage, electricity, transportation) sparked new community struggles that became as important as the more traditional labor union struggles among organized sectors of the labor force.

Meanwhile, in the rural areas, hundreds of thousands of those displaced within the highlands or to the southern coast joined with the landless already living there to form a national movement for land. The reconstituted popular movements of primarily rural indigenous peoples also included human rights groups organized around demands that were openly political and directly related to the ongoing counterinsurgency war. These groups included the Mutual Support Group (Grupo de Apoyo Mutuo, GAM), an organization of wives and mothers of the "disappeared" and other human rights victims; the mainly indigenous widows' organization National Coordinating Committee of Guatemalan Widows (Coordinadora Nacional de Viudas de Guatemala, CONAVIGUA); Council of Ethnic Communities "Everyone Is Equal" (Consejo de Comunidades Etnicas Runujel Junam, CERJ Runujel Junam), founded to empower highland Mayas to resist service in the PACs; and the Council of Displaced Guatemalans (Consejo de Desplazados Guatemaltecos, CONDEG), representing internal refugees. Tens of thousands of Indians also resisted army relocation and control programs by fleeing to remote mountain areas and forming permanent "communities of people in resistance" (Comunidades de Población en Resistencia, CPR), which finally began to gain national and international recognition in the early 1990s.

First among the new characteristics of Guatemala's popular movements in the late 1980s and early 1990s was the centrality of the indigenous population with its double burden of exploitation and ethnic discrimination in both rural and urban settings. This change was reflected in the rapid rise of diverse movements and organizations fighting for a broad range of indigenous rights.[11] A second novelty was the slowly emerging—often invisible—protagonism of women. Third was the growing role of the Catholic Church in bringing together popular movements. Liberation theology was a major influence throughout the 1970s and 1980s; and, even after the appearance and rapid growth of evangelical Protestant groups during the 1980s, the Catholic Church remained a leading force in articulating the demands of the popular movements.

In short, Guatemala experienced the gradual emergence of a bloc of popular and indigenous organizations. The notion of a "bloc" indicates that the social subject is not one class in the traditional sense but a combination of exploited and dominated sectors, whose political expression is a coalition or "front" of popular and indigenous movements. "Popular" refers to a cross-class grouping, incorporating conditions related to (ethnic) identity and (gender-based) reproduction as well as (class-based) exploitation. These movements continued to suffer from many serious weaknesses—above all, continued vulnerability to the endless stream of kidnappings, disappearances, death threats, and assassinations. Their articulation as a social force was also hindered by continuing problems of disunity and inability to organize among the huge informal proletariat. Because they still had to operate semi-underground as a consequence of repression, their advances were often imperceptible. Nevertheless, their continued existence and growth was in itself a form of defiance of the counterinsurgency state.

By the late 1980s the context for political action was also shaped by the resurgence of the URNG. Even while having destroyed much of the URNG's social base in the highlands in the early 1980s, the army had been unable to inflict a "final" defeat upon the insurgent forces or to "win" the war definitively. Hence, the organizations of the URNG survived the holocaust; they remained the nuclei of future resistance even at their low point and gradually began to recover their ability to take initiatives, both militarily and politically. Nevertheless, their inability to resist the army's counteroffensive of the early 1980s, combined with the recomposition of the counterinsurgency state in the mid 1980s, required once again a profound reorganization and redefinition of strategy.

Such redefinitions became necessary in response to the clear lesson of the early 1980s, that military victory over the counterinsurgency forces was a totally unthinkable objective and that the cost of the second round of the war for the civilian population had been so high as to preclude a strategy based simply on continuing the war. Furthermore, in view of the 1985 election and transition to nominal civilian rule, that is, to a potentially legitimate government, the Left had to find new ways of becoming a significant force in civil society. Hence, shortly after the 1985 election, the URNG began to propose negotiations for a political settlement to the war. For the URNG the emphasis on negotiations was part of several larger modifications of strategy: giving more weight to political aspects of the struggle, while at the same time maintaining a military capacity; broadening its social and political alliances; and slowly beginning to recognize the role of popular and indigenous sectors acting *autonomously* and the importance of an ideological pluralism that would allow the popular movements to follow their own organizational dynamic. This response was necessary also because of the growing complexity and the growing plurality of interests in Guatemalan society.

The Context for Beginning a Peace Process

The Guatemalan counterinsurgency project, because of its profound contradictions, was unlikely to be stabilized. Given its intrinsic brutality, it did not and could not win the battle for legitimacy, and its failure to win the war against the guerrilla insurgency had caused discontent and destabilization within the ruling coalition. Also, its economic policies, designed to expand the economy solely through world-market-oriented "non-traditional exports," only intensified social conflicts and eventually limited economic growth precisely because they did nothing to develop the internal market.

By the late 1980s, though by no means in an insurrectionary situation or "ungovernable," Guatemala was in chronic social crisis. The counterinsurgency state made reformism by itself inviable by precluding partial solutions to the staggering problems of poverty and ethnic discrimination. Gradualist approaches to change simply were not permitted. But faced with the deepening of these problems, important sectors of the population made continual efforts to organize in self-defense—increasingly around issues of ethnic discrimination and indigenous rights, as well as poverty. Hence, basic issues of social transformation remained on Guatemala's agenda, although not in the traditional forms.

Though the URNG, for its part, experienced another resurgence during the late 1980s, its "revolutionary" or transformatory project required redefinition. Guatemala was one of the few countries in Latin America where the armed insurgent movement had operated continuously since the 1960s. But armed struggle is not what people choose; after thirty years of counterinsurgency war, and particularly after the holocaust of the early 1980s, the URNG could not simply propose another decade of war. Most important, the URNG realized that the goal of "taking state power" militarily was unthinkable and would be unacceptable to the civilian population. The enormous price already inflicted by the extreme brutality of the Guatemalan army was daunting.[12] And, like the Farabundo Martí Front for National Liberation (Frente Farabundo Martí de Liberación Nacional, FMLN) in El Salvador,[13] the URNG had come to realize that the United States would do to future "Nicaraguas" what it was already doing to the Sandinistas. Faced with these realities and several splits over the prospect of a prolonged war within their organization, the URNG leadership recognized the need for significant modifications of strategy. Hence, after Guatemala's return to civilian rule in 1986, even while continuing the war, the URNG began pressing for political negotiations with the government and army to end the war.

For four years the government stubbornly insisted that the insurgents must first "lay down their arms." But by the beginning of the 1990s, with the war intensifying, even army and government spokesmen were finally forced to acknowledge the significant upsurge in guerrilla actions. The implicit admission that the war could not be "won" militarily by either side created the conditions, beginning in spring 1990, for serious discussions about ending it.

Negotiating Peace

Long before the Guatemalan government and military admitted the impossibility of military victory, the Catholic Church had been pushing for a peaceful solution. During 1989, the Catholic Church sponsored a national dialogue that, although boycotted by the army, the government, and the private sector, expressed a clear national consensus among all other sectors in favor of a substantive political settlement to the war. The dialogue process projected a series of URNG meetings with the political parties and "social sectors" (private enterprise and popular and religious movements) and, finally, with the government and army. The 1990 sessions included a September meeting between the URNG and the umbrella organization of big business, the Coordinating Committee of Agricultural, Commercial, Industrial, and Financial Associations (Comité Coordinador de Asociaciones Comerciales,

Industriales y Financieras, CACIF), an event unthinkable during the previous thirty years. Beyond the formal meetings, the dialogue process opened up spaces within a repressive context for public discussion of issues that had been undiscussable for decades. In this sense, it became an important avenue for beginning to democratize Guatemala.

In early 1991 the newly elected government of Jorge Serrano opened direct negotiations with the URNG. For the first time, top army officials agreed to participate in meetings to set the agenda and procedures for peace talks without demanding that the URNG first disarm—although they still hoped to win URNG demobilization in exchange for minimal, pro forma concessions. During the next year, there were agreements in principle on democratization and partial agreements on human rights. The precariousness of the process became evident when it stagnated in mid 1992 and moved toward total breakdown during the last months of Serrano's crisis-ridden government. The Serrano government turned out to be more interested in imposing a cease-fire deadline than in resolving the substantive issues on the eleven-point agenda (ranging from human rights and demilitarization to indigenous rights and social-economic issues). This stance by the government was unacceptable to the URNG.

The entire peace process was derailed by the May 1993 "Serranazo" or attempted *autogolpe*. Serrano's attempt to seize absolute control (initially but briefly supported by some factions of the army) unleashed a major political and constitutional crisis. After being repudiated by virtually all sectors of civil society and the international community, the Serranazo was resolved through the (most unexpected) ascendance of former human rights ombudsman Ramiro de León Carpio to the presidency.[14]

But the peace process remained at a standstill during the rest of 1993. The new government was closely allied with the dominant wing of the army high command, which supported the idea of civilian presidents but with full autonomy and wide-ranging veto powers for the military. The new government presented unrealistic negotiation proposals that would have discarded previously signed agreements and, in essence, would have required the URNG to disarm without any substantive settlements. Perhaps the army had hoped to use de León Carpio's legitimacy to achieve unilateral surrender by the URNG. These proposals were rejected almost unanimously throughout Guatemalan society (except by the army and private sector) and were viewed as completely nonviable by the international community.

In January 1994 with these tactics having run their course, the negotiations were resumed but this time on a significantly different basis. During the 1991–1993 rounds, Guatemala's peace talks had been moderated by Monsignor Rodolfo Quezada Toruño of the Catholic Bishops' Conference, with the United Nations in an "observer" role. As of January 1994 both sides agreed that the UN should become the moderator; this paved the way for significantly increased involvement by the international community, raising the stakes in the negotiations and giving the entire process a less reversible dynamic.[15]

Furthermore, the January 1994 "Framework Accord" established a clear agenda (which was maintained) and timetable (which proved unrealizable). It also formalized a role for the broad-based multi-sector Assembly of Civil Society (Asamblea de la Sociedad Civil, ASC), which included virtually all organized sectors of civil society (including, for the first time, women's organizations), as well as the major political parties. Only the big business sectors represented in CACIF decided not to participate. Having gained new experience during the Serranazo, these grassroots organizations had become increasingly vocal in demanding participation in the peace process. The ASC was also striking for the diversity or plurality of political-ideological positions represented within its ranks. Unlike El Salvador's popular organizations in relation to the FMLN, the ASC was by no means a simple instrument of the URNG. As the main agreements were being hammered out, the ASC—after itself engaging in a fascinating process of consensus-building among widely divergent positions—offered proposals to the negotiating parties on each issue. While not binding, their proposals had to be taken into account by the two parties, and the URNG adopted many of the ASC proposals as its own negotiating positions.

The formation of the ASC also gave Guatemala's organized popular sectors their first sustained experience (following upon their initial experience during the Serranazo) of participating in and considering themselves part of the political process. This participation was particularly important for sectors that had always rejected electoral participation and prided themselves on their antisystem political culture of protest (*denuncia*) as a manifestation of political resistance. In the particular unfolding of Guatemalan history, the ASC experience was the precursor to the eventual participation by those sectors in the 1995 election.

A breakthrough human rights accord was signed in late March 1994 calling for the immediate establishment of international verification mechanisms to monitor human rights. But for months the government took no steps to comply with its obligations under the accord, and the mandated UN Verification Mission in Guatemala (Misión de las Naciones Unidas de Verificación en Guatemala, MINUGUA) did not arrive until November 1994. At the table, two new accords were signed in June 1994 on the resettling of displaced populations and a watered-down Truth Commission empowered to shed light on (*esclarecer*) past human rights crimes, but without naming the individuals responsible. The latter aspect sparked fierce criticism from popular and human rights organizations. Meanwhile, on the ground, human rights violations worsened, leaving the definite impression that the government was going through the motions of a peace process without intending to change anything.

For these reasons as well as the complexity of the issue itself, it took until March 1995 to reach an agreement on the next theme, identity and rights of indigenous peoples. The signing of this accord was a landmark achievement for a country whose population is 60 percent indigenous. The actual signing, however, was overshadowed by the eruption on March 23 of the scandal in Washington concerning the involvement of a CIA-paid army officer in the murders of a U.S. citizen and a guerrilla commander married to U.S. lawyer Jennifer Harbury—a scandal that remained front-page news for several weeks and left the Guatemalan army even further discredited. Negotiations on the theme of social-economic issues (directly affecting the interests of Guatemala's economic elites) continued throughout 1995, making some progress but without a final resolution during the lame-duck de León Carpio government.

Inside Guatemala, meanwhile, the peace process had a direct effect on the dynamics of the campaign for the November 1995 general election—and vice versa. One of the most important novelties of this electoral process was the URNG's call to vote. In addition, a left-of-center front of popular and indigenous organizations (the "left flank" of the ASC), the New Guatemala Democratic Front (Frente Democrático Nueva Guatemala, FDNG) was formed to participate in the elections. Finally, in August the URNG signed an agreement in which it promised not to disrupt the elections in exchange for a commitment by the major political parties to continue the peace negotiations under a new government and to honor the accords already signed— a crucial committment for the peace process.

In the November 1995 general elections, no presidential candidate received an absolute majority. The major surprise of the election was the stronger-than-expected showing of the newly formed FDNG, which won six seats in Congress. Additionally, alliances between the FDNG and locally based indigenous "civic committees" won several important mayoralties, including Xelajú (Quetzaltenango). A January 1996 run-off for president pitted modernizing conservative Alvaro Arzú against a stand-in for former dictator Efraín Ríos Montt. Arzú won by a scant 2 percent margin.

Even before taking office, Arzú held several direct, secret meetings with the URNG in different venues. Shortly after taking office, he signaled his intention to bring the ongoing peace talks to a successful conclusion. (Ríos Montt's party, by contrast, was openly opposed to negotiation.) In addition to appointing a "peace cabinet," the new president underscored his intention to establish civilian control over the army by undertaking a series of shake-ups in the army high command and the police. These and other actions created a new political climate of confidence and paved the way for an indefinite cease-fire between the rebels and the army in March 1996.

Once the formal peace negotiations were reinitiated, and following intensive consultations with the private sector, an accord on socioeconomic issues was signed in May 1996—this time, finally, with CACIF support. Because of the compromises involved, the accord generated considerable controversy among popular organizations before the ASC eventually endorsed it. The crowning achievement of the peace process was the September 1996 accord on strengthening civilian power and the role of the armed forces in a democratic society. While mandating constitutional reforms, subordinating the army to civilian control, and restricting the army's role to external defense, it called for a new civilian police force to handle all internal security matters. The army's size and budget was also to be reduced.

A serious crisis, with some lasting effects, nearly derailed the entire process in October 1996, when a high-level cadre of ORPA (previously regarded as the most pro-negotiation of the URNG constituent organizations) was discovered to be the author of a high-level kidnapping of the octogenarian Olga de Novella, from one of Guatemala's richest families and a personal friend of the president. The government suspended the peace talks until ORPA's top leader resigned from the negotiating table in November. Once the process was resumed, this time with a deadline (December 29), several operational accords were signed in December. These dealt with a definitive cease-fire, constitutional and electoral reforms, the legal reintegration of the URNG (entailing a partial amnesty for both the URNG and the army), and a timetable for fulfillment of all of the accords. Following the dramatic return of the URNG leadership to Guatemala on December 28, the final peace accord was signed amid considerable domestic and international attention in Guatemala's National Palace on December 29, 1996. Thus ended the first phase of the peace process that the Guatemalan elites had vowed "never" to permit in Guatemala.

How did this "never" turn into acceptance? The UN played a role that no other mediating force could have played in facilitating agreements between the government and the URNG. (See Chapter 8.) In addition, six governments played an important supportive role as the "Group of Friends" of the peace process.[16] Slowly, despite fierce resistances and significant delays, the peace process acquired credibility within Guatemala. To be sure, at many times, its volatility and fragility evoked images of the Middle East negotiations between Israel and the PLO. But with all its difficulties, the logic of the peace process, broadly understood, came to offer Guatemala its best opportunity to democratize a thoroughly exclusionary system, to make important changes that would have been highly unlikely or impossible under any other circumstances.

Even within the recalcitrant CACIF, "modernizing," more pragmatic fractions became invested in the peace process; they recognized that it was the only way to avoid being isolated and left behind in the world of the twenty-first century. For its part, the seemingly all-powerful army, despite all appearances to the contrary, was increasingly on the defensive and had decreasing legitimacy and authority within Guatemala, especially after the failed Serranazo. Internationally, given the changes in the world and in Guatemala since 1990, the United States no longer had any strategic justification for maintaining its alliance with the Guatemalan counterinsurgency army. In short, none of the major Guatemalan players had anywhere to move but forward.

Seen in its totality, the negotiation process was a great step forward for Guatemalan democracy, although not for social justice. The accords constituted a truly negotiated settlement, much like El Salvador's of 1992. Rather than being imposed by victors upon vanquished, they represented a splitting of differences between radically opposed forces, with major concessions from both sides. This exercise in the culture of compromise was a novelty in Guatemala.

Additional process-related gains for democracy accumulated after the signing of the accords. Most of the accords contained important provisions for participation in decision making—including *comisiones paritarias* (parity commisions), with equal representation from the government and indigenous organizations, and a host of other multisectoral commissions. In addition, the implementation of the accords gave rise to a far-reaching practice of *consultas* (consultations) involving some (not all) policymakers in direct interchanges with citizens and social organizations—some of them outside the capital city (also a novelty). Finally, the accords provided innovative mechanisms such as the Women's Forum (Foro de Mujeres) for training and "capacity-building" among those who have never had such opportunities.

Conclusion

In the little more than four decades that had elapsed since the CIA-orchestrated overthrow of the democratic reformist government of Jacobo Arbenz in 1954, Guatemala had made a long and tortuous journey from repression to revolt and extreme repression to negotiation and finally to peace. For the first time since 1954, there were real possibilities for beginning a process of democratic development. This achievement—at a cost of over two hundred thousand civilian lives—was largely a result of the perseverance of several generations of insurgents as well as the halting but recurrent and growing emergence of a resilient and diverse civil society.

As this was being written, despite advances made, the future of Guatemala was by no means clear. Even more than in El Salvador, the accords as signed had not been implemented by the government. In fact, the 1997–1999 battles to gain governmental compliance with what it had signed proved to be even more difficult than the battles that led to the signing of the accords. Furthermore, even after the signing of peace, violence—some of it politically motivated—continued.[17] The most notable example was the 1998 assassination of Bishop Juan Gerardi just two days after he released a report by the Archbishop's Human Rights Office (which he founded) that

attributed over 85 percent of the killings during the war to government soldiers and associated paramilitary forces.[18] Furthermore, Guatemala—like
the rest of the isthmus—was in the throes of neoliberal "reform" with all of
its negative consequences for income distribution and social justice. It was
unclear how true participatory democracy could prosper in an economic
environment still characterized by extreme polarities. In addition, new political developments in 1999 put the implementation of the peace accord
into serious danger.

On the positive side, however, was the newfound determination of large
numbers of Guatemalans to overcome the violence, exclusion, racial discrimination, and socioeconomic disparities of the past, and the effervescent
growth of civil society based on these rising expectations in the 1990s and
into the twenty-first century. In addition, there were significant international pressures, which had the potential to play a decisive role in securing
compliance with the peace accords. Taking all of these forces into consideration, it seemed clear that Guatemalans would use the newly opened political spaces to continue their long-standing struggles for substantive as well
as formal democracy.

Notes

1. The figure 200,000 (used in Susanne Jonas, *The Battle for Guatemala: Rebels,
Death Squads, and U.S. Power* [Boulder, CO: Westview Press, 1991], p. 2) was long
challenged by officials from the Guatemalan and U.S. governments. The most au-
thoritative reports on the human rights atrocities committed during Guatemala's
thirty-six-year war—that of the Guatemalan Archbishop's Office on Human Rights
(1998) and that by the Guatemalan Historical Clarification Commission or "Truth
Commission" (1999)—both use that figure, with the latter suggesting that it might
even be low.
2. It is significant and, now, irrefutable that the U.S. military actually trained
their Latin American counterparts—first and most notably those of Guatemala—in
the techniques of "counterterror," a euphemism for state-sponsored terror—involving widespread torture, assassination, and "disappearances"—designed to silence
opposition by disarticulating "civil society." Though such activities were denied
throughout the cold war, seven training manuals designed in part to teach these
techniques were disclosed by the Department of Defense in September 1996. See
U.S. Department of Defense, "Fact Sheet Concerning Training Manuals Containing
Materials Inconsistent with U.S. Policy" (Washington, DC, September 1996). See
also Dana Priest, "U.S. Instructed Latins on Execution, Torture—Manuals Used
1982–1991, Pentagon Reveals," *Washington Post*, September 21, 1996, A1, A9; Lisa
Haugaard, "How the US Trained Latin America's Military: The Smoking Gun," *Envio*
16, no. 165 (October 1997): 33–38.
3. See, for instance, Richard H. Immerman, *The CIA in Guatemala* (Austin:
University of Texas Press, 1982).
4. Central American Historical Institute, *Update*, August 27, 1987. For more
details see Jonas, *The Battle for Guatemala*, 178.
5. Susanne Jonas, "Dangerous Liaisons: The U.S. in Guatemala," *Foreign Policy*
(Summer 1996): 144–60.

6. Ricardo Falla, *Quiché Rebelde* (Guatemala: Editora Universitaria, 1978).

7. Susanne Jonas, "Elections and Transitions: The Guatemalan and Nicaraguan Cases," and Robert Trudeau, "The Guatemalan Election of 1985: Prospects for Democracy," in John A. Booth and Mitchell A. Seligson, eds., *Elections and Democracy in Central America* (Chapel Hill: University of North Carolina Press, 1989), 126–57, 93–125.

8. Susanne Jonas, "Electoral Problems and the Democratic Project in Guatemala," in Mitchell A. Seligson and John A. Booth, eds., *Elections and Democracy in Central America, Revisited* (Chapel Hill: University of North Carolina Press, 1995), 25–44.

9. See the statistical profile in Jonas, *The Battle for Guatemala*, 177–80.

10. Ibid.

11. For details, see Kay Warren, *Indigenous Movements and Their Critics* (Princeton: Princeton University Press, 1998); Alberto Esquit and Victor Galvez, *The Mayan Movement Today* (Guatemala: FLACSO, 1997).

12. There are serious and complex debates about the responsibility of the guerrillas for provoking the repression against the Maya highlands population in the early 1980s. These issues are raised in a very sophisticated and nuanced analysis in Yvon Le Bot, *La Guerra en tierras mayas* (Mexico: Fondo de Cultura Económica, 1995). See also the discussion at the end of Chapter 1 in Susanne Jonas, *Of Centaurs and Doves: Guatemala's Peace Process* (Boulder, CO: Westview Press, 2000).

13. Coauthor Thomas Walker had the opportunity to interview some FMLN guerrilla spokespersons in Managua in November 1982. They clearly stated that their objective was not to seize control of the government but to fight to force the government into a negotiated settlement. Given what the United States was already doing to the revolutionary government of Nicaragua, outright victory, in the words of Rubén Zamora (whom he also interviewed at the time), would be "ashes in our mouths."

14. See Susanne Jonas, "Text and Subtext of the Guatemalan Political Drama," *LASA Forum* 24, no. 4 (Winter 1994): 3–9.

15. This argument is developed in detail in Chapter 2 of Jonas, *Of Centaurs and Doves*.

16. Comprised of six countries: Mexico, United States, Spain, Norway, and (nominally) Venezuela and Colombia.

17. See Jonas, *Of Centaurs and Doves*.

18. "Guatemala: Never Again?" Central America Report 25, no. 16 (April 30, 1996): 1–3.

2

El Salvador
Revolt and Negotiated Transition

Shawn L. Bird and Philip J. Williams

Two days before the March 1994 elections in a poor neighborhood in San
Salvador, Don Miguel, a member of the local Christian base community,
warned about the possibility of electoral fraud: "If there's a blackout Sunday evening, then you know there's fraud, just like in every other election."
He went on: "Hopefully, it'll be different this time, but then again, these
elections are only one moment in a long journey, *our* journey toward peace
with justice."[1]

Although no blackout occurred on Sunday evening, for many Salvadorans and most international observers, the elections were a great disappointment. After all, these were supposed to be the "elections of the century."
However, they were little different from the flawed elections of the 1980s,
marred by low voter turnout and widespread irregularities on election day.
Despite the peace accords and constant international pressure, the electoral
system had changed very little.

By viewing the 1994 elections as the defining moment of the democratic transition, international observers and scholars were articulating a
view of democratization not shared by Don Miguel and most Salvadorans.
In a sense, Don Miguel demonstrated a more sophisticated, nuanced understanding of El Salvador's democratic transition. In his analysis, the elections did not represent the endpoint of the transition process but instead
reflected the unfinished nature of an ongoing process.

Democratic Transition and Consolidation

The central topic of this volume is "democratic transition," or the movement toward democratic governance. Borrowing from John Booth's work,
"democracy will be treated in the broader classical sense of popular participation in rule, rather than the narrower, electoral focus associated with the

position of the pluralist-elitists."[2] In other words, elections are an important element in democratic development but represent only one of many ways in which citizens can influence government decisions. Thus, when measuring the extent of democracy in any given polity, in addition to analyzing the process by which leaders are selected, we must also consider the opportunities available to citizens to participate in policymaking and to hold elected officials accountable.

To better understand democratic transitions, Guillermo O'Donnell offers the idea of "two transitions,"[3] the first being the crumbling of authoritarian rule, a concurrent political opening, and the initiation of democratic rule. The second transition picks up where the first ended—the establishment of democratic rule—and concludes, if all goes well, with the consolidation of democracy, or the effective functioning of a democratic regime. In segmenting the transition process into two stages, O'Donnell provides a means to more precisely study the phenomenon and differentiate between phases and aspects of the interval period.

It is generally agreed that the Central American states (with the possible exception of Guatemala), by the late 1990s, had successfully progressed through the first of O'Donnell's two transitions. In each case authoritarian regimes had given way to procedurally democratic regimes that later formed a government through a competitive electoral process. In theory, at the end of democratic consolidation a regime would be fully democratic; but just as democratization is a continuous process, so too is democratic consolidation.

As a subject of inquiry, consolidation is more difficult to study than the first stage of transitions; it raises a wider array of problems with a vast number of variables to consider. To get a handle on it, some scholars have taken a minimalist conception of democratic consolidation. O'Donnell, for example, considers a democracy to be consolidated where common citizens *and* elites have agreed to and achieved a lawful, institutionalized, and resilient democratic framework under which to govern themselves and their social relations.[4] Some scholars have developed "turnover tests"—the passing of power from one government to another—to determine when a democracy has achieved consolidation. For example, a democracy is consolidated, according to Samuel Huntington, when the government loses an election to the opposition and the successor government subsequently loses.[5] Other scholars emphasize negative aspects of consolidation in suggesting that if the costs of failing to overturn democracy are excessive and the probabilities of success minimal, actors will stay in the democratic game no matter how much they hate it.[6]

To require a consolidated democracy be free of political crisis and threats is seen by J. Samuel Valenzuela as "insufficient" and "excessively demanding."[7] All democracies, even consolidated ones, are always susceptible to disintegration. Instead, Valenzuela looks at what may undermine a democracy and its institutions, or what he calls "perverse institutionalization." A consolidated democracy is one without perverse elements—the number of which is many.[8]

As more and more scholars have recognized the problematic nature of such a loaded concept as democratic consolidation, a movement has risen advocating the disaggregation of the term. Perhaps the best way to study consolidation is to "disaggregate the concept of democratic regime and focus the analysis on how the component parts operate rather than trying to assess whether the political system overall is consolidated."[9] In doing so, researchers can use existing bodies of literature and theories that have been developed on elements of a democratic regime (elections, parties, legislatures, interest groups, civil-military relations, civil society) when examining their condition. Gary Hoskin speaks for many when he argues that this movement to disaggregate democratic consolidation represents an appealing alternative by drawing on different "islands of theory" that have emerged for studying various dimensions of democracies.[10]

The authors of this study agree in principle with those who advocate a disaggregation of the term "democratic consolidation." Scholars have spent too much intellectual energy on formulating and arguing over definitions of phenomena, such as regime type, stages of transition, and conditions for consolidation, while neglecting the study of the functioning of an effective democracy. Does correctly labeling a particular regime as transitional, semiconsolidated, or consolidated matter as much as understanding its working aspects? For the citizens of these emerging democracies the latter takes precedence. Only by disaggregating democratic consolidation can it be approached in a manner that accounts for variance in the development of different elements of a regime, and only then can questions of how democracy affects ordinary citizens be broached.

Historical Overview

Prior to the 1980s, El Salvador experienced little in the way of democratic development (see Table 1). Though there were periods of limited political reform, they were restricted to urban areas and were never intended to give opposition groups effective political representation.[11] After 1931 when the military assumed direct control of the government, the possibilities for constructing a civilian democratic regime were greatly limited.

As in the other Central American republics, El Salvador witnessed high levels of political violence and instability following independence. Caudillos and their personal armies battled one another over the right to assume public office. Not until the 1870s, with the expansion of coffee production, was some semblance of order established. Even then, it was not until after 1911 that civilians occupied the presidency in an uninterrupted fashion.

Table 1. Salvadoran Heads of State since 1931

Term	Name	Method of Assuming Office
1931–1934	Gen. Maximiliano Hernández Martínez	Coup
1934–35	Gen. Andrés Ignacio Menéndez	Apptd. by Hernández Martínez
1935–1944	Gen. Maximiliano Hernández Martínez	Fraudulent election
1944	Gen. Andrés Ignacio Menéndez	Apptd. by Hernández Martínez
1944–45	Col. Osmín Aguirre y Salinas	Coup
1945–1948	Gen. Salvador Castaneda Castro	Noncompetitive election
1948–1950	Military-civilian junta	Coup
1950–1956	Maj. Oscar Osorio	Semicompetitive election
1956–1960	Lt. Col. José María Lemus	Noncompetitive election
1960–61	Military-civilian junta	Coup
1961–62	Military-civilian junta	Coup
1962	Eusebio Rodolfo Cordón	Apptd. by constituent assembly
1962–1967	Col. Julio Adalberto Rivera	Noncompetitive election
1967–1972	Col. Fidel Sánchez Hernández	Semicompetitive election
1972–1977	Col. Arturo Armando Molina	Fraudulent election
1977–1979	Gen. Carlos Humberto Romero	Fraudulent election
1979–1982	Series of military-civilian juntas	Coup
1982–1984	Alvaro Magaña	Apptd. by constituent assembly
1984–1989	José Napoleón Duarte	Semicompetitive election
1989–1994	Alfredo Cristiani	Semicompetitive election
1994–1999	Armando Calderón Sol	Competitive election
1999–	Francisco Flores	Competitive election

From 1911 to 1927 two prominent coffee- and sugar-producing families (Menéndez-Quiñones) dominated the government. A boom in coffee exports during the 1920s contributed to a more relaxed political environment. During this period the Salvadoran trade union movement emerged to become the strongest in Central America, and the Salvadoran Communist Party was founded.

The limited political opening was short-lived. In December 1931 a group of junior officers, unhappy with President Arturo Araujo's (March–December 1931) handling of the economic crisis, staged a successful coup that ushered in a period of prolonged military rule. Araujo's vice president, General Maximiliano Hernández Martínez, took over as president and set about laying the groundwork for the military's consolidation of power. The fraudulent municipal elections in January 1932 triggered an indigenous uprising that shook the Hernández Martínez regime. The military responded by executing thousands of peasants suspected of participating in the rebellion or aiding the rebels. In the wake of the rebellion, Hernández Martínez won the allegiance of the agro-export elite and developed an extensive paramilitary network in the rural areas, in hopes of prolonging his political control. Nevertheless, during the 1940s a new generation of officers emerged to oppose Hernández Martínez's plans for remaining in power.

A successful coup in 1948 opened up new possibilities for reform. The officers who carried out the coup referred to their movement as a "revolution." Influenced by reformist initiatives in neighboring Guatemala and in Costa Rica, the government led by Major Oscar Osorio (1950–1956) sought to diversify the economy by promoting domestic industry and new agro-exports, and by investing in social programs. It also allowed greater political space for opposition parties to compete in elections. Nevertheless, in many ways the military governments of the 1950s resembled that of Hernández Martínez. The political opening was restricted to urban areas and did not translate into significant representation for opposition parties. The reforms never threatened the economic dominance of the agro-export elite. And finally, the military maintained its pervasive paramilitary structure in the rural areas.

A steep decline in the international price of coffee (1957–1960) contributed to growing social tensions and a full-blown political crisis in 1960. President José María Lemus's (1956–1960) reckless attempts to repress opposition movements prompted a group of officers loyal to former president Osorio to overthrow Lemus in October 1960 and replace him with a civilian-military junta. Unfortunately for the junta, the international environment in 1960 was not conducive to its efforts to open up political space for the Left. The United States, concerned about the Cuban revolution spreading across Latin America, never extended diplomatic recognition. In January 1961 the junta was ousted in a bloodless coup by a group of conservative officers more in tune with U.S. interests.

The military governments of the 1960s found themselves caught between the U.S. insistence on political and economic reforms to prevent revolutionary threats and the agro-export elite's resistance to such reforms. In the context of substantial economic growth stimulated in part by the Central American Common Market, the governments of Colonels Julio Adalberto Rivera (1962–1967) and Fidel Sánchez Hernández (1967–1972) tolerated increased opportunities for opposition groups. By 1968 opposition parties were close to obtaining a majority of seats in the legislature and were poised to mount a significant challenge in the 1972 presidential elections. In fact, because of the opposition's electoral advances, the military had to resort to widespread fraud to secure the election of Colonel Arturo Armando Molina in 1972. Disillusionment with the military's electoral shenanigans was not limited to opposition groups. An unsuccessful coup by reformist officers hoping to prevent Molina from assuming the presidency signaled the growing disenchantment within the military over the slow pace of reforms.

After 1972 reform gradually gave way to repression. President Molina's (1972–1977) tepid land reform program was successfully blocked by conservative landholding interests. The army's paramilitary structure proved ineffective in containing growing opposition during the 1970s. In the countryside, the expulsion of 130,000 Salvadorans by the Honduran government in the aftermath of the Soccer War contributed to increasing land pressures. In urban areas, industrialization failed to provide adequate employment

opportunities for the growing influx of rural migrants. As the 1970s unfolded, the military's political control began to unravel. Increasingly, the
military turned to repression. President Carlos Humberto Romero's (1977–
1979) repressive tactics fueled a spiral of political violence as armed groups
on the Left responded with kidnappings and assassinations of prominent
business and political leaders. By mid 1979 there were five small guerrilla
groups operating in the country.[12] Although the armed Left was split along
ideological and tactical lines, it posed a significant enough threat to prompt
a group of young reformist officers to oust the Romero government in a
coup in October 1979.

The 1979 coup provided a unique opportunity to implement far-
reaching reforms, especially since it enjoyed the support of a spectrum of
opposition groups and key leaders in the Catholic Church.[13] Nevertheless,
within ten weeks of the coup, the junior officers had lost control to a group
of conservative officers only superficially committed to the reform program. Conservative officers were more concerned with the growing threat
posed by the revolutionary Left, which, by the end of 1980, was united under the Farabundo Martí Front for National Liberation (Frente Farabundo
Martí de Liberación Nacional, FMLN).[14] Nevertheless, as the war escalated,
the Salvadoran military increasingly came to depend on U.S. assistance for
its survival. In return, the military would have to show greater respect for
human rights, implement a series of reforms, and permit the election of a
civilian-led government.

Elections without Democracy

For some observers the 1979 coup represented a watershed event. Enrique
Baloyra, writing in 1982, argued that the coup marked the end of "reactionary despotism" in El Salvador, ushering in a series of reforms that undermined continued oligarchic domination.[15] Other scholars agree that the coup
was an important turning point yet stress the continuities as well as the
changes in the wake of the coup.[16] For example, although conservative officers carried out a significant land reform program over the objections of
the agro-export elite, the most important phase of the reform was never
implemented. Moreover, despite the fact that the military agreed to a formal transfer of power to a civilian president, the armed forces managed to
retain their political power throughout the 1980s.[17]

Important political changes took place during this period, but they represented a process of uneven political liberalization, not a regime transition
from authoritarian to democratic rule. These political changes included holding regularly scheduled elections beginning in 1982 and leading to the election of a civilian president in 1984; the drafting of a new constitution in
1983; and the opening of political space to accommodate the Christian Demo-

cratic Party (Partido Demócrata Cristiano, PDC) and its affiliated organizations. Nevertheless, during the 1980s at no time did the military give up its capacity to control outcomes that affected its core interests.

The process of liberalization was made more complicated by the context of the war. Salvadoran military leaders and their U.S. advisors viewed liberalization as part of an overall counterinsurgency program. Thus, the opening and closing of political spaces responded in part to the dynamics of the war. Also influencing the liberalization process was U.S. policy. The Reagan and Bush administrations exerted variable pressure on the regime, especially about human rights abuses.[18]

One of the most important political innovations after 1979 was the decision to organize a series of regularly scheduled elections. While U.S. administration officials pointed to the elections between 1982 and 1991 as proof of a democratic transition in El Salvador, critics of U.S. policy condemned them as "demonstration elections."[19] In assessing the degree to which elections contribute to democratic governance, Booth employs three criteria: breadth of political participation, range of political participation, and depth of political participation. Breadth of participation involves the proportion of citizens that actively engages in politics.[20] Range of participation concerns the diverse ways in which citizens participate in political activities. And depth refers to the autonomy and potential efficacy of political participation.

One obvious measure of the breadth of participation is voter turnout in the elections. Here we find a pattern of sharply declining voter turnout throughout the period (1982–1991). During the 1982 and 1984 elections, turnout ranged from 1.4 million to over 1.5 million voters. For subsequent elections, turnout hovered between 1 million and 1.1 million voters (see Table 2). Turnout as a percentage of registered voters is even more revealing. In the 1982 elections, turnout was 63.6 percent of registered voters; by 1991 it was down to 45.8 percent (Table 2). Thus, by 1991 less than a majority of Salvadoran voters were participating in the electoral process.[21]

In terms of the second criterion, range of participation, the elections did present citizens with greater opportunities for political participation. Nevertheless, these opportunities were extremely limited by the context of the civil war and extensive human rights abuses. As the Salvadoran military and the FMLN battled for control of the countryside, the civilian population was subjected to a growing climate of fear and intimidation. The FMLN targeted regime supporters, especially pro-government mayors. However, the military and security forces were responsible for the most serious abuses.[22] As part of its counterinsurgency program, the Salvadoran military attempted to solidify its control of the countryside and to emasculate popular movements. Leaders of opposition trade unions, peasant organizations, neighborhood associations, and progressive church groups were all targeted. Although the level of human rights abuses by the military and security forces

Table 2. El Salvador: Election Results by Party, 1982–1999

Year	Type	FMLN	CD	PDC	ARENA	PCN	Total Votes[a]	Turnout Rate[b]
1982	L	NP	NP	40.1	29.5	19.2	1,551,687	63.6
1984	P	NP	NP	43.4[c]	29.8	19.3	1,419,493	56.3
1985	L	NP	NP	52.4	29.7	8.4	1,101,606	42.0
1988	L	NP	NP	35.1	48.1	8.5	1,084,132	59.0
1989	P	NP	3.8	36.0	53.8	4.1	1,003,153	39.9
1991	L	NP	12.2	28.0	44.3	9.0	1,051,481	45.8
1994	P[d]	25.0[e]		16.3	49.1[f]	5.3	1,411,320	54.0
	L	21.4	4.5	17.9	45.0	6.2	1,453,299	54.0
	M	21.4	3.4	19.4	44.4	8.0	1,450,434	54.0
1997	L	33.0	3.5	8.4	35.4	8.7	1,176,909	37.0
	M	32.6	2.4	9.1	36.6	9.2	1,169,376	37.0
1999	P	29.1	7.5[g]	5.77	52.0	3.8	1,223,215	38.6

Sources: The 1982–1991 and 1994 municipal results are from Enrique Baloyra, "Elections, Civil War, and Transition in El Salvador, 1982–1994," in Mitchell A. Seligson and John A. Booth, *Elections and Democracy in Central America, Revisited* (Chapel Hill: University of North Carolina Press, 1995), 54. The 1994 presidential and legislative results are from Ricardo Córdova Macias and Andrew Stein, "National and Local Elections in El Salvador 1982–1994," in Henry Dietz and Gil Shidlo, eds., *Urban Elections in Latin America* (Wilmington, DE: Scholarly Resources, 1998), 145. Results and total vote figures for 1997 are from "Resultados Estadísticos de las Elecciones de 1994 y 1997" (San Salvador: TSE-UNDP, 1997). Total votes figures for 1982–1991 are from Richard Stahler-Sholk, "El Salvador's Negotiated Transition: From Low-Intensity Conflict to Low-Intensity Democracy," *Journal of Interamerican Studies and World Affairs* 36, no. 4 (1994): 27. Presidential results and total vote figures for 1999 are from "Consolidado Nacional del Escrutinio Final para Elección de Presidente y Vice-presidente de la República: Elección 1999," Tribunal Supremo Electoral, http://www.tse.gob.sv/Cuadroef.htm.

Notes: Results are expressed as percentages. Only major parties are included. L = legislative elections; P = presidential elections; M = municipal elections; NP = did not participate. Names of parties: Farabundo Martí Front for National Liberation (Frente Farabundo Martí de Liberación Nacional, FMLN); Democratic Convergence (Convergencia Democrática, CD); Christian Democratic Party (Partido Demócrata Cristiano, PDC); Nationalist Republican Alliance (Alianza Republicana Nacionalista, ARENA); and National Conciliation Party (Partido de Conciliación Nacional, PCN).

[a]Includes blank and spoiled ballots. Percentages are calculated on the basis of valid votes only.

[b]This rate equals total votes as a percentage of total registered voters.

[c]The PDC went on to win in the second round of voting over ARENA (53.6 percent to 46.4 percent).

[d]First round of voting only.

[e]The FMLN, CD, and National Revolutionary Movement (Movimiento Nacional Revolucionario, MNR) ran together in a coalition on the presidential ballot.

[f]ARENA won the second round over the FMLN (68.3 percent to 31.7 percent).

[g]The CD ran together in a coalition with the Democratic Party (Partido Demócrata, PD), Popular Labor Party (Partido Popular Laborista, PPL), and the Christian Democratic Unity Movement (Movimiento de Unificación Demócrata Cristiano, MUDC).

peaked by 1983, they continued, albeit at lower levels, for some time, thereafter. Moreover, throughout the period of the civil war, the military High Command refused to punish those officers responsible for the abuses.

In addition to the limitations on participation in political activities, the elections from 1982 to 1991 presented voters with a limited scope of choices. In this sense, electoral participation was shallow. Unlike in elections during the 1970s, the Christian Democrats were able to compete and win elections at the national level. Nevertheless, the left of the political spectrum was not represented until the 1989 presidential elections, when Guillermo Ungo, a member of the political wing of the FMLN, competed as a candidate. The return of Ungo and other social democratic leaders to El Salvador in 1987 resulted in the formation of a new opposition coalition, the Democratic Convergence (Convergencia Democrática, CD).[23] Despite the decision of the CD to compete in the elections, Ungo and his supporters were severely limited in their ability to campaign. The climate of fear and intimidation that reigned throughout most of the country made it difficult for the CD to get its message across to voters. Moreover, because of the use of translucent, sequentially numbered ballots and clear plastic ballot boxes, voters had little guarantee that their vote would remain secret. The climate of fear was still present during the legislative and municipal elections in 1991, making it difficult for the CD to campaign or field candidates outside of the capital.[24]

The depth of participation also was limited in that elections between 1982 and 1991 failed to significantly influence government policy. For example, despite the fact that in his 1984 presidential campaign José Napoleón Duarte ran on a platform endorsing negotiations with the FMLN and further political and economic reforms, the "chief result of the 1984 election, like that of 1982, was a major escalation of the war, made possible through a dramatic increase in U.S. aid."[25] Not surprisingly, there was a significant decline in voter turnout in subsequent elections, most likely reflecting "decreasing voter confidence in the efficacy of the elections, particularly at resolving the war and in improving the economy."[26]

A fourth criterion can be added to the three used by Booth to assess the relationship between elections and democratization: the degree to which elections contribute to a political compromise among the country's principal political actors. Terry Karl argues correctly that, while an institutional compromise over the basic "ground rules" of the new political regime was fundamental in the Salvadoran case, it was not a sufficient basis for a democratic transition.[27] Because of the deep societal divisions resulting from the war, a substantive compromise was also necessary, including issues such as past human rights abuses, land reform, incorporation of the FMLN into the political process, and the future of the two contending armies. Nevertheless, elections during the 1980s were used by the regime and the Reagan administration as an alternative to negotiating these issues with the FMLN.

Excluding the FMLN from the electoral process made a political compromise unlikely, if not impossible.

The signing of the 1992 peace accords between the government of El Salvador and the FMLN represented a significant breakthrough toward achieving a substantive compromise between the country's principal political forces. Support for a negotiated settlement gained momentum in the wake of the FMLN's November 1989 offensive. The Salvadoran High Command's lack of preparedness and its fatal decision to murder the six Jesuit priests during the offensive damaged its credibility, fueled internal factionalism, and jeopardized future U.S. assistance. At the regional and international level, the Central American peace process under the leadership of Oscar Arias and the Bush administration's more pragmatic approach created new opportunities for a peace agreement. Finally, war weariness and continued economic decline contributed to growing support for negotiations, including among leaders of the moderate faction of the governing Nationalist Republican Alliance (Alianza Republicana Nacionalista, ARENA) party.

Beyond the Peace Accords

On January 16, 1992, representatives of the FMLN and the Salvadoran government signed a comprehensive peace agreement, including electoral, judicial, socioeconomic, military, and police reforms. By addressing these substantive issues and providing for a process whereby the FMLN could participate in the political process, the accords went a long way in moving the country toward a genuine process of democratization.

Elections, Electoral Reform, and Party System

It was not until the peace accords were signed that genuinely free, fair, and competitive elections became a real possibility. To ensure that the 1994 elections would truly mark a break with the past, the accords included a number of electoral reforms that guaranteed, at a minimum, procedurally democratic elections.

The 1994 Elections. The elections of the century turned out to be an important step in establishing procedural democracy in El Salvador; however, the results were less than historic, irregularities during the registration period and on election day continued, and turnout levels were disappointing. The presidential candidate of the incumbent ARENA, Armando Calderón Sol, was forced into a second round after he fell just short of an absolute majority in the first round. ARENA held onto the presidency with a convincing (68.3 percent to 31.7 percent) victory in the second round (Table 2). The FMLN achieved more tangible gains in the legislative election. It secured 21 of the 84 National Assembly seats, making it the second strongest party in the country. ARENA garnered 39 seats, short of a majority; however, by allying with other parties on the right, it retained a working majority in the legislature. At the municipal level, ARENA made a strong showing winning 207 of El Salvador's 262 municipalities. The FMLN's victory in only 15 municipalities was the most sobering result of the 1994 election for the former guerrillas. In sum, other than introducing the FMLN as a new countervailing force to ARENA in the legislature and a weakening of the PDC, the 1994 elections did not greatly alter the distribution of political power.

As an exercise in democratic development, the 1994 elections did signal a step in the right direction. On the positive side, the elections went off without widespread fraud or irregularities, pre-election campaign political violence was confined to isolated incidents, and all parties abided by the official results. On the negative side, procedural problems plagued the voter registration process in the months leading up to the elections. It is estimated that those excluded from participating in the 1994 elections were equivalent to at least 20 percent of those voting.[28] In addition, ARENA outspent the FMLN U.S.$12 million to $270,000 during the campaign, allowing ARENA to have a major advantage in advertising time on television and radio than the FMLN.[29] Many placed blame for these numbers squarely on the shoulders of the Supreme Electoral Tribunal (Tribunal Supremo Electoral, TSE), the governing body overseeing Salvadoran elections, because of its unbalanced nature and use of questionable formulas for determining the distribution of funds.[30] It is this type of "technical fraud," rather than the more blatant forms of the past, that earned the 1994 contest less than glowing assessments.

As a showcase for democratic participation, the 1994 elections were a disappointment, especially given the high expectations. As it turns out just over 51 percent of registered voters cast ballots in March 1994; the presidential run-off held a month later saw a 46 percent turnout rate. These numbers reflected only slight improvement in terms of the breadth of participation for the "elections of the century" (Table 2).

Heading the list of reasons for the low voter turnout were procedural irregularities, followed by the impact of death squad activities in the months leading up to the elections and the fact that the election did not carry a sense of urgency as, for example, the 1990 Nicaraguan elections did. A resumption of the civil war seemed unlikely, the economy was starting to rebound, and a flood of remittances from abroad helped bolster Salvadorans' standard of living. In short, the 1994 elections, while attracting considerable international attention, did not generate significantly more interest among Salvadorans than had previous ones.

The 1997 Elections. After the 1994 contest it was clear that more extensive reforms were needed. A presidential commission was formed in 1995 to discuss further reforms and it issued a series of recommendations.[31]

Little ever came of the recommendations because ARENA used its dominance in the Assembly to stall the reforms. In fact, the next year ARENA, with the help of the PDC, pushed through an alternative electoral reform that amended the electoral code so as to restrict the number of small parties.[32] Instead of addressing the inadequacies of the existing registration process and assignment of polling places—both of which hold down turnout and disadvantage marginalized sectors—ARENA favored a more restrictive electoral process.

The legislative and municipal elections of 1997 were another opportunity to assess democratic development since the signing of the accords. Again, there was mixed evidence in this regard. Most important, Hector Silva, the FMLN candidate, scored a convincing win over ARENA's incumbent mayor, Mario Valiente, in the San Salvador mayoral race. In a positive sign, once it was clear that ARENA was going to lose the capital, Valiente conceded publicly and early to Silva, as did President Calderón Sol. This marked the first time ARENA had to concede a major electoral defeat to its former enemies. Such "firsts" were important for a country still recovering from a deeply polarizing civil war.

Other results of the 1997 election were significant as well. The FMLN and ARENA received about equal percentages of the total vote, each around 35 percent (Table 2). This translated into 28 seats in the Assembly for ARENA and 27 for the FMLN. The FMLN posted even more dramatic victories in the municipal elections, winning 6 of the 14 department capitals, and 53 of the 262 municipalities. As a result of these victories the Left now controlled the local government of more than 50 percent of Salvadorans. The FMLN's success in 1997 brought a greater balance of power between the Left and the Right.

Despite the historic results of the 1997 elections, they did not provide evidence of meaningful electoral reform. Voter turnout was even more disappointing than in 1994 since it fell to 37 percent (Table 2). This drop can be accounted for, in part, by the fact that they were not presidential elections and carried less national attention. Still, many had hoped that the less charged political atmosphere would have resulted in greater participation. Low voter turnout had an influence on the election results. ARENA officials claimed that absenteeism was the principal cause of their party's poor showing. Many traditional ARENA supporters were said to have stayed home out of overconfidence. In addition, there was general dissatisfaction with the party because of a number of recent policy initiatives and a slumping economy.[33]

The 1999 Elections and Current Electoral Conditions. A number of persistent problems continued to dog El Salvador's democratic consolidation in the run-up to the 1999 elections. Public opinion polls indicated low levels of citizen support for the political system. One-third of the population, for whatever reason, did not participate in the political system, and the TSE continued to come under fire for its procedural complexity and questionable integrity.[34] El Salvador suffered from citizen distrust of government institutions, apathy toward politics, and public doubt about the government's and parties' ability to solve pressing issues such as crime and economic inequality. These were serious obstacles to consolidation.

Not surprisingly, the turnout (38.6 percent) for the 1999 presidential election was only slightly better than that in 1997. Low turnout appeared to favor the incumbent ARENA, whose presidential candidate, Francisco Flores, won a majority (52 percent) in first-round voting. Neither Flores nor Facundo Guardado (FMLN) succeeded in energizing the electorate. Internal divisions at the FMLN's party convention to select presidential and vice presidential candidates raised questions about the party's ability to govern effectively. Although ARENA presented itself as the more cohesive and experienced party, it—like the FMLN—offered only vague solutions to the country's most pressing problems.

Finally, while some of El Salvador's political parties showed signs of growing institutional cohesiveness in the wake of the 1999 elections, their failure to establish stable roots in society indicated that the Salvadoran party system was still far from becoming institutionalized.[35] It must be acknowledged, however, that the party system made significant strides in the 1990s. The system seemed to be moving rapidly to a bipolar configuration, with the FMLN dominating the Left and ARENA controlling the Right. The traditionally strong centrist party—the PDC—experienced a dramatic decline in recent elections (see Table 2) and found itself increasingly squeezed out as the FMLN and ARENA moderated their platforms. The bipolarization of the Salvadoran party system, still present in the 1999 elections, hurt small and centrist parties the most but pointed to the fact that the ideological distance between the two major parties was shrinking.[36]

Enhancing Municipal Governance

At the conclusion of the civil war it was generally agreed that local governments needed to be strengthened if democratic consolidation was to move forward. Like most Latin American states, El Salvador had a history of a strong, centralized system of governance. This arrangement contributed to a situation where local governments had little functional power, serving as administrative liaisons for the activities of central government ministries and providing only supplementary services.[37] In addition, state resources were inadequate for addressing local needs, with El Salvador's 262 municipalities receiving less than 1 percent of the national budget. Moreover, municipalities lacked any means to generate revenues for themselves, relying instead on transfers from the central government and foreign aid donations.[38]

Municipalities in El Salvador are generally small and lack the financial means to provide their residents with basic services. In 1998, more than three-quarters (201 out of 262) of them had populations under 20,000. These largely rural municipalities had trouble raising local revenues because they did not have local sources of income—only 8.1 percent of small municipalities' total resources came from local sources. Larger, more urban communities found it easier to generate funds; for example, a recent study found an 8-to-1 or 9-to-1 urban-rural difference in taxes raised per capita. [39] Moreover, the destruction incurred by small rural communities during the civil war exacerbated the inequality between small and large municipalities.[40]

In recognition of the inherent weakness of local governments, several measures were implemented to strengthen municipalities as part of an overall decentralization process. The 1983 constitution provided for municipal autonomy by acknowledging municipalities as autonomous in economic, technical, and political terms. Further, the 1986 Municipal Code spelled out the limits of municipal competence and powers. And, in 1986 the Salvadoran government initiated the Municipalities in Action (MIA) program. Originally an initiative of the U.S. Agency for International Development with counterinsurgency elements, MIA evolved into an effective program to shift resources to localities. Thus, even before the end of the civil war, Salvadoran municipalities had started to receive greater attention.

MIA centered its program on the *cabildo abierto* (municipal assembly), a Salvadoran version of a town meeting. At these regularly held gatherings, municipal officials reported on the implementation of community programs and residents could propose new projects. MIA encouraged a second mechanism, *consultas populares* (popular consultations), by which local initiatives were discussed publicly before implementation. And finally, *asociaciones comunales* (community groups) of at least twenty-five members were granted official recognition and were to serve as advisors to the municipal council. These bodies were intended to foster citizen participation in local government; however, implementation of these municipal bodies was uneven and their effectiveness questioned.[41]

One obstacle to greater citizen participation was the way in which leaders of local governments were determined. According to the electoral code, the party or coalition that won a simple plurality of the vote in a local election received the mayorship and all the municipal council seats. This "winner-takes-all" arrangement favored large parties because they overwhelmingly dominated control of local government. Electoral rules such as these allowed for parties who lost by a slim margin to remain totally excluded from local government for the next three years.

In an effort to make local government more pluralistic, a number of voices[42] called for proportional representation in municipal council elections, thereby providing greater opposition party representation on the council. Another proposed reform was to open up council sessions to the public to ensure more honest and efficient functioning of local government. And finally, to strengthen municipal autonomy, the government needed to undertake tax reform in a way that would provide municipalities with their own sources of funding.[43] These municipal reforms, if implemented, had the potential to create a greater balance of political power between national and local government and to make municipal government more responsive to citizens' needs.

Military and Police Reforms

During the negotiations leading to the peace accords, the question of the armed forces was a major sticking point. Especially problematic was the issue of past human rights abuses by military officers. The peace accords went a long way toward addressing the problem of impunity and laid out an impressive blueprint for subjecting the military to democratic control and the rule of law. "Under the peace accords, the military's constitutional role no longer included public security; the security forces were dissolved and a new civilian police force created under executive control; the military-controlled intelligence agency was disbanded and a new one set up under civilian control; the military academy was now accountable to a civilian-military council; and, for the first time in history, officers had to submit to an external evaluation conducted by civilians."[44]

Not surprisingly, members of the armed forces contested the implementation of some of these reforms. Especially controversial was the work of the Ad Hoc Commission, which was charged with evaluating the entire officer corps; especially officers' past record on human rights, their professional competence, and their ability to adapt to a democratic society. Control over internal promotions, assignments, and discipline had been a traditional core prerogative of the Salvadoran military. Thus, the work of the Ad Hoc Commission was interpreted by many officers as an attack on the institution. When the commission presented its report in September 1992, the military High Command (several of whom were singled out for removal) refused to carry out the recommendations. After much pressure by the Clinton administration (including conditioning $11 million in military assistance on full compliance with the commission's recommendations) and the UN, the High Command eventually relinquished in March 1993.[45]

The dismantling of the security forces and the creation of the new National Civilian Police (Policía Nacional Civil, PNC) was similarly problematic.[46] First, the High Command delayed in disbanding the security forces and then incorporated the National Guard and Treasury Police structurally intact into the army. Second, the military was not cooperative in supporting the creation of the new police force. The High Command's unwillingness to provide a suitable location for the new police academy delayed its scheduled opening by four months. In addition, the military refused to hand over equipment provided by the U.S. administration's police aid program. Because of these delays, the process of deploying the PNC and dismantling the old National Police was not complete by the time of the 1994 elections.

Consequently, during the electoral process the PNC was deployed in only about half the country, with the National Police responsible for public security in the rest.

By the end of 1994 the National Police's demobilization was completed, as were the rest of the military reforms agreed to by the government and the FMLN. Despite the uneven nature of the implementation phase, the reforms succeeded in significantly circumscribing the military's political prerogatives and influence. Nevertheless, the accords did not go far enough in ensuring civilian supremacy over the armed forces. The military lost many of its prerogatives, but it retained much of its institutional autonomy intact. For example, the military maintained complete control over defense policy; the minister of defense was still an active-duty officer; legislative oversight of the defense budget and internal promotions remained weak; and, despite its constitutional role having been limited to national defense, the military continued to be involved in public security and intelligence gathering.[47] Further reforms, then, were needed to make the armed forces accountable to elected officials. Although military officers were unlikely to embrace additional reforms, civilian leadership, combined with the constant pressure of organized groups in civil society and of international actors, could open up new opportunities in the future.

Socioeconomic Conditions and Trends

The peace accords, while initiating reform in several different aspects of Salvadoran society, did not adequately address economic issues. The underlying conditions that drove people to openly challenge the regime in the 1980s were left largely unresolved. One area of economic reform that the accords did address to some extent was land ownership. They provided for a land transfer program that was to distribute land to former combatants from both sides of the conflict, and to those who had cultivated land in war zones. Approximately 47,500 heads of households were originally to receive land, but that number dropped closer to 35,000. The transfers were slow and plagued with problems, but by the end of 1996 the transfers were complete.[48]

Agriculture remained critically important; it still employed 27 percent of the labor force (more than any other sector), provided one-third of export earnings, and satisfied 70 percent of domestic food needs.[49] One of the most contentious issues after the peace accords was debt burden relief for small landowners and agrarian reform cooperatives. In 1996 the Assembly passed legislation forgiving 70 percent of the outstanding debt of agrarian reform cooperatives, while providing financing for the rest.[50] Agriculture, however, was fast becoming a smaller sector relative to others. In 1980, for example, agricultural activities accounted for 38 percent of the GDP; by 1995 this had dropped to 14 percent. At the same time, the nonagricultural economy became increasingly dominant, especially under the Cristiani administration. Alfredo Cristiani, a prominent member of the economic elite, initiated a series of neoliberal policies promoting export-led growth. In addition to traditional exports, the government supported the expansion of nontraditional exports such as tomatoes, yucca, watermelons, oranges, and sesame seed. The fastest growing export sector during the first half of the 1990s was the *maquila* industries, mainly textiles and clothing imported for assembly and re-exported to the United States. Exports from *maquilas* grew from $198 million in 1992 to $1.2 billion in 1998,[51] accounting for close to 50 percent of total export earnings—more than three times that of coffee.[52] Although *maquilas* employed over fifty thousand Salvadorans, the pay was low, working conditions were poor, and *maquilas* hired almost exclusively young women with little formal education.

Neoliberal policies in the 1990s also focused on privatization. The Salvadoran government was in the process of privatizing key state industries such as banking, the state pensions system, telecommunications, and electricity companies. After two years of legislative setbacks, the privatization of the all-important state-run telecommunications industry was finalized in July 1998.

The ARENA government claimed that its policies were producing positive results. For example, the economy grew at an average of 6.8 percent from 1992 through 1995, helped by the return of private investment and remittances from relatives in the United States. The economy did experience an eighteen-month recession from 1996 to mid 1997, but grew at 3.2 percent in 1998 and 1.8 percent in 1999.[53] Inflation declined from a rate of 10 percent in 1995 to 2.5 percent in 1998. Thus, according to macroeconomic indicators, the Salvadoran economy has enjoyed steady expansion with low inflation since 1992.

Unfortunately, life for most Salvadorans did not improve measurably over the same period. Finding secure employment was difficult. While the official unemployment rate stood at 8 percent in 1997, underemployment was estimated at 50 percent of the labor force. Moreover, about 70 percent of the working population received less than the minimum wage.[54] As a consequence the informal sector grew tremendously and income disparity worsened. Many Salvadorans came to rely increasingly on remittances; a poll found that 26 percent of the population depended on money received from abroad.[55] Remittances totaled $1.24 billion in 1999, equal to over 50 percent of export earnings.[56]

The peace accords ushered in a period of growth for those well situated to benefit from neoliberal policies and participate in a more diversified economy. Sadly, this applied to only a small percentage of Salvadorans. For the rest, peace and economic reforms brought little material gains. The country suffered from an explosion of organized crime and gang activity. El Salvador recently gained the unfortunate distinction of having the highest murder rate per capita in Central America. Polls showed that crime and economic problems were the most worrisome issues for Salvadorans. Yet few Salvadorans believed that the government was capable of solving these problems.[57]

Conclusion

Despite the political opening during the 1980s, it was not until the peace accords were signed in 1992 that a genuine democratic transition became possible. Although the 1994 election signaled the culmination of the first transition, it also highlighted some of the formidable tasks awaiting the second transition: the stage of democratic consolidation. While great progress was achieved in laying the institutional and procedural foundations for democracy, the challenge of increasing opportunities for citizen participation became an intractable problem. For example, while the electoral system was becoming more institutionalized, the political system, in its entirety, was seen as less than effective by most Salvadorans. Evidence of this was the low level of voter turnout that continued to plague the electoral process. Moreover, although efforts to empower local government represented an encouraging development, the central government demonstrated little willingness to channel more resources to municipalities.

Whether Salvadoran democracy would live up to the expectations of Don Miguel remained to be seen. Much would depend on the ability and desire of political leaders at the national and local level to foster greater levels of citizen participation in the decision-making process. This in turn could lead to more effective governmental institutions that address Salvadorans' most basic, yet pressing problems. Only then, would Don Miguel's dream of "peace with justice" become reality for all Salvadorans.

Notes

1. Anonymous interview with base community member, Mejicanos, March 17, 1994.

2. John A. Booth, "Introduction. Elections and Democracy in Central America: A Framework for Analysis," in Mitchell A. Seligson and John A. Booth, eds., *Elections and Democracy in Central America, Revisited* (Chapel Hill: University of North Carolina Press, 1995), 7.

3. Guillermo O'Donnell, "Transitions, Continuities, and Paradoxes," in Scott Mainwaring, Guillermo O'Donnell, and J. Samuel Valenzuela, eds., *Issues in Democratic Consolidation: The New South American Democracies in Comparative Perspective* (South Bend, IN: University of Notre Dame Press, 1992), 17–56.

4. Ibid., 48–49.

5. Samuel P. Huntington, *The Third Wave: Democratization in the Late Twentieth Century* (Norman: University of Oklahoma Press, 1991).

6. Ben Ross Schneider, "Democratic Consolidations: Some Broad Comparisons and Sweeping Arguments," *Latin American Research Review* 30, no. 2 (1995): 220.

7. J. Samuel Valenzuela, "Democratic Consolidation in Post-Transitional Settings," in Mainwaring, O'Donnell, and Valenzuela, *Issues in Democratic Consolidation*, 59.

8. Valenzuela lists the most threatening as: (1) nondemocratically generated tutelary powers, (2) the existence of reserved domains of authority and decision making, (3) major discriminations in the electoral process, and (4) means other than free elections whereby it is possible to constitute governments. Ibid., 62–68.

9. Schneider, "Democratic Consolidations," 220–21.

10. Gary Hoskin, "Democratization in Latin America," *Latin American Research Review* 32, no. 3 (1997): 223.

11. This section draws primarily from Philip Williams and Knut Walter, *Militarization and Demilitarization in El Salvador's Transition to Democracy* (Pittsburgh: University of Pittsburgh Press, 1997), chaps. 2–4.

12. For more on the origins and evolution of the revolutionary movement in El Salvador, see Tommie Sue Montgomery, *Revolution in El Salvador: From Civil Strife to Civil Peace* (Boulder, CO: Westview Press, 1995), chap. 4.

13. The first junta and its cabinet included representatives from the Foro Popular—an alliance of opposition parties, trade unions, and peasant organizations—and from the private sector. It also received the endorsement of the Archbishop of San Salvador, Oscar Romero.

14. The FMLN consisted of the following revolutionary organizations: Popular Forces of Liberation (Fuerzas Populares de Liberación, FPL); National Resistance (Resistencia Nacional, RN); Revolutionary Army of the People (Ejército Revolucionario del Pueblo, ERP); Revolutionary Party of Central American Workers (Partido Revolucionario de Trabaja dores Centroamericanos, PRTC); and the Communist Party of El Salvador (Partido Comunista Salvadoreño, PCS).

15. Enrique Baloyra, *El Salvador in Transition* (Chapel Hill: University of North Carolina Press, 1982).

16. Montgomery, *Revolution in El Salvador.*

17. See Williams and Walter, *Militarization and Demilitarization*, chap. 6.

18. See Cynthia Arnson, *Crossroads: Congress, the President, and Central America* (University Park: Penn State University Press, 1993).

19. See, especially, Frank Brodhead and Edward Herman, *Demonstration Elections: U.S.-Staged Elections in the Dominican Republic, Vietnam, and El Salvador* (Boston: South End Press, 1984).

20. Booth, "Introduction," 1–21.

21. Baloyra suggests a number of factors that contributed to declining turnout: decreasing voter confidence in the efficacy of the elections, decreasing confidence in political parties, guerrilla violence, and the complicated registration process. Enrique Baloyra, "Elections, Civil War, and Transition in El Salvador, 1982–1994," in Seligson and Booth, *Elections and Democracy*, 51–56.

22. The UN Truth Commission attributed 85 percent of the abuses to the military and security forces. United Nations, *De la locura a la esperanza: Informe de la Comision de la Verdad para El Salvador* (New York: UN Department of Public Information, March 1993).

23. The parties making up the CD were: National Revolutionary Movement (Movimiento Nacionalista Revolucionario, MNR), Popular Social Christian Movement (Movimiento Popular Social Cristiano, MPSC), and Social Democratic Party (Partido Social Demócrata, PSD).

24. Baloyra, "Elections, Civil War, and Transition."

25. Terry Karl, "Exporting Democracy: The Unanticipated Effects of U.S. Electoral Policy in El Salvador," in Nora Hamilton et al., *Crisis in Central America*

(Boulder, CO: Westview Press, 1988), 180. Direct U.S. military assistance to El Salvador jumped from $81.3 million in 1983 to $196.6 million in 1984.

26. Baloyra, "Elections, Civil War, and Transition," 52.

27. Karl, "Exporting Democracy," 187.

28. Jack Spence, David Dye, and George Vickers, *El Salvador's Elections of the Century: Results, Recommendations, and Analysis* (Cambridge, MA: Hemisphere Initiatives, 1994), 7.

29. Richard Stahler-Sholk, "El Salvador's Negotiated Transition: From Low-Intensity Conflict to Low-Intensity Democracy," *Journal of Interamerican Studies and World Affairs* 36, no. 4 (Winter 1994): 24.

30. Although more pluralistic than during the 1980s, the TSE continued to be highly partisan and was dominated by parties on the right. Moreover, the TSE used a complicated campaign finance formula that allowed parties to borrow against money the government would provide after the election. A party's borrowing capacity was determined by performance in previous elections.

31. The commission offered four main recommendations: unitary documents, residential voting, professionalizing the TSE, and proportional representation in municipal elections.

32. See Jack Spence, David R. Dye, Mike Lanchin, and Geoff Thale, *Chapúltepec: Five Years Later* (Cambridge, MA: Hemisphere Initiatives, 1997), 11.

33. In June 1995 the ARENA government raised the national value-added tax from 10 to 13 percent. In late 1995, it issued Decree 471, which eliminated several hundred government jobs.

34. Ricardo Córdova Macias and Andrew Stein, "National and Local Elections in El Salvador, 1982–1994," in Henry Dietz and Gil Shidlo, eds., *Urban Elections in Latin America* (Wilmington, DE: Scholarly Resources, 1998), 152–55.

35. With the exception of the PDC and the PCN, most parties are relatively new, having been formed in the 1980s. Consequently, the level of party affiliation is generally low and most parties have weak ties to organized sectors of civil society.

36. Córdova and Stein, "National and Local Elections," 144.

37. R. Andrew Nickson, *Local Government in Latin America* (Boulder, CO: Lynne Rienner, 1995).

38. In 1993 half of local governments' funds came from foreign aid. Kevin Murray, *Rescuing Reconstruction: The Debate on Post-War Economic Recovery in El Salvador* (Cambridge, MA: Hemisphere Initiatives, 1994), 35.

39. Córdova and Stein, "National and Local Elections," 153.

40. Ibid. Government reconstruction funds were distributed according to municipalities' population size.

41. See Murray, *Rescuing Reconstruction*; Nickson, *Local Government*.

42. See Córdova and Stein, "National and Local Elections," and *El Salvador: Election Observation Report* (Washington, DC: International Republican Institute, 1997).

43. Ibid., 154–55.

44. Williams and Walter, *Militarization and Demilitarization*, 1.

45. For a detailed discussion of the implementation of the reforms, ibid., chap. 7.

46. See William Stanley, *Risking Failure: The Problems and Promises of the New Civilian Police in El Salvador* (Boston: HI/WOLA, 1993).

47. In the context of increasing criminal violence after the peace accords, the military participated in "dissuasive" patrols along highways and in support of outgunned police units. In the intelligence area, although a new civilian-led intelli-

gence agency was created to replace the military's intelligence agency, the Ministry of Defense continued to be responsible for training civilian and military intelligence personnel. Williams and Walter, *Militarization and Demilitarization*, 166–67.

48. For more on the agrarian question, see T. David Mason, "Take Two Acres and Call Me in the Morning: Is Land Reform a Prescription for Peasant Unrest?" *The Journal of Politics* 60, no. 1 (1998): 199–231.

49. *Country Profile: Guatemala, El Salvador* (London: Economist Intelligence Unit, 1997), 84.

50. After the 1997 elections, the Assembly passed legislation that would forgive 100 percent of the debt for small farmers and cooperatives, but Calderón vetoed it and the opposition failed to override the veto.

51. *Country Report El Salvador*, Economist Intelligence Unit, February 4, 2000, http://www.eiu.com.

52. Ibid.

53. Ibid.

54. The minimum wage at the end of 1997 ranged from U.S. $68 to $131 a month, depending on the type of work. The overall poverty rate for 1996 was estimated at 51 percent of the population. *Proceso* 18, nos. 788 (December 24, 1997) and 801 (April 1, 1998).

55. *Country Profile: Guatemala, El Salvador, 1st Quarter* (London: Economist Intelligence Unit, 1998), 35.

56. *Country Report El Salvador*. Other social indicators pointed to uneven development; for example, 30 percent of Salvadorans were illiterate, 45 percent lacked access to safe water, and 60 percent lacked access to health care. UN Development Program, *Human Development Report* (New York: Oxford University Press, 1996).

57. "Los salvadoreños evalúan el año '97," Instituto Universitario de Opinión Pública (IUDOP), San Salvador, December 11, 1997, http://uca.edu.sv/publica/iudop/principal.htm.

3

Honduras
Militarism and Democratization in Troubled Waters

*J. Mark Ruhl**

Honduras, unlike its Central American neighbors, never became engulfed in civil war during the late 1970s and 1980s. Several small guerrilla groups did begin operation during this period, but none won significant popular support or ever posed a threat to the Honduran government's survival. Although Honduras shared many of the social and economic problems that contributed to national revolts in neighboring countries, its distinctive political traditions promoted stability. Honduran political and military elites historically were much less repressive than their counterparts in Nicaragua, El Salvador, or Guatemala and more willing to implement modest reforms to accommodate popular demands.

Electoral politics returned to Honduras during the early 1980s. Unfortunately, the nation's democratic transition from military dictatorship to democracy was more apparent than real. Behind a formal democratic facade, the Honduran military continued to be the dominant political actor. In fact, the armed forces grew stronger than ever as U.S. military aid soared in exchange for Honduras's willingness to host the Nicaraguan Contras. With the end of the cold war and the Central American civil wars, however, the United States drastically cut its military assistance to Honduras and became a strong critic of the armed forces. As the United States reversed its policies, Honduran civil society and civilian politicians grew bolder in contesting military prerogatives. In a series of dramatic reforms, the military was stripped of many of its privileges and much of its political influence. The political decline of the armed forces enabled Honduras to complete its

*The author wishes to thank Don Schulz and Kurt Weyland for their comments on an earlier version of this chapter.

long transition from authoritarian rule to procedural democracy in the late 1990s.[1]

Democratic consolidation, however, still remained a distant goal. Civilian and military elites had not yet fully and permanently committed themselves to democratic politics, and the Honduran mass population was increasingly disenchanted with democracy. Despite democratization and neoliberal economic reforms, most ordinary Hondurans saw little improvement in their traditionally poor living conditions. With a GNP per capita of only about U.S.$600 in 1998 and with 70 percent of the population living below the poverty line, this Pennsylvania-sized nation (112,088 square kilometers) of 5.9 million was the third poorest in the Americas.[2] Moreover, the massive damage done to the Honduran economy by Hurricane Mitch in late 1998 worsened the country's already difficult economic circumstances.

Sources of Political Stability: Historical Contrasts between Honduras and Its Neighbors

Compared with El Salvador, Guatemala, or Nicaragua, Honduras was an oasis of relative political stability during the late 1970s and 1980s. Although the repression of popular sector groups did increase, Honduran political and military leaders acted with far more restraint than elites in neighboring countries. Despite the deteriorating political climate, labor unions, peasant groups, and other opposition forces continued to work within the existing system. This less polarized and more accommodative elite-mass relationship was, in large part, a product of the country's distinctive late-nineteenth-century and twentieth-century history.

Honduras was the only Central American country in which coffee did not become the principal export by the late nineteenth century. No cohesive, politically dominant coffee oligarchy intent on capturing peasant lands and labor ever formed. Instead of promoting coffee, late-nineteenth-century Liberal reformers such as President Marco Aurelio Soto (1876–1883) collaborated with U.S. silver mining ventures. Other enterprising Honduran elites moved to the largely unoccupied North Coast to establish banana export enterprises.[3] The vast majority of Honduras's large landowners continued to raise cattle for local markets. None of these elite economic activities threatened the peasantry. In fact, because of the country's small population relative to its size, Honduran peasants had no difficulty acquiring lands to cultivate until well into the twentieth century. Although there was little friction between Honduran peasants and large landowners in this period, intra-elite political conflicts over state control were more persistent and more violent in Honduras than in any other Central American country.[4]

United Fruit and other U.S. companies arrived at the turn of the century to expand the banana export industry on the North Coast. They built huge plantations but displaced few peasants. The workers on these banana plantations gradually organized and formed the core of what would become Central America's strongest trade union movement. Although banana companies gained great influence over Honduran governments, they could not always count on Honduran authorities to suppress striking workers. Dictator Tiburcio Carías Andino (1932–1949) of the National Party (see table) proved a dependable ally of United Fruit, but leaders of the weaker Liberal Party tended to be more friendly to labor.[5] In addition, Carías's National Party successor Juan Manuel Gálvez (1949–1954) was a political moderate who negotiated a reasonably equitable settlement to the critical 1954 banana workers' strike. Such concessions discouraged radicalism within the banana worker unions, which affiliated with pro-U.S. international labor federations. In addition, a new commercial and industrial elite with an important immigrant Arab component that formed on the North Coast benefited from increased worker purchasing power and often endorsed banana union demands.[6] This cross-class coalition of progressive urban entrepreneurs and organized workers had no counterpart in neighboring countries. The reformist North Coast coalition provided crucial support to the resurgent Liberals led by social democrat Ramón Villeda Morales during the 1950s and early 1960s and to the populist military regime of General Oswaldo López Arellano in the 1970s.

Honduran Presidents since 1932

Term	Name	Party
1932–1949	Tiburcio Carías Andino	National Party
1949–1954	Juan Manuel Gálvez Durón	National Party
1954–1956	Julio Lozano Díaz	National Party
1956–57	Military Junta	Armed forces
1957–1963	Ramón Villeda Morales	Liberal Party
1963–1971	Gen. Oswaldo López Arellano	Armed forces
1971–72	Ramón Ernesto Cruz Uclés	National Party
1972–1975	Gen. Oswaldo López Arellano	Armed forces
1975–1978	Gen. Juan Melgar Castro	Armed forces
1978–1982	Gen. Policarpo Paz García	Armed forces
1982–1986	Roberto Suazo Córdova	Liberal Party
1986–1990	José Azcona del Hoyo	Liberal Party
1990–1994	Rafael Leonardo Callejas	National Party
1994–1998	Carlos Roberto Reina	Liberal Party
1998–	Carlos Flores Facussé	Liberal Party

The Rise of the Honduran Military

The Honduran military was a late arrival on the political scene. Civilian elite divisions and the lack of serious elite-mass conflicts delayed the creation of a professional military in Honduras until the 1940s. The U.S.-trained military, however, soon became an important political player. Soldiers first intervened in politics in 1956 to depose Julio Lozano Díaz, an interim president who had become unpopular with both traditional parties. The armed forces governed for over a year and then held constituent assembly elections that resulted in a landslide victory for the Liberals. Before leaving power, the military negotiated a constitutional guarantee of institutional autonomy. The 1957 constitution deprived the incoming president of his right to choose or to remove the chief of the armed forces or to give orders to the military except through its commander.

Reformist President Villeda Morales (1957–1963) instituted a new labor code and a social security system. He also launched a small agrarian reform in response to land scarcity problems that had developed in the late 1940s because of population growth and the rapid expansion of new agricultural exports (cotton, beef, sugar, coffee). Although coffee was grown on small and medium-sized farms in Honduras, cotton plantations and modern cattle ranches were large-scale enterprises that illegally enclosed public lands traditionally farmed by the peasantry.[7] Villeda's reformism was opposed by the new agricultural export elites and conservative rural bosses in his own party. He also angered the military by founding an armed Civil Guard under Liberal control. Although the Liberals' candidate to succeed Villeda, Modesto Rodas Alvarado, represented the traditionalist wing of the party, he pledged continued reform and promised to end the armed forces' autonomy. In response, the military allied itself with the National Party and intervened in 1963 to prevent a certain Liberal victory. The Civil Guard was replaced by a national police force commanded by regular military officers.

General Oswaldo López Arellano ruled Honduras from 1963 to 1971 in league with National Party boss Ricardo Zuñiga Agustinus. López initially repressed the new peasant groups that had organized to resist land enclosures. He also clashed with North Coast business and labor organizations. By 1967, however, the politically pragmatic air force general had begun to allow some peasant groups to retake enclosed properties. He also tried to defuse the rural land tenure crisis by evicting tens of thousands of Salvadoran peasants who had moved into Honduras because of the much more acute land scarcity situation in their own country. During the subsequent war with El Salvador in 1969, Honduran peasants, trade unions, and North Coast entrepreneurs won military approval when they rallied patriotically to support the armed forces.[8] The following year, López broke with the National Party and formed a new progressive political alliance with these groups. When a bipartisan civilian government elected in 1971 headed by Ramón Cruz failed to enact reforms, General López staged another military coup in late 1972.

From 1972 to 1975, López led a populist military regime that redistributed land to about one-fifth of the peasants identified as landless or land poor[9] at a time when the governments of El Salvador, Nicaragua, and Guatemala still fiercely opposed peasant organization and land redistribution.

The Honduran military's more conciliatory policy effectively co-opted peasant organizations that gained land[10] and persuaded other groups to keep pressing their demands within acceptable political channels. The military government also enlarged the economic role of the Honduran state and provided trade protection for North Coast entrepreneurs who had been battered by their Central American Common Market (CACM) competitors. Industrial growth had been slower in Honduras than in any of the other CACM nations, but fortunately, this meant that urban inequalities also had not grown as quickly.[11]

General López's policies won wide popular support for the military, but his monopolization of power within the armed forces caused dissension. After an internal struggle, López was forced to give up the post of armed forces chief in 1975, and a new constituent law of the armed forces created the Superior Council of the Armed Forces (Consejo Superior de las Fuerzas Armadas, CONSUFFAA) to serve as a collegial decision-making body for the military. Shortly thereafter, López also lost the presidency after being accused of taking a bribe from a U.S. banana company. Recently appointed armed forces chief Colonel Juan Melgar Castro (1975–1978) became president. Under conservative officers like Melgar and his successor as head of the armed forces, General Policarpo Paz García, the military again moved closer to the National Party and large landowner interests. General Paz (1978–1982) replaced Melgar in the presidency after an internal coup in 1978 (see table).

Although both Melgar and Paz, at times, repressed popular sector protests, the healthy pluralism that had come to characterize Honduran civil society persisted. Basic civil and political liberties remained intact and relatively few human rights abuses occurred. Trade unions still pressed their demands, and real wages increased for the urban working class during the late 1970s.[12] The Honduran government also continued to spend more on education and health care than any of its three neighbors. Though the pace of agrarian reform slowed considerably under Melgar and especially Paz, land redistribution did not end. At a time when the repressive excesses of the armed forces in neighboring countries were radicalizing opposition forces, the Honduran military still acted with restraint and maintained a dialogue with popular sector groups. The behavior of Honduras's military rulers was entirely consistent with the nation's authoritarian but accommodative political traditions.

Counterfeit Democratization in the 1980s

The military's popularity faded in the late 1970s. Peasant and labor support eroded as social reform slowed, while the private sector blamed military mismanagement for rising fiscal deficits and foreign debt. In 1979, after the collapse of the Somoza regime in Nicaragua, the Carter administration stepped up its campaign to persuade the Honduran military to return to the barracks. After receiving assurances of increased U.S. military and economic aid, the armed forces agreed to leave. General Paz, however, kept tight control over the transition process which began in 1980 with constituent assembly elections.

The Liberal Party defeated the military-linked National Party in the 1980 race, winning 52 percent of valid votes to their rival's 44 percent.[13] In an election marked by high turnout, a new reformist Innovation and Unity Party (Partido de Innovación y Unidad, PINU) collected the remaining votes. These results were interpreted as a rebuke to the military. Nevertheless, General Paz stayed on as chief executive with a civil-military cabinet weighted against the Liberals and demanded that the constitutional assembly maintain the armed forces' autonomous status. In the 1982 constitution, the armed forces chief was selected, not by the president, but by the Honduran Congress from a three-person list of nominees provided by CONSUFFAA. He could be dismissed only by a two-thirds congressional vote. Presidential orders to the armed forces still had to be approved by the armed forces chief. General Paz also compelled the two leading presidential candidates to agree to a list of military demands that included a veto over cabinet appointments, exclusive control of external and internal security policy, and a ban on investigations into military corruption.[14]

The 1981 elections again stimulated a large and enthusiastic turnout. The presidential race pitted longtime National Party boss Ricardo Zuñiga against Roberto Suazo Córdova, an unknown country doctor from the conservative wing of the Liberal Party. Antimilitary sentiment contributed to another Liberal victory with an even larger margin (54 percent to 42 percent). PINU and a new left-of-center Christian Democratic Party (Partido Demócrata Cristiano de Honduras, PDCH) divided the remaining votes. Honduran electoral rules prevented split-ticket voting (until 1997) so that in addition to winning the presidency the Liberals captured a large majority in Congress.

In January 1982, Roberto Suazo Córdova (1982–1986) became the first civilian president in a decade, but any hopes that his inauguration would bring genuine democratization soon evaporated. Indeed, the military grew even more formidable than before as the United States converted Honduras into a platform from which to implement its Central America policy. In return for allowing the Nicaraguan Contras to be based in Honduras, the Reagan administration gave the Hondurans unprecedented military and economic assistance. Military aid skyrocketed from $3.9 million in 1980 to $77.5 million in 1984, enabling the armed forces to expand to over 26,000 men and to improve their equipment and training.[15] Frequent joint exercises with U.S. forces also raised the Honduran military's professional capabilities. Rather than trying to reduce the political influence of the expanding armed forces, President Suazo formed a close alliance with General Gustavo Alvarez Martínez who became the country's new military strongman.

General Alvarez was one of the Honduran army's most professional and most fervently anticommunist officers. He was intensely committed to the overthrow of the Sandinista government in Nicaragua. On his own initiative, he had been aiding anti-Sandinista rebels since early 1980 hoping that Nicaraguan rebel forces would provoke a Sandinista attack on Honduran territory that could be used as a pretext for a U.S. invasion.[16] Alvarez also was determined to eliminate the small Marxist guerrilla organizations that had formed in Honduras. The most important of these were the Morazanist Front for the Liberation of Honduras (Frente Morazanista para la Liberación de Honduras, FMLH), which had about three hundred armed fighters at its height, and the smaller Cinchoneros Popular Liberation Movement (Movimiento Popular de Liberación Cinchoneros, MPLC) and Lorenzo Zelaya Popular Revolutionary Front (Fuerzas Populares Revolucionarias Lorenzo Zelaya, FPR-LZ). These three groups carried out sporadic bombings, kidnappings, political assassinations, and attacks on U.S. military personnel but never attracted appreciable popular support.

The Argentine-trained Alvarez began a systematic "dirty war" against suspected subversives soon after he became armed forces chief. Battalion 3-16, a special counterterrorist unit, along with the National Directorate of Investigations (Dirección Nacional de Investigaciones, DNI) and other Public Security Force (Fuerza de Seguridad Pública, FUSEP) police elements carried out a campaign of torture and assassination to destroy the Honduran guerrillas as well as any groups providing support to leftist insurgents in El Salvador. The security forces also infiltrated unions, student groups, and peasant organizations suspected of radical political leanings. Although the number of individuals "disappeared" by Honduran death squads was small in comparison with the thousands who suffered a similar fate in neighboring countries, such extreme violence by government forces constituted a sharp break with Honduras's less polarized political traditions. Much of the private sector and middle class, however, tacitly accepted the dirty war as a necessary evil to combat the revolutionary threat to the region. Most of the rest of Honduran civil society with the exception of some courageous human rights organizations such as the Committee for the Defense of Human Rights (Comité para la Defensa de los Derechos Humanos, CODEH) were too frightened to resist.[17] The vast majority of civilian politicians either supported the military's repressive policies or kept silent.

President Suazo and the U.S. embassy lost their principal military ally when a bloodless military coup deposed General Alvarez in 1984. The most important reasons for Alvarez's fall were his professional arrogance and his quest for total control over the armed forces.[18] Collegial direction of the armed forces by CONSUFFAA resumed under new armed forces chief

General Walter López Reyes as the military factionalized more deeply into generational and personalist cliques. The armed forces began to drive a harder bargain with the United States over Contra aid and ended an Alvarez-negotiated program to train Salvadoran soldiers in Honduras. Although frictions between the military and its U.S. and Contra partners increased, the Honduran armed forces continued to collaborate with U.S. policy. American officials boosted military aid to an all-time high of $81.1 million in 1986 and continued to turn a blind eye to military corruption and human rights violations. During López Reyes's tenure as armed forces chief, the repression of internal dissent did subside. The military allowed somewhat greater political space to civilian authorities and civil society. Honduras's traditional political pluralism began to reassert itself.

Civilian Politics in a "Democradura"

Honduras failed to make substantial progress toward democratization during the early 1980s not only because of the military's supremacy but also because of the failings of civilian political leaders such as President Suazo Córdova. Like most Honduran politicians, Suazo had entered politics in order to acquire wealth and power for himself and *chamba* (patronage) for his followers, not to achieve any particular policy goals or to strengthen the country's political institutions.[19] Corruption was widespread in his administration, and policy making was based on short-term power calculations. Suazo resisted U.S. embassy pressures for a neoliberal austerity program, for example, not so much because he disagreed with its economic logic, but because its adoption would have damaged his popularity and reduced the government spoils on which he depended. Suazo also correctly calculated that as long as Honduras was the lynchpin in U.S. Central America policy, the United States would always provide the funds needed to stave off economic collapse. When new elections approached, President Suazo used bribery and his control of the Supreme Court and National Electoral Tribunal to interfere in the presidential nomination process. His attempts to retain office beyond the one-term limit or to impose a pliable ally worsened factional divisions within both parties and led to a constitutional clash with Congress. Much of Honduran civil society mobilized to protest his abuse of power, but it was military mediation strongly backed by the United States that ultimately resolved the crisis. A compromise agreement permitted all party factions to run candidates in the 1985 election.

The four Liberal factions as a whole out-polled the three National Party factions by 51 percent to 45.5 percent in 1985; hence the Liberal winning the most votes (27.5 percent), José Azcona del Hoyo (1986–1990), became president. President Azcona, a civil engineer and Suazo opponent, was much more respectful of constitutional rules than his corrupt predecessor.[20] Nevertheless, his public policy achievements were few. A traditional politician from the conservative side of the party, Azcona showed little interest in developing coherent policy initiatives. In addition, the divided Liberal Party never provided him with a reliable base of congressional support. For a time, he formed a coalition with National Party leader Rafael Callejas, who had won the most votes in the 1985 presidential race, but beyond the division of patronage appointments this arrangement accomplished little.

As Honduras's fiscal and balance of payments deficits mounted during the late 1980s, Azcona did strongly oppose U.S. pressures for neoliberal economic reform. With the Contras declining in importance, however, the United States no longer tolerated Honduran economic intransigence and saw to it that international financial institutions denied further funding. The nation's foreign reserves were soon exhausted, making it impossible to import enough energy and other needed inputs to sustain economic growth. Unemployment and inflation ballooned while labor unrest spread rapidly. As the Contras became increasingly unpopular, the Liberal president also demonstrated a degree of autonomy from the United States in the Central American peace process. However, President Azcona never challenged the powerful Honduran armed forces.

After a CONSUFFAA majority removed General López Reyes in 1986, in part for being too accommodating to civilians, hardline General Humberto Regalado Hernández became chief of the armed forces. Political disappearances again increased and military corruption reached new extremes. Allegedly, Regalado and other senior officers enriched themselves by misappropriating military funds and by participating in the international narcotics trade.[21] Honduras had by this time become an important transshipment point for Colombian cocaine, and the new drug money further divided the officer corps. The Azcona government was too weak to challenge General Regalado and the politically dominant armed forces over their linkages to narcotics trafficking or their human rights violations. Although the military allowed Azcona and the Liberal Congress to take charge of nonsecurity-related policy, key decisions about internal or external security were still largely a product of negotiations between the military and the U.S. embassy.[22] As the decade came to a close, Honduras was a classic example of what Guillermo O'Donnell and Philippe Schmitter have called a "democradura"—a nominally democratic country that actually is dominated by its armed forces.[23]

The Decline of the Military

Although the democratic electoral process that President Suazo had undermined began to strengthen in the late 1980s, the most important advances in democratization were achieved by curbing the power of the military during the 1990s. The end of the cold war and the collapse of communism removed the principal security threats that justified the existence of the Honduran armed forces.[24] The Central American civil wars came to an end, and by 1991 virtually all Honduran guerrillas had accepted amnesty. The subsequent downsizing of the Nicaraguan and Salvadoran armies made it hard to rationalize a large Honduran army. Any lingering concerns about a security threat from El Salvador largely disappeared when the World Court resolved remaining border disputes in 1992. In this post–cold war context, U.S. policymakers began to see the Honduran army, not as an ally against communism, but as a corrupt and costly obstacle to democratization. American military aid plummeted, and the U.S. Embassy became strongly critical of the armed forces. Encouraged by the new U.S. embassy stance, student groups, unions, human rights organizations, business associations, and the Catholic Church collaborated in publicly attacking the military's power and prerogatives. Investigative journalists fueled the growing antimilitary movement with regular exposés of military corruption, human rights abuses, and other criminal activity. The participation of private sector business groups such as the powerful Honduran Council of Private Enterprise (Consejo Hondureño de la Empresa Privada, COHEP) in the antimilitary coalition was especially important. Tired of the expense of financing the corrupt military and no longer fearful of regional revolution, Honduran business organizations joined in demanding that the armed forces be downsized and subordinated to civilian authority. This unusually broad antimilitary coalition gradually persuaded traditional party politicians to challenge the armed forces on a range of issues. The decline of the military began during the administration of National Party leader Rafael Callejas but greatly accelerated under his Liberal successor, Carlos Reina.

The Rafael Callejas Administration, 1990–1994

Rafael Leonardo Callejas, a U.S.-trained agricultural economist from a prominent landowning family, won the presidency in 1989 with 51 percent of the vote as Hondurans penalized the Liberals for the deepening economic crisis of the late 1980s. Liberal Carlos Flores Facussé, a newspaper publisher from an important Arab-Honduran family of North Coast industrialists, finished a distant second with 43 percent. Callejas's inauguration was a milestone in the nation's democratic transition because it represented the first democratic transfer of power between competing political parties in more than a half-century. The rightist Callejas, however, was a loyal friend of the military and had no plans to weaken the armed forces. Actions by the United States and Honduran civil society forced his hand.

Beginning in 1990 the United States made sharp cuts in its military aid to Honduras, which fell from $41.1 million in 1989 to only $2.7 million by 1993. In addition, after the military attempted to cover up a rape and murder allegedly committed by a Honduran colonel, U.S. ambassador Cresencio Arcos began a public campaign against military impunity. This U.S. policy reversal promoted the growth of a vocal antimilitary movement that drew from almost all segments of Honduran civil society. Under increasing external and internal pressure, Callejas named Leo Valladares, a widely respected law professor, to the new post of human rights commissioner and appointed members to the Ad Hoc Commission for Institutional Reform headed by Archbishop Oscar Andrés Rodríguez. The Ad Hoc Commission investigated the military's FUSEP police branch, which had been implicated in many crimes, and recommended that its notorious DNI be replaced by an independent investigative agency. Later, the human rights commissioner published a report detailing the military's responsibility for the disappearances of 184 persons during the 1980s.[25] Faced with the opposition of a broad antimilitary coalition that included former allies such as the U.S. embassy and the Honduran private sector, the military gradually began to give ground. Putting aside his earlier belligerence toward the military's critics, armed forces chief General Luis Discua Elvir adopted a more conciliatory tone and formally accepted the recommendations of the Ad Hoc Commission. The colonel accused in the rape and murder case as well as another senior officer implicated in narcotics trafficking were turned over to civilian authorities and later convicted.

The once unassailable Honduran military was put on the defensive while Callejas was president, but the National Party leader deserved scant praise for this development. The U.S.-led international credit boycott of Honduras also left him little choice but to impose the orthodox economic reforms Honduras so long had resisted. Callejas cut the nation's chronic fiscal deficit by shrinking the size of the overlarge bureaucracy and by increasing taxes and charges for public services. His structural adjustment program also liberalized trade and drastically devalued the nation's currency.[26] These policies restored external financial support, reduced inflation, and, after a sharp recession, reignited economic growth. In addition, Callejas's pro-business reputation helped to attract new foreign investment to maquiladora assembly plants on the North Coast. Although trade unionists and other popular sector groups saw their real incomes shrink and protested neoliberal policies, Callejas used his excellent public relations skills to persuade most Hondurans that his harsh economic reforms were necessary. Unfortunately, during his final year in office, the president subverted his own program by raising government capital spending by almost 50 percent and by distributing large wage increases to public employees.[27] These ill-considered moves drove the fiscal deficit back up to an unmanageable 10 percent of GDP and rekindled inflation. Callejas's policy reversal sent the country back into economic crisis and forced the long-suffering Honduran public to endure a much longer period of economic hardship. Many believe that increased capital spending made it possible for Callejas and other members of his cabinet to collect hefty kickbacks from contractors. This is only one of the many charges of official corruption that have been leveled against what many

Hondurans regard as the most corrupt administration in their country's modern history.

The Carlos Reina Administration, 1994–1998

The Liberals returned to power and Honduras completed its second consecutive democratic turnover of parties when Carlos Roberto Reina, a sixty-seven-year-old former diplomat, won the 1993 election by a margin of 53 percent to 43 percent over Oswaldo Ramos Soto. As a social democrat from the Liberal Left and former president of the Inter-American Court of Human Rights, Reina was determined to reduce military power further. Following the recommendations of the Ad Hoc Commission, Reina quickly replaced the DNI with a new, U.S.-trained Directorate of Criminal Investigation (Dirección de Investigación Criminal, DIC) under a new civilian Public Ministry. In addition, the president endorsed a constitutional reform that, by late 1997, removed the entire national police force from military command for the first time since 1963. Carlos Flores Facussé, the Liberal president of Congress and leader of the largest Liberal congressional faction, played a key role in creating the new National Civilian Police (Policía Nacional Civil, PNC).

The separation of the police from the military was a major achievement, but Reina's most popular accomplishment was his passage of constitutional reforms in 1994 and 1995 that abolished press-gang recruitment by the armed forces. The new all-volunteer system caused a rapid decline in the size of the armed forces. Low military salaries and the inability to resort to forced recruitment shrank the armed forces to only about twelve thousand men by early 1997 (of whom almost six thousand were police who would soon be under civilian leadership).[28] Despite protests from the high command, Reina also cut the military budget from $50 million in 1993 to $35 million by 1996. U.S. military aid, which fell to only $425,000 in 1997, provided little cushion. Military units no longer had sufficient funds to carry out basic functions. Military officers' salaries eroded so seriously that many younger officers resigned.

Reina also denied the armed forces major sources of illicit funding when he ended the military's longstanding control of the Honduran telecommunications system, the immigration department, and the merchant marine. The military, however, still operated the controversial Military Pension Institute (Instituto de Previsión Militar, IPM), which owned enterprises whose total book value ranked it as the fifth largest financial group in the country.[29] The IPM gave military officers undue economic influence, but the institute was weakened by chronic liquidity problems allegedly caused by profit skimming by some of the retired and active-duty officers directing it. Remaining IPM profits were distributed to its retired beneficiaries rather than to the armed forces budget.

Finally, in contrast to earlier Honduran presidents, Reina took advantage of the few military-appointment privileges granted to him by the constitution. He chose a reformist military professional hated by corrupt armed forces chief Discua to be the head of his presidential guard and selected a highly respected U.S. Army War College graduate as his minister of defense after explicitly rejecting every alternative candidate proposed by the high command.

Although President Reina greatly reduced the power and prerogatives of the armed forces, he was unable to subordinate the military fully to civilian authority. During 1995 about two dozen current or former military personnel were called to testify in Honduran courts about 1980s human rights abuses, but nearly all refused to cooperate and fled prosecution. Many fugitive officers went into hiding on military bases, and the armed forces refused to turn them over to civilian authorities. The military argued that its personnel were shielded from prosecution by amnesties passed during the Callejas administration. Honduran courts made inconsistent rulings on this issue. In the interest of national reconciliation, Reina sometimes appeared to favor amnesty for the accused military personnel. He made no attempt to force the armed forces to give up fugitive officers.

Military intelligence officers also reportedly collaborated with rightwing Cuban exiles in 1995 and 1996 in a series of bombings that targeted President Reina, the Supreme Court, Congress, and human rights groups.[30] In addition, there were death threats against judges assigned to human rights cases involving military personnel. Several possible witnesses died in suspect circumstances. Although military coup threats had become unconvincing by the late 1990s because of the anticipated reaction of the United States and civil society to a military takeover and the unreliability of enlisted forces, these actions made clear that military officers still had the power to intimidate their enemies. Some officers also continued to defy civilian authority by participating in bank robberies, car theft rings, narcotics trafficking, and other ordinary criminal activity, although they faced an increasing risk of arrest and prosecution for such nonpolitical crimes.

In addition to trimming military power, the Reina administration capably implemented the nation's structural economic reform program. After some early indecision and renewed pressure from international lenders, the Liberal government instituted austerity measures to rectify the economic crisis left by Callejas. The recession that followed, coupled with a severe, drought-induced energy shortage, cost Reina much of his popular support. Moreover, his attempts to control government personnel costs precipitated frequent strikes by unionized public school teachers and hospital workers. His need to raise fuel prices and public service charges also brought protests from the public at large. Although greater concessions were made to organized labor than the International Monetary Fund (IMF) recommended and no important state enterprises were privatized, the Liberal government made a concerted effort to meet most IMF guidelines. The fiscal deficit was quickly reduced and the economy resumed growth by 1995, although inflation did not subside until 1997. By the end of Reina's term, the Honduran economy was stronger than it had been in many years; foreign investment was on the increase, and real income was finally rising. Unusually high coffee export prices, falling oil import prices, and earnings from the booming maquiladora industries raised Honduras's foreign exchange reserves to record levels, making the country's heavy $4 billion foreign debt a little easier to manage.

The Carlos Flores Administration, 1998–2002

After an issueless 1997 campaign, Liberal congressional leader Carlos Flores Facussé easily defeated former Tegucigalpa mayor Nora Gúnera de Melgar, the candidate of a deeply factionalized National Party by 53 percent of the vote to 43 percent. Flores's victory was the fourth Liberal triumph in the five presidential contests held since the restoration of civilian government. The Liberals also won a majority in Congress with 67 seats to the Nationals' 55 seats in the first election to permit split-ticket voting.[31] Three minor parties divided the remaining six seats.

During his first months in office, President Flores sought to build on the demilitarization and economic reform policies of his predecessor. Most important, he won an agreement from armed forces chief General Mario Hung Pacheco to a constitutional reform that brought the military under the direct control of the president through the defense minister for the first time since 1957. Both the post of armed forces chief and CONSUFFAA were abolished by this reform, which was passed twice (as constitutionally required) by the Honduran Congress, in September 1998 and January 1999. Although the reform generated dissension within the military over the distribution of command positions under the new institutional arrangement, most of the officer corps accepted their formal subordination to the president. Some analysts argued that military acquiescence was won in return for Flores's support for applying existing amnesty laws to military personnel accused in pending 1980s human rights cases.[32] In addition, as crime rates continued to rise, Flores backed the interim civilian junta directing the national police, now merged with the more professional DIC, in its efforts to purge corrupt senior officers and others guilty of criminal conduct. He also promised to double the size of the new PNC and to improve its pay and equipment.

Flores initially stayed in the good graces of international financial institutions by deepening the country's neoliberal structural economic reform program despite problems associated with a new drought and energy shortages caused by El Niño. He continued fiscal austerity and initiated the country's first serious privatization program. Although Flores often spoke of the need to alleviate the misery of the country's poor majority, the conservative president believed that the solution to poverty lay not in redistribution but in stimulating new private sector investment. His tax reform lowered taxes on businesses but increased the value-added tax paid by all.

Under Flores, the Honduran economy was growing at a vigorous 5 percent rate in 1998, but it came to an abrupt halt in October of that year when Hurricane Mitch destroyed 80 percent of the country's economic infrastructure and most of its agricultural production. Early damage estimates put the nation's losses at $3 billion, a sum equal to about three-quarters of the entire Honduran GDP. Generous international economic assistance and debt relief allowed the Flores administration to begin the rebuilding process, but the task ahead posed an enormous challenge to the Liberal government.

Problems of Democratic Consolidation

By early 1999, Honduras had completed the transition to procedural democracy that had begun almost two decades earlier.[33] A system of free and fair elections open to all adults finally had become institutionalized and an acceptable level of civil and political liberties had been attained. Honduras's pluralist civil society was well established. Although the armed forces still enjoyed considerable institutional autonomy, their political influence had declined dramatically. The downsized, demoralized military no longer posed a credible coup threat. The end of military dominance and the observance of electoral rules by all competing civilian political elites were historic achievements. Nevertheless, few Hondurans were rejoicing in their democratic good fortune. Instead, they were increasingly disillusioned with the poor quality of what passed for democratic governance in Honduras.

In the late 1990s, it appeared that democratic consolidation would be difficult to achieve in Honduras. The ongoing spoils battle among Honduran politicians was still intense, and their new willingness to respect electoral rules stood to be seriously tested if the United States and its allies were ever to lose interest in maintaining electoral democracy. Honduran politicians believed that they would be severely penalized by the United States and the international community if they gained power by electoral fraud or force. Even the least democratically minded had learned to play the electoral game by its rules. Thus, it was difficult to know what proportion of the Honduran political class had really come to believe in these rules as the best way to permanently keep the struggle for *chamba* from raging out of control. The level of trust among competing political factions was still low. Although Honduran general elections were now free of serious fraud, several primary elections, which attracted almost no international attention, had been marred by charges of vote tampering.

Military elites also obviously represented an obstacle to democratic consolidation. Many senior army officers were unreconciled to their loss of power. They had little respect for the civilian political class that they perceived to be even more self-interested and venal than themselves. The military grudgingly accepted a series of major political defeats in the 1990s culminating in their constitutional subordination to civil authority only because, without its former external or internal allies, it had little choice. Some analysts hoped that civil-military relations would improve as the current generation of senior military officers retired, but any future breakdown in electoral rule observance could open political space for the armed forces again. Others worried that widespread, sustained popular-sector unrest directed against the failure of elected governments to improve social conditions could also revive the military's sagging political fortunes. They reasoned that if the expanded PNC proved unable to manage such a situation, the army might again become an important ally of a fearful economic elite or, as was admittedly unimaginable in the late 1990s, of an angry popular sector.

Juan Linz and Alfred Stepan argue that democratic consolidation requires that the mass public as well as political elites accept the democratic process as legitimate and as the "only game in town."[34] However, just as Honduran political and military elites were learning to abide by democratic rules in the late 1990s, ordinary Hondurans seemed to have become increasingly ambivalent about democracy. In a 1996 survey of public opinion in Latin American countries, Hondurans voiced less enthusiasm for democracy than any other Latin Americans interviewed.[35] Hondurans said that they preferred democracy over authoritarianism by a 42 to 14 percent margin. However, fully 30 percent of the population said that they did not care what sort of government they lived under. Although they continued to turn out to vote in respectable numbers (75 percent voted in 1997) and told interviewers that they would still be willing to defend the current democratic system if it were threatened, the politically cynical Hondurans also demonstrated the lowest level of belief in the efficacy of voting.

Hondurans were becoming disenchanted with their political system during the late 1990s because their "low-quality" democracy[36] bore little resemblance to the established democratic regimes of western Europe or the United States. Corruption may have declined during the Reina administration, but it was still widespread. Few public officials were ever punished. The criminal justice system, from the police to the courts, was itself corrupt and unable to defend the rule of law. The government's ability to manage the Honduran economy had improved in recent years, but inequalities had increased with the imposition of neoliberal economic reforms. Most Hondurans remained extremely poor; nearly half subsisted on less than one dollar a day.[37] Honduran governments also had failed to deal effectively with rising crime, which had become the number one issue of concern to the Honduran public. Furthermore, the traditional patron-client political parties had remained focused on capturing the spoils of office rather than on developing coherent policy alternatives for dealing with these critical national problems. They poorly represented the lively pluralism of Honduran civil society. Under these circumstances, it was little wonder that many citizen groups increasingly resorted to direct action to pressure the government instead of working through politicians and parties. During the 1990s, urban slum dwellers, indigenous groups, peasant organizations, and trade unions repeatedly marched on the capital or blocked key road junctions to demand government assistance.

For Honduran democracy to consolidate, it was clear in the late 1990s that the country's political elites would have to dramatically change their traditional values and behavior. Elected officials would have to concentrate more on policy making than on *chamba*. They would also have to be ready to be held accountable for their actions by a stronger and more independent judiciary. Such fundamental changes in elite political culture never come easily. Moreover, political leaders would have to find ways to convince most Hondurans that their elected government could really improve the lives of ordinary people. The Reina administration had abolished the hated military press gangs and created the DIC and PNC, which promised to reduce crime, but it had done little to ensure that the country's poor majority would one day share in the benefits of economic growth.

In this context, the vast devastation caused by Hurricane Mitch in late 1998 created a critical political challenge for Honduran elites. Effective use of international relief funds to rebuild the country and to provide aid to the thousands who had lost everything could raise the legitimacy of democratic government. On the other hand, elite corruption and incompetence at this critical juncture in the nation's history could worsen mass cynicism and disillusionment.

Conclusion

Honduras's distinctive political culture of elite restraint and accommodation enabled the country to avoid the political violence that convulsed its Central American neighbors beginning in the late 1970s. However, Honduran traditions of authoritarian politics and military dominance slowed the democratization process of the early 1980s. The politically powerful, U.S.-backed armed forces continued to rule despite the restoration of democratic elections. In addition, most Honduran civilian politicians showed scarcely more respect for democratic principles than did the armed forces. Leaders of the two traditional parties concentrated on amassing spoils rather than on developing effective public policy. The initial executive succession provoked a constitutional crisis when the incumbent president illegally interfered in the electoral process.

The end of the cold war and the Central American civil wars brought about changes in U.S. policy that greatly accelerated Honduras's democratic transition during the 1990s. The United States turned on its former friends in the Honduran military and helped a broad antimilitary coalition dislodge the armed forces from their dominant political position. Civilian leaders also gradually began to show greater respect for basic democratic rules beginning in the late 1980s. The holding of three consecutive free and fair elections (1989, 1993, 1997) without presidential interference produced two democratic turnovers between competing parties and institutionalized the electoral system.

Honduras's completed transition to procedural democracy was a major accomplishment after so many decades of military dominance. However, as the century came to a close, the consolidation of Honduran democracy appeared to present a more difficult problem. The civilian political class had learned to abide by the results of democratic elections, but the depth of its commitment to electoral democracy was still uncertain. In addition, many senior military officers remained unreconciled to growing civilian control over their institution. In July 1999, President Flores dismissed the armed forces chief of staff and several other high-ranking officers who had recently clashed with the civilian defense minister over personnel issues. The mass public also was increasingly disenchanted with democracy because of the low quality of democratic governance in Honduras in the late 1990s. Corruption by public officials was widespread and seldom punished. Street crime had exploded to overwhelm an antiquated and corrupt criminal justice system. The government had improved its macroeconomic policy making, yet poverty and inequality continued to grow as neoliberal economic reforms were implemented. Moreover, it was still unclear in early 2000 if the Honduran political elite could efficiently and honestly manage the multiyear national reconstruction task that faced the country in the wake of Hurricane Mitch.

Notes

1. I define "democracy" in procedural terms following guidelines in Larry Diamond, Juan J. Linz, and Seymour Martin Lipset, eds., *Politics in Developing Countries: Comparing Experiences with Democracy* (Boulder, CO: Lynne Rienner, 1995), 6–9. I assume that a democracy has become consolidated when both elites and the mass public accept the democratic system as legitimate and as the "only game in town." This definition is drawn from Juan J. Linz and Alfred Stepan, *Problems of Democratic Transition and Consolidation: Southern Europe, South America, and Post-Communist Europe* (Baltimore: Johns Hopkins University Press, 1996), 5–6.

2. The World Bank, *World Development Report 1997* (New York: Oxford University Press, 1997), 214. At purchasing power parity, the Honduran GNP per capita would be about $1,900.

3. Dario A. Euraque, *Reinterpreting the Banana Republic: Region and State in Honduras, 1870–1972* (Chapel Hill: University of North Carolina Press, 1996), 5–13.

4. Victor Bulmer-Thomas, *The Political Economy of Central America since 1920* (New York: Cambridge University Press, 1987), 17–18.

5. Euraque, *Reinterpreting the Banana Republic*, 52–59.

6. Ibid., 96–97.

7. William H. Durham, *Scarcity and Survival in Central America: Ecological Origins of the Soccer War* (Stanford: Stanford University Press, 1979), 117–23.

8. Euraque, *Reinterpreting the Banana Republic*, 137–40.

9. J. Mark Ruhl, "Agrarian Structure and Political Stability in Honduras," *Journal of Interamerican Studies and World Affairs* 26, no. 1 (February 1984): 55.

10. Rachel Sieder, "Honduras: The Politics of Exception and Military Reformism, 1972–1978," *Journal of Latin American Studies* 27, no. 1 (February 1995), 120–21.

11. John A. Booth, "Socioeconomic and Political Roots of National Revolts in Central America," *Latin American Research Review* 26, no. 1 (1991): 47.

12. Bulmer-Thomas *Political Economy of Central America*, 215, 219.

13. Electoral data for 1980–1989 are taken from the Honduras chapter in Ronald H. McDonald and J. Mark Ruhl, *Party Politics and Elections in Latin America* (Boulder, CO: Westview Press, 1989), 111–22.

14. Donald E. Schulz and Deborah S. Schulz, *The United States, Honduras, and the Crisis in Central America* (Boulder, CO: Westview Press, 1994), 71–72.

15. U.S. military aid figures cited in this chapter are from J. Mark Ruhl, "Redefining Civil-Military Relations in Honduras," *Journal of Interamerican Studies and World Affairs* 38, no. 1 (Spring 1996): 39, 44; and Adam Isacson, *Altered States: Security and Demilitarization in Central America* (Washington, DC: Center for International Policy and Arias Foundation for Peace and Human Progress, 1997), 173.

16. Schulz and Schulz, *The United States, Honduras and the Crisis*, 65.

17. Victor Meza, "The Military: Willing to Deal," *NACLA Report on the Americas* 22, no. 1 (January–February 1988): 16.

18. Schulz and Schulz, *The United States, Honduras, and the Crisis*, 99–102.

19. Mark B. Rosenberg, "Can Democracy Survive the Democrats? From Transition to Consolidation in Honduras," in John A. Booth and Mitchell A. Seligson, eds., *Elections and Democracy in Central America* (Chapel Hill: University of North Carolina Press, 1989), 41–56.

20. On the Azcona administration, see J. Mark Ruhl, "Honduras," in James M. Malloy and Eduardo A. Gamarra, eds., *Latin America and Caribbean Contemporary Record, Volume 8 (1988–89)* (New York: Holmes and Meier, 1996), B271–B284.

21. Schulz and Schulz, *The United States, Honduras, and the Crisis*, 169–70, 271–72.

22. Mark B. Rosenberg, "Narcos and Politicos: The Politics of Drug Trafficking in Honduras," *Journal of Interamerican Studies and World Affairs* 30, nos. 2, 3 (Summer–Fall 1988): 152–53.

23. Guillermo O'Donnell and Philippe C. Schmitter, *Transitions from Authoritarian Rule: Tentative Conclusions about Uncertain Democracies* (Baltimore: Johns Hopkins University Press, 1986), 9.

24. The analysis of Honduran politics in the 1990s draws heavily from Ruhl, "Redefining Civil-Military Relations," 41–53; and J. Mark Ruhl, "Doubting Democracy in Honduras," *Current History* 96, no. 607 (February 1997): 82–86.

25. Center for Justice and International Law and Human Rights Watch/Americas, *The Facts Speak for Themselves: Preliminary Report on Disappearances of the National Commissioner for the Protection of Human Rights in Honduras* (New York: Human Rights Watch, 1994).

26. The discussion of Honduran economic performance draws on Ruhl, "Doubting Democracy," 84–85.

27. Economic statistics are from the Economic Commission for Latin America and the Caribbean (CEPAL), *Estudio económico de América Latina y el Caribe, 1993: Honduras* (Santiago, Chile: United Nations, 1995) and subsequent UN studies.

28. Military size and budgetary data are from Isacson, *Altered States*, 62–63, 173.

29. Ibid., 65.

30. *Miami Herald*, September 28, 1997.

31. *Honduras This Week*, January 3, 1998.

32. *La Prensa*, September 21 and 23, 1998; *Central America Report*, October 2, 1998.

33. Freedom House raised Honduras to its "free" (democratic) category in 1997. (Their rating is based on expert assessment of political rights and civil liberties.) See Adrian Karatnycky, ed., *Freedom in the World : The Annual Survey of Political Rights and Civil Liberties, 1997–1998* (New Brunswick, NJ: Transaction, 1998), 271.

34. Linz and Stepan, *Problems of Democratic Transition*, 5–6.

35. Marta Lagos, "Latin America's Smiling Mask," *Journal of Democracy* 8, no. 3 (July 1997): 13–133.

36. Variations in the quality of democracies are discussed in Linz and Stepan, *Problems of Democratic Transition*, 6.

37. World Bank, *World Development Report*, 214.

4

Nicaragua
Transition through Revolution

Thomas W. Walker

Nicaragua's political evolution was similar in many ways to that of other Central American countries yet dramatically unique in others. As in El Salvador and Guatemala, Nicaragua inherited a very unequal society from the days of the Spanish Conquest and, as in those two states, the intransigence of twentieth-century elites made insurrection and revolution virtually inevitable as a vehicle for making space for democracy. In addition, after the transition to democracy, Nicaragua and all other Central American countries found themselves in the paradoxical position of attempting to maintain or consolidate democracy with its essential elements of popular participation while, at the same time, implementing neoliberalism—a very nonparticipatory, income-concentrating economic system. However, Nicaragua was also notably unique in that, only there, was the transition to democracy achieved through a successful guerrilla insurgency and subsequent period of revolutionary rule.

Situated in the center of Central America, Nicaragua is a small country with 57,143 square miles of territory and a population of 4.48 million in 1998—roughly equivalent to the U.S. state of Alabama with 50,750 square miles and 4.9 million people. But it is also very poor: its 1998 GDP per capita was $430 (that of the United States was over $31,000, or more than 72 times greater). In fact, by the late 1990s Nicaragua was the poorest country per capita in Central America and either the second or third poorest in Latin America.[1] Given the fact that it is blessed with abundant fertile land, rich

Some of the material in this chapter is from the introduction to Thomas W. Walker, ed., *Nicaragua without Illusions: Regime Transition and Structural Adjustment in the 1990s* (Wilmington, DE: Scholarly Resources, 1997); and (with the permission of the publisher and my coauthor) from the author's contribution to the update of Chapter 6, on Nicaragua, in John A. Booth and Thomas W. Walker, *Understanding Central America*, 3d ed. (Boulder, CO: Westview Press, 1999), 69–100.

mineral and energy resources, and access to two oceans, all of this seems paradoxical until we consider that country's history.

Historical Background

The Introduction to this volume describes how social and economic patterns established during the conquest and the colonial period—and accentuated under the Liberal "reforms" of the nineteenth century—caused a concentration of income and perpetuated the poverty of the masses in the three Central American countries that would experience armed insurrection in the late twentieth century. Those patterns would become even more severe in the first half of the twentieth century. The regime that oversaw this period of continued income concentration in Nicaragua was that of the Somoza family (1937–1979).

As the United States withdrew after its occupation of Nicaragua from 1912 to 1933, command of the U.S.-created surrogate army, the "Nicaraguan" National Guard, was turned over for the first time to a Nicaraguan. A bright, congenial young man who spoke fluent English, Anastasio Somoza-García had ingratiated himself with the occupying Americans.[2] Once in command of the country's military, he quickly consolidated his power. Augusto Cesar Sandino—the nationalist guerrilla leader who had forced a withdrawal of U.S. troops in 1932—was assassinated in 1934, a coup and rigged election took place in 1936, and the Liberal caudillo was formally inaugurated as president on January 1, 1937.[3] Thus began the longest-lived dynastic dictatorship in Latin American history (see table). Somoza himself would run the country until assassinated in 1956. His eldest son, Luis Somoza-Debayle, would then rule directly or through puppet presidents until 1967. Luis's younger brother, Anastasio Somoza-Debayle, would then take up the reins of power until overthrown by mass-based insurrection in 1979.

Nicaraguan Heads of State, 1937–Present

Term	Name	Method of Assuming Office
1937–1956	Anastasio Somoza-García (and puppets)	Coup/rigged elections
1956–1967	Luis Somoza-Debayle (and puppets)	Rigged elections
1967–1979	Anastasio Somoza-Debayle (and puppet Triumvirate)	Rigged elections
1979–1985	Junta of National Reconstruction (Daniel Ortega Saavedra, Head)	Armed insurrection
1985–1990	Daniel Ortega Saavedra	Competitive election
1990–1997	Violeta Barrios de Chamorro	Competitive election
1997–	Arnoldo Alemán	Competitive election

The personalities and governing style of the three Somozas differed one from the other. The father was a sort of populist dictator; Luis liked the appearance of "democracy" and 1960s developmentalism; and the younger Anastasio was an intemperate, greedy man more prone to the use of force. Nevertheless, the Somoza formula for governing was simple and fairly constant during most of the forty-three years of family rule. It rested on three pillars: co-optation of key domestic elites, direct control of the National Guard, and the support of the United States.

The Somoza system accentuated class differences and social problems. The socially regressive agro-export economy, developed in the nineteenth century, was made even more exploitative as a new wave of peasant farmers was displaced to make way for the production of cotton in the 1950s. As more and more land was cultivated to produce export products, less and less food was produced for consumption by an ever-expanding population. Per capita income remained below average even for impoverished Latin America, with the lower 50 percent of the population in the late 1970s probably having access to under $300 per person per year. Social conditions, as seen in high infant mortality and illiteracy rates and very low average life expectancy, were horrendous. Meanwhile, the Somoza family fortune, which had consisted of a small, run-down coffee farm in the early 1930s, had risen to at least a half billion dollars by the time the last Somoza was toppled. Corruption and abuse of power, not unusual business acumen, clearly accounted for most of that sum.

The Overthrow of Somoza

In the early 1970s the Somoza system began to unravel and, on July 19, 1979, was finally toppled by a mass-based insurrection. Several single-factor explanations have been offered for why this insurrection, unlike so many others in Latin America, succeeded. But, as Timothy Wickham-Crowley shows, none is adequate in itself.[4] Instead, he claims that four broad conditions were met in Nicaragua (and Cuba in 1959) that were not all present in any of the many other Latin American countries that had experienced insurrection since the late 1950s. Basically, Nicaragua had the right social conditions; a target regime so despicable that it had managed to alienate most of its political base; temporarily, the right international environment; and an intelligent and flexible guerrilla movement.

That the social conditions in Nicaragua in the 1970s were ripe for revolution needs little elaboration. Much of the rural population consisted of extremely impoverished people—such as migrant farm workers, squatters, and share croppers—living in very precarious circumstances. The harsh and exploitative character of agro-export had driven many poor people into urban areas in search of a better life. There, most ended up in slums with poor employment opportunities and little access to social services. In Managua, their situation was made even more desperate following an earthquake in 1972 that destroyed most of the city. Though the dictatorship received over $100 million in international relief aid, precious little ever went to relieving the suffering of the city's poor majority. In all, by the late 1970s, most Nicaraguans were impoverished and desperate and owed little to the existing system.

The second factor that contributed to the success of the revolution was that it faced the ideal type of foe: in Wickham-Crowley's words, a "mafia-cracy." The last of the Somozas was a self-centered, tyrannical man who lacked the political skills of his father and his older brother. His behavior following the 1972 earthquake alienated one of the important pillars of the Somoza system, the domestic elite. He saw the influx of international aid and the spending programs created in the demolition and reconstruction of Managua as an opportunity to enrich himself and his cronies. Accordingly, he bullied his way into key sectors of the economy (demolition, cement, concrete, construction, among others) and had the government award his enterprises lucrative contracts. He also allowed the National Guard to misappropriate and sell food and other material relief supplies. In so doing, he lost the support of most civilian elites. Thus, by 1977, when the Carter administration successfully pressured the dictator to reinstate freedom of the press, Pedro Joaquín Chamorro's Conservative opposition daily *La Prensa* had a field day detailing the corruption and greed of the regime. Chamorro's assassination the following January made any rapprochement between the elites and the regime impossible.

The third important factor that contributed (unwittingly) to the success of the insurrection was a temporary moderation in U.S. cold war policy. Unlike administrations immediately before or after it, the Carter administration placed considerable rhetorical emphasis on human rights. Accordingly, although the Somoza regime tried to accommodate Washington in certain cosmetic ways, the United States eventually cut off military aid and cut back on nonmilitary assistance. Even though Israel (the biggest U.S. foreign aid recipient in the world) immediately replaced the United States as Somoza's arms supplier with no audible objection from Washington, the symbolic significance of the change in U.S. aid policy was profound. The dictator and his cronies were demoralized and the insurgents and their backers were energized. In the end, though the Carter administration abhorred the idea of a rebel victory and even made a last-minute plea for the Organization of American States to send a "peacekeeping" force (to block such an outcome),[5] the United States at least refrained from direct military intervention.

The final factor was the nature of the insurgency itself. The Sandinista Front for National Liberation (Frente Sandinista de Liberación Nacional,

FSLN) was formed in 1961 by a small group of Marxist students who had left the Nicaraguan Socialist Party, which they saw to be too closely controlled by the Soviet Union. Inspired by Sandino and the Cuban revolution, they adopted a rural guerrilla *foco* approach to insurgency. Never numbering more than a few dozen in the 1960s, most Sandinista cadre were killed in a rural confrontation with government forces at Pancasán in August 1967. The surviving Sandinistas then adopted a strategy of "the accumulation of force in silence" according to which, for seven years, they worked quietly among university students and the urban and rural poor.

Meanwhile, the Latin American Bishops meeting in Medellín, Colombia, in 1978 had called on all religious personnel to make a "preferential option for the poor" (Chapter 9). Among other things, they were to spread the Church's liberating message to the masses by training Lay Delegates of the Word and creating "Christian base communities" (Comunidades Eclesiales de Base, CEB) in which small groups of ordinary people would discuss the "social gospel." When the bishops' directives were implemented in Nicaragua in the late 1960s and early 1970s, the regime, seeing the resultant grassroots activity as subversive, reacted with violence that sometimes resulted in deaths. Ironically, this helped the rebel cause by convincing many Catholics that there was no way to bring justice to Nicaragua except through armed struggle. From then on, the insurgent effort would blend both nationalist Marxist and progressive Catholic elements and thus considerably broaden its appeal.

Though the Sandinistas would stage one spectacularly successful hostage-ransom operation in 1974 and a flurry of attacks on urban areas in 1977, the insurgency did not really catch fire until late 1978. In August of that year, the FSLN staged another successful hostage-ransom operation, this time holding the National Legislative Palace in the heart of Managua for several days until the regime agreed to several humiliating concessions. The following month, inspired by this event, groups of young people in several important cities set up barricades and fought off the National Guard for up to two weeks. The National Guard defeated the poorly armed insurgents at the cost of several thousand civilian lives, but, from then on, both the regime and the people knew that the overthrow of the system was imminent. The FSLN, whose leadership had been squabbling for several years over insurrectionary tactics, finally came together around an effective multiclass strategy that combined rural and urban tactics. And a big influx of recruits quickly swelled the FSLN's formal army from a few hundred to several thousand. The demoralized Somoza elite and officers corps began transferring assets out of the country. Early the following summer, the FSLN declared its "final offensive" as well-coordinated fighting broke out on six "fronts" in various parts of the country. As the National Guard imploded, the FSLN announced the liberation of one city after another. On July 17,

1979, Somoza fled to Miami. Two days later, the FSLN marched into Managua and accepted the surrender of what remained of the Guard.

In all, the FSLN had shown considerable skill and flexibility in its struggle against the dictatorship. It had changed strategies and tactics until it finally found a formula that worked. It had integrated new groups, such as progressive Catholics, into its ranks and had sought multiclass support. And it had demonstrated great skill in public relations by sending spokespersons around the world to gain international backing and running a rebel radio station that reached not only Nicaraguans but could also be heard as far away as the United States.

The Sandinista Period

The Sandinista leadership that came to power in 1979, though revolutionary, was well aware that there were a number of important constraints on what it could and should do. The Latin American Catholic Church had recently made its "preferential option for the poor" and thus could not simply be dismissed as a reactionary enemy of the people. Socialism in the Soviet Union and the Eastern Bloc was beginning to lose its glow. Castro, while in many ways a genuine hero for most Sandinistas, had been in power long enough to have made many mistakes (for example, the cult of personality, oversocialization of the economy, restrictions on political freedoms, overbureaucratization, and a tendency on occasion to unnecessarily twist the U.S. tiger's tail) that the Sandinistas wanted to avoid.

The FSLN was determined to carry out a Nicaraguan revolution responding to Nicaragua's own domestic and international reality at that critical point in time (*coyuntura*). Not only would the Sandinistas immediately issue decrees to prevent the emergence of the veneration of a strongman but, throughout their administration, they would be far more respectful of civil and political rights than other revolutionary regimes and, indeed, than most Latin American governments. They would pursue a mixed economy that, though perhaps overregulated by the state, would allow the bulk of production to remain in private hands. And they would embark on a foreign policy intended to maintain cordial relations with all countries, regardless of form of government, wishing to have relations with Nicaragua.

It is useful to divide the ten and a half years of Sandinista rule into two roughly equal segments: the transitional Government of National Reconstruction (July 1979 to January 1985) and the Constitutional period (January 1985 to April 1990).[6] The first period was a time of innovation, experimentation, and some excesses yet considerable success in a number of categories. In the second period, the U.S.-organized Contra war, although never a military threat, inflicted such heavy economic, fiscal, and human damage that the revolution began to unravel and the system lost credibility to the point that it was eventually voted out of office.

The Government of National Reconstruction, 1979–1985

The most convenient way to discuss the first subperiod of Sandinista rule is to examine it under four categories: economic, social, political, and international. Though Marxist Leninists in some respects, most Sandinistas realized from the start that it would be foolish for a small nation such as theirs in the heart of the Western Hemisphere to try to move to a socialist, command economy. Instead, they opted for a "mixed economy" in which the bulk of production would remain in the hands of a now more heavily regulated private sector. True, the properties of the Somozas and their cronies were quickly nationalized as were those assets that appeared abandoned by wealthy people who had panicked and emigrated to other countries. But the public sector never accounted for more than 40 percent of the productive capacity of the country. Indeed, though this policy tended to become a casualty of escalating mutual suspicion, the government actually used loans, favorable exchange rates, and other means to try to encourage those entrepreneurs who remained in the country to behave as a productive, "patriotic bourgeoisie."[7]

Confiscated properties were turned into state farms, peasant cooperatives, and, to a lesser extent, individual plots. Though the initially heavy emphasis on state farms and cooperatives disappointed many peasants, it is clear that far more peasants had access to land—cooperative or individual—than in the past and that, as a result, for those few years until the Contra war disrupted production, Nicaragua became much more self-sufficient in domestic food production than at any time in recent memory.

During these years, Sandinista policy makers also attempted to avoid international economic isolation. Accordingly, the new government immediately announced its willingness to service the huge and onerous foreign debt left behind by the Somozas. It also sought to maintain or establish trade and aid relations with all countries regardless of regime type.

The results of these policies were generally positive if measured in terms of growth in gross domestic product (GDP) per capita. Indeed, from 1979 through 1983 Nicaragua experienced an overall growth in GDP per capita of 7 percent while Central America as a whole suffered a decline of 14.7 percent.[8] It was only in the wake of the full impact of the Contra war and the U.S.-orchestrated cutoff of World Bank and Inter-American Development Bank loans that the Nicaraguan economy first stagnated (1984) and then began a sharp decline (1985).

These years were also a time of innovative and effective social policies. Social security and social welfare were radically expanded. Agrarian reform gave to more than one hundred thousand peasant families access to land in either individual plots or, more commonly, cooperatives. But perhaps most impressive were the programs in health and education. Here, the enthusiastic voluntary efforts of tens of thousands of young people were harnessed to carry out one of the world's most ambitious and successful literacy crusades (1980) and an equally impressive grassroots program of preventive medicine (beginning in 1981). Even the report issued by the Kissinger Commission—appointed by President Ronald Reagan with the obvious purpose of justifying U.S. policy in Central America—admitted that "Nicaragua's government has made significant gains against illiteracy and disease."[9]

The first half decade of Sandinista rule also featured experimentation, innovation, and some significant success in the area of politics and government. One of the most striking phenomena of these years was an explosion in grassroots organizational activity. Though some Sandinista leaders believed in a top-down, Leninist approach to politics and government, many were very enthusiastic about what they saw as true participatory democracy. Accordingly, they encouraged the growth of organizations representing neighborhoods, women, youth, urban and rural workers, and peasants. They allowed them significant autonomy, channeled resources through them to the people, and gave them formal representation in governmental decision-making bodies and on the Council of State—the corporative structure that served as the country's legislature until 1985. In turn, these organizations played a central role in the implementation of social programs and boosted production.[10] By late 1984, an in-house U.S. embassy report placed membership in grassroots organizations at seven to eight hundred thousand, the equivalent of about half of the country's population aged sixteen or over.[11]

The revolution also moved during this time from transitional government, through elections, to constitutional government. The first institutions of government consisted of a multiperson executive (junta), a corporative legislature or Council of State (appointed in 1980), and a judiciary branch comprised of the usual lower and higher courts plus People's Anti-Somocista Tribunals set up first to process charges against Somoza-era war criminals and later to deal with captured or suspected Contras. Though these branches were staffed by persons having a variety of political orientations and class backgrounds, all were appointed by the nine-person Sandinista Directorate.

Meanwhile, in the early 1980s, the Council of State debated and ultimately passed a parties law and an electoral law. Modeled on western European practices, these laws were drafted in close consultation with the Swedish Electoral Commission. The elections themselves were moved forward from 1985 to November 4, 1984, in order to preempt the perceived possibility that the United States might use an alleged lack of democracy in Nicaragua as a pretext for invasion during Reagan's second political "honeymoon" following his expected reelection two days later. In the most widely internationally observed election in Latin America to that point, one in which 75 percent of the electorate participated, FSLN presidential candidate Daniel Ortega Saavedra and Sandinista Constituent Assembly candidates won

63 percent of the votes (67 percent of valid votes) in an open contest against six parties, three to the right of the Sandinistas and three to their left.[12]

The worst problems Nicaragua encountered in the early 1980s were in foreign affairs. The Sandinistas had wanted to preserve or promote good relations with all countries willing to have relations with their government. In some respects they were successful. Within a year they had doubled the number of countries with which Nicaragua had diplomatic involvement. Their country quickly joined the Nonaligned Movement and in October 1982 won a nonpermanent seat on the UN Security Council. Nevertheless, relations with the United States, the hemisphere's major power, went sour almost immediately. While the Sandinista victory was accepted with frigid resignation by the Carter administration, it was treated as a threatening extension of Soviet-backed communism by the Reagan administration, which took office eighteen months later. Although there was little objective reality to this frightening specter, it played to an important political constituency in the United States and would, therefore, motivate U.S. policy toward Managua until the Sandinistas left office.[13]

The Reagan administration's assault on Nicaragua was multifaceted.[14] Among other activities, it involved training, equipping, and directing a Nicaraguan exile counterrevolutionary (Contra) army to fight against its own government; using U.S. influence in the World Bank and the Inter-American Development Bank to cut off all normal lending to the upstart republic; and orchestrating a massive anti-Sandinista propaganda campaign typified by frequent distortion and outright fabrication.

U.S. behavior in relation to the Nicaraguan election of 1984 gives a good glimpse of the use of propaganda as a weapon. Apparently fearing that the still very popular FSLN would win and be legitimized by free elections, the Reagan administration denounced the 1984 elections as a "Soviet-style farce" as soon as they were announced late in 1983. Then "teaser" candidate Arturo Cruz, at the time a highly paid CIA asset with connections to the Contras, was employed to show apparent interest in running, campaign without formally registering, and then withdraw with great fanfare claiming that conditions for a free election did not exist. Later, one of the six registered opposition candidates was persuaded by the U.S. embassy to withdraw at the last moment—again with great drama. Finally, immediately after the election, when it became obvious that observer reports from credible delegations such as the British Parliament and House of Lords, the Irish Parliament, and Willy Brandt representing the Socialist International were likely to find the Nicaraguan elections clean and valid, director of the CIA William Casey arranged dramatic government "leaks" of a wholly fabricated story that Soviet-built MiG jet fighters were en route to Nicaragua aboard Socialist bloc freighters. As surely intended, this caused a great alarm in the U.S. media reminiscent of that of the Cuban Missile Crisis of 1962 and prevented less dramatic news about Nicaragua, such as the favorable international election observer reports, from even being mentioned.[15]

The Constitutional Period, 1985–1990

The second half of the Sandinista period was a time of significant achievement as well as serious economic, social, and political setback for the revolution. First, despite the fact that the country was fighting a war against the Contras, the Sandinistas continued to show a relatively high level of respect for human rights—certainly in comparison with the three Central American countries to the north.[16] In addition, the new governmental system was formally institutionalized. The Constituent Assembly, elected in 1984, wrote a constitution that, after considerable debate, national and international consultation, and modification, was promulgated in 1987.[17] That same year, the Assembly also formalized an innovative autonomy law for the peoples of the Atlantic coast. Later, new laws related to parties and election were passed (1988) and amended (1989) to honor the constitutional mandate for an election in 1990. The election itself took place that February 25 under unprecedentedly heavy international observation and was universally certified as clean and valid. Two months later, the losing FSLN turned over power to the victorious opposition.

But this was also a time of setbacks that ultimately led to the Sandinista defeat at the polls. For one, the economy went into a free fall beginning in the mid 1980s. This plunge was largely due to the direct and indirect cost of the Contra war and related U.S. programs of economic strangulation. But Sandinista economic policy, which became ever more erratic in the face of the hopelessness of the situation, did not help. The wild printing of unbacked currency to finance the war led to hyperinflation that passed 33,000 percent in 1988. And, though the Sandinistas themselves implemented structural reforms that year and the next that brought inflation down to 1,690 percent for 1989,[18] the unemployment and social pain those policies caused was enormous.

This period also saw real decay in the innovative social programs first implemented in the early 1980s. This decay was partly the result of a shift in budgetary priorities from social programs to the war. But it also reflected the success of Contra strategy that deliberately targeted government social services and personnel. Detailed war casualty statistics compiled by the government for its internal use indicate that 130 teachers, 40 doctors and nurses, 152 technicians, and 41 other professionals were among the 30,865 Nicaraguans killed in the war.[19] In practical terms, this meant that large sectors of rural Nicaragua were deprived of the government services they had come to expect in the early 1980s.

Finally, grassroots participatory democracy, a vibrant feature of the early 1980s, suffered a serious decline in the second half of the decade.[20] One reason may have been the fact that the deliberately corporatist Council of State, which had given formal representation to mass organizations early in the revolution, was replaced in 1985 by a Constituent Assembly based on traditional geographic representation. Then, too, the worsening economic situation in the late 1980s meant that ordinary people were now so busy trying to survive that they had less time for grassroots activity and that the government now had far fewer resources to channel to the people through such organizations. Finally, the Sandinistas themselves—desperate to win the war and revive production—increasingly used the grassroots organizations for their own ends. This "tasking" from above tended to deprive the organizations of their autonomy and, hence, their legitimacy in the eyes of ordinary people. Accordingly, by 1990 the neighborhood committee movement and the women's organization had virtually collapsed. Only the farmer's organization, which had maintained much of its autonomy, was still doing well.

This deteriorating situation provided an incentive for Washington to modify its posture in relation to elections in Nicaragua. In 1984, the Reagan administration had worked to discredit and encourage abstention from a clean election it knew the opposition could not possibly win. In the late 1980s, however, the Bush administration would adopt a two-track policy. On one hand, with an eye to the possibility that opinion polls might be right and that the Sandinistas would win, it frequently criticized the elections as unfair.[21] On the other, sensing that a Sandinista defeat was at least a possibility, it encouraged the opposition to participate and to unify as a coalition. Leaving nothing to chance, Washington, in the words of one State Department official, decided to "micromanage the opposition."[22] U.S. diplomats barraged the opposition with tactical advice, and tens of millions of dollars in covert (CIA) and overt (National Endowment for Democracy) funds were provided or promised. Because this money would be available only to parties and politicians who joined the National Opposition Union (Unión Nacional Opositora, UNO) or to "nonpartisan" civic organizations that, in fact, shared overlapping directorates with UNO, an extremely fractious and diverse collection of microparties and politicians stayed more or less unified throughout the campaign period.[23] In addition, in an apparent effort to warn Nicaraguan voters of the consequences of retaining the Sandinistas in power, the Contra war itself was dramatically escalated. These strategies worked: on February 25, 1990, UNO and its presidential candidate Violeta Barrios de Chamorro won an impressive 55 percent of the valid vote.

Nicaragua in the 1990s

Characteristically, official Washington, much of U.S. media, and many people in the monied opposition in Nicaragua jubilantly hailed the inauguration of Violeta de Chamorro as a watershed passage for Nicaragua from Marxist totalitarian dictatorship to Western-style democracy. That description, however, wildly distorts and rounds off the edges of reality. Nicaragua's transition had begun over a decade earlier and had yet to be fully consolidated as this was being written.

In 1994, Philip J. Williams published an article that presents a much more nuanced and accurate interpretation.[24] He argues that, after the overthrow of Somoza in 1979, the revolutionary government had introduced two types of democracy in succession—"popular revolutionary democracy," typified by the mushrooming and effervescent activity of grassroots organizations in the early 1980s, and more traditional electoral and constitutional democracy that began in 1984 and continues today. He concludes that "the unique legacy of ten years of revolution makes the consolidation of electoral democracy alone much more problematic in Nicaragua than in other Latin American cases."[25] In other words, unlike, for example, the cases of Chile, Argentina, and Brazil, where formal democracy had returned immediately after long periods of violently demobilizing dictatorships, post-Sandinista governments in Nicaragua would have to contend with widespread and often raucous, even chaotic grassroots participation of ordinary Nicaraguans who had become empowered citizens in the 1980s. Nicaraguan politics would be "messier"—less elite—but arguably more democratic than elsewhere.

Williams was correct as far as he went; but the legacy of the 1980s proved to be even more complicated than he describes. The U.S.-sponsored Contra war and associated programs of "black" and "gray" propaganda,[26] as well as some of the reactions of the Sandinistas to them, had also left the poison of deep polarization and hatred within Nicaraguan society. Even with the more positive legacies described by Williams, this would make the consolidation of democracy in post-1990 Nicaragua very difficult.

The Chamorro Years, 1990–1997

The Chamorro years are hard to evaluate.[27] On one hand, the new administration was truly reactionary in social and economic matters and the poor majority suffered noticeably.[28] Indeed, according to the United Nations Development Program's "Human Development Index" (which is based on per capita income and social indicators such as education levels and life expectancy), Nicaragua had dropped from 85th in the world when Chamorro took office to 117th by the time she left.[29] On the other hand, her administration did succeed in taming inflation and, after several years, achieving modest economic growth. What is most laudable, however, President Chamorro was a peacemaker who believed that binding up the political wounds of the Nicaraguan family was an essential prerequisite for both successful governance in the short run and democratic consolidation in the future.

Economic and Social Policy

It would be unfair to say that the Chamorro administration introduced economic neoliberalism to Nicaragua. In fact, the Sandinistas had implemented harsh "structural reforms" in the late 1980s in response to the hyperinflation caused mainly by spending on the Contra war. But the new administration embraced neoliberalism with enthusiasm and intensified its implementation. Government properties were privatized, government expenditures cut, budgets were balanced, and tariff barriers were lowered.

Though these policies curbed inflation and eventually resulted in slight economic growth, they inevitably pummeled the poor majority. Such measures as the downsizing of government, cutbacks in social services, privatization of state enterprises, and the credit emphasis on agro-export rather than peasant production of domestic foodstuffs combined to exacerbate the misery of ordinary Nicaraguans. Unemployment, underemployment, drug addiction, crime rates, homelessness (especially among children), and domestic violence all soared.

Further aggravating the social picture, the demobilization of the Contras and the bulk of the national armed forces threw tens of thousands of young men—with little training or experience in anything except violence—into the streets. Though the Chamorro administration promised former combatants land and resettlement benefits in the peace agreements of 1990, it ultimately fell far short of fully meeting these obligations. Sporadically, throughout the 1990s, rearmed Contras ("Recontras"), former Sandinista military ("Recompas"), and mixed units of both ("Revueltos")[30] engaged in renewed guerrilla activity or banditry in rural areas. Though organized armed conflict tended to decline after the mid 1990s, there were still instances of it even in the late 1990s.[31]

Politics and Government

Given the fact that Nicaragua in its two recent wars—the War of Liberation (1978–79) and the Contra war (1981–1990)—had lost almost 3 percent of its population, it is not surprising that the period of the Chamorro administration was marked with intense political invective and conflict that sometimes turned violent. Indeed, what is really surprising is the fact that this period also saw considerable progress toward national reconciliation and democratic consolidation.

Grassroots organizations—representing the poor majority of Nicaraguans—played a significant role in the politics of this period. The Rural Worker's Association, the National Union of Farmers and Ranchers, and mixed Contra/Compa groups of former combatants, were involved in the negotiations regarding the privatization of state farms, successfully insisting that some of the land be deeded to former workers and excombatants.

The National Worker's Front did the same in the privatization of urban state-owned properties. At other times, when the government was unresponsive, these and other groups staged marches, demonstrations, and strikes to force government respect for the interests of ordinary people.

Meanwhile, the Chamorro administration steadfastly eschewed pressures from the United States (from 1990 through 1993) and right-wing members of UNO to engage in a vengeful "desandinization" program. Instead, the president wisely allowed Sandinista General Humberto Ortega to remain at the head of the military. Assured in this way that there would not be an anti-Sandinista bloodbath, the FSLN accepted the demobilization of the army from over eighty thousand to fewer than fifteen thousand. In addition, the Chamorro government, the FSLN leadership, and a wide spectrum of politicians engaged in frequent bargaining, negotiation, and pact making. This ultimately resulted in a majority consensus in the National Assembly that made possible the promulgation of a new military code (1994) increasing civilian control over the military, some revisions of the 1987 Constitution (1995) that, among other things, prohibited reelection of the president and curbed the powers of that office, and the passage of Property Stability Law 209 (1996) setting a framework for dealing with property disputes arising out of the revolutionary period. Clean elections held on the Atlantic coast in 1994 also seemed to bode well for a successful consolidation of democracy.

However, all may not have been as well as it seemed. The bulk of the UNO coalition that had brought Violeta Chamorro to power in 1990 was soon alienated by her attempts at pact making, especially her gestures of reconciliation toward the Sandinistas. Many of their leaders had won positions as mayors in Nicaragua's largest cities. Nurtured by funds from the U.S. Agency for International Development (USAID) destined exclusively for municipalities that had voted the Sandinistas out, these individuals engaged in public works and neopopulist politics that won them wide popular support. Under their leadership, the old Liberal Party—the majority party of Nicaragua until it became corrupted by the Somozas—was resuscitated as various splinter Liberal parties were fused under the banner of the Liberal Alliance. The Liberals did well in the Atlantic coast elections of 1994 and they would win the national elections of 1996.

The 1996 Election

For one who had been an official observer at the elections of 1984 and 1990, I found the character of the 1996 election, which I also observed, to be a disappointment. In the politically polarized atmosphere of Nicaragua at the time, the right wing had insisted on a series of last-minute changes in the electoral law and in the personnel of the Supreme Electoral Council. The procedural modifications were hard to operationalize on such short notice and the changes in personnel introduced many people into the system who were inexperienced or lacking in commitment to democracy. Each step of the election was flawed by anomalies—from registration, throughout the campaign, to election day voting and post-election vote counting.

The worst problems occurred in the vote counting following the closing of the polls. Here there were so many irregularities that it took the Supreme Electoral Council over a month to announce official results. Such confusion reigned in some places that the entire tallies of hundreds of voting stations were ultimately thrown out. Perhaps significantly, the bulk of them occurred in the three departments—Managua, Jinotega, and Matagalpa—whose electoral councils were under newly appointed Liberal presidents. Against this background, the Liberal Alliance was triumphant. Its presidential candidate, Arnoldo Alemán, beat perennial FSLN candidate Daniel Ortega by 51 as opposed to 37.7 percent of the vote. In the National Assembly, the Liberals took 42 seats as opposed to 36 for the FSLN and 15 divided among nine minor parties. Both Ortega and the presidential candidate who placed third denounced the Liberal victory as illegitimate.[32]

Though the anomalies that had occurred may not have affected the final outcome significantly, they could hardly have had a positive impact on the civic attitude of ordinary Nicaraguans. An impressive 86 percent of the electorate appears to have voted.[33] Yet, for those citizens who became "nonvoters" as a result of local tally annulments and most others who heard the denouncements and saw images of widespread confusion and possible corruption through the media, the sense of voter efficacy must have been significantly diminished.

The Alemán Administration

The fifty-year-old lawyer-farmer who was inaugurated president in January 1997 had been a Liberal since the days of the Somozas. Though he had developed a burning hatred for the Sandinistas, he was widely rumored to have made a financial killing during the revolution purchasing heavily subsidized veterinary medicines in Nicaragua and shipping them to neighboring countries for sale at much higher market prices.[34] Elected to the Managua City Council in 1990, he then engaged in complicated deal making—some of it quite deceitful—to get himself appointed mayor by his peers. In that position he governed as a sort of "neopopulist" (see below). Using USAID funds to carry out highly visible public works for which he took full credit, he employed the politically faithful, mixed with and proclaimed his concern for the poor, and identified the Sandinistas as the cause of most of the country's problems. With financial and moral support from the Cuban and Nicaraguan exile communities in Miami, he and other Liberal mayors worked to create the Liberal Alliance out of various Liberal microparties that had survived the fall of Somoza.

Ironically, the Liberal victory of 1996 was also facilitated by the behavior of some leaders of FSLN itself in the 1990s. These people had weakened the image of the party by engaging in a legal but unseemly property grab (dubbed "la piñata") during their lame duck months early in 1990 and again by clinging to the leadership of the party when challenged in 1994. The break-off of the Renovating Sandinista Movement (Movimiento Renovadora Sandinista, MRS) into a separate party in 1995 took most of the middle-level leadership out of the FSLN just as the united and well-financed Liberals were gearing up for the 1996 election.

The Alemán administration—as this was being written at the halfway mark—had been a disappointment for anyone concerned with democratic consolidation in Nicaragua. It had been marked by extreme polarization, confrontation, administrative incompetence, and persistent charges of unprecedented corruption. The disastrous impact of Hurricane Mitch in October 1998 only highlighted and accentuated these failings.

In many ways, Arnoldo Alemán was a quintessential neopopulist—a category of leader that had emerged in various parts of Latin America by the end of the century.[35] Like the populists of earlier decades (Getulio Vargas in Brazil, Juan Perón in Argentina, José María Velasco Ibarra in Ecuador), the neopopulists used personal charisma and dramatic rhetoric to appeal—almost as secular messiahs—to large blocks of socially and economically marginalized and stressed citizens. Characteristically, they championed the weak and vulnerable (the "people") as against the evil and "repugnant other" (often, though not always, the privileged classes).[36] Unlike the old populists who promoted labor unions and other organs of civil society, neopopulists (such as Carlos Menem in Argentina, Alberto Fujimori in Peru, and Abdala Bucaram in Ecuador) appealed directly to the politically unorganized sectors of society. Indeed, such leaders actually feared and disliked organized civil society, be it in the form of grassroots civic organizations (of peasants, workers, or women, for example) or nongovernmental organizations (NGO)—national and international—providing assistance to the latter. And, finally, unlike the old populists with their schemes for government intervention in the economy, the neopopulists—though usually elected on platforms criticizing neoliberal economics—often eventually adopted neoliberalism (discussed in Chapter 10) and, indeed, found that, in the short run at least, the implementation of structural reforms was popular with their marginalized supporters.[37]

Nicaragua of the 1990s was ripe for the emergence—though perhaps not the long-term success—of neopopulism. The U.S.-orchestrated Contra war and related programs of economic strangulation had ruined the economy and created an ever-growing segment of impoverished people, including informal sector vendors, unemployed workers, and demobilized combatants. Most of these were not members of organized civil society. In addition, massive U.S.-generated anti-Sandinista propaganda promoted in the

1980s through local and international media, the Catholic Church hierarchy, and opposition parties—together with Sandinista inability to bring peace and solve the country's economic problems—had demonized the Sandinistas in the eyes of many. Thus neopopulism in Nicaragua had both an accessible base of stressed, angry but unorganized people to which to appeal and a ready-made "repugnant other" (the Sandinistas) to serve as a target in mobilizing that anger. Added to this, as noted earlier, the neopopulists were helped by the USAID programs in the early 1990s (from which pro-Sandinista municipalities were excluded) and by popular reaction to Sandinista excesses starting with the "piñata" in 1990 and continuing throughout the decade as a tiny group of old revolutionaries clung stubbornly to the reins of party power.

Thus, Alemán rose to power—and initially attempted to rule—as a neopopulist. Harboring an intense hatred of the Sandinistas and not having played a central role in the bargaining and consensus-building that went into the National Assembly's rewriting of the "rules of the game" in the mid 1990s, Alemán and his Liberal plurality in the legislature immediately called into question the legitimacy of the 1994 Military Code, the 1995 amendments to the 1987 Constitution, and the 1996 Property Stability Law 2092. In addition, seeing the Sandinistas as unredeemable evil, they maneuvered to deprive them of the full number of seats on the executive body of the National Assembly to which they appeared entitled.

These moves resulted in months of chaos featuring general strikes, demonstrations, raucous and hate-filled invective, renewed armed insurgency, FSLN boycotts of the Assembly, constitutional challenges, sporadic attempts at public dialogue, and behind-the-scenes bargaining between the leaders of the two major political forces. On the positive side, grassroots organizations representing peasants and urban workers were again active in defending their interests—especially as they related to the property issue.

Eventually, pressure—both international and domestic—for a compromise solution became irresistible and Alemán was forced to adopt a new strategy that would add behind-the-scenes deals with his Sandinista enemies to his neopopulist public posture. In fall 1997, private negotiations between legal teams representing the FSLN and the government culminated in an agreement on the thorniest issue of the 1990s, that of property. In November after only four hours of debate, 73 of the 93 members of the National Assembly voted to approve the Law of Urban and Rural Reformed Property.[38]

For a while it appeared that with the settlement of the property issue a "new normalcy" was beginning to emerge in Nicaragua. In a short span of time the government announced a badly needed program of rural credit for small farmers; the IMF agreed to renew support for Nicaragua that had been suspended for two years; and an international Consultative Group consisting of various countries and organizations pledged $1.8 billion over a period of four years to promote macroeconomic stability, the development of the farming sector, and governability. In addition, another round of clean—though not well attended—local elections were held in the Atlantic region.

However, the impression that Nicaraguan politics had taken a more sanguine turn quickly evaporated. Soon the leaders of the two major parties each suffered personal scandals. Alemán was engulfed in escalating charges of corruption. First came the "Narcojet" scandal in which traces of cocaine were found in a rented (previously stolen) jet that had been serving as the "presidential plane" since December 1997. Then, in February 1999, Comptroller General Agustín Jarquín announced the results of an investigation of the president's personal assets that showed that Alemán's personal fortune had grown by 900 percent from 1990 to 1996. For his part, in 1998, Ortega suddenly found himself accused by his thirty-year-old stepdaughter of having sexually abused her for almost twenty years.

While both Ortega and Alemán would survive the scandals and retain control of their respective political movements, their behavior hurt their parties and dramatically eroded their popularity. In April 1999 nearly half of those questioned in an *Envio* survey saw the Alemán administration as "the most corrupt government in Nicaragua's history,"[39] and a CID-Gallup Poll of public opinion found that fully 77 percent of Nicaraguans had doubts about their president's honesty.[40] In the latter poll, public support for the two major parties—FSLN and Liberal—had dropped to 20 percent each.[41]

On top of this, support for Alemán and the Liberals was also hurt by their poor handling of the disaster visited on Nicaragua by Hurricane Mitch in October 1998. Over twenty-four hundred people were killed and nearly a fifth of Nicaragua's population left homeless. Economic damages totaled over $1.5 billion.[42] Working with a civil service stripped to the bone by a decade of neoliberal downsizing and further debilitated by corruption, cronyism, and incompetence, the Alemán administration was painfully slow in helping those hurt by the disaster. Further, as a neopopulist, Alemán channeled Nicaraguan public relief aid through local governments where Liberals were in power or through Liberal party organizations where they were not. He even attempted at first to deflect the flow of international assistance away from NGOs (seen by him as Sandinista) that he could not control.[43]

The increasingly weak position of both Alemán and Ortega would lead in turn to a strange series of pacted agreements between the two arch enemies.[44] Whereas the agreement on the 1997 property law could be seen as serving a national good, it would be hard to defend subsequent deals between the two caudillos in such terms. While publicly attacking each other in the most visceral terms, Alemán and Ortega now made deals that simply served their own or their party's narrow interest. Backed by an FSLN-Liberal majority in Congress, they agreed, among other matters, to appoint a poorly qualified FSLN-Liberal Party faithful to fill the long-vacant office of Human Rights Ombudsman; to expand and "pack" the Office of the Comptroller with similarly partisan individuals; to change the electoral laws in ways designed to protect their two-party hegemony and discourage third parties; and to modify the constitution to allow, among other things, for the reelection of the president.

As this was being written, Nicaragua appeared to be at a critical political juncture. Once dramatically dissimilar, the Liberals and what was left of the FSLN had, by the end of the century, become much more alike. Since the days of Somoza, the Liberal movement had long been essentially a vehicle for personal aggrandizement and ambition. Now in the late 1990s, a tiny remnant of the original FSLN controlled a party that had seen the defection of most of its middle- and upper-level cadre and a near-complete dissolution of its once strong relationship with the various organs of civil society created in the 1970s and 1980s. In the wake of Hurricane Mitch, the bulk of the grassroots organizations created during Sandinista rule simply gave up on both their government and the FSLN—instead, vigorously pulling together with national and international NGOs to confront the common disaster.[45] By 1999, various groups disgusted by the behavior of the Liberals and the FSLN were talking of creating a third force, "The Fatherland Movement," which, perhaps with Comptroller Agustín Jarquín as its presidential candidate, could challenge the established parties in the 2001 general election. Nevertheless, though discredited and isolated, the two major parties and their respective leaders still had sufficient power, and at least two more years, to pose some threat to their country's new democratic institutions.

Conclusion

Nicaragua's transition to democracy was unique and, in some ways, fragile. It was not, as U.S. conventional wisdom would have us believe, something that happened suddenly in 1990 when the U.S.-sponsored Contra war finally forced the "totalitarian" Sandinistas to allow free elections. That interpretation is propaganda-driven, cold war nonsense. In fact, the transition in Nicaragua was made possible by the insurrectionary overthrow of a U.S. client dictator in 1979 and was implemented largely by the Sandinista governments of the 1980s. Indeed, if anything, U.S. behavior in the 1980s contributed dramatically to the social and economic distress and political hatred that would make democratic consolidation in the 1990s more difficult.

The Sandinista period, despite U.S. behavior, bequeathed the very positive legacies of participatory democracy and formal electoral institutions. These legacies survived through the Chamorro administration and into that of Alemán. Indeed, though the country's formal democratic institutions were in some danger of being modified and "pacted" away in FSLN-Liberal bargaining, they were still, at the time of this writing, quite strong. Equally important, civil society—invigorated by the challenge of Hurricane Mitch and enraged by the behavior of the government and the two major parties—was stronger than ever.

Clearly all was not well as Nicaragua entered the new millennium. The use of public office for self-aggrandizement—universal in the old Somoza system but practically nonexistent during most of the Sandinista period—had reappeared late in the Sandinista period and had steadily increased throughout subsequent administrations. In addition, the "two-party system" that had emerged in Nicaragua in the 1990s had performed poorly and was discredited. Thus, paradoxically, though Nicaraguan voters retained almost touching faith in elections, their image of politicians in general was very low. Finally, the negative legacy of hatred and distrust flowing from the Contra war and related phenomena in the 1980s had so polarized the country and stressed such a large portion of its population that it actually helped generate Central America's first example of neopopulism and, in doing so, constituted a serious obstacle to democratic consolidation.

Nevertheless, the existence of a vigorous civil society, a raucous and aggressive free press, good electoral laws and constitutionally based institutions gave cause for some hope for the survival of democracy. In addition, with the end of the cold war, the international community had come to exert tremendous pressure for the preservation of democratic forms—pressure that even leaders with the most scant instinct for democracy were unlikely to openly defy.

Notes

1. Only Haitians are clearly poorer. Though Cuba's GDP per capita figures would formally put it second from the bottom, they misrepresent the reality of Cuban life in that they do not include the many free government services Cuban citizens receive.

2. For a study of the life and reign of the first of the Somoza dictators, see Knut Walter, *The Regime of Anastasio Somoza: 1936–1956* (Chapel Hill: University of North Carolina Press, 1993).

3. Please refer to the section titled "The Common History of the Original Five" in the Introduction for the discussion of the term "liberal." As noted there, "Liberal" in the Latin American context is very unlike "liberal" in the United States.

4. Timothy P. Wickham-Crowley, *Guerrillas and Revolution in Latin America: A Comparative Study of Insurgents and Regimes since 1956* (Princeton: Princeton University Press, 1992).

5. For an examination of U.S. policy toward Nicaragua in this period, see Morris H. Morley, *Washington, Somoza, and the Sandinistas: State and Regime in U.S. Policy toward Nicaragua, 1969–1981* (New York: Cambridge University Press, 1994).

6. Though a formal constitution did not come into being until 1987, I choose to call this the "Constitutional period" because, during all of these five years, the country was ruled by an elected president and the Constituent Assembly.

7. See Rose Spalding, *Capitalists and Revolution in Nicaragua: Opposition and Accommodation, 1979–1993* (Chapel Hill: University of North Carolina Press, 1994).

8. For the sources behind these statistics and discussion of the Sandinista economic model, see Michael E. Conroy, "Economic Legacy and Policies: Performance and Critique," in Thomas W. Walker, ed., *Nicaragua: The First Five Years* (New York: Praeger, 1985), 219–44.

9. Kissinger Commission, *Report of the National Bipartisan Commission on Central America* (Washington, DC: U.S. Government Printing Office, 1984), 30.

10. See Luis Héctor Serra, "The Grass-Roots Organizations," in Walker, *Nicaragua: The First Five Years*, 65–89.

11. This information was revealed by an official of the U.S. embassy to a group of which I was a part on June 25, 1985.

12. For a description of that election and citation of observer delegation reports, see Thomas W. Walker, *Nicaragua: The Land of Sandino*, 3d ed. (Boulder, CO: Westview Press, 1991), 50.

13. For a discussion of these matters, see Mary B. Vanderlaan, *Revolution and Foreign Policy in Nicaragua* (Boulder, CO: Westview Press, 1986).

14. See Thomas W. Walker, ed., *Reagan versus the Sandinistas: The Undeclared War on Nicaragua* (Boulder, CO: Westview Press, 1987).

15. For documentation of the assertions in this paragraph see Walker, *Nicaragua: The Land of Sandino*, 50–51, and accompanying endnotes.

16. For a solid examination of human rights in Nicaragua during the entire Sandinista period, see Michael Linfield, "Human Rights" in Thomas W. Walker, ed., *Revolution and Counterrevolution in Nicaragua* (Boulder, CO: Westview Press, 1991), 275–94.

17. See Kenneth J. Mijeski, ed., *The Nicaraguan Constitution of 1987: English Translation and Commentary*, Ohio University Monographs in International Studies (Athens: Ohio University Press, 1991).

18. Both inflation figures are from UN Comisión Económica para América Latina y el Caribe, "Balance Preliminar de la Economía de la América Latina y el Caribe, 1990," *Notas Sobre la Economía y el Desarrollo*, no. 500/501 (December 1990): 27.

19. These statistics are from eight pages of charts provided to me by the Ministry of the Presidency in January 1990. In various trips into the war zone, I personally saw numerous rural clinics, schools, and food-storage facilities that had been destroyed by the Contras.

20. Luis Héctor Serra, "The Grass-Roots Organizations," in Walker, *Revolution and Counterrevolution in Nicaragua*, 49–76.

21. For example, "Quayle Calls Nicaragua's Plans for Elections in 1990 Just a 'Sham,' " *New York Times*, June 13, 1989.

22. An unidentified State Department official as quoted in "Chamorro Takes a Chance," *Time* magazine, May 7, 1990.

23. See William I. Robinson, *A Faustian Bargain: The U.S. Involvement in the Nicaraguan Elections and American Foreign Policy in the Post-Cold War Era* (Boulder, CO: Westview Press, 1992).

24. Philip J. Williams, "Dual Transitions from Authoritarian Rule: Popular and Electoral Democracy in Nicaragua," *Comparative Politics*, January 1994, 169–85.

25. Ibid., 172.

26. "Black" propaganda usually refers to complete lies or inventions, whereas "gray" propaganda involves distortion.

27. For a comprehensive examination of this period see Thomas W. Walker, ed., *Nicaragua without Illusions: Regime Transition and Structural Adjustment in the 1990s* (Wilmington, DE: Scholarly Resources, 1997).

28. In this context, "reactionary" is a better word than "conservative" since, in social and economic matters, the new administration was not trying to conserve what it had inherited from the Sandinistas but rather to "turn the clock back" to a real or imagined past.

29. As cited in Nitlapan-Envio Team, "President Alemán: First Moves, First Signals," *ENVIO* 16, no. 187–88 (February–March, 1987): 3–4.

30. *Recompa* comes from the word *compa*, which is short for *compañero* or comrade in arms, a term often used for Sandinista soldiers. *Revueltos* is used in other contexts for scrambled eggs.

31. See, for instance, "Nicaragua: Atlantic Coast Groups Rearm," *Central America Report*, June 11, 1998, 3.

32. For information concerning the election, see "Epilogue: The 1996 National Elections," in Walker, *Nicaragua without Illusions*, 305–11.

33. The official figure for voter turnout did not include voters in stations where the tallies were annulled.

34. From an author interview with Ricardo Chavarría, former Vice Minister of Social Welfare (INSSBI), July 18, 1998.

35. For good discussions of this interesting phenomenon, see Carlos de la Torre, "Populism and Democracy: Political Discourses and Cultures in Contemporary Ecuador," *Latin American Perspectives* 24, no. 3 (May 1997): 12–24; Kurt Weyland, "Neopopulism and Neoliberalism in Latin America: Unexpected Affinities," *Studies in Comparative International Development* 31, no. 3 (Fall 1996): 3–31.

36. De la Torre, "Populism and Democracy," 19–20.

37. See Weyland, "Neopopulism and Neoliberalism."

38. Nitlapán-Envio Team, "An Accord Besieged by Discord," *Envio* 16, no. 196 (November 1997): 3–4.

39. "After Stockholm and before the Pact," *Envio* 18, no. 215 (June 1999): 4.

40. "Nicaragua: Government and FSLN Weakened by Protests," *Central America Report*, May 14, 1999, 2.

41. "Nicaragua: FSLN Hard liners Maintain Control," *Central America Report*, June 18, 1999, 7.

42. "Nicaragua: Mitch Redefines Political and Social Scenario," *Central America Report*, May 28, 1999, 6.

43. Ricardo Chavarría, Executive Director of the Instituto de Promoción Humana (Nicaragua's oldest nongovernmental organization), in a lengthy e-mail communication with the author on January 14, 1999.

44. Strange as this turn of events may seem, it actually was predicted as a strong possibility by Nicaraguan political observer Oscar René Vargas in an interview with the Hemisphere Initiatives/Washington Office on Latin America election observer team (of which I was a member) in October 1996.

45. "Nicaragua: Mitch Redefines."

5

Costa Rica
Buffeted Democracy

John A. Booth

Despite national myths to the contrary, Costa Rican democracy did not develop in the nineteenth century and did not arise from an egalitarian distribution of resources or racial homogeneity.[1] Nineteenth- and early-twentieth-century Costa Rica often deviated greatly from the mythical image of civilian rule, political stability, and developing electoral democracy. Instead, Costa Rican democracy arose from a combination of increasingly powerful social forces, driven by socioeconomic diversity and political discord that forced the adoption of democratic institutions at mid twentieth century.

Costa Rican democracy consolidated in the 1950s and achieved remarkable stability for several decades. The political system was buffeted by a series of challenges that began in the 1970s—regional political turmoil and conflict with neighboring Nicaragua, a national economic and debt crisis, and sharply increased domestic unrest and terrorism—some of which continued through the subsequent two decades. Although Costa Rica's institutions proved remarkably resilient, these difficult challenges nevertheless transformed the nation's political and economic systems. The resulting changes may have somewhat weakened Costa Rica's democratic practice.

The Development of Costa Rican Democracy

Significant Spanish settlement of Costa Rica's *meseta central* (central valley) began in earnest around 1560 but remained relatively slow in the mineral-poor colony. Indigenous peoples died out from disease, fled from the Spaniards, or assimilated into the emerging society by intermarriage. The colonists imported African slaves for agricultural workers, but Costa Rica suffered a persistent agricultural labor shortage that kept rural wages high during much of the colonial era. Though economic inequality in Costa Rican society remained less severe than in many neighboring nations, significant economic and social differentiation developed.[2] The colony's criollo aristocracy, descendants of the conquerors and colonial land grantees, owned extensive lands and dominated a larger society of slaves, indigenous peoples, and free mestizo (indigenous-European mixed race) artisans, laborers of various sorts, and subsistence farmers.

Certain features of colonial life probably contributed somewhat to the eventual development of democracy.[3] First, Costa Rica never developed the extensive quasi-feudal hacienda system of other Latin American countries, which typically operated with labor coerced by the army and police. Second, because of a persistent labor shortage, family farming and free rural wage labor survived and kept peasants relatively free and prosperous. Third, Costa Rica's isolation from the seat of colonial government in Guatemala gave the political elite some experience with self-government because *cabildos* (local councils) developed in much of the country. Fourth, the emergent aristocratic factions of Conservatives and Liberals active in the *cabildos* remained relatively civil with each other, while elsewhere in Central America Liberal-Conservative conflict became violent after Independence.

Political life in Costa Rica, a province of the Central American Federal Republic, began quietly in 1823. Even when Liberal-Conservative conflict raged in the rest of the federation, a quick Liberal victory kept things relatively calm in Costa Rica. When the federation collapsed, Costa Rica followed a practice already established during the federal period—the indirect election, often marred by fraud, of president and legislators from among the landowning elite. In 1838, however, Braulio Carrillo seized power and declared himself "dictator for life" and took Costa Rica out of the federation. Civil life deteriorated rapidly. Carrillo's enemies attempted to oust him in 1842, but their leader, General Francisco Morazán Quesada, was captured and executed.

For many ensuing decades, Costa Rica remained politically unstable. From 1824 through 1905, roughly a quarter of Costa Rican presidents served no more than a year in office, one in six was toppled by a coup, and over one-third of the period was spent under military rule (see Table 1). Generals ruled Costa Rica more than half the time between 1835 and 1899. "During this period there were six different constitutions and there were numerous changes of government with military support. Civilian governments, generally of short duration, were usually elected indirectly."[4]

Colonel Tomás Guardia, a Liberal, seized power in 1870 and embarked on a modernizing project that included railroad construction, constitutional reform, the promotion of education, and military professionalization and expansion. The Conservatives declined and virtually disappeared, leaving anticlerical Liberal coffee-grower factions to squabble over power after

Guardia died in 1882. Costa Rican political elites continued to compete for power through indirect, often fraudulent elections. Gradually increasing literacy, the product of the Liberals' education efforts, expanded the population of men able to vote.[5] Popular mobilization in support of a new Catholic Party candidate in 1889 forced the military to respect an opposition election victory. Albeit by rioting rather than voting, this incident marked the first time ordinary citizens (angered by heretofore rare hard times) meaningfully affected politics.

Table 1. Characteristics of Costa Rican Presidencies, 1824–1998

	1824–1905	*1906–1949*	*1950–1998*
Mean presidency length (yrs.)	2.7	3.1	4.0
Civilian only	2.3	3.2	4.0
Military only	4.8	1.5	0.0
Percentage under military rule	36%	7%	0%
Percentage of presidents serving less than one year	24%	14%	0%
Percentage of presidencies ended by coup	17%	14%	0%
Mean voter turnout of population	—ª	14.5%	40.3%

Source: Table from John A. Booth, *Costa Rica: Quest for Democracy* (Boulder, CO: Westview Press, 1998), 41. Table data from Harold H. Bonilla, *Los presidentes: Tomo I* and *Tomo II* (San José: Universidad Estatal a Distancia-Editorial Costa Rica, 1979).
ªNot available; estimated at consistently below 10 percent.

As the twentieth century began, increasing ethnic diversity (laborers from Jamaica, China, Italy, and elsewhere came to work on the railroads) and economic diversification (due to urbanization, increased external trade, and transportation modernization) led to labor organization and strikes. Boom-and-bust cycles, the worst being the Great Depression, generated much class conflict and political turmoil among rapidly growing working and middle classes. Labor unions formed the Reformist Party (Partido Reformista, PR) to contest the 1923 election. Though PR candidate Jorge Volio lost, the party's social democratic platform and its cooperation with unions and progressive Catholics provided a foretaste of future political alliances. The Costa Rican Communist Party, formed in 1931, organized banana workers, won a major strike in 1934 against United Fruit Company, and gave birth to a powerful labor confederation. Though weaker than the Communists and organized labor, middle-class civil society also expanded rapidly during the 1930s.

Confrontation between coffee grower-dominated elite politics and these rising social forces reached a critical stage in the 1940s. Competition among elite factions in the early twentieth century led to direct presidential elections, and expanding literacy continued to increase the electorate. Presidents Cleto González Víquez and Ricardo Jiménez Oreamuno reciprocally tolerated each other's opposition election campaigns and thus improved standards for political fair play. Military plotters seized power in 1917 but were ousted in 1919 by a combination of a revolt by exiled elites and popular turmoil. Despite the return to civilian rule, elections during the next three decades remained frequently fraudulent. Elite factions manipulated electoral rules in hopes of managing growing turmoil in civil society.

In 1940 social Christian reformer and *cafetalero* (coffee grower) Rafael Angel Calderón Guardia became president under the Republican (Republicano) Party banner. He implemented social security reforms that alienated his *cafetalero* allies, including much of his own party. Fighting for political survival, Calderón forged a populist alliance with the Communist Party, its unions, and archbishop Victor Sanabria. The coalition, successful in the 1942 legislative election, quickly enacted a labor code and recognized the right to strike. Calderón attempted to retain control of the political system as class and political tensions escalated. His vice president, Teodoro Picado Michalski, succeeded Calderón in the presidency while the labor Left intimidated growing middle-class and elite opposition.

Calderón's campaign for a second presidential term in 1948 brought these conflicts to a head. Seeking to placate political opponents, the regime set up a national election board and gave control over it to the opposition. Otilio Ulate Blanco of the National Union Party (Partido de Unión Nacional, PUN) ran against Calderón and won with the aid of significant fraud. Calderonista deputies, a majority in the new Congress, refused to certify Ulate's victory. This provided the pretext awaited by social democrat José Figueres Ferrer, who had for several years been agitating against the populist coalition regime and preparing to revolt. In 1948 Figueres and his National Liberation Army rebelled and defeated the regime, army, and unions in a short but bloody civil war.[6]

Figueres and the National Liberation junta ruled for eighteen months. They repressed labor but implemented key social democratic reforms and retained the labor and social security laws passed under Calderón. The junta fared badly in a constituent assembly election, which Ulate's PUN dominated. Two critical Constitutional reforms enacted in 1949 framed the subsequent democracy—abolition of the armed forces and the creation of an independent electoral agency, the Supreme Electoral Tribunal (Tribunal Supremo Electoral, TSE). The Liberation junta relinquished power to Ulate in 1949.

An interelite accord eventually arose from this complex and turbulent political situation.[7] The accord supplemented the formal constitutional rules that provided for clean elections and eliminated the army as a danger to civilian rule. With the election fraud and rule manipulation behind them, a broad array of political elites of various social classes gradually embraced democratic rules of the game. Cooperation and accommodation of various economic and political forces became the rule: rather than staying in power by force, Figueres and the Liberationists handed power to Ulate and the PUN, the putative victors in the 1948 election. The junta and Ulate's government left Calderón's labor and social security policies in place to placate working- and middle-class elements. The social democratic rebels then converted their movement into the National Liberation Party (Partido de Liberación Nacional, PLN), which contested the 1953 election and won.

In sum, increasing socioeconomic diversity (new products, infrastructure, ethnic groups, class relations, and external economic links) generated working-class and middle-class social forces that, driven by economic hard times, increased in organization and mobilization. However, though political elites repeatedly refined election rules and expanded popular access to the system, these changes failed to bring stability. Calderón's coalition with Communist-led labor and the Church shattered the hegemony and class unity of the coffee elite but was itself soon destroyed by countervailing middle-sector and upper-class forces in the 1948 civil war. The PLN in the 1950s forged a new liberal-democratic regime marked by an inclusive interelite accord on fair elections as the only means to compete for power. Ultimately the emergent elite consensus, social democratic development model, and widespread popular political participation stabilized the system and produced a consolidated democratic regime.

Costa Rican Democracy in Practice

Constitution and Government

The 1949 Constitution, in force ever since, established the polity upon the principles of popular sovereignty, equality of citizens before the law, and limited government. It divided power among legislative, executive, judicial, and electoral branches of government, each with some restraints upon the others.[8] The abolition of a standing military eliminated the likelihood of military disruption of the constitutional order, placed formal power holders and contenders on a relatively equal footing, and encouraged unfettered citizen participation. The Constitution provided extensive political rights and guarantees to citizens, including broad freedom of written and spoken expression, movement, religion, association, and petition of government; freedom from self-incrimination, cruel or unusual punishment, and double jeopardy; and the right to due process, privacy, and free access to information from the government.[9] Moving well beyond these political rights and liberties, the Constitution also granted social and economic rights: government protection for families and for mothers and minor children, equal rights between marriage partners, and equal parental obligation to children born within or outside of wedlock; the economic rights to organize, bargain collectively, and strike; equal pay for equal work, minimum wages, overtime pay, paid vacation, housing, and a system of public health care.

The Constitution established the Legislative Assembly (Asamblea Legislativa) with fifty-seven deputies elected by proportional representation from the nation's seven provinces and vested it with powers that made it one of Latin America's strongest legislatures. The Assembly had the power to legislate, approve the budget, tax, declare war, and amend the Constitution. Its checks upon the executive branch included the power to require information from cabinet ministers, investigate, impeach, censure, and remove executive officials, regulate presidential foreign travel, override vetoes, appoint the powerful national comptroller, and appoint Supreme Court and TSE magistrates. Despite these checks, provisions barring immediate reelection of deputies (or any other public official) and weak legislative staffing undermined the Assembly's expertise and weakened it relative to the executive. Problems arising from national economic difficulties curtailed Legislative Assembly power in the 1970s and 1980s, especially its influence over economic policy. As presidents used legislated decree powers and executive rule-making to enact neoliberal policies required of Costa Rica by international lenders, legislative policy initiation, particularly in fiscal matters, declined as deputies shifted attention toward minor pork barrel legislation.[10]

The formal legislative-executive balance of power in the 1949 Constitution favored the Assembly, but the 1980s economic crisis shifted the power pendulum toward the executive branch. So marked was this switch that, in just ten years, the executive branch of Costa Rica's government became as strong as it had formerly been weak.[11] The 1949 Constitution provided that the president should serve a single four-year term and should share authority with cabinet ministers (the Council of Government) in foreign policy, appointment, budgeting, legislative initiative, and even the veto. The council, not the president, could name ambassadors and heads of autonomous bureaucracies, grant clemency, and request the Assembly to raise military forces or negotiate peace. Despite such restraints, the executive branch roughly tripled its output of decrees and rules between the 1960s and 1980s, greatly increasing presidential power over public policy.[12] The size of the executive branch increased steadily from the 1950s into the 1980s—government employment tripled, and government workers increased from 6 percent to almost 10 percent of the economically active population. Autonomous bureaucratic agencies (outside the central ministries) that delivered key public services (electricity, telephone service, water) grew faster than central ministries. However, public sector cutbacks mandated by neoliberal reforms after the mid 1980s shrank the executive branch and eroded education, health, and infrastructure programs.[13]

The Constitution gave Costa Rica's Supreme Court of Justice (Corte Suprema de Justicia, CSJ) effective power to restrain both the executive and legislative branches (judicial review of proposed and enacted legislation and executive decrees and behavior) and authority to appoint lower courts.

The CSJ regularly exercised these powers, and it and other courts provided considerable protection to citizens' rights, including those that allow open political participation. Costa Ricans recurred to litigation with growing frequency from the 1960s through the 1990s, more than quadrupling the number of cases handled during that period. The Legislative Assembly and the CSJ extensively reorganized the courts to cope with the growing case load.[14]

The Party System and Elections

The 1949 Constitution guaranteed citizens the right to form parties to compete for power. In the 1950s the system became effectively two-party dominant, although that dominance did not fully consolidate itself until the 1980s. Proportional representation permitted regional and other small parties to win some Legislative Assembly seats and to survive despite small bases. The number of parties with at least one deputy rose from four in 1953 to six in 1998, but the number of seats going to parties other than the dominant PLN or its main opponent, the Unity coalition (succeeded in 1983 by the Social Christian Unity Party—Partido Unidad Social Cristiana, PUSC), declined over that period. The number of presidential candidates rose from two in 1953 to twelve in 1998, but, as of this writing, only the PLN or Unity-PUSC had won the presidency since 1953.[15]

Thus, by 1990 only two groups effectively competed for the presidency— the social democratic PLN and the PUSC—and they alternated in power. In thirteen post-civil war governments from 1949 through 1998, the PLN held the presidency seven times, and either the Unity coalition or PUSC held it six times (Table 2). The PLN won a majority of seats in seven of twelve Assemblies elected between 1953 and 1998 (Table 2). This party alternation occurred because many voters did not identify with one particular political party and made voting choices based upon candidate personality or programs. Moreover, one survey reported that 60 percent of even strong party identifiers endorsed a change of ruling party every four years despite their party allegiance.[16] John Peeler contends that "it is inconceivable that liberal democracy could have been maintained in [Costa Rica] without . . . the regular practice of alternation of parties in the presidency."[17] The two large parties consistently did disproportionately better than smaller parties in the public funding of election campaigns.

The National Liberation Party was preeminent in Costa Rican politics in the second half of the twentieth century. Its original social democratic ideology attracted a middle- and working-class base with programs—largely enacted into public policy—that gave the state a large role in managing the economy, redistributing income, and providing numerous subsidized services to citizens. Beginning in the late 1980s the PLN effectively abandoned its long-championed social democratic economic program and replaced it with one more in line with neoliberalism, free markets, and a curtailed public sector.[18] PLN social democratic traditionalists resisted this program change within the party and in the Legislative Assembly.[19]

Table 2. Party Control of Presidency and Legislative Assembly, 1949–2000

Term	President, Party[a]	Winner's % of Presidential Vote	Winner's Party with Legislative Majority[b]
1949–1953	Otilio Ulate Blanco, PUN	54	yes
1953–1958	José Figueres Ferrer, PLN	65	yes
1958–1962	Mario Echandi Jiménez, PUN	46	no
1962–1966	Francisco Orlich B., PLN	50	yes
1966–1970	José Joaquín Trejos Fernández, Unif./Unity	51	no
1970–1974	José Figueres Ferrer, PLN	55	yes
1974–1978	Daniel Oduber Quirós, PLN	43	no
1978–1982	Rodrigo Carazo Odio, Unif./Unity	50	no
1982–1986	Luis Alberto Monge Alvarez, PLN	59	yes
1986–1990	Oscar Arias Sánchez, PLN	52	yes
1990–1994	Rafàel Angel Calderón Fournier, PUSC	51	yes
1994–1998	José Figueres Olsen, PLN	50	no
1998–2000	Miguel Angel Rodríguez Echeverría, PUSC	47	no

Source: Table drawn from John A. Booth, "Costa Rica: The Roots of Democratic Stability," in Larry Diamond, Jonathan Hartlyn, and Juan J. Linz, eds., *Democracy in Developing Countries: Latin America* (Boulder, CO: Lynne Rienner, 1999), table 9.2; and John A. Booth, *Costa Rica: Quest for Democracy* (Boulder, CO: Westview Press, 1998), table 4.2.
[a]Parties: PLN = National Liberation, PUN = National Union, PUSC = Social Christian Unity, Unif./Unity = "Unification" or "Unity" party coalition.
[b]The Assembly has 57 seats; 28 constitute a majority.

In 1983 most of the parties of the Unity coalition merged to form the PUSC, which became the nation's second great centrist party. The PUSC and its predecessor coalition drew votes from all social classes, but their leadership came mainly from the national commercial and agricultural bourgeoisie. Although the PUSC drew upon a social Christian antecedent that included the Catholic Union Party of the late 1800s, the Reformist Party of the 1920s, and Calderón's coalition of the 1940s, the PUSC's effective ideology embraced neoliberalism.[20]

In sum, Costa Rica developed a political party system dominated by two strong, moderate (centrist) parties, with several other small and regional parties. Indeed, the PLN and PUSC became more alike as the former moved toward the ideological center in the 1980s and 1990s. Meanwhile, leftist parties lost support, leaving voters with a narrower array of policy choices. Although some experts hold that just such dominance by two strong, centrist parties may contribute importantly to democratic consolidation, the increasing sameness of the PLN and PUSC likely underlay voter anger that caused an 11 percent voter turnout decline in 1998.[21]

Elections and Campaigns

Starting in 1949, Costa Rica elected all public officials every fourth year for coterminous terms, and the Supreme Electoral Tribunal conducted all elections and managed the voter registration system and national registry. The TSE—as independent of both government and parties as functionally possible—consists of three magistrates and six *suplentes* (literally, "reserve" magistrates) appointed by the Supreme Court of Justice.[22] The 1949 Constitution barred electoral legislation during the six months prior to an election and vested the TSE with authority to review and approve electoral legislation drafted by the Legislative Assembly (which had the power to override a TSE veto only by a two-thirds majority) and to act as the sole adminis-trative, regulatory, investigative, and appellate institution in all electoral matters.

Campaigns, legally limited to six months' duration, are typically energetic, enthusiastic, and seemingly all-encompassing.[23] Both the PLN and PUSC use open (all-citizen) primary elections to nominate candidates. Prior to the advent of television and public opinion polling, Costa Rican campaigns involved intense party mobilization of voters by person-to-person electioneering in neighborhoods and workplaces. At first, public funding of campaigns enabled small and regional parties to compete with the larger, national parties. The effective domination of elections by the PLN and Unity-PUSC (they jointly captured an average of nearly 95 percent of the votes in two-thirds of the elections from 1953 through 1998),[24] their capacity to raise funding independently of government financing, and the particulars of the public campaign finance scheme,[25] however, gradually eliminated small-party competitiveness at the national level. During the 1980s, the two major parties began employing U.S. campaign consultants and techniques. The increased television campaigning and poll-driven advertising that resulted eliminated much of the face-to-face campaigning and apparently undermined a long-standing tradition of civility between major candidates—especially in 1994 and 1998.[26]

Voting became mandatory in the 1960s. Election turnout thereafter remained above 80 percent, until 1998 when several groups, including libertarian and Far Left parties, urged voters to abstain. Their arguments resonated with popular frustration over economic problems, corruption, and incivility between candidates, and turnout in 1998 declined to 71.2 percent.[27]

Free and fair elections are an essential element of representative democracy because they allow citizens to evaluate and reject or accept candidates for public office without fear of retaliation. After 1949, Costa Ricans voted with confidence that the TSE would count their votes accurately. So excellent was its work that one authority would remark that the TSE "has all but eradicated the incidence of fraud in Costa Rican elections. Costa Rica's reputation for fairness and honesty in elections is one of the highest in the world."[28] However, the changing style of campaigning, the growing role of private money in campaigns, and the increasing dominance of the PUSC and PLN and similarity of their programs frustrated many Costa Ricans. The significance of these tendencies for Costa Rican democracy remained to be determined, but the possibility that they underlay the abstention from the 1998 election by one-seventh of the usual electorate suggested potentially serious problems.

The Evolving Political Economy

The victorious National Liberation junta adopted the foundations of a new development model in 1948–49. Retaining the previous labor and social security reforms to placate organized workers, the junta nationalized the banking and insurance systems. It courted the middle and working classes by including extensive social protections into the new Constitution. Later, after winning the 1953 election, the newly constituted PLN further elaborated the social democratic development model. An economically activist state began to redistribute income toward the middle class, increase social services and economic regulation, and aggressively promote economic growth.[29] By the 1960s, Costa Rica had committed itself to import substitution industrialization and regional economic integration through the Central American Common Market (CACM). The public sector expanded as the government assumed new functions, delivered new services, and broadened educational opportunity to provide itself trained workers.

This development model, aided by several decades of growth of the world economy, transformed Costa Rica. The CACM attracted foreign aid to improve roads, ports, and public services, and domestic and foreign investment increased sharply. Gross domestic product (GDP), a measure of overall economic activity, quintupled between 1950 and 1975, while GDP per capita more than doubled from $372 to $779. Although agriculture remained crucial to export earnings, its share of overall economic activity shrank steadily after 1950 while manufacturing's share rose. The government's portion of GDP roughly doubled between 1950 and 1970.[30]

Despite decades of success, the social democratic model failed in the 1980s and was attacked from within and abroad. When oil prices rose drastically in 1973 and thereafter, the sudden growth of the trade deficit created a balance of payments problem that depressed the economy.[31] Virtually everything Costa Rica consumed became more costly as the effects of inflation rippled through the economy while real wages fell. Demand for goods and services shrank, causing private-sector layoffs that further depressed demand for consumer goods.[32]

Government policies temporarily cushioned early effects of the oil shock but eventually created a worse problem. Rather than raise taxes or scale back spending to fit revenue (and thus deepen the recession), the government kept spending. The national budget deficit peaked in 1980 at around 8 percent of GDP. To finance this ballooning fiscal deficit Costa Rica borrowed heavily from abroad. Foreign loans permitted the government to keep up its own consumption and subsidize state enterprises, the private sector, and consumers. For a few years foreign borrowing maintained foreign currency liquidity and staved off a deeper recession.

Costa Rica thus sank ever deeper into debt, which ultimately triggered an even deeper recession and great political change. Foreign debt, expressed as a percentage of GDP, rose from 11.5 percent in 1970 to 147.0 percent in 1982, and interest payments on it consumed a third of export earnings by the early 1980s.[33] The entire Central American economy went into recession with Costa Rica in the mid 1970s, and the resulting political turmoil frightened away domestic and foreign capital, collapsed the CACM, and wrecked Costa Rica's regional export markets. Costa Rica began to devalue the colón. This action raised import prices, slowed commerce, and exacerbated inflation. Exchange controls and higher interest rates imposed to prevent capital flight further slowed growth and increased unemployment. But these policies proved insufficient, and in July 1981 Costa Rica defaulted on its foreign debt. The colón spiraled downward, eventually falling to 157 to the dollar in 1994 (from 8.6 per dollar in 1980). This large, protracted devaluation further raised prices and depressed real wages.

When Luis Alberto Monge took office in May 1982 his administration reacted to these calamities by seeking to stabilize the economy. The escalating regional geopolitical crisis offered a temporary escape. Monge traded Costa Rican cooperation with the U.S. effort to overthrow Nicaragua's Sandinista government for U.S. aid—$1.14 billion between 1981 and 1988, a tenfold increase over the previous eight-year period. This windfall, along with the implementation of macroeconomic controls, promoted a quick but artificial recovery[34] that merely postponed confronting the trade deficit, ballooning external debt, and other problems with the social democratic development model. (Furthermore, cooperation with the Reagan administration's anti-Sandinista policy also brought Nicaragua's turbulent politics into Costa Rica through the mobilization of violent exile groups and their Costa Rican supporters and opponents. Domestic turmoil soon included numerous terrorist acts, destructive protests, the formation of paramilitary forces, and threats of coups.)[35]

In 1985 a second, more drastic phase of economic transformation began, based upon structural adjustment programs imposed by the World Bank and other international lenders (Chapter 10). These programs promoted reactivation and a transformation of the economy through reinsertion into the international market by the exportation of nontraditional products to areas outside of Central America.[36] This neoliberal attack on the social democratic development model, engineered mainly by external lenders assisted by local economic interests, soon forced Costa Rica to reduce the size of the state and its role as entrepreneur, regulator, and service provider and to stimulate new exports, open itself to foreign capital, and attract foreign investment by lowering labor costs through devaluations.

The international banking community's leverage came from the massive external debt that Costa Rica desperately needed to refinance on more favorable terms. In exchange for further assistance, these lenders forced Costa Rica to abandon in stages the social democratic development model. Costa Rica made three successive agreements on structural adjustment programs (SAP) with the International Monetary Fund, World Bank, United States, and European Community. SAP I, approved in 1985, pursued the objectives of reducing the state's economic role, the number of government employees, and public spending.[37] SAP II, signed in 1989, continued SAP I objectives and policies and added new goals: tax reform; elimination of subsidies to public services, railroads, and refining; promotion of nontraditional exports; and tariff reduction. The effects of these programs included a cut in the government's share of GDP from 11.1 percent in 1985 to 9.9 percent in 1990, privatization of numerous firms, reduced budget deficits, reduced debt service, partially privatized banking, and increased fees for public services.

Having thus forced Costa Rica to abandon the social democratic development model, external lenders then employed SAP III in the mid 1990s to consolidate the neoliberal model. The task proved increasingly difficult politically, however, as victims of the policies rallied against their high social costs. Lenders pressed PUSC president Rafael Angel Calderón Fournier (1990–1994) for deeper cuts in public spending and employment, further privatization of banking and insurance, lowered trade barriers, and greater stimulation of nontraditional exports.[38] By the beginning of the administration of José María Figueres Olsen (PLN)[39] in 1994 protests were swelling. Health and education spending had been cut dramatically, undermining program quality and cutting human capital investment. Teachers went on strike for over a month in mid 1995 but failed to win most of their goals. Other public sector unions denounced the impact of budget cuts on public employees and their pension plans. PLN social democratic traditionalists resisted full privatizing of the national telephone-electric company, forcing the president to backtrack somewhat. Citizens of the port city of Limón, hit hard by port privatization, protested violently in June 1996. Other angry Costa Ricans also took to the streets. President Figueres Olsen felt the brunt of their anger, earning the lowest presidential approval ratings in memory.[40] Hamstrung without a PLN legislative majority, Figueres Olsen had the grim task of pressing the Assembly to dismantle the social guarantees and development model built by his father in the 1950s. Like several predecessors, he often resorted to executive decree to override the balky legislature and placate international lenders.

Challenges to Costa Rican Democracy

The previous discussion highlights several factors that posed ongoing challenges to democracy in Costa Rica. Some arose from the change in economic development strategy that significantly altered state strength and the services that Costa Ricans had come to expect. Others arose from the interaction of the restructured state with established citizen attitudes and patterns of political participation.

Political Economy and Institutions

Costa Rica revolutionized its political economy, abandoning social democracy for neoliberalism. The country scaled back the regulatory state and its many restrictions on business and increased economic freedom. External lenders forced the debt-addicted state to address its financial weaknesses and operate the economy more responsibly. Although the new freedom would bring new risks, a smaller, leaner government and freer private sector could help Costa Rica find an advantageous new niche in the international economy.

In terms of social justice, however, the neoliberal revolution augured ill. Though the neoliberal model brought no dramatic short-term changes in income distribution, early evidence suggested that income might soon begin shifting back toward the wealthy.[41] By limiting the state's ability and will to redistribute income toward the middle and poorer classes, neoliberalism threatened socioeconomic justice by promoting inequality and poverty. Structural adjustment delivered (and promised more) cutbacks in public spending, investment, and program quality in education, health, and other public services. Such policies began to erode the standards of living, resources, health, and skills of middle- and working-class citizens and thus threaten the social development that had made Costa Rica distinctive among developing nations.

What might the transition to neoliberalism imply for democracy itself? On the positive side, a leaner and less debt-reliant government and economy promised a stronger and healthier state that might eventually fortify democratic institutions. Privatization and deregulation would establish new economic interests that would stimulate new forces in civil society to increase citizen demand making and government responsiveness.

On the negative side, neoliberalism brought certain reductions in Costa Rican democracy. First, structural adjustment was imposed mainly by outsiders, a process that on its face failed to meet any reasonable test of democratic decision making. Second, in order to implement structural adjustment, the executive branch resorted increasingly to legislation by decree and bureaucratic rule making. This tactic took away from the people's representatives in the Legislative Assembly much of their constitutionally assigned lawmaking responsibility, causing another significant setback for democratic governance.

Finally, Costa Rica's neoliberal revolution curtailed the electorate's prior influence on economic policy by leaving more economic decisions in the hands of domestic and foreign private investors and intergovernmental lenders. At the end of the 1990s it appeared likely that the new private interests representing both the winners and losers from economic restructuring would generate new citizen organization and mobilization, which would strengthen civil society. Time alone would reveal whether recent retrenchments in the quality and subject matter of Costa Rican democracy might be compensated by such a strengthening of civil society and its various effects.[42] In the short run, the once great ability of the Costa Rican middle sector to shape and benefit from economic policy under social democracy diminished as neoliberalism transferred much of this political and economic power to economic elites by reducing government's economic role.

Political Participation

Classical democratic theory defines democracy in terms of widespread citizen involvement in rule through diverse political activities. Surveys since the 1970s have portrayed Costa Ricans as active participants in politics at levels and in patterns comparable to those found in industrialized countries.[43] Modes of participation resembled those found elsewhere—voting, campaigning, organizational and communal activity, and contacting officials. At odds with Costa Rica's pacific image, however, participation in the late twentieth century sometimes took unconventional, confrontational, and even violent forms. Citizens from every sector of society, including those demanding housing and others protesting everything from bus fare hikes to foreign policy, as well as informal sector workers, banana union members, teachers, health workers, and landless laborers took to the streets to protest, demonstrate, and demand policy change. From time to time Costa Ricans threatened violence and organized paramilitary groups. From the 1970s onward, some engaged in acts of violence including riots, bombings, and assassination.

The government usually welcomed and rewarded participation. It encouraged conventional political activity and often responded favorably to peaceful citizen demands through the national budget, legislation, and administrative action. The state also sometimes rewarded and thus encouraged unconventional activity, even including violent confrontations with authorities, by changing public policy when challenged by protests. Although the government's response to terrorism was typically measured but firmly negative, security officials tolerated and even encouraged the formation of rightist paramilitary forces during the 1980s.[44] While such turbulence reached menacing levels during the mid 1980s as protagonists in the Nicaraguan revolution and U.S.-backed counterrevolution and their Costa Rican allies repeatedly clashed, it subsided after the 1987 Central American Peace Accord.

In sum, under their democratic regime, the citizenry of Costa Rica and the state continuously conducted open, sometimes contentious dialogue. Expecting attention, citizens mobilized and petitioned the state. The state dedicated personnel, programs, and resources to attend to citizen demands and thus reinforced Costa Ricans' willingness to make demands of government. This dialogue took place through the formal representative channels (citizens petitioning municipal councils and legislative deputies), through parties' efforts to mobilize support and co-opt other organizations as they contested for ruling power, and through an almost ritualized direct communication between mobilized citizen protesters and public officials.

Although central to democracy, political participation as practiced in Costa Rica late in the century challenged democracy in two ways. The first challenge was that citizens' very activism sometimes appeared to threaten the institutional political order—the constitutional framework of limited government. As citizens protested and challenged and made increasingly vociferous demands and the government tried to accommodate these demands, state resources shrank markedly. A smaller government had fewer programs, services, and subsidies with which to placate escalating demands driven by hard times and regional political turmoil. During the 1980s official fears of internal turbulence and of dangerous neighbors led to increased spending on the police and officially tolerated paramilitary groups. This combination of problems suggested the Huntingtonian scenario that an excess of citizen participation for a given institutional capacity to maintain order might lead to political decay.[45] Had serious political decay occurred in Costa Rica in the mid 1980s, it might have taken various forms—a collapse of the interelite accord on democratic rules, a coup attempt, elite-led violence through the paramilitaries, mass turmoil causing a breakdown of public order, or increased governmental repression. None of these scenarios materialized, however, and the risk of their occurring seems to have greatly diminished in the 1990s.

The second, more recent challenge to democracy was the withdrawal of 11 percent of the normal electorate (usually 82 percent, down to 71 percent) in 1998 after an abstentionist campaign.[46] With evident effect, several groups urged Costa Ricans to refrain from voting in order to protest economic problems, campaign quality, and the paucity of party and policy options. Former president Oscar Arias Sánchez denounced the parties and their 1998 election campaigns for deficiencies of ideas and excesses of vitriol. His disgust may have mirrored citizens' own, which easily could have contributed to voter abstention. Were some Costa Ricans beginning to lose faith in their vaunted electoral institutions and democratic processes? It remains to be determined whether this significant exit of participants marked a major erosion of Costa Rican democracy, and whether it constituted an isolated phenomenon or signaled a longer-term decline in participation.

Political Culture

Political theorists contend that citizen and elite political culture play important roles in sustaining democracy. Citizen norms supporting democracy shape the behavior of citizens and constrain elites, while elite commitment to democracy helps establish and maintain a democratic institutional order.

Late-twentieth-century survey research and other analyses identified several key features of Costa Rican political culture:[47] The legitimacy of the Costa Rican political system had long been high and support for the democratic regime widespread. Citizens strongly supported fundamental democratic liberties and opposed disruptive tactics and antidemocratic methods. The political culture had a conservative bent—citizens wished to retain the democratic system. The public supported the alternation of parties in office, viewed as a way to restrain party power.[48] Though citizens demonstrated strong anticommunist biases, political elites had not systematically denied political rights to the Left, nor would a majority of citizens have supported such a denial.

Elites and masses largely shared the same political values. Elites usually manifested greater commitment to democratic liberties than the general urban public and approved less of antidemocratic tactics. One study from the late 1990s reported that political elites appeared no more change-oriented than the mass public.[49] Institutions and shared norms appear to have worked together to restrain elites with antidemocratic impulses.

While this picture makes clear that Costa Rican political culture sustains institutional democracy, certain cultural values suggest pockets of dissonance. Surveys reported some citizens who supported political confrontation, demonstrations, and violent protest, and some who justified antidemocratic political methods. Careful scrutiny of such attitudes in the mid 1990s suggests, however, that they were more instrumental than part of a truly antidemocratic subculture. That is, endorsing civil disobedience derived not from hostility to democracy but from citizens' knowledge that government often responded favorably to confrontation. Indeed, even members of those social sectors that were most likely to engage in civil disobedience (the Far Left, communal activists, and youth) on balance opposed disruptive tactics and strongly supported democratic liberties.[50]

In sum, evidence on Costa Rican political culture suggests that most citizens and elites valued and preferred to keep democracy. Indeed, instrumentalist norms favoring civil disobedience, protest, and confrontation with government—values held by certain politically disadvantaged minorities—

likely developed because of the encouragement given by a traditionally tolerant, seldom-repressive, and policy-responsive government. Ironically, it appeared as of this writing that the challenge to Costa Rican democracy that might arise from such a regime-encouraged protest culture was that, conditioned as they had been to confront government when it displeased them, Costa Ricans, while appearing at the polls in shrinking numbers, might demand too much too often for the new neoliberal state, which had laid aside many of the traditional tools for placating citizen demands (subsidies, services, and employment) during a period in which recovery from a twenty-year recession remained far from complete. Had the institutional capacity of the government to meet demands diminished too soon, before Costa Ricans had learned to expect less of the state? Did this increase the risk of political decay, of citizen demand swamping institutional capacity to keep order and deliver prosperity? Might Costa Ricans ultimately become disgruntled with the democratic regime if it continued to fail to satisfy their political demands?

At the turn of the century, it was too early to conclude that increased protest and declining voter turnout constituted a serious problem for Costa Rican democracy. Indeed, democratic theorists such as Thomas Jefferson regarded vigorous civil society and protest behavior as essential to democracy because they force government to be attentive to popular preferences.

Conclusions

Clashing political and class forces in the 1940s established the contemporary Costa Rican democratic polity, which thereafter operated with extensive participation by citizens, fair elections, and a restrained yet policy-responsive government. For decades, Costa Rica constituted a consolidated national-level democracy with considerable citizen involvement, a wide range of policies subject to citizen input, and consistent potential for citizens to affect public policy. Moreover, its overall prospects for continued consolidated democracy appeared fairly good at the close of the twentieth century. The country met many of the criteria experts believe favor democratic consolidation:[51] Costa Rica had a presidential system dominated by two competitive, centrist parties. Its electoral agency was highly competent and honest. The security forces posed little threat to civilian rule. The state was capable, legitimate, and able to govern with little repression. Despite some internal racial and religious differences, Costa Rica was relatively homogeneous culturally and ethnically; many of its social cleavages were crosscutting. Most citizens and elites preferred a consensual set of democratic political rules. Costa Rica's neighbors were also civilian democracies, and major international actors impinging upon Costa Rica preferred democracy in the region.

Significant changes occurred in the 1980s: the Legislative Assembly lost policy-making influence to the executive branch, organizational and ideological diversity among the parties diminished, citizen involvement declined while the power of monied special interests in election campaigns grew, and the government relinquished authority over the economy. These changes diminished the extent to which—and array of policies over which—citizens exercised influence and thus somewhat reduced democracy. But by no means did such changes destroy or undermine the consolidated democratic regime, which as of this writing remained fairly resilient and stable despite the intense geopolitical and economic strains it experienced during the 1980s.

Certain democratic consolidation factors, however, posed continuing risks worth noting. Persistent economic inequalities had worsened with late-twentieth-century economic crises and appeared likely to intensify further. The government retained some ability to ameliorate the effects of poverty, but neoliberalism had stripped it of many policy instruments. Economic growth, strong in the 1950s through the early 1970s, had become erratic, and prospects for sustained economic recovery under neoliberalism remained uncertain.

These changes raised ongoing questions about the future of the political system, underlying what one might characterize as the "paradox of Costa Rican democracy": the adoption of the neoliberal development model might invigorate the economy, but it also would certainly make it more volatile for ordinary citizens since future governments would do less for them than past ones had. In moments of economic stress would demands exceed the capacity of the state and economy to satisfy the public? Might a failure of economic recovery or a recurrence of hard times lead to so much citizen mobilization that it would undermine institutional stability? Could a poorly performing, resource-limited democratic regime indefinitely retain the loyalty of citizens who believe that confrontational tactics should pay off but that voting and the traditional parties have lost some of their efficacy? This, then, is the paradox (and the irony) of Costa Rican democracy—that it could some day fall victim to its own success by encouraging citizens to expect and demand too much.

Notes

1. Lowell Gudmundson's *Costa Rica before Coffee: Society and Economy on the Eve of the Export Boom* (Baton Rouge: Louisiana State University Press, 1986) explores the myth, traces the origins and ideological purpose, and debunks it.

2. This section is drawn heavily from John A. Booth, *Costa Rica: Quest for Democracy* (Boulder, CO: Westview Press, 1998), chap. 3. The main historical sources on colonial Costa Rica are Gudmundson, *Costa Rica before Coffee* and Elizabeth Fonseca, *Costa Rica colonial: La tierra y el hombre* (San José: Editorial Universitaria Centroamericana, 1984).

3. On colonial era politics, see Samuel Stone, *La dinastía de los conquistadores* (San José: Editorial Universidad de Costa Rica-Editorial Universitaria Centroamericana, 1975), 52–73.

4. Bernhard Thibaut, "Costa Rica," in Dieter Nohlen, ed., *Enciclopedia electoral Latinoamericana y del Caribe* (San José, Costa Rica: Instituto Interamericano de Derechos Humanos, 1993), 183 (author's translation). On national politics of the period 1824–1905, see Booth, *Costa Rica: Quest for Democracy*, 38–42.

5. That is, literate males could vote in the first stage of indirect elections, to choose electors who actually elected the president.

6. Material on this period and the democratization process is drawn from various sources, including Booth, *Costa Rica: Quest for Democracy*, chap. 3; John Peeler, *Latin American Democracies: Colombia, Costa Rica, Venezuela* (Chapel Hill: University of North Carolina Press, 1985); Deborah J. Yashar, *Demanding Democracy: Reform and Reaction in Costa Rica and Guatemala, 1870s–1950s* (Stanford: Stanford University Press, 1997); Fabrice Lehoucq, "The Origins of Democracy in Costa Rica" (Ph.D. diss., Duke University, 1992).

7. John Peeler, *Latin American Democracies: Colombia, Costa Rica, Venezuela* (Chapel Hill: University of North Carolina Press, 1985), 100–110.

8. The electoral branch is the TSE, which controls elections and resolves all electoral disputes.

9. See *Constitución política de la República de Costa Rica* (San José: Imprenta Nacional, 1978); Booth, *Costa Rica: Quest for Democracy*, 56–66.

10. Carlos José Gutiérrez, "Cambios en el sistema jurídico costarricense," in José Manuel Villasuso, ed., *El nuevo rostro de Costa Rica* (San José: Centro de Estudios Democráticos de América Latina, 1992), 359–84. Gutiérrez shows that the mean number of laws passed per year by the Assembly fell by more than two-thirds between the 1960s and late 1980s.

11. Miguel Angel Rodríguez Echeverría, "El poder político y el poder económico," in Asociación Nacional de Fomento Económico (ANFE), *El modelo político costarricense* (San José: ANFE, 1984), 153–65.

12. Gutiérrez, "Cambios en el sistema," 28–30; Fernando Guier Esquivel, "Sistema presidencialista y sistema parlamentario," in ANFE, *El modelo político costarricense*, 20–22.

13. Booth, *Costa Rica: Quest for Democracy*, 63–64, 166–70.

14. Ibid., 64–66.

15. Ibid., tables 4.1 and 4.2.

16. Mario Carvajal Herrera, *Actitudes políticas del costarricense* (San José: Editorial Costa Rica, 1978), 156–57; and Mavis Hiltunen de Biesanz, Richard Biesanz, and Karen Zubris de Biesanz, *Los costarricenses* (San José: Editorial Universidad Estatal a Distancia, 1979), 587–88. Data on party control of the presidency and Assembly from Booth, *Costa Rica: Quest for Democracy*, tables 4.1 and 4.2.

17. Peeler, *Latin American Democracies*, 113.

18. Jorge Rovira Mas, "Costa Rica," *Boletín Electoral Latinoamericano*, January–June, 1994, 49–50; Regine Stiechen, "Cambios en la orientación política-ideológica de los partidos políticos en la década de los '80," in Villasuso, ed., *El nuevo rostro*, 265–75.

19. Bruce M. Wilson, *Costa Rica: Politics, Economy, and Democracy* (Boulder, CO: Lynne Rienner, 1998), chap. 5.

20. Stiechen, "Cambios en la orientación política-ideológica," and Oscar Aguilar B., "Una nueva vía política social-cristiana," in Villasuso, *El nuevo rostro*, 265–76 and 277–86, respectively.

21. Wilson, *Costa Rica*, 158–59; Booth, *Costa Rica: Quest for Democracy*, 78.

22. During election times, the TSE's normal complement of three magistrates expands by two, selected by the TSE from among the *suplentes*. Magistrates and *suplentes* serve staggered six-year terms.

23. "Pre-campaigns" for party nomination, however, go on for almost two years prior to nomination.

24. Booth, *Costa Rica: Quest for Democracy*, 70.

25. Small parties (as defined by low votes in prior elections) receive public funds for election campaigns, but payment comes after the election and is based on votes received—thus requiring them to borrow in the short run. The PLN and PUSC, based on prior votes, typically qualify for advance disbursement of public campaign funds and thus enjoy an advantage in campaigns.

26. Booth, *Costa Rica: Quest for Democracy*, 72–76.

27. Ibid., table 3.4 and p. 78.

28. Charles D. Ameringer, *Democracy in Costa Rica* (New York: Praeger, 1982), 51.

29. Jorge Rovira M., "El nuevo estilo nacional de desarrollo," in Villasuso, *El nuevo rostro*, 242–45.

30. Booth, *Costa Rica: Quest for Democracy*, 156–59.

31. Victor Bulmer-Thomas, *The Political Economy of Central America since 1920* (Cambridge: Cambridge University Press, 1987), table A14.

32. Booth, *Costa Rica: Quest for Democracy*, 158–63.

33. Ibid., 160–61.

34. Carlos Castro Valverde, "Sector público y ajuste estructural en Costa Rica (1983–1992)," in Trevor Evans, ed., *La transformación neoliberal del sector público* (Managua, Nicaragua: Latino Editores, 1995), 49.

35. Booth, *Costa Rica: Quest for Democracy*, 118–21, 183–91; Martha Honey, *Hostile Acts: U.S. Policy in Costa Rica in the 1980s* (Gainesville: University Press of Florida, 1994), chaps. 8–13.

36. Castro Valverde, "Sector público y ajuste," 51; Wilson, *Costa Rica*, chap. 5; Mary A. Clark, "Transnational Alliances and Development Policy in Latin America: Nontraditional Export Promotion in Costa Rica," *Latin American Research Review* 32, no. 2 (1997): 71–97.

37. This section drawn mainly from Clark, "Transitional Alliances," 51–56.

38. Ibid.; Mary A. Clark, "Nontraditional Export Promotion in Costa Rica: Sustaining Export-Led Growth," *Journal of Interamerican Studies and World Affairs* 37, no. 2 (1995): 181–220; "Costa Rica," in Inter-American Development Bank, *1990 Report*, 92; Castro Valverde, "Sector público y ajuste," 55–56.

39. José María Figueres Olsen is the son of the PLN's founder, José Figueres Ferrer.

40. "Costa Rica," *Mesoamerica*, November 1995, 4.

41. Booth, *Costa Rica: Quest for Democracy*, 83–86.

42. See Chapter 11, this volume, for further discussion of civil society's potential positive and negative effects.

43. Booth, *Costa Rica: Quest for Democracy*, chap. 6; John A. Booth and Patricia Bayer Richard, "Repression, Participation, and Democratic Norms in Urban Central America," *American Journal of Political Science* 40 (November 1996): 1205–32; John A. Booth and Patricia Bayer Richard, "Civil Society, Political Capital, and Democratization in Central America," *Journal of Politics* 60 (August 1998): 780–800; and Mitchell A. Seligson, Annabelle Conroy, Ricardo Córdova Rivas, Orlando J. Pérez, and Andrew J. Stein, "Who Votes in Central America? A Comparative Analysis," in Mitchell A. Seligson and John A. Booth, eds., *Elections and Democ-*

racy in Central America, Revisited (Chapel Hill: University of North Carolina Press, 1995).

44. The formation of rightist paramilitary forces was tolerated and even encouraged by top security officials and was intended to counteract domestic leftist groups and offset growing Nicaraguan military power. See Booth, *Costa Rica: Quest for Democracy*, 119–22.

45. Samuel P. Huntington, *Political Order in Changing Societies* (New Haven: Yale University Press, 1968), chap. 1.

46. Booth, *Costa Rica: Quest for Democracy*, 125.

47. Ibid., chap. 7; Carvajal Herrera, *Actitudes políticas*; Richard Biesanz, Karen Zubris Biesanz, and Mavis Hiltunen Biesanz, *The Costa Ricans* (Englewood Cliffs, NJ: Prentice-Hall, 1988); Booth and Richard, "Repression," table 5; Mitchell A. Seligson and Miguel Gómez B., "Ordinary Elections in Extraordinary Times: The Political Economy of Voting in Costa Rica," in John A. Booth and Mitchell A. Seligson, eds., *Elections and Democracy in Central America* (Chapel Hill: University of North Carolina Press, 1989), 158–84.

48. Carvajal Herrera, *Actitudes políticas*, 156; Biesanz, Biesanz, and Biesanz, *The Costa Ricans*, 186–87.

49. Booth, *Costa Rica: Quest for Democracy*, chap. 7, table 7.7.

50. These attitudinal scales measure support ranging from low to high levels. Certain cohorts of citizens scored higher on antidemocratic norms and support for civil disobedience than the population mean, but the overall score for both the population and these cohorts still fell in the pro-democracy end of the scales. See ibid., table 7.7.

51. These criteria are drawn mainly from Larry Diamond and Juan Linz, "Introduction," in Larry Diamond, Juan Linz, and Seymour Martin Lipset, *Democracy in Developing Countries*, vol. 4, *Latin America* (Boulder, CO: Lynne Rienner, 1989); Samuel P. Huntington, *The Third Wave: Democratization in the Late Twentieth Century* (Norman: University of Oklahoma Press, 1991); Peeler, *Latin American Democracies*.

6

Panama
Militarism and Imposed Transition

Steve C. Ropp

The Republic of Panama is a four-hundred-mile-long country that looks something like a letter *S* lying on its side. To the west are Costa Rica and the rest of Central America, while to the east and south lies the vast expanse of South America. Panama is quite small, roughly the size of West Virginia. But paradoxically this lack of territorial size has given the country global importance. Less than fifty miles across at its narrowest point, Panama unites the Atlantic Ocean, which lies to its north, with the Pacific Ocean to its south.

Panamanian history can be neatly divided into three major periods. The first lasted from 1513 until 1821 when Panama declared its independence from Spain and chose to adhere to the newly formed South American country of Colombia. The second lasted from 1821 until 1903 when Panama declared independence from Colombia. And the third began with the establishment of the independent Republic of Panama in 1903 and continues to the present. During the second and third periods, developments on the isthmus were heavily influenced by French and later U.S. efforts to construct a canal.[1]

Panama's government has been very unstable since independence was achieved in 1903, and "democracy" has remained an illusive concept. This fact is perhaps best illustrated by the long list of presidents who have been removed from office during the twentieth century, and by two decades of military rule during which presidents served at the behest of the Panamanian officer corps (see table).

At best, it might be argued that, since 1903, Panama has been undergoing a "continuous transition toward democracy." At worst, it might be argued that Panama has undergone no transition at all, and that the various discrete political events in Panama's political history that outside observers have interpreted as steps in the direction toward democracy were in fact not steps at all. From a somewhat different historical point of view, the "politics of continuous transition" looks a lot like politics as usual. And what requires explanation is not so much the process of change but the historical continuities.

Presidents of Panama since 1904

Year Elected	
1904	Manuel Amador Guerrero
1908	José D. Obaldía
1912	Belisario Porras
1916	Ramón M. Valdés
1920	Belisario Porras
1924	Rodolfo Chiari
1928	F. H. Arosemena (removed from office)
1932	Harmodio Arias Madrid
1936	Juan D. Arosemena
1940	Arnulfo Arias Madrid (removed from office)
1945	Enrique Jiménez
1948	Domingo Díaz
1952	Arnulfo Arias Madrid (removed from office)
1952	José Antonio Remón Cantera
1956	Ernesto de la Guardia
1960	Rodolfo Chiari
1964	Marco A. Robles
1968	Arnulfo Arias Madrid (removed from office)

During Years of Military Rule
(Under General Omar Torrijos Herrera, 1968–1981)

1972	Demetrio Lakas
1978	Arístides Royo (removed from office)

(Under General Manuel Antonio Noriega, 1981–1989)

1984	Nicolás Ardito Barletta (removed from office)
1985	Eric Arturo Delvalle (removed from office)

Following the End of Military Rule

1989	Guillermo Endara
1994	Ernesto Pérez Balladares

Regardless of one's perspective on the transition issue, no effort to explain Panama's political process could be complete without taking into account the major role played by the United States during the twentieth century as the region's hegemonic military and economic power. Nowhere else in the Caribbean Basin was the United States literally present at the creation of a new state or so continuously and directly involved "on the ground." And Panama is among a handful of countries in the region where the United States has consistently used armed intervention to achieve its foreign policy goals.[2]

This chapter argues that, while the United States has long sought to impose its political values and institutions on Panama, that country's leaders historically have resisted such imposition for a variety of reasons and in numerous ways, and they have shaped state policies and institutions to serve their own rather than U.S. interests. Moreover, these leaders have been able to avoid some of the political costs that they believe to be associated with intermittent U.S. efforts to impose procedural democracy, a form of electoral democracy that would call for extensive competition among all organized groups in society, as well as for a sufficient degree of civil liberties to ensure that such competition would regularly take place.[3]

Most of the reasons Latin American states (including Panama) are thought to be resistant to U.S. attempts to impose democracy have been discussed extensively in the literature on democratization. Some observers stress the fact that regional culture is inherently authoritarian and thus inclined toward nondemocratic solutions to political problems. Others emphasize the fact that broad historical patterns of economic growth and industrial expansion in twentieth-century Latin America have not been supportive of the sustained growth of democratic regimes in the region. And recently, there has been a suggestion that Washington's own concern with the promotion of neoliberal economic reforms and structural adjustment packages in Latin America has spawned a new generation of neopopulist authoritarian leaders.[4]

Although all of these factors may have played a role in Panama's seeming inability to move beyond "the politics of continuous transition," this chapter focuses on one that has received comparatively little attention. Under circumstances where the Panamanian state has historically been contested "high ground" for two quite different national identity projects (discussed in detail below), state leaders sought to gain and to hold onto political power at all cost. While their tactics and techniques for doing so varied considerably (from direct use of the police to very sophisticated electoral fraud), the goals remained the same. Politicians sought to consolidate the particular identity project with which they were associated through the practice of electoral *continuismo* (the use of electoral manipulation or outright fraud to remain in office).

In attempting to avoid U.S. imposition of procedural democracy and hence to maintain themselves in power, Panamanian politicians had to cope with an ever-changing array of constraints and opportunities presented to them by the United States. Their decision making was further complicated by the fact that various U.S. administrations did not consistently support democratization but often instead used the concept pragmatically and strategically to promote stability and thus protect U.S. interests. The presence of the Panama Canal meant that the United States always had a deep sense of concern for the security implications of political developments on the isthmus, a concern that endured despite major changes in international security conditions and in the structure of the international system. At the same time, there was on occasion a genuine (if secondary) concern with the promotion of democracy that manifested itself in efforts to prevent authoritarian leaders from coming to power, or to prod existing authoritarians into becoming more democratic.

After the 1989 U.S. military invasion, Panamanian political leaders operated in an international environment where retaining their hold on power through electoral manipulation was seemingly made more difficult by changes in the post–cold war international system. On one hand, U.S. security concerns were somewhat allayed by the collapse of the Soviet Union, thus suggesting that concern with democratization in countries such as Panama could occupy a more prominent place in U.S. policy. On the other hand, the worldwide legitimacy that global values such as democracy and human rights had achieved in the modern era made it more difficult for those who wished to adopt authoritarian domestic practices to openly do so.[5]

Contested National Identity

Why have the intermittent U.S. efforts to impose democracy failed so badly in the past, and are they more likely to succeed following the 1989 invasion? Laurence Whitehead's observations on the subject of imposition help to explain the relatively modest success experienced by the United States in its various intermittent efforts to democratize Panama. In a very useful book chapter written a decade ago on efforts to "export" democracy, Whitehead notes that the United States has assumed that Latin American countries are nation states with well-defined identities.[6] "Unfortunately, this intuitively plausible [U.S.] model of the democratization process assumes the prior existence of a well-defined nation state in which no major problems of nation identity remain pending. . . . [The dubious nature of this assumption means that] . . . the imposition of democracy in the region has often proved a problematic and frustrating experience."[7]

The ways in which long-standing national identity problems in a very new Panamanian state continually frustrated U.S. efforts to impose democracy by placing a premium on the acquisition and retention of power by local politicians should be stressed. In Latin America and indeed throughout much of the world, national identities are fragile and highly contested social constructs that require considerable time and effort to create and maintain. Under such conditions, local politicians are aware that a major goal of any successful regime must be to create and maintain a coherent national identity construct that can authenticate and legitimize the regime and like-minded successors. Furthermore, since this process takes decades, the regime and its individual leaders must stay in power long enough to firmly ground their particular vision of the national identity in the public conscience.

This analysis of the problems associated with contested national identity draws heavily on a new generation of scholarship regarding nationalism. Much of the recent literature focuses on nationalism as a socially constructed and maintained form of collective identity rather than as a primordial given with roots in some ancient discoverable past. From this perspective, the creation of the new Panamanian state in 1903 and associated Panamanian nationality required not so much works of objective scholarship as acts of political will. The struggle over contested national identity (between two quite different "imagined Panamas") appears to have had major consequences for politics and for past U.S. efforts to impose democratic institutions and practice on the isthmus.[8]

Contested National Identity and Resistance to Democracy in Panama, 1903–1968

National identity has received relatively little attention in discussions of what makes for a stable democracy. However, students of Latin America are increasingly making use of the literature on identities to examine and explain a broad range of associated political phenomena such as nationalism and the nature of social movements.[9] Julie Skurski suggests that the struggle for political power in Latin America can best be understood as a struggle between competing cultural and ethnic groups to control the "high ground" of political discourse and hence legitimate representations of national identity. Her study of early twentieth-century Venezuela demonstrates how an ascendant middle class used an imaginatively reconfigured view of Venezuelan national identity (based on *mestizaje*, or racial mixing) to successfully challenge the monopolistic view of national identity historically associated with the Creole elite.[10] Skurski's analysis thus suggests that contests over the fundamental nature of national identity may play an important role in the process of state-level political change.

But what more specifically is the relationship between the existence of a contested identity project in Panama and the increased difficulty of establishing a stable democracy there? One might suggest that a country's failure to resolve its most basic questions of identity dramatically raises the stakes in democratic elections. For example, in most stable democracies, the candidates of various political parties accept the basic premises on which their particular system of government is founded as well as the deeper sense of values and national identity that underlies that system. They are thus free to argue "minor" points of value difference or resource allocation. But if there is no fundamental agreement about the nature of the national identity or its most basic forms of cultural representation at the societal level, politicians end up talking past each other and seeking ways to give their particular political "voice" more extended representation in government. Such lack of agreement characterizes the United States, for example, prior to the Civil War where a conflict that was partially over identity put great stress on our democratic republic.

Panama's long history of contested identity and its equally long history of civilian *continuismo* and military authoritarianism suggests that there may be a connection between the two. Since the fundamental nature of the national identity has been contested, and since high office has thus been viewed as a "bully pulpit" from which the politics of identity could be preached, the stakes involved in attaining (or being denied) such office have been very high. These high stakes in turn have led to efforts by civilian politicians representing competing identity projects to use force as a means for achieving power, and a variety of forceful as well as pseudo-democratic techniques for prolonging their stay in office once there. It has meant as well that sporadic U.S. efforts from the earliest years to impose democratic practices have met with very limited success.

Panama's History of Contested Identity

Since colonial times, the territorial entity and associated population we call "Panama" has been shaped by global forces operating largely beyond local control. Regionally hegemonic states (beginning with Spain) sought to shape the isthmus in their own image and to use Panama for their own economic purposes. At the same time, the small racially and culturally mixed group of people who resided on the isthmus attempted to harness these global forces to serve their own interests.

This tension between the global and the local led to the creation during the nineteenth and twentieth centuries of two quite distinct and highly contested identity projects (self-conscious works in progress) that we have come to call Panama. Both of these projects were local responses to evolving global material conditions and ideals of the times. Both involved local groups attempting to construct and maintain a vision of the state's collective identity that they could impose on residents of the isthmus as a whole.

One local group of urban whites living in the transit area sought to strengthen their particular identity project by developing a dense network of ties to powerful actors within the larger global system. At first, these ties were to French businessmen who hoped to construct a sea-level canal linking the Atlantic to the Pacific. Then, during the twentieth century, ties to the United States became particularly important as this urban white group attempted to use another white-governed great power as a counterweight to Hispanicized blacks and mestizos who questioned their "cultural authenticity" and hence their right to rule.

Originally, Panama was a small colonial administrative unit in which a distinct isthmian sense of identity (separate from Spain) hardly existed. It is important to note that this colonial Panama (1513–1821) contained a very racially and ethnically mixed population of white Europeans (predominantly of Spanish decent), blacks (including many escaped slaves), mulattos, indigenous peoples, and mestizos. Later, this population was to become even more mixed with the addition of large numbers of Chinese and black English-speaking West Indians brought in to help construct the Panama Canal.

With regard to the development of an independent sense of identity, the first Panama to emerge in the nineteenth century was a province within the newly created country of Colombia. In this Panama, ideas about identity largely derived from the writings of white Hispanics residing in the transit zone around Panama City. This small group of well-educated intellectuals attempted to ground Panama's emerging sense of collective identity in the belief that the isthmus was blessed with topographical features that destined it to become a major center of global trade. More specifically, this vision of Panama as a global emporium was influenced by the positivist writings of Benjamin Constant, who believed that cities allow for the deepest and most meaningful expression of society's aspirations. The "nation," as institutionalized through territorial structures, is nothing more than an idealized and socially constructed abstraction. Thus, the identity project of these white urban groups centered on the vision of Panama as a white, Europeanized, globally embedded city-state.[11]

In the name of this vision of Panama as a global emporium, urban commercial groups attempted to create a sense of collective identity that could support a broad movement for federal autonomy or independence from the more "traditional" country of Colombia.[12] However, this group's view of authentic Panamanian identity excluded broad sectors of the isthmus's racially mixed population. Rather than looking inward and "downward" to the lower classes for validity and authenticity, they looked outward to the region's great powers. And once they realized that construction of a transisthmian canal lay beyond the organizational powers of the Colombian state, they linked their local sense of identity even more closely to the broader global vision of international cooperation and unity being promoted by an ascendant United States.[13]

The second Panama emerged as a distinct identity project somewhat later and differed substantially from the first in terms of its material base. Its immediate origins lay in the unhappiness of mestizos living in the interior provinces about their cultural alienation from the non-Hispanicized racial and ethnic population inhabiting the transit area, and their lack of access to economic benefits deriving from completion of the Panama Canal. During the 1920s Panamanian intellectuals such as José D. Moscote and José Daniel Crespo used a variant of positivist ideology as the intellectual foundation for their conscious effort to "Hispanicize" Panama's sense of collective identity.[14] Stress was placed on the use of public schools as an instrument for culturally integrating the isthmian population and thus attempting to ensure racial and class harmony within the institutional framework of a cohesive nation-state. Within this intellectual context the University of Panama opened its doors, giving full voice to those groups associated with this second identity project.

For purposes of this analysis, Panama's first identity project is hereafter referred to as "globalized Panama" and the second as "integral Panama." Integral Panama differed in some very significant ways from globalized Panama. Unlike the Hispanic-led but more generally white cosmopolitan leaders of urban Panama, the rural mestizos wanted a Panama that was Hispanic and mestizo to its very core. This second vision of Panama's true identity spawned the movement in 1923 called Community Action (Acción Comunal). Unlike the first identity project with its emphasis on Panama's broad place within and openness to the world, Community Action emphasized a narrow and culturally exclusive view of national identity and cultural authenticity.[15]

Beginning in the 1940s, Arnulfo Arias and the Panameñista Party came to represent this narrower view of nationhood.[16] Following his election to the presidency in 1940, Arias held a plebiscite to consider a new constitution under the terms of which large segments of the racially and ethnically mixed urban population would become disenfranchised. Furthermore, he legally redefined the meaning of "Panamanian" to exclude large numbers of blacks who had recently immigrated to Panama and others who did not speak Spanish. During these years Panamanian culture was respecified to reflect the customs of residents of the interior provinces, and symbols of the fully territorialized nation-state assumed much greater prominence.[17]

The leaders of the two identity projects differed most fundamentally about how important race and ethnicity should be in determining the "essence" of the national identity. For those who led globalized Panama, questions of race and ethnicity were dealt with as if they had been brought before members of a city council. These matters had no intrinsic importance with regard to defining membership in the national community but mattered only insofar as the urban tensions that race and ethnicity might generate could have an adverse impact on the community's ability to efficiently and effectively conduct its business.

In contrast, the leaders of integral Panama treated race and ethnicity as central features in any discussion of national identity. A "hierarchy of belonging" was reflected in the cultural symbols of the Panameñista Party. Those people who most clearly belonged to this community came from Panama's cultural heartland (the interior provinces), were mestizo, and spoke Spanish. For the Panameñistas, people who remained largely "unimagined" as citizens included large numbers of English-speaking urban blacks, Chinese, and the cosmopolitan population of white Hispanics and non-Hispanics living in the transit area.

Frustrated U.S. Efforts at Democratization in a Context of Contested National Identity, 1903–1968

In the years following Panama's creation as a distinct country, the United States played a critical role in political affairs and in related efforts to promote and impose democracy. These efforts had three basic characteristics. First, the United States used a variety of imperialistic tools to influence Panamanian behavior. Article 136 of Panama's first Constitution (as well as the 1903 treaty) gave the United States the right to intervene militarily in order to "reestablish public peace and constitutional order." Such legally authorized intervention was a simple matter logistically since the United States maintained troops in the Canal Zone, and Panama's civilian leaders had been persuaded to abolish their army. Military influence was strengthened by economic influence, which derived fundamentally from the fact that Panama's currency was tied after 1904 to the U.S. dollar.[18]

A second characteristic of U.S. efforts to promote democracy was a consistent bias in favor of groups associated with globalized Panama. From the very beginning, a natural affinity existed between the white urban groups that saw Panama as a global emporium and white policy makers in Washington, DC. The fact that these policy makers favored a globally open Panama does not necessarily mean that representatives of integral Panama were prevented from competing in democratic elections. But there was a clear pattern of bias in favor of looking the other way when representatives of globalized Panama acted undemocratically and in favor of quickly using military or economic power against leaders of integral Panama when they behaved in a similar manner.

Third, while U.S. efforts to promote democracy were overwhelmingly intrusive, they also tended to be erratic and episodic. In this regard, they responded to changing sentiment concerning foreign involvement by the United States overseas, as well as to the calls of various Panamanian politicians (in and out of office) for intervention. The historical evidence suggests that U.S. willingness to intervene in Panama's internal affairs was often as much the result of the pleadings of threatened local politicians for help in ensuring "fair elections" as it was of U.S. desires to control Panama.[19]

U.S. involvement in Panama's electoral process began in 1908 when an investigative commission was established to ensure that elections for Liberal and Conservative candidates would be held in an orderly fashion. Orderliness was maintained, but the many different racial and ethnic voices waiting to be heard in national politics at the time were largely muted because of the alliance of interests between a regionally ascendant United States and dominant white factions in Panama's two major political parties. Furthermore, the fact that the Liberals were more closely tied than were the Conservatives to an electoral base of black and mixed-race peoples gave the

Conservatives an early edge with some avowedly racist U.S. policy makers. Both parties were considered acceptable, however, as long as they maintained a certain modicum of electoral dignity and showed the world their predominantly white "face."[20]

Because elite leaders of Panama's two political parties both looked to U.S. policy makers for help, and because Panama had yet to develop state-level institutions capable of representing broadly based racial and ethnic groups within society, the period from Panamanian independence in 1903 until the 1920s might best be described as dominated by the "politics of suppressed identity." Political conflict tended to take place at the highest and most superficial level, centering on the personalities of individual Liberal and Conservative leaders. Given the lack of an army, a university, or any other major institutional avenue for the articulation of alternative imagined national identities, the political representatives of globalized Panama reigned supreme.[21]

During this earliest phase of Panamanian state history, identity politics did not play a central role in elections because the strong convergence in the material interests of the United States and globalized Panama prevented those representing alternative visions of the nation from successfully contesting for political power. However, this situation changed gradually in the 1920s as the United States began to tire of its intrusive role in Central American affairs and turned toward the more pressing issues of economic depression and pending global war.

Thus, the U.S. government stood passively by in 1931 when members of Community Action staged a coup, removing the president from office and replacing him with one of their own.[22] For the next decade, U.S. officials watched nervously as Arnulfo Arias and members of his Panameñista Party sought to ground their alternative identity project in Panamanian law and practice. Only in late 1941 did they move to encourage a coup against Arias, an action that was prompted largely by his intensely nationalistic stance with regard to U.S. military basing agreements in a context of global war.[23]

The early post–World War II years saw a series of unsuccessful efforts by the United States to impose democracy on Panama. Such efforts became particularly sporadic and half-hearted once the cold war had begun in earnest. Throughout Latin America, cold war security concerns increasingly privileged local militaries in their domestic struggle for institutional ascendancy. In Panama, such concerns led to the conversion of the National Police into the National Guard in 1953 with all its soon-to-be-realized negative implications for Panamanian politics. Thereafter the U.S. government consistently looked the other way as the National Guard accumulated more institutional power. Its acquiescence in this process of power acquisition and to the 1968 military coup that was its eventual result, as well as to two subsequent decades of military rule, is best explained as issues of cold war security.[24]

In sum, various special characteristics of the relationship of the United States with the new state of Panama resulted in efforts to impose democracy that were extremely intrusive (even by U.S. regional standards) but also erratic and dependent on U.S. priorities and interests at any given time. From 1903 until 1931, the U.S. government became deeply involved in efforts to shape in its own image not just Panama's political system but Panamanian society. Government officials, constrained by North America's perception of its own white racial identity, too easily assumed that the representatives of urban globalized Panama with whom they regularly dealt were the only "real" Panamanians. This led to early attempts to support democracy that, while sometimes well intentioned, regularly favored the Conservatives and that portion of the Liberal Party not closely associated with black and mixed-race peoples. The result was a superficial "politics of suppressed identity" in Panama that conveyed an impression that the personality of candidates was all that really mattered.

When this facade of a commonly agreed-upon Panamanian identity was ruptured in the 1930s, the United States faced an entirely new set of problems that led to even more intrusive and erratic behavior during subsequent decades. Now, policy makers had to contend with a previously suppressed identity project of such immense popularity that it could not simply be wished away. When Arnulfo Arias directly challenged the security interests of the United States during the 1940s, U.S. policy makers aided in the removal of this elected president. From that time forward until the late 1960s, the difficult question for U.S. policy makers was how to reconcile a commitment to democracy with the fact that it was regularly producing victories for this strongly nationalistic representative of integral Panama.[25] Such reconciliation generally took place by ignoring the commitment to democracy.

Military Rule and the Partial Centering of Panamanian Identity, 1968–1989

During the late nineteenth and early twentieth centuries, there were no domestic institutions to give "voice" to the visioning processes of the majority of Panama's mestizo, black, mulatto, and indigenous population. Within this institutional vacuum the white intellectuals living in the transit zone were able to envision a globally embedded city largely detached from the racially mixed population to which they believed it was haphazardly and unnecessarily attached.

When spokesmen for integral Panama emerged, however, in the 1920s to challenge the visionary ascendancy of globalized Panama, the situation with regard to the creation of institutional bases from which to imagine "alternative Panamas" changed dramatically. A new university and a wide array of state institutions were established during the 1930s, 1940s, and 1950s. Many had as their primary goal the creation of a new developmental state that could guide Panama's process of industrial economic growth.

From the standpoint of influencing Panama's evolving sense of collective identity, the most important institution to emerge during these years was the army. It had been disbanded in 1904 because it was viewed as a threat to the shared U.S.-Panamanian vision of a peaceful and domesticated city-state serving the interests of the larger global community. However, through a slow evolutionary process, the army was reconstituted out of the small police force that had taken its place. By the early 1950s, the National Police had been turned into the National Guard, and a colonel had been elected president with military backing.[26]

After a turbulent period of unstable government associated with extremely polarized identity processes, the military coup launched against Arnulfo Arias brought General Omar Torrijos to power in 1968. Torrijos quickly built a political base of support among a wide range of urban and rural racial and ethnic groups. Farm collectives were formed, labor unions organized, and the government expanded dramatically to accommodate popular needs for services. On the basis of this broad domestic alliance as well as external support from multinational banks a military regime was constructed that would last for over two decades.[27]

This long period of authoritarion military rule was crucial to the formation of the Panamanian identity because the highly polarized political struggle between representatives of globalized Panama and integral Panama was now subject to discipline. Equally important, the Panamanian military came to power with its own vision of the national identity. Initially unarticulated, it was not so much an intellectual vision as one embedded in the "bones" and instincts of several generations of officers and enlisted men drawn from every conceivable racial and ethnic group within the middle and lower classes. We might call this third and latest identity project "militarized Panama."[28]

Scholars who study the role of the military in Latin America and elsewhere have long recognized the contribution that military institutions and practices make to the process of national identity formation.[29] Particularly in countries that only recently achieved independence from the early twentieth century's colonial powers, local armies have often provided an overarching sense of collective identity that bridges the often-substantial gap between various racial and ethnic groups.

From this perspective, Panama's military can be viewed as having partially reconfigured the national identity by providing a view of race and ethnicity that was simultaneously more exclusionary and more inclusionary than those provided by the political leadership of globalized Panama and integral Panama. The former offered a vision of Panamanian identity that was far too broad in that it reached beyond the boundaries of the country itself, and the latter offered one that was too narrow in its reliance on visions of nationalism derived from life in a few interior provinces. In contrast, the Panamanian military provided a vision of the national identity that centered on the image of a strong developmental state designed to serve a racially mixed population within well-defined ("hard") state borders.

While Panama was certainly not democratic during these decades of military rule, the military did establish a variety of new political institutions that had the effect of generating some of the preconditions for the establishment of procedural democracy. Among these preconditions were a more universally held sense of citizenship. Under General Torrijos, the National Assembly (an urban elite-dominated institution) was replaced with a much larger legislature whose members were elected from the country's 505 widely dispersed municipal subdistricts. Also, an official party was formed to broadly incorporate the widely diverse racial and ethnic constituencies reflected within the military itself. Thus, an indirect consequence of the military's attempt to extend its political reach to the most remote corners of the realm was to establish the material preconditions for a universal view of citizenship that encompassed the population of those remote corners.[30]

Transition in the Late Twentieth Century

Although twenty years of Panamanian militarism had the effect of reducing the degree of polarization over identity politics and partially educating the public to expect regular elections, it also produced an increasingly brutal and corrupt group of military "politicians." From 1968 until his death in a plane crash in 1981, General Omar Torrijos, from behind puppet presidents, ruled Panama with an iron fist covered by a velvet glove. Although the military was a repressive and thoroughly corrupt institution during these years, the government can most accurately be described as a "soft dictatorship" when compared with authoritarian regimes to the south such as Argentina and Chile. General Torrijos remained popular among a broad cross section of Panama's population because of his populist economic policies and his successful effort in 1977 to negotiate new treaties with the United States. And because of a wish to see these new treaties succeed, the Carter administration reinforced the positive view of the military government abroad.

When General Torrijos died, however, he was eventually replaced by the ruthless and considerably more corrupt head of the military's intelligence services. General Manuel Antonio Noriega quickly consolidated his grip on power and began to reverse the slow and already tentative process of political liberalization that had been initiated in 1975 by his predecessor. In the mid 1980s, relations with the United States began to deteriorate for a variety of reasons that had little to do with U.S. concern with authoritarian government in Panama. General Noriega was viewed in Washington as an untrustworthy ally in Central America's civil wars, as a military leader incapable of ruling without "excessive" use of force, and as deeply involved in drug trafficking at a time when the U.S. public was becoming more and more concerned with this issue.[31]

From 1985 until 1988, the Reagan administration applied increasing diplomatic and economic pressure on General Noriega to step down. But by the time George Bush took office early in 1989, it had become clear that nothing short of military force was likely to accomplish this end. Although diplomatic and economic pressure continued to be applied throughout 1989, attention shifted to planning for the "imposition option." In the early morning hours of December 20, 1989, President Bush launched the largest U.S. military operation since the end of the Vietnam War in 1975. "Operation Just Cause" succeeded in quickly overpowering the Panamanian military and eventually resulted in General Noriega's extradition and trial on drug-trafficking charges in the United States.

"Operation Just Cause" was a stunning military success. And yet the very fact that democracy had to be imposed by military force suggests that past U.S. efforts to impart its political values to Panama had all been monumental failures. After two decades of military rule, it proved necessary not only to dismantle a vast array of authoritarian institutions that empowered General Noriega politically but also to provide outside military protection for the new set of democratic leaders who replaced him.

The government that took power in the wake of "Operation Just Cause" was led by Guillermo Endara, head of the Democratic Civic Opposition Alliance (Alianza Democrática de Oposición Civilista, ADOC) and the real winner of the May 1989 elections. President Endara and his two vice presidents came to power strictly as a result of U.S. military intervention. They were sworn in on a U.S. military base, their first public pronouncements were issued over U.S. fax machines, and they move around Panama City using U.S.-provided transportation.[32] Ironically, much less U.S. military force had been used to support the installation of Panama's first independent civilian government in 1904 than was necessary to install another civilian one after more than eight decades of intermittent U.S. efforts to promote democratization.[33]

With regard to its impact on subsequent efforts to bring democracy to Panama, the U.S. military invasion was clearly more important for what it managed to tear down than for what it succeeded in building up. Most important, the invasion succeeded in removing the military leadership from power and in partially dismantling the bureaucratic infrastructure that allowed it to govern for more than two decades.[34] After such a long period of military governance, a whole generation of Panamanians had become accustomed to the "inevitability" of military rule. The U.S. invasion made it clear that any Panamanian government, whether civilian or military, still governed at the discretion of decision makers in Washington.

Beyond removing some of the personal and institutional impediments that had rendered substantive democracy impossible, the United States also contributed to subsequent democratizing efforts by throwing a protective military blanket over the fledgling Endara government. Soon after the U.S. invasion, members of the old military regime threatened the government by mounting several coup attempts. The most serious of these came in December 1990, when Colonel Eduardo Herrera Hassan, a former member of the Defense Force, and thirty of his fellow officers seized national police headquarters. The Bush administration's response to these threats was to grant Panama's new government de facto protectorate status. When Endara requested military help, four hundred U.S. troops were used to quell the unrest.[35]

As for broader U.S. support for Panama's fledgling democracy, various forms of external economic aid increased dramatically immediately following the invasion. Congress authorized an emergency aid package to deal with critical needs for housing and infrastructure, and it was followed by a larger package of assistance to Panamanian financial institutions and social sectors that vaulted Panama to first place among all regional aid recipients.[36] However, the U.S. government's initial enthusiastic support for Panamanian democracy quickly began to wane as a result of increasing budgetary pressures and perceptions of success in this democratic endeavor. By the time President Ernesto Pérez Balladares took office in 1994, levels of U.S. aid were modest even by regional standards.[37]

Paradoxically, then, both the twenty-year period of military rule and the subsequent U.S. military invasion that ended it had the effect of clearing the way for the ongoing attempt to create democracy in Panama. Whether this attempt would ultimately prove successful was a matter of debate, and only time would tell.

As of mid 1999, Panama had had two presidents since the 1989 U.S. invasion. The first, Guillermo Endara, quickly turned his attention to the ailing national economy, a task that required restoration of the government's shattered international financial credibility. Since international lending institutions such as the International Monetary Fund demanded reduction of the government deficit as the price for new loans, Endara attempted to reduce the size of the government bureaucracy. However, these efforts were largely unsuccessful and very little change had taken place by the time he left office in 1994.[38]

Endara's successor, Pérez Balladares, was a member of the Democratic Revolutionary Party (Partido Revolucionario Democrático, PRD) that had been founded by General Omar Torrijos in 1975. Pérez Balladares attempted to follow up on the tentative steps that Endara had taken to restore economic stability. Major moves included opening up the national economy to global competition and forcing more substantial reductions in the size of the public sector. He also attempted to change the progressive labor legislation that had been enacted under military rule but without much success.[39]

What is most striking about these two post-invasion presidencies is that neither political leader attempted to mobilize constituents based primarily on the old identity politics. As a Panameñista of long standing, President Endara easily could have reverted to the kind of identity rhetoric associated with integral Panama in order to deal with the considerable unhappiness among members of his party over a lack of government jobs. Similarly, President Pérez Balladares could have called upon the PRD faithful of militarized Panama to recall the heritage of racial and class unity that supported their political project. Noticeably absent in both cases was any evocation of the collective identities that gave these two large-scale identity movements their underlying sense of unity and strength.

A major reason for the lack of attention to identity politics during both presidential administrations was surely the sea change in global economic thinking that took place during the 1980s with regard to the appropriate national strategies for promoting growth. With the end of the cold war, a "Washington consensus" emerged that suggested that economic growth would best be achieved through neoliberal reforms that stressed smaller government bureaucracies, balanced budgets, and expanded exports (Chapter 10). With neoliberal economic thinking temporarily dominating the global debate concerning economic development, neither Panamanian president could successfully appeal to his popular constituency by raising "irrelevant" issues such as race, ethnicity, and sense of national belonging.[40]

Did the absence of identity politics for most of the 1990s suggest that democracy would soon be consolidated in Panama? One hopeful sign was the muted nature of the debate over national identity during the May 1999 presidential elections. While two of the candidates (Mireya Moscoso and Martin Torrijos) had strong personal links to integral and militarized Panama, respectively, neither made them the centerpiece of his campaign. From this perspective, the fact that these recent presidential elections were peaceful and democratic could be partially attributed to the decreased electoral influence of identity issues.[41]

Notes

1. Although there are many good books dealing with the role of the great powers in construction of the Panama Canal, the best (and certainly the most readable) is David McCullough, *The Path between the Seas: The Creation of the Panama Canal, 1870–1914* (New York: Simon and Schuster, 1977).

2. Steve C. Ropp, "The Bush Administration and the Invasion of Panama: Explaining the Choice and Timing of the Military Option," in John D. Martz, ed.,

United States Policy in Latin America: A Decade of Crisis and Challenge (Lincoln: University of Nebraska Press, 1995), 80–81.

3. The concept of procedural democracy is discussed in Joseph A. Schumpeter, *Capitalism, Socialism, and Democracy*, 2d ed. (New York: Harper, 1947); and Robert A. Dahl, *Polyarchy: Participation and Opposition* (New Haven: Yale University Press, 1971).

4. The literature on democratization is now so extensive that it would require a separate chapter to discuss it adequately. Moreover, problems of definition and conceptualization still abound. For a good recent appraisal of some of these remaining problems, see David Collier and Steven Levitsky, "Democracy with Adjectives: Conceptual Innovation in Comparative Research," in *World Politics* 49, no. 3 (April 1997).

5. In this regard, see Thomas Risse, Steve C. Ropp, and Kathryn Sikkink, eds., *The Power of Human Rights: International Norms and Domestic Political Change* (Cambridge, England: Cambridge University Press, 1999).

6. Laurence Whitehead, "The Imposition of Democracy," in Abraham F. Lowenthal, ed., *Exporting Democracy: The United States and Latin America* (Baltimore: Johns Hopkins University Press, 1991), 217.

7. Ibid., 220.

8. The idea of "imagined" nations derives from the seminal work of Benedict Anderson, *Imagined Communities: Reflections on the Origins and Spread of Nationalism*, 2d ed. (London: Verso, 1991).

9. Recent works on identity politics include Sarah Radcliffe and Sallie Westwood, *Remaking the Nation: Place, Identity, and Politics in Latin America* (London: Routledge, 1996); Arlene Dávila, *Sponsored Identities: Cultural Politics in Puerto Rico* (Philadelphia: Temple University Press, 1997); Sonia E. Alvarez, Evelina Dagnino, and Arturo Escobar, eds., *Cultures of Politics, Politics of Cultures: Revisioning Latin American Social Movements* (Boulder, CO: Westview Press, 1998); Julie Skurski, "The Ambiguities of Authenticity in Latin America: Dona Barbara and the Construction of National Identity," in Geoff Eley and Ronald Grigor Suny, eds., *Becoming National* (New York: Oxford University Press, 1996).

10. Skurski, "Ambiguities of Authenticity," 371–72.

11. Panamanian scholar Ricaurte Soler wrote extensively about Panama's sense of collective identity and generally viewed it as having formed around the nineteenth century idea of "modernity." This belief in "modernity" (including its rational, secular, and materialistic aspects) lent support to the idea of nation states as the embodiment of the collective aspirations of a homogenous population of citizens. Ricaurte Soler, *Formas ideológicas de la nación Panameña* (San José, Costa Rica: Editorial Universitaria Centroamericana, 1972).

12. The classic work on Panama's federalist philosophy and aspirations is Justo Arosemena, *Estado Federal de Panamá* (Panama City: Ediciones Manfer, 1998), first published in the 1840s. Arosemena believes that a great city always lies at the heart of a great state, and "real" states are thus by nature small. He views most nineteenth-century Latin American states as unnatural agglomerations of conquering and conquered peoples—technically speaking, as empires (3–11).

13. Alfredo Figueroa Navarro, *Dominio y sociedad en el Panamá Colombiano* (Panamá City: Impresora Panamá, 1978), 357–59.

14. Soler, *Formas ideológicas*, 72–75.

15. Steve C. Ropp, *Panamanian Politics: From Guarded Nation to National Guard* (Stanford: Hoover Institution Press, 1981), 21–23. Arlene Dávila's brilliant analysis of Puerto Rican identity processes suggests that conflict between urban and rural views of national identity is widespread in Latin America. The interior

provinces of many Latin American countries provided a space within which images of the nation could be shaped apart from those held by the urban-based colonial bureaucracy. Often, these images from the interior associated nationality more closely with white and Hispanic cultural characteristics. See Dávila, *Sponsored Identities*, 268, n. 8.

16. The best historical work on Community Action and the Panameñista movement is Jorge Conte Porras's *Requiem por la Revolución* (San José, Costa Rica: Litografia e Imprenta LIL, 1990). Conte Porras is explicit in his recognition of this movement as an identity movement, stating that "the ascension of Dr. Harmodio Arias Madrid to the Presidency of the Republic [in 1932] responded to the prolonged generational movement that appeared simultaneously with a growing sense of national identity" (161).

17. For example, Arias required all members of his cabinet to wear traditional folk dress during symbolically important cultural events such as Carnaval. Ibid., 191.

18. Walter LaFeber, *The Panama Canal: The Crisis in Historical Perspective* (New York: Oxford University Press, 1978), 68–70.

19. There are a number of good books dealing with U.S. involvement during the years immediately following Panama's independence. See in particular G. A. Mellander, *The United States and Panama: The Intriguing Formative Years* (Danville, IL: Interstate Printers and Publishers, 1971). For a good summary of the recent historiography, see Celestino Andreas Araúz and Patricia Pizzurno, "El intervencionismo diplomático, político y militar," *El Panamá América*, March 1999 supplement, *Historia de las relaciones entre Panamá y Los Estados Unidos*.

20. President William Howard Taft was particularly concerned with the possibility that the election of a Liberal president would destabilize the isthmus. The Conservatives were seen as a white "party of property," while the Liberals were viewed as too closely allied with a resentful population of potentially rebellious blacks and mulattos. LaFeber, *Panama Canal*, 51.

21. Here, I agree with the general conclusion of Orlando J. Pérez about the personalistic nature of politics during this period. See Orlando J. Pérez, "Election under Crisis: Background to Panama in the 1980s," in Mitchell A. Seligson and John A. Booth, eds., *Elections and Democracy in Central America, Revisited* (Chapel Hill: University of North Carolina Press, 1995), 123–25.

22. Michael L. Conniff, *Panama and the United States: The Forced Alliance* (Athens: University of Georgia Press, 1992), 91.

23. Ibid., 92–93.

24. On cold war security logic, see Peter H. Smith, *Talons of the Eagle: Dynamics of U.S.–Latin American Relations* (New York: Oxford University Press, 1996), 188–214.

25. Arias was by far the most important figure in Panamanian politics from 1940 when he was first elected president until he was removed from office through a military coup in 1968. Whether running for president himself or brokering political deals behind the scenes when excluded from electoral process, he and his Panameñistas framed the debate on national identity.

26. Thomas L. Pearcy, *We Answer Only to God: Politics and the Military in Panama, 1903–1947* (Albuquerque: University of New Mexico Press, 1998), 137–42.

27. For an explanation of the military regime's longevity that stresses external factors, see Steve C. Ropp, "Explaining the Long-Term Maintenance of a Military Regime: Panama before the U.S. Invasion," *World Politics* 44, no. 2 (January 1992).

28. Sarah Radcliffe and Sallie Westwood suggest that there are three basic state-level sources for imagining the national identity—intellectuals, soldiers, and politicians. I find this three-way distinction to be rather artificial because there is often a prolific borrowing of ideas among these three groups, particularly in countries where there is less role differentiation. Thus, it is hard to determine whether General Omar Torrijos was more a professional soldier or a skilled politician (he was certainly no intellectual). Radcliffe and Westwood, *Remaking the Nation*, 9–10.

29. For a seminal work on the subject of military institutions and processes of national identity formation, see Morris Janowitz, *The Military in the Political Development of New Nations* (Chicago: University of Chicago Press, 1964).

30. In the language of identity politics, military rule succeeded in producing a more centered sense of national identity and common citizenry. Those who saw no place for themselves in the territorially and racially exclusive vision of integral Panama could now do so. And those who felt themselves on the margins of globalized Panama's more cosmopolitan culture, could now do the same.

31. One of the major events behind this shift in U.S. policy was the discovery of the headless body of Dr. Hugo Spadafora along the Costa Rican border in fall 1985. Spadafora, a well-known guerrilla internationalist who had served under General Torrijos, had been openly critical of General Noriega. Evidence suggested that Noriega plotted with several other officers to have Spadafora killed while Noriega was in Europe.

32. Tom Barry and John Lindsay-Poland, *Inside Panama* (Albuquerque, NM: Interhemispheric Resource Center Press, 1995), 22.

33. Prior to and during the Panamanian uprising against Colombia in 1903, President Theodore Roosevelt positioned the USS *Nashville* off the Panamanian port city of Colón, and U.S. sailors were used to help persuade Colombian troops to leave the insurrectionists alone. LaFeber, *The Panama Canal*, 32–33. In contrast, the U.S. invasion of 1989 led to much greater loss of life.

34. One should not overemphasize the extent to which the power of the Panamanian security forces had been reduced by the U.S. invasion. As of 1999, there were still some thirteen thousand members engaged in a wide variety of police and military activities.

35. Steve C. Ropp, "Things Fall Apart: Panama after Noriega," *Current History* 92, no. 572 (March 1993): 105. In analyses of Panama's post-invasion process of democratization, not nearly enough attention has been paid to the issue of U.S. willingness to use military force if necessary to prevent possible military or civilian coups. This omission is probably due to the fact that information on possible coup attempts is usually closely held within the U.S. and Panamanian intelligence communities and thus not available for use and reference by scholars.

36. Barry and Lindsay-Poland, *Inside Panama*, 149.

37. Ibid., 151.

38. Steve C. Ropp, "Panama: Cycles of Elitist Democracy and Authoritarian Populism," in Howard Wiarda and Harvey F. Kline, eds., *Latin American Politics and Development*, 4th ed. (Boulder, CO: Westview Press, 1996), 514.

39. Steve C. Ropp, "Panama: Tailoring a New Image," *Current History* 96, no. 607 (February 1997): 57.

40. It is also important to note that many of the institutions that had been associated with the process of national identity formation saw an erosion of their position during the 1990s. These included the University of Panama, the Panameñista Party, and (most definitely) the military.

41. Despite the absence of identity politics during the 1990s, there are signs that this issue lies just below the surface. The Panamanian press is constantly lamenting the absence of attention to cultural matters and the "loss" of national identity. And it is revealing that the highly respected journal *Tareas* recently devoted a full issue to the problem of Panamanian identity. See "El proyecto de Nación y Tareas," *Tareas* 100 (September–December 1998): 9–144.

II

The Forces

7

External Actors
Other States

*Richard Stahler-Sholk**

After the Sandinistas lost the 1990 elections to the U.S.-backed National Opposition Union (Unión Nacional Opositora, UNO) coalition, Sandinista guerrilla commander Dora María Téllez was asked whether the U.S. government was now pouring aid into Nicaragua. She replied, "The gringos haven't really given much aid—they've only threatened to!"[1] Her ironic reply captures some of the contradictory aspects of the role of external state actors in the Central American transitions of the 1990s. U.S. hegemony in a broad sense continued to be a relevant framework for understanding the international context of Central American politics. Yet the end of the cold war and the rise of globalization called for reexamining the changing roles and priorities of the United States and other actors in managing the global system.

The standard "transitions to democracy" literature, applied to Central America, portrays the regime changes of the 1990s as part of a global Huntingtonian "third wave" of democratization. According to this "transitology" interpretation, democratization was promoted by a resurgence of self-confident U.S. interventionism and Soviet decline and reinforced by global pressure for economic liberalization. Variants on this orthodoxy suggest that U.S. support for democratization came about only through the persistence of domestic and international critics of U.S. policy, and that the path to democratization was cleared by the independent decline of revolutionary momentum within the region.[2] This school—emphasizing a moderate middle as agents of reform, and the international community as a positive and significant force for democratization—bears many of the hallmarks of the

*Support for a research trip to Central America in July 1998 was provided by Eastern Michigan University/Provost's New Faculty Research Award. Thanks also to Jack Spence, Loli De Zúnega, and David Holiday for helping with interview contacts, and Rose Spalding for valuable comments.

modernization theory and nation-building of yesteryear. It assumes the United States is a major global promoter of democracy, the Soviet Union was a principal obstacle, and the expansion of market-oriented development is a key facilitating condition. It is based on an equilibrium model of society, privileging order over equality. This school implicitly assumes a natural tendency toward harmonious convergence around consensual democratic ideals.

In a provocative alternative perspective, William Robinson argues that the U.S. shift to promoting formal political democracy (polyarchy) in the 1980s and 1990s is essentially the new ideology for protecting the interests of transnational elites in an era of globalized production. Drawing on world-systems theory and a neo-Gramscian perspective on hegemony in international relations, Robinson suggests that "democracy promotion" has served to legitimize states adopting neoliberal programs, which exclude the majorities from actual democratic participation and control over fundamental decision making.[3]

This second perspective can be usefully adapted, allowing room for local resistance against imperialism and transnational capital. Though the outcomes are not all structurally determined, this perspective views democratization as a conflictual process, even one that required armed struggle in Central America. U.S. "democracy promotion" must be seen in historical context. This critical historical analysis suggests that the cold war was not just a bipolar global contest played out in Third World regions such as Central America but rather a useful ideological construct for legitimizing U.S. domination of the global system since World War II. The emergence of new European- and Japan-led economic poles in a period of accelerating globalization, and the imperial overreach in U.S. efforts to quell radical movements throughout the Third World, were already forcing a reformulation of the ideological underpinnings of U.S. global hegemony a decade before the Berlin Wall came down.

This critical perspective also distinguishes between market opening and democratization. In fact, the neoliberal policies promoted by Central American governments and their principal international backers in the 1990s tend to reinforce the political power of a narrow, internationally oriented fraction of capitalists, with problematical implications for democracy. Rather than assuming a harmonious confluence of political and economic liberalizations leading to a single path labeled "transition," we might identify three transitions under way in Central America: (1) from war to peace, (2) from authoritarianism to electoral democracy, and (3) democratic consolidation, or the transition to sustainable democracy.

External actors, eventually including the United States, finally supported the first two transitions (toward peace and competitive elections); but progress toward democracy was won by popular struggles, not conceded by foreign powers. U.S. support for elections in the 1980s was intertwined with the U.S. domestic politics of mobilizing resources for counterinsurgency. The very contradictions of this "reform with repression" model opened space for both the popular-revolutionary movements in the region and the anti-interventionist movements abroad, adding to pressure for negotiated peace.

The third transition—democratic consolidation—involves an ongoing struggle between the neoliberal vision of a lean and "modern" state organized to facilitate integration into global markets and an alternative vision of mass participatory democracy in which the state must respond to organized demands from below. This phase is unstable because it involves overlapping contests over both the new rules of the political game (procedure) and a basic social compact defining the type of democracy (substance), all under the shadow of possible authoritarian regression.[4] Given the authoritarian context of the transitions, institutionalizing procedural competition alone—under regimes bent on demobilizing the popular classes and reducing the breadth and depth of participation—would bring a very incomplete type of "democracy."[5] Indeed, sustainable democracy arguably requires the effective extension of citizenship to the masses of the population who have been socioeconomically excluded, implying a social struggle with a substantive content.[6]

Healthy skepticism about the essentially authoritarian transitions to "low-intensity democracy" in the 1990s does not preclude cautious optimism about the continued struggle for the third transition, that is, for substantive democratization in Central America. Ironically, it took a revolutionary challenge to win electoral democracy, but the rest of the revolutionary project by the late 1990s remained in contest.[7] After the signing of peace accords and the first competitive elections, external actors continued to try to shape political outcomes, albeit with changing resource commitments and priorities; but so did domestic social subjects, including those mobilized by the revolutionary movements. This perspective was summarized by graffiti of the Guatemalan former guerrillas near the campus of the University of San Carlos: "Signing [the peace accords] is political struggle, not surrender." External states formed part of the context of that struggle, but their influence was not necessarily determinant, nor consistently favorable to democratization.

Central America and the U.S. Hegemonic Project

Historically, U.S. attention to Central America was sporadically intense, linked to U.S. international aspirations, for example, to hemispheric hegemony since the late nineteenth century and global hegemony after World War II.[8] U.S. economic aid surged in response to revolution in the 1980s, then plummeted in the 1990s—from a peak in El Salvador of $462 million in 1987 to $41 million in 1997; and in Nicaragua from $553 million in 1991 after the Sandinista defeat to $37 million in 1998, with projections for continued decline (aside from the temporary and insufficient response in 1999 to the devastation of Hurricane Mitch).[9] Given such large fluctuations, it would be misleading to assess U.S. "democracy promotion" in the 1990s separately from the massive U.S. involvement of the 1980s.

Neutralizing Revolution

During the 1980s a central objective of U.S. policy was to neutralize radical revolution in the region. The "pacification" of Central America, directed against the popular and revolutionary forces on the left, involved a disproportionate outlay of U.S. resources, totaling $1.8 billion in direct military aid (excluding military exercises and Contra aid) and $8 billion in economic aid in the 1980–1992 period.[10] Much of that "economic" aid—particularly the Economic Support Fund (ESF), which provided unrestricted balance of payments support to countries of strategic interest to the United States— was a thinly disguised extension of "low-intensity warfare."[11] Revolution had put Central America near the top of the U.S. foreign policy agenda; by the mid 1980s, tiny El Salvador was the third largest recipient of U.S. aid after Israel and Egypt. The country and sectoral distribution of aid to Central America suggests that U.S. aid, which represented 71 percent of the total to the region in the 1980s, was shaped more by the politics of counterinsurgency than by development needs.[12]

The U.S. counterinsurgency strategy for Central America in the 1980s faced external and domestic opposition. In response to European and Latin American government initiatives promoting negotiated alternatives, leaked National Security Council documents revealed U.S. efforts to isolate Mexico, derail third-party mediation, and co-opt the negotiations.[13] U.S. efforts to engineer the election of moderate centrists stumbled over counterrevolutionary priorities, which meant collaboration with antidemocratic rightist forces. Growing public and Congressional opposition to U.S. policy in Central America increased pressure to prioritize human rights, social reforms, and political democratization, which led to some aid for reforms and interruptions in military aid. The November 1989 offensive by the Farabundo Martí Front for National Liberation (Frente Farabundo Martí de Liberación Nacional, FMLN), which nearly took San Salvador, and the killing of the Jesuits by a U.S.-trained military unit dramatized the ineffectiveness of U.S. policy and combined with other factors coming together to favor negotiations.

While acquiescing to the transition from armed conflict to negotiated peace, the United States still preserved military options, pending assurances that revolutionary outcomes were neutralized. In the period between the 1988 Sandinista-initiated ceasefire and 1990 Nicaraguan elections, the United States insisted on a series of modifications of the electoral rules to the disadvantage of the Sandinista Front for National Liberation (Frente

Sandinista de Liberación Nacional, FSLN) (including allowing foreign campaign financing) yet refused to end Contra aid as the Central American presidents had agreed. As the election approached, the United States intervened directly in support of the opposition.[14] The Bush administration also indirectly shaped voters' perceived options by (1) using the carrot of promised aid if the anti-Sandinista UNO coalition won, and the stick of the still-mobilized Contras, (2) withholding judgment on the legitimacy of the electoral process before seeing the results (unlike in the 1984 elections, which the United States condemned in advance as unfair when it was clear the Sandinistas would win), and (3) invading Panama in December 1989, sending a message about U.S. intolerance for troublesome governments in the region. With the only revolutionary government in Central America electorally removed in 1990, the United States could support the "peace process," leading to accords signed in El Salvador (January 1992) and Guatemala (December 1996).

The FSLN, immediately following its 1990 electoral defeat, still had a strong social base of mobilized grassroots supporters, and the largest political bloc following the breakup of the U.S.-sponsored UNO electoral coalition. Desandinization seemed more of a U.S. priority than supporting peaceful transition in Nicaragua. U.S. hostility to the negotiated FSLN/Chamorro transition accords after 1990 focused on the continuation of Sandinista Humberto Ortega as head of the army. Yet Ortega's presence facilitated the army's peaceful acceptance of its own drastic downsizing, from 96,000 troops in 1990 to 15,000 by 1992. Much later, after the FSLN's political strength had declined, U.S. officials acknowledged that the army had been effectively transformed into a nonpartisan, professional institution.[15] Meanwhile, U.S. hostility toward the de facto "modernizing right"/FSLN governing alliance strengthened the populist right after 1990. Arnoldo Alemán, of dubious democratic commitment, became president in 1996 in an election marred by irregularities—a retreat from the procedural fairness of the much-observed 1990 election.

In El Salvador, the United States was less concerned about the FMLN, which had disbanded its armed structures in 1992. When the military almost derailed the peace accords by refusing to remove members of the high command cited by the Truth Commission for human rights violations, the U.S. halted military aid to press for the officers' removal but was otherwise ambivalent about insisting the armed forces be fully subordinated to civilian control.[16] With the FMLN politically divided by the 1994 elections, the U.S. limited its involvement to modest efforts to co-opt the centrist breakaway from the FMLN led by Joaquín Villalobos; and Armando Calderón Sol, representing the traditional right-wing of the National Republican Alliance (Alianza Republicana Nacionalista, ARENA), won the presidency handily. However, the FMLN rebounded in the 1997 legislative and municipal elections to capture about as much of the vote as ARENA, including the capital of San Salvador. U.S. officials—once again looking to co-opt a resurgent left—began waxing enthusiastic about the "Plan for the Nation" (Plan de Nación), issued in January 1998 by a coalition of internationally oriented capitalists, professionals, and former FMLN social democrats.[17]

In Guatemala, the National Revolutionary Unity (Unidad Revolucionaria Nacional Guatemalteca, URNG) guerrillas had been decimated by the scorched-earth counterinsurgency of the 1980s. Peace accords reflected their weakness, providing for only a one-third reduction in the armed forces and vaguely defined social reforms. The United States did not support the 1993 Serrano *autogolpe* (self-coup) initially backed by some military hardliners, but Washington also refused to push for demilitarization as part of the peace negotiations or even to endorse European calls for abolition of the army-controlled "civilian self-defense patrols."[18] During this time of mixed U.S. messages to the Guatemalan military, the current defense minister estimated that only 50 percent of the officers would permit a negotiated solution in 1991, rising to perhaps 90 percent acquiescence by the time the accords were signed in December 1996.[19] Besides this "military veto," the fragile democratization process was also clouded by the right-wing populist Guatemalan Republican Front (Frente Republicano Guatemalteco, FRG) party's campaign to revise the constitution to allow the candidacy of General Efraín Ríos Montt, head of the repressive government installed by coup in 1982.

The URNG failed to reorganize immediately for electoral competition, but the leftist New Guatemala Democratic Front (Frente Democrático Nueva Guatemala, FDNG) tested the limited political opening, winning six of eighty seats in November 1995 congressional elections. The URNG's weakness left some supporters dismayed by the ex-guerrilla leadership's close collaboration with the neoliberal National Advancement Party (Partido de Avanzada Nacional, PAN) party of President Alvaro Arzú and technocrats from the UN Verification Mission in Guatemala (Misión de las Naciones Unidas de Verificación en Guatemala, MINUGUA). The United States generally preferred this informal alliance to the FRG but cared little about the 1999 election results since the URNG was militarily disbanded and politically weak. Indeed, U.S. criticism of the government's failure to implement the peace accords was stronger than the URNG reaction, which was "very muted, delayed, and pro forma."[20] Comparing the three cases of Nicaragua, El Salvador, and Guatemala, the U.S. support for negotiated transitions to peace depended on the extent to which the revolutionary Left was disarmed and politically weak.

The Democracy Offensive

Post-World War II U.S. policy in the region, from John F. Kennedy's Alliance for Progress to Jimmy Carter's human rights policies, promoted market-oriented economic development plus counterinsurgency. It was the

Reagan administration that launched the main "democracy offensive," coupling resurgent interventionism with a rhetorical commitment to exporting "democracy." During the peak of intervention in Central America, the United States created the National Endowment for Democracy (NED) in 1983, and the Office of Democratic Initiatives within the U.S. Agency for International Development (USAID) in 1984.[21] As the revolutionary armed conflicts declined in the late 1980s and 1990s, these U.S. agencies and resources were dedicated to low-budget intervention in the ongoing struggle over the definition of democracy, in five areas.

ELECTIONS. U.S. pressure encouraged elections in Central America in the 1980s while the United States was also a major actor in ongoing armed conflicts. In El Salvador in the early 1980s, U.S.-promoted electoralism represented a setback for democracy, creating an illusion of reforms designed to rationalize more military aid to an exclusionary and repressive regime. In Nicaragua, the U.S.-backed Contra war undermined Sandinista efforts to combine electoral pluralism with mass participatory democracy.[22] The United States denounced the 1984 Nicaraguan elections that the Sandinistas won as unfair, contrary to the conclusions of most other international observers, and intervened extensively on behalf of the anti-Sandinista coalition that won the 1990 election.

Negotiated ceasefires in the 1990s allowed more parties to participate in elections, and U.S. aid improved their procedural quality. Despite this aid, elections alone did not bring democracy. Voter registration and identification procedures remained seriously deficient in post-conflict El Salvador and Guatemala. Participation was low in Guatemala, where the URNG had only begun organizing to run candidates for 1999, and the ruling PAN party blocked efforts to move the elections from the middle of the harvest season in November, effectively excluding migrant agricultural workers (half the potential electorate). Moreover, the URNG's decision to focus on electoral politics meant shifting cadre out of unions and other popular organizing efforts during the struggle over implementation of the peace accords,[23] a tradeoff that the FMLN had faced in El Salvador in 1994 in the post–peace accord "elections of the century." The Left coalition in the 1994 Salvadoran election won only one-quarter of the presidential vote and 6 percent of mayoral elections. Learning from its mistakes, however, in the March 1997 Salvadoran election the FMLN won 27 (compared with the rightist alliance ARENA's 28) of 84 legislative seats; and alone or in coalition, gained control of 53 of 262 municipalities, including the capital city of San Salvador.

In Nicaragua, problems of fraud returned in the 1996 election, probably not altering the presidential results but undermining electoral legitimacy. Some external election monitors were too quick to endorse the elections before the problems were adequately investigated. Moreover, when pre-election polls showed Sandinista candidate Daniel Ortega catching up with Arnoldo Alemán, the U.S. State Department began issuing anti-Ortega

statements in a blatant attempt to influence the results. One Sandinista foreign relations specialist concluded ruefully that the United States remained
uncommitted to democracy: "Now U.S. diplomats are less like proconsuls,
and more like used car salesmen."[24] Despite the Sandinistas' internal divisions and disastrous failure to revitalize the party after 1990, official results of the October 1996 election still gave the FSLN 38 percent to the
Liberal Alliance's 51 percent; and the FSLN won 42 of 93 Assembly seats
and 51 of 145 municipalities.[25] Notwithstanding the democratic deficiencies of Nicaraguan parties and elections, the revolution had mobilized popular organizations in a way that changed the political landscape.

The suspension of armed conflict and introduction of competitive elections did not resolve the structural causes of revolution, including highly
unequal distribution of land and wealth and concentrations of unaccount-
able power in the hands of elites and their repressive agents. Institutions of
civil society, including political parties, that had been destroyed or driven
underground did not spring up overnight, and many doubted whether elections would lead to sustainable democracy in which majorities would exercise effective control over decisions affecting their everyday lives.

JUDICIAL AND POLICE REFORMS. These reforms were an important
part of the negotiated transitions to political democracy, given the widespread human rights violations with impunity and the counterinsurgency
orientation of domestic security forces that characterized many Central
American countries in the 1980s.[26] Complex issues to be negotiated and
monitored included selection and training of judicial personnel and police;
incorporation of ex-combatants into the new police, and the appropriate
human rights screening standards; and accountability and punishment (or
amnesty or pardon) for past human rights abuses.

U.S. funding—plus that of Spain and Sweden and the UN—provided
significant support for police and judicial training in Nicaragua and El Salvador. The United States offered courses through the International Criminal
Investigative Training and Assistance Program (ICITAP), relaxing prohibi-
tions imposed by Congress in the 1970s on aid to foreign police forces in
reaction to gross human rights violations.[27] To get a 1997 exemption for
Nicaragua, USAID convinced Congress that the United States would be able
to influence police behavior only if it had an aid program.[28] This was an old
and problematical argument, as U.S. training had not necessarily improved
the human rights records of public security forces in Latin America in the
past.[29]

External aid in the short run did not solve the public security problem
in the region, which by the late 1990s continued to plague the transition to
liberal democracy in Central America. The AID missions noted significant
remaining shortcomings in the administration of justice and electoral reform, even as aid levels declined drastically.[30] Despite initial hope for the
new Civilian National Police in El Salvador, public confidence declined

after an officer was videotaped robbing a bank. Rampant violent crime threatened the precarious transitions to political democracy, particularly when the Far Right responded with militarized police or vigilante measures.[31] In Nicaragua, the line between political violence and violent common crime was often blurry in the 1990s.[32] In Guatemala, the April 1998 killing of Monsignor Juan José Gerardi after the Archbishop's office released its exhaustive human rights investigative report, more than a year after the signing of peace accords, reinforced general skepticism that the rule of law had in fact been established.

With aid and training programs fragmented among various donors, on one hand, U.S. programs sometimes undercut UN efforts to condition aid on human rights improvement in the administration of justice and policing.[33] On the other hand, U.S. efforts to condition aid on democratic reforms could be parried by the recipient governments' simply not drawing on the funds allocated to programs that the political elites disliked.[34] Leverage was further reduced as international attention (and funding, in the case of U.S. aid) decreased.

U.S. promotion of judicial reform was also contradicted by U.S. government reluctance to declassify documents that could clarify responsibility for past abuses. This reluctance perpetuated impunity and undermined democratic accountability. In El Salvador, the United States delayed declassification of documents that might have hurt ARENA's electoral showing and then disingenuously released tens of thousands of pages of unsorted documents at the last minute before the elections. In Guatemala, where the negotiated accords did not include the equivalent of an internationally supervised truth commission, civil society groups attempted to fill in, including the Recuperation of Historical Memory (Recuperación de la Memoria Histórica, REMHI) project of the Archdiocese, and the Commission for Historical Clarification (Comisión para el Esclarecimiento Histórico, CEH). U.S. officials claimed to have released "most" of the declassified Guatemalan documents, but cited budgetary constraints and lack of specificity in document requests as obstacles to further cooperation with the CEH.[35] In Nicaragua, rearmed groups had largely disappeared and political killings ended by 1998, but there was still no real accountability, since all the investigative bodies had some political affiliation, and the U.S. embassy in Managua was the most partisan in the region. In Honduras, U.S. officials covered up human rights abuses by military units.[36]

DEMILITARIZATION. The United States was necessarily a key actor because of its massive military aid and involvement in the 1980s. At a minimum, the size and functions of the armed forces would have to be adapted to peacetime and the military institution subordinated to elected civilian authority. The end of armed conflict brought major reductions in the size of the armed forces of Nicaragua and El Salvador, and a much more modest reduction in Guatemala, but armies were not abolished as in the pact that ended Costa Rica's 1948 civil war. Still, the decline in U.S. military aid helped protect the electoral status quo: after the FMLN's strong showing in the 1997 elections, one Christian Democrat noted that "democracy was saved by the negative route. The government wanted to alter the election results, but couldn't find anyone to do it for them. The army wasn't in the business of overturning elections anymore."[37]

U.S. military aid to Central America continued in the 1990s, albeit at decreased levels. This aid included arms sales; training; bases in Honduras and Panama; and growing "civic action," joint military exercises, and "counternarcotics" programs. The School of the Americas, which had trained large numbers of Central American troops in the 1980s—including some notorious human rights abusers, using manuals on torture techniques that the United States later retracted[38]—continued to train Central Americans. Guatemala, El Salvador, and Nicaragua were the top three recipients in 1997 of Expanded International Military Education and Training funds, a program ostensibly designed to improve systems of military justice to promote human rights and subordination to civilian authority.[39] Critics doubted whether such military aid, even reoriented, actually contributed to democracy. Moreover, the expansion of the military's mission into such areas as road building and drug policing reinforced an already overgrown institution.

The United States made a significant contribution to programs for the "reinsertion" of ex-combatants into productive civilian life. As Chapter 8 details, the UN and the Organization of American States (OAS) initially played the main roles in overseeing the demobilization of fighters and destruction of arms, with the United States providing some assistance in specific areas such as demining. U.S. and other aid in the 1990s financed land, credit, job training, and employment-generating productive projects for ex-combatants. However, such programs, even when successful at the micro level, were inadequate to repair a decade of war destruction or revamp the region's unviable economic model.

In Nicaragua, the Chamorro government, whose election the United States had supported in 1990, sowed conflict by promising the same land twice, that is, returning confiscated properties to large landowners (thus displacing beneficiaries of Sandinista agrarian reform) and providing land to former Contras. Tensions were accentuated by the fact that the OAS commission overseeing demobilization had a mandate only to help the former Nicaraguan Resistance (RN, or Contras); and resources were strained as RN families and noncombatant supporters claimed rights to land, while international funds fell short of donor promises.[40] The United States not only failed to prioritize funding for resettlement in Nicaragua but also aggravated the problem by pressing for the return of confiscated properties to former (generally wealthy) owners.

In El Salvador, U.S. aid included substantial amounts for reinsertion of ex-combatants from both the armed forces and guerrillas. However, poverty remained a problem among this population, and wounded veterans received inadequate attention, leading to street demonstrations that were violently repressed by the government. A land transfer program benefited significant numbers of ex-combatants with small plots. However, without adequate credit and technical assistance to offer a viable livelihood, conflict continued.[41]

In Guatemala, the URNG forces were so decimated by scorched-earth policies before the peace accords that there were under three thousand demobilized, of whom perhaps only a few hundred were full-time combatants, so the U.S. government and other donors could claim relatively quick success in demobilization.[42] However, resettlement of the much larger numbers of URNG supporters and others, displaced or herded into "development poles," posed a much more complex problem of demilitarization of the counterinsurgency state. Attacks on returning refugees in the early 1990s left doubts about the military's commitment to a negotiated peace. Even assuming U.S. willingness, conditioning aid on demilitarization was problematical. The prevailing ideology even among pro–peace process members of the high command was that they were victims of Soviet-sponsored aggression, that the army had defended an anticommunist constitutional order, and that they had won the war without U.S. help.[43]

In all three post-conflict demobilizations, foot soldiers on both sides of the armed conflicts resented the much more generous resettlement packages that their commanders had negotiated for themselves, including externally funded training seminars and scholarships. The strategy of buying off military and guerrilla leaders to prevent their rearming was short-sighted, neglecting the socioeconomic problems of the mainly peasant troops. The U.S. aid strategy (much more so than that of European and other donors) leaned toward quick disbursement of funds to avoid an authoritarian regression, rather than holding up monies to enforce human rights and other conditions. Critics argued that the front-loading of funds represented a missed opportunity to use external finance for "peace conditionality."[44]

REFORM ("MODERNIZATION") OF THE STATE. U.S. aid in the 1990s included assistance in drafting new constitutional and legal frameworks, training judicial personnel and legislators, and improving public administration, especially local government. These programs were part of a broader trend toward incorporating concepts of "good governance" or "governability" into international development assistance. Donor efforts to shape public policy and define "good governance" stemmed from neoliberal ideology, emphasizing individual property and contract rights. This market-driven vision of "modernization of the state," involving privatization and cutbacks of public services, fit well with U.S. objectives of molding Central American "democracy" while spending much less on aid.

Under pressure from U.S.-backed international financial institutions to meet fiscal austerity targets, governments found it more politically expedient to cut peace expenditures than touch the military budget or increase taxes on the wealthy. In El Salvador, where costs of reinsertion of ex-combatants and building democratic institutions (for example, civilian police, judicial systems, and human rights offices) exceeded initial estimates, international donors expected a reluctant government to mobilize more domestic resources to fill the gap. One government official reportedly told USAID they would never have signed the peace accords if they had known the actual costs in advance.[45] In 1998 to the dismay of donors, the government tried to eliminate the office of human rights prosecutor in the name of budget cutting.[46]

In Guatemala, perhaps learning from the Salvadoran case, socioeconomic policy issues were explicitly included in the negotiated peace agreement. However, the agreements were sufficiently vague, and the Guatemalan military and more reactionary capitalists (organized in the business peak association, the Chamber of Agricultural, Commercial, Industrial, and Financial Associations—Comité Coordinador de Asociaciones Comerciales, Industriales y Financieras, CACIF) strong enough to block progress in key areas of demilitarization, indigenous rights, and fiscal reform. In a country with one of the lowest rates and most regressive structures of taxation in Latin America (under 8 percent of gross domestic product [GDP], with indirect taxes representing 76 percent of revenues), CACIF managed to overturn even a temporary two-year property tax; defying the peace accord provision for "progressive" taxation rising to 12 percent of GDP by 2000, and international pressure for fiscal reform.[47] The United States and other donors tended to favor the modernizing capitalists (neoliberals) who wanted a minimalist state but who accepted the basic premises of the twentieth century welfare state. In the Guatemalan context, even that minimum would require a substantial increase in the mobilization of public resources for social spending, essential for extending citizenship rights to the poor (mainly indigenous) majority of the Guatemalan population.[48] However, this concept was anathema to the right-wing FRG party of General Ríos Montt. Moreover, international pressure for fiscal reform may have only boosted the nationalist credentials of the Far Right, which was not committed to either the peace accords or the neoliberalism of President Arzú's PAN.

In Nicaragua, U.S. policies on law and property rights sent mixed messages. Washington first ignored the World Court's 1986 ruling that the Contra war violated international law, then withdrew from the court's jurisdiction to evade assessment of damages, then used promises of aid to induce the Chamorro government to retroactively withdraw Nicaragua's World Court case. The issue of property rights was explosive following Nicaragua's unprecedented electoral transfer of power in 1990, from a revolutionary government that had initiated sweeping agrarian reform and other redistribution. Former president Jimmy Carter attempted to mediate, but Senator Jesse Helms—chair of the Foreign Relations Committee—aggravated tensions by blocking aid to support property claims of U.S. citizens, many of whom were Nicaraguans who had become U.S. citizens only after their holdings were confiscated.[49]

In each of these cases, the definition of "good government" was not neutral. Even in improving financial management to eliminate corruption, external influence was always selective. For example, during the Duarte administration in El Salvador, U.S. support for the Christian Democrats meant turning a blind eye to widespread public corruption. After the 1992 peace accords when the United States and other donors became stricter about financial accountability, the ARENA government used the tightened procedures in a discriminatory fashion to delay disbursements to foreign-funded projects in FMLN-controlled municipal governments.[50] In Nicaragua, U.S. officials in 1998 saw "no proven corruption yet" in the Alemán administration, a view that contrasted markedly with that of other international aid agencies.[51] In Guatemala, USAID's financial reporting requirements were a particular obstacle to funding for smaller local nongovernment organizations (NGOs), and some organizations were reluctant to open their files to U.S. government agencies when the fear of death squads still lingered.[52]

Wherever external aid flows represented a significant portion of government budgets, the selection of intermediary institutions was a powerful instrument of "nation-building." The model was Costa Rica in the 1980s, where the current president Oscar Arias had frankly noted that as long as the Sandinista comandantes remained in Nicaragua, Costa Rica could expect $200 million per year in economic aid.[53] This U.S. aid was conditioned on neoliberal reforms, including privatization and export promotion. The "local counterpart currency" generated by USAID programs, and the windfall from subsidized privatization sales, were administered by what an Arias advisor later denounced as a "parallel state," complete with virtual government ministries, directed by the U.S.-sponsored Costa Rican Coalition for Development Initiatives (Coalición de Iniciativas de Desarrollo, CINDE). Similar business councils and related networks of parallel state institutions—Salvadoran Foundation for Economic and Social Development (Fundación Salvadoreña para el Desarrollo Económico y Social, FUSADES) in El Salvador, CACIF and Guatemalan Chamber of Business (Cámara Empresarial de Guatemala, CAEM) in Guatemala, Superior Council of Private Enterprise (Consejo Superior de la Empresa Privada, COSEP) and later Association of Nicaraguan Producers and Exporters of Non-Traditional Products (Asociación de Productores y Exportadores Nicaragüenses de Productos No Tradicionales, APENN) in Nicaragua—were created or promoted by USAID throughout Central America.[54] These networks promoted development strategies with regressive distributive impacts and shifted control over development policy away from elected governments toward externally selected social institutions.

DEVELOPMENT OF CIVIL SOCIETY. Given the weakness of the state in post-conflict Central America, the role of civil society in the reconstruction process took on political significance. As the United States and other do-nors channeled funds and support through NGOs, the "transition to democ-racy" became a struggle against co-optation or externally imposed criteria shaping the correlation of forces in civil society.

In Nicaragua, the post-1990 governments and some external actors, particularly the United States, avoided Sandinista-mobilized grassroots or-ganizations. As these groups clashed with the policies of the more conser-vative Chamorro and Alemán governments, the United States saw them as disruptive instruments of an antidemocratic party.[55] Yet many of these groups were actually becoming more autonomous from the Sandinista party, an-other hopeful sign of substantive democratization.[56]

In El Salvador, where grassroots organizations linked to the FMLN had established a vibrant organizational presence in the former conflict zones, USAID—in contrast to European donors—sought to avoid reinforcing the Left, even when these "opposition" NGOs were best positioned to deliver community services. This selection was particularly evident in the large amounts of funding disbursed under the National Reconstruction Plan, where the U.S.-favored institutions were the successors of the old "Municipalities in Action" counterinsurgency program.[57] U.S. support for the ARENA government's decision to channel reconstruction funds through the government's Secretariat of National Reconstruction—rather than the UN Development Program (UNDP), as agreed to in the peace accords—under-mined the Left's NGOs. The discrimination softened after ARENA won the 1994 election, but the winner-take-all format of the 1994 municipal elec-tions often shut the FMLN out of participation in local development coun-cils. USAID officials acknowledged that the FMLN generally did a good job administering local development projects after the party won a third of the municipalities in the 1997 election[58]—another sign of a new democratic space being created by activists mobilized in the revolutionary process.

In Guatemala as in El Salvador, U.S. aid programs did not formally exclude the foundations and NGOs affiliated with the former guerrillas, and in fact worked smoothly with them on programs for reinsertion of ex-combatants. However, USAID's exhaustive reporting requirements tended to favor establishment-oriented groups over those that had more grassroots organizing history. For example, one project in Huehuetenango involved workshops for rural teachers and community leaders to explain people's rights under the new peace accords. While the civic education goals sug-gested community empowerment and democratization, the Christian Democrat–leaning NGO was based far away in the capital city, and training often fell apart for lack of an organizational presence in and around the communities served.[59]

In Guatemala, one promising offshoot of the peace process was the for-mation of an independent coordinating forum of NGOs, which took its case for a more participatory model of development directly to the Consultative

Group (CG) of donors. The forum criticized the government's attempt to exclude them from the CG meeting in Brussels in January 1997, its failure to obtain more than $400 million of $1.9 billion in external financing originally contemplated for the peace process, and the government's insistence that the $700 million that foreign donors expected in domestic resources come from privatization rather than tax reform. Demanding a public debate on these issues, they insisted that modernization of the state should mean democratization.[60]

This vision of democratization from within civil society was not so much promoted externally as it was formulated from the grassroots in reaction to the externally supported implementation of peace accords. If governments were going to be negotiating public policy with foreign donors, civil society demanded to be represented too. While some saw grassroots activism as a problem of governability, others saw active participation by a diversity of civil society agents in shaping public policy as the very essence of democratization.

The UNDP shared the latter view with Central Americans who argued that as long as extreme physical and economic insecurity were a part of everyday life for the majorities, competitive elections would not lead to democratic consolidation.[61] As UN officials noted, economic austerity and state rollback conflicted with reconstruction and social policies, necessary to build a minimum of national consensus.[62] Donor efforts to channel funds to "targeted social compensation" did not alter deep structural inequalities, and donors faced traditional elites building patronage machines, as did Arnoldo Alemán as mayor of Managua (1990-1996) and then president.[63] European governments were less insistent than the U.S. government in conditioning aid on adherence to neoliberal orthodoxy in the 1990s. However, growing multilateral (especially the Inter-American Development Bank [IDB] and the World Bank) finance (see table) made funds available strictly on the basis of economic orthodoxy, thus undercutting efforts by bilateral aid administrators to condition aid on the fulfillment of peace accord provisions.[64]

The debate over development strategy reflected the struggle to shape Central America's "third transition," democratic consolidation. Critics of the U.S.-backed neoliberal model noted that rather than stimulating production and job-creation, fostering broad economic and political participation, it had created a mini-boom in commerce and financial services for a narrow elite, whose import-intensive consumption was artificially boosted by unsustainable inflows of family remittances and foreign aid.[65] Alternative visions of participatory democracy were being formulated not so much by ex-guerrilla-organizations-turned-political-parties as by the popular organizations initially mobilized in the revolutionary process: the unions and women's movement in Nicaragua, the FDNG in Guatemala, and a variety of Salvadoran popular organizations.[66]

Official Development Assistance to Central America, 1980–1997 (millions of U.S. $)

	Annual Averages									
	1980–1984	*1985–1989*	*1990*	*1991*	*1992*	*1993*	*1994*	*1995*	*1996*	*1997*
United States	341.8	719.6	740.0	809.0	592.0	406.0	294.0	208.0	86.0	161.0
Europe[a]	122.2	265.0	481.3	550.8	587.9	539.6	636.8	817.6	1055.0	556.1
Austria	5.1	4.7	7.9	20.8	4.7	16.8	19.6	20.5	16.5	12.5
Belgium	1.3	3.1	5.1	6.2	6.7	8.4	6.9	10.7	8.1	8.2
Denmark	1.3	7.0	15.4	25.5	25.8	27.9	25.5	32.7	39.4	42.4
Finland	1.9	10.7	13.4	25.9	14.3	8.2	5.3	6.7	5.2	7.7
France	8.1	21.1	13.1	14.2	34.4	25.4	20.2	38.6	22.9	14.0
Germany	31.4	67.8	104.9	121.8	130.4	96.7	120.2	261.5	487.3	105.1
Ireland	0.0	0.0	0.0	0.0	0.1	0.2	0.6	1.2	0.8	1.5
Italy	4.9	44.7	64.2	60.4	46.2	35.0	127.1	22.8	27.8	10.0
Luxembourg	0.0	0.0	0.0	0.5	0.2	2.9	3.7	0.0	4.3	4.1
Netherlands	26.5	42.8	83.7	29.0	63.1	67.3	61.8	109.3	85.0	77.2
Norway	3.3	17.6	40.8	32.7	35.6	26.4	32.1	43.9	44.3	40.9
Portugal	0.0	0.0	0.0	0.0	0.0	0.0	0.0	0.0	0.2	0.0
Spain	0.0	7.2	27.2	48.5	31.4	50.4	57.6	77.5	90.0	85.5
Sweden	9.7	35.3	40.5	71.6	80.4	55.5	45.7	51.5	69.7	44.8
Switzerland	6.8	13.5	12.8	34.0	27.8	14.6	25.0	33.8	24.1	11.5

United Kingdom	2.4	3.7	4.7	4.5	5.3	6.8	9.9	6.2	7.5	5.4
EC/EU multilateral	19.4	31.7	47.6	55.2	81.5	97.1	75.6	100.7	121.9	85.3
Japan bilateral	14.4	44.4	139.6	148.0	179.3	147.6	181.4	201.1	231.8	201.7
Canada	17.4	24.5	26.7	36.3	28.3	31.8	24.7	19.6	26.5	23.7
Other	0.0	0.8	0.2	0.2	0.3	0.5	0.6	0.3	10.5	10.9
IDB	146.1	64.4	76.2	56.1	121.1	81.8	134.6	113.7	191.6	90.8
World Bank	19.3	-0.8	-3.0	98.0	130.9	66.7	112.3	92.3	116.5	141.5
UNDP	11.4	13.8	17.3	24.8	31.8	44.9	45.4	50.7	60.5	83.3
Other multilateral[b]	54.0	80.7	87.3	87.5	93.4	69.0	88.9	115.5	69.7	55.6
Total	726.7	1212.2	1565.6	1810.7	1765.0	1387.9	1518.7	1618.8	1848.1	1324.6

Source: Calculated from OECD/DAC (Organization for Economic Cooperation and Development/Development Assistance Committee), *Geographical Distribution of Financial Flows to Aid Recipients* (Paris: OECD, various years).

Note: The figures in this table represent total Official Development Assistance (ODA) net disbursements from OECD/DAC countries plus multilateral aid, to Costa Rica, El Salvador, Guatemala, Honduras, and Nicaragua.

[a] Includes European Communities/European Union.
[b] Excludes European Communities/European Union.

Restoring Hemispheric Hegemony

The intense U.S. intervention in Central America in the 1980s was not undertaken because the Sandinistas might invade Harlingen, Texas, or revolutions threatened the Panama Canal or Caribbean "sea lanes," or banana supplies might be interrupted. In General Alexander Haig's memorable phrase, the United States had "drawn the line" in Central America and, having done so, created a U.S. interest in the outcome of the revolutions. The region became a test of the post-Vietnam U.S. ability to project its power to achieve declared objectives internationally, that is, to maintain global hegemony.

With the negotiated peace in the 1990s and declining international attention to Central America, preserving hegemony was defined more in terms of issues such as drug trafficking, immigration, and intellectual property rights. These were global regulation issues, involving market-driven flows that transcended borders; Central American government policies could not be neatly separated from the effects of U.S. domestic and foreign policies. For example, with the $4.5 billion in family remittances by Salvadorans living in the United States exceeding the $3.3 billion total of U.S. aid to El Salvador in the 1978–1994 period,[67] U.S. immigration policies had enormous impact on socioeconomic stability in El Salvador. But hegemony meant that the United States would define the nature of the problem and arrange consensus about the solutions.

After the 1990 Sandinista electoral defeat, no Central American government was far out of step with U.S. policies. Even the ripple of dissent represented by the Esquipulas initiative of Central American presidents had become moot. One litmus test for U.S. ability to coordinate hemispheric policies had long been the campaign to isolate Cuba, and on this score the Alemán government bent over backward to reverse the course charted in the Sandinista era, to evident U.S. delight. The Somoza government had previously offered Nicaragua as a beachhead for efforts to overthrow the Castro government, and Cuban-American contributors to Alemán's election campaign seemed to nurture hopes that Nicaragua would return to this traditional role as an adjunct to U.S. policy. El Salvador's ARENA government indulged in anti-Cuba posturing, although Salvadoran capitalists (reportedly including former president Alfredo Cristiani of ARENA) actively took advantage of Cuba's market opening.

U.S. efforts to reestablish hegemony also involved changing the image of U.S. involvement in Central America. The United States had paid international political costs in the 1980s for its unpopular campaign to defeat revolutionary and popular movements, particularly for support or acquiescence in repression. Joining international efforts in support of peace processes in the 1990s was a relatively low-cost way to shift attention from the past. U.S. aid efforts along these lines were supplemented by programs such as United States Information Agency (USIA) scholarships for Central Americans to come to the United States, and the Peace Corps, which returned to Nicaragua after a long absence in the Sandinista years and had one hundred volunteers there by 1998. Any assessment of the overall U.S. role in Central America would be incomplete without consideration of the earlier phase of intense involvement in the 1980s, as well as the complementary or competing agendas of other outside actors.

Other State Actors in Central America

The states that played significant roles in Central America's transitions might be usefully grouped into four categories, defined by two variables: major versus minor (the latter consisting of those whose involvement was unsustained in the 1990s), and support for the basic U.S. agenda (deradicalization and globalization).[68] In the first quadrant of major actors reinforcing the U.S. goals would be Japan, an often overlooked actor with aid levels exceeding U.S. aid in the 1990s. Europe would fall into the second category, of major actors that departed from the U.S. agenda, promoting negotiated peace and democratization when U.S. priorities were elsewhere. The third category, lesser actors supporting counterrevolution and market opening, included Israel, Argentina under military rule, and Taiwan. A fourth group of states did not sustain their involvement but countered the U.S. agenda in significant ways. These states included Cuba and the Soviet Union, less extensively involved than cold war rhetoric claimed in supporting revolution, and other Latin American countries (particularly the Contadora Group) plus Canada, supporting negotiated alternatives.

Japan's Complementary Agenda

Japanese aid policy has been traditionally conservative and organized around Japanese commercial interests. After the kidnaping of several Japanese businessmen in El Salvador in the 1970s, Japanese involvement in the 1980s concentrated on Honduras, Costa Rica, and Panama. However, following the peace negotiations of the 1990s, Japan committed large amounts of aid to El Salvador, Guatemala, and Nicaragua. At the March 1992 Consultative Group meeting of donors to El Salvador right after the signing of peace accords, Japan pledged $100 million of the total $810 million promised by the international community, and by 1996 had actually approved $207 million.[69] Japanese aid to Nicaragua in the 1990–1998 period totaled $295 million.[70] In Guatemala, Japan promised significant support for implementation of the December 1996 peace accords and by the end of 1997 had disbursed $29 million, second only to the U.S. disbursement ($33 million) among bilateral funders.[71] Japanese aid to Central America surpassed U.S. aid after 1995 (see table).

Japan's involvement in Central America was considerably less than these aid figures suggest, however. Japan's aid had a much higher loan component and smaller grant component than other sources and was concentrated in a few big infrastructure projects. Of Japan's $207 million in aid to El Salvador in 1992–1996, $204 million was for infrastructure, of which $95 million was for rebuilding two major bridges; and 95 percent was loans rather than grants.[72] Compared with U.S. or European aid, Japan had little hands-on involvement in the details of the region's transitions, much less political conditionality. Although Japan's embassy was the largest in Managua and the largest Japanese embassy building in Latin America, it housed only nine diplomats; the impressive facility was considered a necessary incentive to induce diplomats to serve in a "hazardous" region.

High levels of Japanese aid to Central America in the 1990s could not be explained by strategic or economic interests in the region, which were minimal. Despite persistent speculation and occasional glimmers of investor interest in several new canal construction schemes, the Japanese government remained wary of instability in the region, and financial commitments leveled off in 1998 as Japan faced its worst financial crisis since World War II. Rather, Japan mainly derived political benefit, principally in the higher priority area of Japanese-U.S. relations. Since July 1993, Japan and the United States had inaugurated a "Common Agenda for Cooperation in Global Perspective," coordinating their international aid programs. Japanese aid helped the United States pull its chestnuts out of the Central American fire, a kind of "peace with honor" as U.S. commitments declined. Besides winning U.S. gratitude, Japan quietly accumulated political chips at low cost among small countries, whose votes might eventually support a Japanese bid for a permanent seat on the UN Security Council.[73]

European Support for Peace

European states played an important role in promoting a negotiated alternative in the 1980s to the U.S.-sponsored efforts to militarily defeat revolutions in Central America, and in bolstering the Latin American initiatives of the Contadora Group and later the Esquipulas process of negotiations among the Central America presidents.[74] France took an early lead, issuing a joint declaration with Mexico in 1981 recognizing the legitimate combatant status of the FMLN in El Salvador and even contracted to sell arms to the Nicaraguan government fighting the U.S.-backed Contras (but reneged under U.S. pressure). The San José meetings of European and Central American foreign ministers, begun in 1984 in the Costa Rican capital, served as a forum to advocate a negotiated regional solution to the conflicts and to coordinate European aid for peaceful development.

This European involvement did not imply support for revolutionary options in Central America or a break with the overall European support for the U.S.-dominated cold war global order. European countries sought to play a mediating role between the United States and Central America because it gave them some international projection, served as a bargaining card with the United States for other important issues, and proved politically useful for demonstrating both independence from U.S. foreign policy and the emergence of European foreign policy coordination.[75] It also provided an opportunity to demonstrate general support for the Third World (important for European commercial and political ties with former colonies) and to promote the ideals of regional integration that had historic relevance in Central America as well as Europe. On this last point, the European interest was only a variation on the U.S. theme of promoting free trade.

European economic aid rose sharply after 1984 when the San José dialogue began and continued to increase at a more modest rate after 1991 when U.S. aid peaked. By 1993 European aid exceeded U.S. aid to Central America. Offsetting the counterinsurgency objectives of U.S. aid, a major portion of European funds went to the Sandinista government in Nicaragua in the 1980s, particularly from Nordic countries (especially Sweden) and the Netherlands, which were sympathetic to the development of cooperatives and policies expanding social welfare. The Nordic countries actually contributed more than the figures show, since they channeled most of their aid through NGOs and the UNDP. Among bilateral European donors, the largest were Germany, the Netherlands, Italy, and Sweden. Countries that increased their aid to important levels in the 1990s included Spain (which had joined the European Community or EC in 1986), France, and Denmark. Europe also expanded its multilateral aid commitments to Central America, from the EC's $88 million in 1985 to the European Union's (EU) $230 million in 1996.[76]

European aid agencies seemed more inclined than the United States to use their growing relative importance in Central America as leverage to encourage implementation of peace accords, although EU officials preferred to avoid the term "conditionality."[77] However, Central American governments in the 1990s often resisted development plans that they could not control from above. Conditioning aid on substantive progress was also complicated by the ambiguous terms on which the region's armed conflicts were brought to a negotiated end. Consequently, the execution rates of EU projects were often very low, especially in Nicaragua and Guatemala.[78]

A distinctive feature of European aid was the NGO component, estimated in 1992 at over one-third of official bilateral aid from European governments.[79] Some (for example, the German Ebert, Adenauer, and Naumann foundations) were linked to political parties, while other NGOs had some particular vision of development, often oriented toward grassroots participation and empowerment. The main recipients were Nicaragua in the 1980s, El Salvador after 1990, and Guatemala after 1991; a shift apparently reflecting not only relative need but also the prospects for social change and the availability of acceptable counterpart agencies. For many donors, Nicaragua's attractiveness as a laboratory for alternative development strategies disappeared when the Sandinistas left office.[80]

Despite the progressive orientation of aid, European trade concessions prioritized Eastern Europe, followed by former colonial preferences under the Lomé Convention, and only then Central America followed by the rest of Latin America. Although the San José dialogue eventually produced some trade concessions in 1991 and 1996, 56 percent of Central American exports to Europe were bananas, excluded from the Generalized System of Preferences.[81] Overall, considering the European role in the collapse of the International Coffee Agreement in 1989 and European banana import quotas introduced in 1993, one study estimated that the negative effects of European trade policies exceeded the value of all European bilateral and multilateral aid to Central America.[82] Considering also the European countries' general support for neoliberal structural adjustment programs, their vision of sustainable democratic development was not radically different from U.S. policy.

Spain became the third largest European source of economic aid in 1995. It took an active part in supporting demilitarization and (along with the United States) providing training to El Salvador's new Civilian National Police. Following the Esquipulas II regional peace initiative, the first talks between the Guatemalan government and URNG guerrillas were held in Madrid in October 1987, eventually leading to the signing of accords in Madrid, Stockholm, and Oslo in December 1996 that ended the Guatemalan armed conflict. Spain joined the "Group of Friends" (along with the United States, Norway, Colombia, and Venezuela) invited to support the UN mediation and monitoring of the Guatemalan peace accords.

For Spain, an active policy of promoting peace and democratic development in Central America was the outgrowth of a long process of post-Franco foreign policy transition. Spain sought a place as a middle power on the world stage, based on special relations with Europe, Latin America, and the Mediterranean-Middle East region.[83] The Spanish government established a new subsecretariat of state for external cooperation with "Iberoamerica" in 1982, organized a series of Iberoamerican summit meetings, and invested heavily in the 1992 celebration of the quincentennial of Spain's "encounter" with the Americas.[84]

Within the Spanish government, some saw support for democratic transition in Central America as an opportunity to showcase Spain's new experience with democratization, to bolster ties with the Social Democratic and Christian Democratic internationals, and to demonstrate externally Spain's democratic credentials for joining the European Community in 1986. Spain also continued to press for European trade preferences for Central and Latin America, arguing that former Spanish domains should be no less favored than the former French colonies under the Lomé Convention, or the British

Commonwealth countries. This campaign yielded few results for Central America, but it was a useful bargaining chip for Spain, to be strategically ceded in exchange for other concessions that Spain really wanted for its own terms of accession to the European Community.[85] Aid to the small Central American region produced political payoffs domestically and with the rest of "Iberoamerica," as well as leverage in Europe and prominence internationally.

Minor Backers of Counterinsurgency and Globalization

Taiwan, along with Argentina, had provided training and assistance to the Guatemalan military in the period when the United States had suspended military aid over the issue of human rights abuse. In the first year after the signing of the peace accords, Taiwan's $20 million aid disbursement to Guatemala made Taiwan the fifth largest source of external finance, after the IDB, the United States, Japan, and the EU.[86]

Taiwanese and South Korean direct foreign investment in the Central American free zones became important in the 1990s. Low labor costs and the absence of a history of armed conflict seemed to be factors of attraction to the maquiladoras in Honduras, where some ninety thousand workers (mainly young women) worked in textile and other assembly plants by 1998. Taiwan's aid was mainly politically motivated: by the end of the 1990s, after South Africa and even South Korea switched diplomatic relations from Taiwan to the People's Republic of China, only about twenty countries maintained ties with Taiwan, mostly small Central American and Caribbean countries. While some Taiwanese aid programs in Central America were in productive sectors such as agricultural technical assistance, the most visible projects were highly politicized construction gifts shunned by other development donors, such as expansion of Central American foreign ministry installations and presidential palaces. In Nicaragua, where Taiwan was financing a multi-million-dollar palace for President Alemán on the former Plaza of the Revolution, diplomatic relations were switched back from the People's Republic of China to Taiwan.

Israel in the late 1970s and 1980s provided counterinsurgency training and equipment to the Guatemalan military, partly offsetting the effect of the interruption of U.S. military aid. The Guatemalan military replaced the M-1 rifle with the Israeli Galil as the standard infantry rifle in 1980, switching back to the U.S.-made M-16 in 1988. Unlike Taiwan, however, Israel did not maintain a major aid program in Central America in the 1990s.

Argentina's military government, with a "national security doctrine" of intense anticommunist ideology and experience in its own "dirty war," became extensively involved in covert counterinsurgency operations in Central America in the late 1970s and early 1980s.[87] In addition to helping organize and train the first Contra forces in Nicaragua, the most repressive parts of the Argentine state apparatus supplied training to the Salvadoran, Guatemalan, and Honduran militaries. During the Reagan administration, the United States coordinated covertly with the Argentine military, so that external support for counterinsurgency was maintained even during periods of U.S. Congressional suspension of aid to the Nicaraguan Contras and to the Guatemalan military. The promiscuous sharing of counterinsurgency techniques in the region undermined efforts to inculcate respect for human rights and accountability in the Central American militaries.

Questioning the U.S. Agenda: The Soviet Union, Cuba, and Other Latin American States

During the Reagan administration, the Soviet Union and Cuba were often portrayed as the major sponsors if not causes of the Central American revolutions. More serious independent analysis suggested that the Soviet Union never made the kind of commitment to Central America that it had once made to the Cuban revolution, and that Cuba's involvement in Central America was on its own initiative.[88] The inflated image of Cuban-Soviet involvement served to rationalize the much more extensive intervention of the United States.

Central American revolutionaries were influenced by the example of the Cuban revolution but did not simply imitate the Cuban model, as evidenced by the Sandinista government's eclecticism. During the formative phases of Central America's guerrilla struggles, Cuba reportedly played a significant role in encouraging and brokering unification of factions within each country's revolutionary movements. Throughout the armed conflicts, Cuba provided a sanctuary and meeting place for Central American revolutionaries (a role Nicaragua also played after the 1979 Sandinista victory), as well as other support including medical treatment. Cuba was one source of arms for the Sandinista struggle against Somoza, along with other countries such as Panama and Venezuela (and Costa Rica, which served as a conduit).

Economic aid from the socialist countries to Nicaragua totaled $215 million in the 1979–1986 period, while Western aid totaled $365 million. After the Sandinista government's attempts to purchase arms from the United States and France were rebuffed, the Soviet Union provided large grants of military hardware, which the U.S. Defense Department estimated at $500 million per year in 1986–1988 at the height of the Contra war.[89] After the United States imposed a trade embargo in 1985 and cut Nicaragua off from other financial sources, the Soviet Union became the largest source of loans in the late 1980s, although these were mostly tied credits that failed to halt Nicaragua's economic deterioration.

By the end of the 1980s, economic problems in the Soviet Union and Cuba and the political upheavals in the Soviet bloc sharply reduced their involvement in Central America. With the Esquipulas regional peace negotiations under way, Soviet Foreign Minister Eduard Shevardnadze communicated to U.S. Secretary of State Howard Baker that the USSR was suspending military aid to Nicaragua and supported the negotiation process. Cuba also made it clear that it was reassessing its role in Central America and supported a negotiated solution.[90]

The Cuban and Soviet reduction of commitments and endorsement of negotiations helped move revolutionaries to the negotiating table, just as declining U.S. involvement affected calculations of actors on the other side. Also, this withdrawal further undercut the rationale for continued U.S. involvement in the armed conflict. In the 1990s, the main role of the successor state in Russia was in forgiving large amounts of debt contracted by Nicaragua with the former Soviet Union. Cuba attempted to continue some technical assistance to Nicaragua in health and education during the 1990–1996 Chamorro government but was rebuffed by the new Alemán administration.

Several nonrevolutionary Latin American countries had supported the Sandinista revolutionary movement in the 1970s. Regional support for the prospect of a popular uprising to overthrow the U.S.-backed Somoza dictatorship became evident in June 1979, when the OAS broke precedent by rejecting U.S. proposals for an OAS "peacekeeping" force to stop the Sandinista revolutionary victory.

The Contadora Group (Mexico, Colombia, Venezuela, and Panama), formed in 1983, played an important part in opposing external military intervention and supporting peace negotiations in Central America. The original group was joined in 1985 by the Lima Support Group (Brazil, Argentina, Peru, and Uruguay), marking a growing regional consensus for an alternative to U.S. policies. The Contadora Group in part reflected the emergence of a group of Latin American would-be middle powers aiming to expand their international influence. Mexico and Venezuela's involvement was boosted by oil revenues. The Mexican government followed a tradition of placating domestic constituencies by demonstrating revolutionary–anti-imperialist credentials abroad; and Venezuela's Christian Democratic and Social Democratic parties were inclined toward solidarity with their Central American homologues.[91]

Besides supporting a negotiated solution, Mexico and Venezuela also played an important role in providing economic aid that deviated from the counterinsurgency logic of U.S. aid in the 1980s. Through the 1980 San José Accord, Mexico and Venezuela supplied oil on concessional terms, including to Sandinista Nicaragua (later suspended as Mexico experienced economic and political pressure in the mid 1980s).

This relatively brief period of Latin American activism in Central America in the late 1970s and early 1980s was important in several ways. It had a mutually reinforcing effect with similar Western European initiatives, in helping sustain (and perhaps encourage pluralism in) the Sandinista revolution and promote regional peace negotiations over U.S. opposition. By the late 1980s, oil price drops and the debt crisis reduced Latin American aid. However, Mexico continued to play a political role into the 1990s in hosting peace talks.

In January 1991, Mexico and the Central American governments met in Tuxtla Gutiérrez, Chiapas, in the first of a series of summits over North American free trade. After Mexico's entry into the North American Free Trade Agreement in January 1994 and devaluation of the Mexican peso in December 1994, the Tuxtla dialogue took on added urgency for Central American countries, which were increasingly concerned by the impact of cheap Mexican imports as they liberalized their economies. However, the urgency was not reciprocal; Mexico's interest in Central America was declining, a trend that continued with the signing of the Guatemalan peace accord in December 1996 and the repatriation of Guatemalan refugees in Mexico.

Canada also supported negotiated alternatives to U.S. policies in the 1980s, albeit through channels less visible than the European San José meetings or the Latin American Contadora Group. Canadian aid to Nicaragua was important during the Sandinista period, probably more than the figures suggest because much of the aid was provided by Canadian NGOs or quasi-NGOs. Following the signing of peace accords, Canada approved U.S.$22 million in grant aid for Salvadoran reconstruction in 1992–1995, and committed U.S.$25 million to support implementation of the Guatemalan accords in 1997–2000.[92] Because Canada preferred to channel aid through local NGOs rather than the Salvadoran government, these smaller aid flows helped preserve space for civil society organizations shut out by the larger funders.

In this panorama of external state actors in Central America, a few patterns can be discerned. The intensity and motives of each state's involvement were varied and shifting and sometimes become clearer with hindsight. Leverage was not necessarily proportional to the expenditure of resources, and the impact of each state's involvement was partly aimed at other external actors. In the 1990s, the volume of aid from Japan, Europe, and the international financial institutions overtook U.S. aid (mainly because of the latter's sharp decline); but U.S. political influence remained considerable, and these increasingly salient actors largely supported the neoliberal agenda.

The Outlook as Central America Drops Off the Map

The cold war exaggerated and distorted the focus on external actors in what used to be called the Central American crisis. U.S. intervention had a major impact on the region in the late 1970s and 1980s, but the United States did not exactly achieve its main objective of militarily defeating the revolutionary movements in the region. Other states intervened with agendas that did not entirely coincide with U.S. policy, and the outcomes were more ambiguous than most had hoped or feared, shaped by the dynamic interaction of internal and external forces.[93]

After the cold war, U.S. involvement in Central America seemed to fall off sharply, with U.S. aid to the region even falling below European and Japanese levels. Upon closer examination, however, U.S. influence remained substantial, and there was also less of a sea change in U.S. policy objectives than might appear.

The social forces that contended in armed conflict in the region had to adjust in the 1990s to a new political framework of formally equal electoral competition, set against a backdrop of personal insecurity, widespread poverty, and growing inequality that tended to undermine the substantive content of citizenship rights. In that new political context, the legacy of the revolutionary era was not just in the political parties that succeeded guerrilla organizations, but perhaps more importantly in the ideological and organizational transformations that had occurred throughout civil society. Extra-regional states would continue to play major roles in post-conflict reconstruction. However, the bulk of financial leverage had passed to the international financial institutions overseeing neoliberal structural adjustment programs. The nature of Central America's ongoing transition would depend on the struggle to democratize civil society and to challenge the technocratic vision of "modernization of the state" that excluded popular participation.

The orthodox "transition to democracy" perspective would predict that the repetition of competitive elections and the development of civic culture will be mutually reinforcing, leading to the consolidation of democracy in Central America. From this perspective, external actors will reduce their supportive roles as the problem of democratization recedes. From an alternative, critical perspective, those mobilized in the revolutionary process will resist efforts to demobilize them in the name of governability and neoliberal efficiency. The resulting struggles—involving domestic politics, but also interacting with transnational structures of capital, international institutions, and external states—will define the region's political dynamics. In this view, democratization will only advance as a continuation of the demands unleashed by the revolutionary movements of the last decade, to expand the scope for participation from below in the construction of a more just society.

Notes

1. Dora María Téllez lecture at Pitzer College, Claremont, CA, November 12, 1992.

2. Jorge I. Domínguez, "Democratic Transitions in Central America and Panama," in Jorge I. Domínguez and Marc Lindenberg, eds., *Democratic Transitions in Central America* (Gainesville: University Press of Florida, 1997), 1–31;

Laurence Whitehead, "Pacification and Reconstruction in Central America: The International Components," in Rachel Sieder, ed., *Central America: Fragile Transition* (New York: St. Martin's, 1996).

3. William I. Robinson, *Promoting Polyarchy: Globalization, U.S. Intervention, and Hegemony* (Cambridge: Cambridge University Press, 1996); "(Mal)Development in Central America: Globalization and Social Change," *Development and Change* 29, no. 3 (July 1998): 467–97.

4. For discussion of these dilemmas, see Guillermo O'Donnell, "Transitions, Continuities, and Paradoxes," in Scott Mainwaring, Guillermo O'Donnell, and J. Samuel Valenzuela, eds., *Issues in Democratic Consolidation: The New South American Democracies in Comparative Perspective* (South Bend, IN: University of Notre Dame Press, 1992), 17–56; Terry Karl, "Dilemmas of Democratization in Latin America," *Comparative Politics* 23, no. 1 (October 1990): 1–21; Adam Przeworski, ed., *Sustainable Democracy* (Oxford: Oxford University Press, 1995).

5. See Edelberto Torres-Rivas, "Authoritarian Transition to Democracy in Central America," in Jan Flora and Edelberto Torres-Rivas, eds., *Sociology of Developing Societies: Central America* (New York: Monthly Review, 1989), 193–209; John A. Booth, "Elections and Democracy in Central America: A Framework for Analysis," in Mitchell A. Seligson and John A. Booth, eds., *Elections and Democracy in Central America, Revisited* (Chapel Hill: University of North Carolina Press, 1995); Terry Karl, "The Hybrid Regimes of Central America," *Journal of Democracy* 6, no. 3 (July 1995):72–86; William A. Barnes, "Incomplete Democracy in Central America: Polarization and Voter Turnout in Nicaragua and El Salvador," *Journal of Interamerican Studies and World Affairs* 40, no. 3 (Fall 1998): 63–101.

6. Susanne Jonas, "Electoral Problems and the Democratic Project in Guatemala," in Seligson and Booth, *Elections and Democracy*, 25–44; Carlos M. Vilas, "Participation, Inequality, and the Whereabouts of Democracy," in Douglas A. Chalmers et al., eds., *The New Politics of Inequality in Latin America: Rethinking Participation and Representation* (New York: Oxford University Press, 1997), 3–42. This understanding of democratic consolidation as a conflictual process of "deepening democracy" beyond its minimal electoral-liberal components is not shared by those transitologists who object that it is open-ended and hard to measure; see Andreas Schedler, "What Is Democratic Consolidation?" *Journal of Democracy* 9, no. 2 (April 1998): 91–107.

7. Carlos M. Vilas, "Prospects for Democratization in a Post-Revolutionary Setting: Central America," *Journal of Latin American Studies* 28, no. 2 (May 1996): 461–503.

8. John H. Coatsworth, *Central America and the United States: The Clients and the Colossus* (New York: Twayne, 1994).

9. Data supplied by USAID (San Salvador and Managua: July 9 and 16, 1998). See also William M. LeoGrande, "Central America's Agony," *The Nation,* January 25, 1999, 21–24.

10. James Dunkerley, *The Pacification of Central America: Political Change in the Isthmus, 1987–1993* (New York: Verso, 1994), 145.

11. Tom Barry and Deb Preusch, *The Soft War: Uses and Abuses of U.S. Economic Aid in Central America* (New York: Grove, 1988).

12. Manuel Orozco, "Aiding Central America: The Three Contexts of Aid," *Revista Relaciones Internacionales* (Universidad Nacional Heredia, Costa Rica), nos. 51–53 (2d–4th trimester, 1995): 47– 61.

13. William M. LeoGrande, *Our Own Backyard: The United States in Central America, 1977–1992* (Chapel Hill: University of North Carolina Press, 1998).

14. William I. Robinson, *A Faustian Bargain: U.S. Intervention in the Nicaraguan Elections and American Foreign Policy in the Post–Cold War Era* (Boulder, CO: Westview, 1992).

15. Kevin Whitaker, political counselor, U.S. embassy, interview by author, Managua, July 16, 1998.

16. Philip J. Williams and Knut Walter, *Militarization and Democratization in El Salvador's Transition to Democracy* (Pittsburgh: University of Pittsburgh Press, 1997), 141–53.

17. Stephen Grant, USAID, interview by author, San Salvador, July 9, 1998. See Comisión Nacional de Desarrollo, "Bases para el Plan de Nación" (San Salvador, January 16, 1998). The document proposes themes for a national dialogue on politics, education and culture, socioeconomic issues, citizen participation, and state institutions.

18. Susanne Jonas, "Dangerous Liaisons: The U.S. in Guatemala," *Foreign Policy* 103 (Summer 1996): 144–60.

19. Gen. Julio Balconi, former minister of defense, interview by author, Guatemala, July 7, 1998.

20. James Benson, deputy political counselor, U.S. embassy, interview by author, Guatemala, July 6, 1998. See also Jack Spence et al., "Promise and Reality: Implementation of the Guatemalan Peace Accords" (Cambridge, MA: Hemisphere Initiatives, August 1998).

21. Cynthia J. Arnson and Johanna Mendelson Forman, "Projecting Democracy in Central America: Old Wine, New Bottles," in Louis W. Goodman et al., eds., *Political Parties and Democracy in Central America* (Boulder, CO: Westview Press, 1992), 237–66.

22. Terry Karl, "Imposing Consent: Electoralism versus Democracy in El Salvador," in Paul W. Drake and Eduardo Silva, eds., *Elections and Democratization in Latin America, 1980–1985* (San Diego: UCSD, 1986); Philip J. Williams, "Dual Transitions from Authoritarian Rule: Popular and Electoral Democracy in Nicaragua," *Comparative Politics* 26, no. 2 (January 1994): 169–85.

23. Carmen Rosa DeLeón, executive director, Instituto de Enseñanza para el Desarrollo Sostenible-IEPADES, interview by author, Guatemala, July 3, 1998; Edmond Mulet, secretary-general, Unión del Centro Nacional-UCN, interview by author, Guatemala, July 6, 1998. See also Edelberto Torres-Rivas, ed., *Guatemala, izquierdas en transición* (Guatemala: FLACSO, 1997).

24. Alejandro Bendaña, director, Centro de Estudios Internacionales-CEI, interview by author, Managua, July 18, 1998.

25. Hemisphere Initiatives/Washington Office on Latin America, "Democracy Weakened? A Report on the October 20, 1996 Nicaraguan Elections" (Cambridge, MA, November 22, 1997), 14.

26. William D. Stanley, *The Protection Racket State: Elite Politics, Military Extortion, and Civil War in El Salvador* (Philadelphia: Temple University Press, 1996).

27. Adam Isacson and Joy Olson, *Just the Facts: A Civilian's Guide to U.S. Defense and Security Assistance to Latin America and the Caribbean* (Washington, DC: Latin America Working Group, 1998).

28. Alexandria Panehal, chief, Office of Democratic Initiatives, USAID, interview by author, Managua, July 16, 1998.

29. Washington Office on Latin America, "Demilitarizing Public Order: The International Community, Police Reform and Human Rights in Central America and Haiti" (Washington, DC, November 1995).

30. Gregory Sprow, political counselor, U.S. embassy, interview by author, San Salvador, July 9, 1998.

31. Jack Spence et al., "Chapúltepec: Five Years Later—El Salvador's Political Reality and Uncertain Future" (Cambridge, MA: Hemisphere Initiatives, January 16, 1997), 10, 16–20.

32. David R. Dye et al., "Contesting Everything, Winning Nothing: The Search for Consensus in Nicaragua, 1990–1995" (Cambridge, MA: Hemisphere Initiatives, November 1995), 39–40.

33. Gino Costa, "The United Nations and Reform of the Police in El Salvador," *International Peacekeeping* 2, no. 3 (Autumn 1995): 365–90.

34. Roger Carignan, acting economic counselor, U.S. embassy, interview by author, Guatemala, July 6, 1998.

35. Benson, interview.

36. Tim Golden, "CIA Says It Knew of Honduran Abuses," *New York Times*, October 24, 1998.

37. Héctor Dada, director, FLACSO, interview by author, San Salvador: July 13, 1998.

38. See SOA Watch, http://www.soaw.org/manuals/; Latin America Working Group, http://www.igc.apc.org/lawg/soafull.html (accessed March 22, 2000).

39. Isacson and Olson, *Just the Facts*, 29–31.

40. Dye et al., "Contesting Everything," 32–42.

41. Spence et al., "Chapúltepec," 36–42.

42. Benson, interview.

43. Balconi, interview.

44. James K. Boyce, "External Resource Mobilization," in James K. Boyce, ed., *Economic Policy for Building Peace: The Lessons of El Salvador* (Boulder, CO: Lynne Rienner, 1996), 140–50; Herman Rosa and Michael W. Foley, "Pledges for Aid: Multilateral Donors and Support for Post-War Reconstruction and Systemic Transformation; El Salvador Draft Report" (New York: NYU Center on International Cooperation and SSRC, April 1998), 42–43.

45. Quoted in Rosa and Foley, "Pledges," 39.

46. Edgar Varela, executive officer, UNDP, interview by author, San Salvador, July 13, 1998.

47. Alexander Segovia, economist, MINUGUA, interview by author, Guatemala, July 7, 1998.

48. United Nations Development Program, *Guatemala: Los contrastes del desarrollo humano, 1998* (Guatemala: UNDP, 1998).

49. Dye et al., "Contesting Everything," 20–32.

50. Byron Hugo López, projects manager, Mayor's Office, interview by author, San Salvador, July 13, 1998; René Canjura, FMLN mayor, interview by author, Nejapa, July 12, 1998.

51. Whitaker, interview. By contrast, UNDP, European Union, and Japanese officials privately described the Alemán administration's corruption and blatantly political shake-ups in government ministries.

52. De León, interview.

53. Barry and Preusch, *Soft War*, 25.

54. Carlos Sojo, *La utopía del estado mínimo: Influencia de AID en Costa Rica en los años ochenta* (Managua: CRIES, 1991); Herman Rosa, *AID y las transformaciones globales en El Salvador* (Managua: CRIES, 1993); Jorge R. Escoto and Manfredo Marroquín, *La AID en Guatemala* (Managua: CRIES, 1992); Angel Saldomando, *El retorno de la AID: El caso de Nicaragua* (Managua: CRIES, 1992). For

further analysis of the recomposition of the capitalist class in the Nicaraguan case, see Rose J. Spalding, *Capitalists and Revolution in Nicaragua: Opposition and Accommodation, 1979–1993* (Chapel Hill: University of North Carolina Press, 1994).

55. Whitaker, interview.

56. Minor Sinclair, ed., *The New Politics of Survival: Grassroots Movements in Central America* (New York: Monthly Review, 1995).

57. Kevin Murray et al., "Rescuing Reconstruction: The Debate on Post-War Economic Recovery in El Salvador" (Cambridge, MA: Hemisphere Initiatives, May 1994); Michael W. Foley, "Laying the Groundwork: The Struggle for Civil Society in El Salvador," *Journal of Interamerican Studies and World Affairs* 31, no. 1 (Spring 1996): 74–81.

58. Deborah Kennedy-Iraheta, Office of Democratic Initiatives, USAID, interview by author, San Salvador, July 9, 1998.

59. Conversations by author with personnel on civic education project, Huehuetenango, July 4–5, 1998.

60. De León, interview.

61. UNDP, *Central America: Development in Peace and Democracy* (San José, Costa Rica: 1998).

62. Alvaro DeSoto and Graciana del Castillo, "Obstacles to Peacebuilding," *Foreign Policy* 94 (Spring 1994): 69–83.

63. European Union project officer, interview by author, Managua, July. 21, 1998; Jack McCarthy, USAID, interview by author, Guatemala, July 7, 1998; Varela, interview.

64. Jérome Veil, advisor, European Union, interview by author, Guatemala, July 7, 1998; Herman Rosa and Jorge Peña, "El Banco Mundial, el BID y la reforma económica en Centroamérica," PRISMA (San Salvador) (November–December 1995).

65. Michael E. Conroy, Douglas L. Murray, and Peter M. Rosset, *A Cautionary Tale: Failed U.S. Development Policy in Central America* (Boulder, CO: Lynne Rienner, 1996).

66. Sinclair, *New Politics*; Susanne Jonas, "Guatemala's Peace Accords: An End and a Beginning," *NACLA Report on the Americas* (May–June 1997); Richard Stahler-Sholk, "Structural Adjustment and Resistance: The Political Economy of Nicaragua under Chamorro," in Gary Prevost and Harry E. Vanden, eds., *The Undermining of the Sandinista Revolution* (New York: St. Martin's, 1997).

67. Manuel Orozco, Rodolfo de la Garza, and Miguel Baraona, "Inmigración y remesas familiares," *Cuaderno de Ciencias Sociales* (FLASCO, San José, Costa Rica) 98 (March 1997): 55.

68. Thanks to Rose Spalding for suggesting this classification.

69. Rosa and Foley, "Pledges," 26–31.

70. Minoru Arimoto, Japan International Cooperation Agency, interview by author, Managua, July 17, 1998.

71. Thomas Carothers and Juan Alberto Fuentes, "La cooperación internacional en Guatemala," consultancy report for Institute for Democracy and Electoral Assistance, Sweden (Guatemala, June 1998), 4.

72. Rosa and Foley, "Pledges," 31–37.

73. Arimoto, interview; Bendaña, interview.

74. Jack Child, *The Central American Peace Process, 1983–1991* (Boulder, CO: Lynne Rienner, 1992).

75. Joaquín Roy, ed., *The Reconstruction of Central America: The Role of the European Community* (Miami: North-South Center, 1992).

76. Finn Hansen, "La cooperación de la Unión Europea hacia Centroamérica: Tendencias ante el nuevo milenio," *Pensamiento Propio* (Managua), no. 25 (September–December 1997): 6.

77. Veil, interview.

78. Hansen, "La cooperación," 10–12; René Escoto, Project Officer, European Union, interview by author, Managua, July 21, 1998. By the end of 1997, only $329 million had been disbursed to Guatemala of the $2.473 billion promised for 1997–2000 at the January 1997 Consultative Group meeting in Brussels; Carothers and Fuentes, "La cooperación," 2–4.

79. Kees Biekart, "La cooperación no-gubernamental europea hacia Centroamérica: La experiencia de los ochenta y las tendencias en los noventa," PRISMA (San Salvador), (November 1994): 16–19.

80. Escoto, interview.

81. European Union, "La Unión Europea: Diálogo con América Central y Panamá" (San José, Costa Rica, 1997), 2.

82. Finn Hansen, *Relaciones Europa-Centroamérica: Ayuda externa y comercio desfavorable* (Managua: CRIES, 1996), 4.

83. Manuel Montobbio, chargé d'affaires, Spanish embassy, interview by author, Guatemala, July 2, 1998.

84. Joaquín María de Arístegui, interim chargé d'affaires, Spanish embassy, interview by author, San Salvador, July 13, 1998.

85. Montobbio, interview.

86. Carothers and Fuentes, "La cooperación," 4.

87. Ariel C. Armony, *Argentina, the United States, and the Anti-Communist Crusade in Central America, 1977–1984* (Athens: Ohio University Press, 1997).

88. Wayne S. Smith, "The Soviet Union and Cuba in Central America: Guardians against Democracy?" in Goodman et al., *Political Parties*, 287–306.

89. Harry E. Vanden, "Foreign Policy," in Thomas W. Walker, ed., *Revolution and Counterrevolution in Nicaragua* (Boulder, CO: Westview Press, 1991), 312.

90. Julio Carranza, "New Challenges for Cuban Policy toward Central America," *Latin American Perspectives* 20, no. 1 (Winter 1993).

91. Terry Karl, "Mexico, Venezuela, and the Contadora Initiative," in Morris J. Blachman et al., eds., *Confronting Revolution: Security through Diplomacy in Central America* (New York: Pantheon, 1986).

92. Rosa and Foley, "Pledges," 30; Carothers and Fuentes, "La cooperación," 2.

93. For some contributions to the reassessment of the legacy of Central America's revolutionary era, see the special issue of *Latin American Perspectives* 26, no. 2 (March 1999).

8

External Actors
The United Nations and
the Organization of American States

*Jack Child**

The balance sheet on the role of the United Nations and the Organization of American States (OAS) in the Central American peace process is a positive one. It would be hard to imagine the relative peace Central America has come to experience without the contribution of these two international organizations. All wars and conflicts eventually end, but without the UN and the OAS, peace might have been pushed far into the future with potentially disastrous impact on the lives of hundreds of thousands of Central Americans.

The UN and OAS involvement in the Central American peace process changed the approach of these two organizations to the various facets of conflict resolution. Instead of the previous simple and easily definable categories of "peacekeeping," "peacemaking," and "peace building" (see the definitions contained in Figures 1 and 2), theoreticians and practitioners of conflict resolution now speak of "multifaceted" or "multidisciplinary" approaches.

The basic contribution of these two international organizations was to provide effective and credible third-party neutral verifiers and guarantors of the Esquipulas peace agreement signed by the Central American nations. Their intervention came at a time when a convergence of several factors was leading the major players in the conflict to actively seek a peaceful solution.

*The author would like to express appreciation to the U.S. Institute of Peace for support of earlier research on this subject, and to three friends and colleagues: Tom Walker for this project, and for his leadership in organizing the unforgettable LASA trips to Nicaragua; and Tommie Sue Montgomery and Tricia Juhn for sharing advance copies of manuscripts.

The success of the Esquipulas process, aided by the UN and the OAS, stands in contrast to the frustrated and even failed efforts of the Contadora process that preceded it. The Contadora nations (Mexico, Colombia, Venezuela, and Panama) were not perceived as being effective or credible by many of the parties involved in the conflict. The Reagan administration, in particular, mistrusted their efforts and would not permit the Contadora process to proceed. Indeed, the United States government believed that a military victory was still possible.

But with the ending of the cold war and the advent of the more pragmatic administration of George Bush, U.S. attitudes toward a peaceful outcome softened. Close collaboration between the secretaries-general of the UN and the OAS, and the efforts of nations such as Canada and Spain, coupled with a general war-weariness in Central America, led the principal players in the conflict to understand that the best chance for regional peace in a decade had arrived with the signing of the Esquipulas agreement between the Central American nations themselves in 1987. A key element in this realization was the belief that the United Nations and the OAS could adequately verify the agreements and gain the trust and confidence of warring parties, which had very little trust and confidence in each other.

For the UN the involvement included components of the usual permanent offices of various of its agencies that normally are represented in Central America, such as the UN Development Program (UNDP), the UN High Commissioner for Refugees (UNHCR), the UN Economic, Social, and Cultural Organization (UNESCO), and the United Nations Children's Fund (UNICEF). But the major UN involvement was anything but routine. It began with the UN Observer Group in Central America (Misión de Observadores de las Naciones Unidas en Centroamérica, ONUCA), which, though present in the five core countries, had its most significant operations in Nicaragua. The UN was also involved in Honduras in persuading the "Contras" to return to Nicaragua, at which point their resettlement became the responsibility of the OAS. The UN Nicaraguan involvement included observation of the key 1990 presidential election through the United Nations Observer Mission to Verify Elections in Nicaragua (Misión de Observadores de las Naciones Unidas en Verificación de Elecciones en Nicaragua, ONUVEN). When ONUCA was phased out, many of its personnel and much of its equipment were used to create the second major peacekeeping verification effort, United Nations Observer Mission in El Salvador (Misión de Observadores de las Naciones Unidas en El Salvador, ONUSAL). Finally, when the peace process moved ahead in Guatemala, the UN was also present in the form of the United Nations Mission in Guatemala (Misión de las Naciones Unidas en Guatemala, MINUGUA). Taken collectively, this UN involvement was a major unprecedented and sustained effort to create, keep, and build the peace in this troubled region. Apart from the contribution made to the welfare (and indeed survival) of countless Central Americans, the effort also changed the nature of UN peacekeeping and the attitude of various nations toward the organization.

OAS involvement in Central America was also unprecedented and significant, even though it did not have the scope and impact of UN involvement. Historically, OAS peacekeeping efforts had been relatively small and dominated by the United States, which usually provided most of the funding and controlled the key logistical effort, including transportation, communications, and management. The only prior major OAS peacekeeping effort had been the 1965 Inter-American Peace Force in the Dominican Republic, widely seen as a thin multinational fig leaf for a unilateral U.S. initiative.

In Central America in the late 1980s and early 1990s the OAS operated with much greater independence from the United States, even though it was U.S. money that financed many of the OAS efforts, especially the Contra resettlement and aid program known as the International Support and Verification Commission (Comisión Internacional de Apoyo y Verificación, CIAV-OAS). The OAS was also involved in monitoring the key 1990 election and in assisting the peaceful transition through its Unit for the Promotion of Democracy (Unidad para la Promoción de la Democracia, UPD). Later the UPD collaborated in a Central American demining effort with a frequently ignored entity of the OAS, the Inter-American Defense Board (IADB).

The major UN (and to lesser extent, OAS) involvement in the Central American peace process also brought in actors that previously had been little involved in Latin American development and conflict resolution, most notably Canada and Spain, both of which participated in ONUCA and ONUSAL in a major way. For other nations, such as Venezuela and Argentina, the UN peacekeeping effort was their first large-scale venture in this area, and for the latter country it was part of a process of institutional and national rehabilitation after the terrible years of the "dirty war."

For the United States government, the UN and OAS involvement in Central America represented a perceived threat to national interests during the Reagan administration. With the shift to a more pragmatic Bush administration, and some nudging from Congress and public opinion, there emerged a grudging recognition that this UN and OAS involvement, coupled with the demise of the Soviet Union and the end of the cold war, might represent the best possible endgame for the years of deepening immersion in the Central American conflict. A key issue for the United States was the verification of the various peace proposals. During the Reagan years the verification issue was manipulated to stall the peace process using the argument that the other side would find ways to cheat unless impossibly strict verification procedures were employed. When, with the help of the Canadians, the UN was able to mount a credible and reasonable verification instrument in ONUCA, the Bush administration was grateful for the contribution and supported the UN. The U.S. relationship with the OAS, described below, was curious and unprecedented: the United States funded the Contra resettlement and support effort using an ad hoc OAS instrument, the CIAV-OAS, which was sometimes caught between the wishes of its chief funder and its bureaucratic masters in the OAS.

The experiences of the UN and the OAS in Central America in these years modified previous approaches to peacekeeping and peacemaking. The traditional notion of peacekeeping as a third-party neutral interposition between two nation-state adversaries gave way to a more complex and challenging notion of a multifaceted effort involving traditional peacekeeping, but also the resettlement of combatants, the verification of elections, the investigation of human rights violations, and the building of trust between former adversaries.[1]

The Central American peace process, and the involvement of these two international organizations, also introduced a series of approaches to conflict resolution that previously had been little known in the area. These included the notion of creating "zones of peace" and of using confidence-building measures (to include better communications between potential adversaries and respect for human rights) to make conflict less likely. Ultimately, there was hope that Central America would some day look more like Costa Rica and less like the Guatemala of the 1980s, a process that would mean new definitions of national defense in which the military would have a much reduced role in internal security, would give up its historic control of police forces, and would accept reductions in size and budgets.

The Creation of ONUCA

The UN Security Council formally created ONUCA when it approved Resolution 644 of November 7, 1989.[2] ONUCA's original mandate (which was later expanded) was to verify the cessation of aid to irregular forces and insurrectional movements and verify the nonutilization of any state's territory to commit aggression against another state. ONUCA's initial mandate, composition, and operational concept reflected the UN reluctance to get involved in internal conflicts.[3] It was to be a verification and peace-observing mission, not a full-scale peacekeeping interposition mission, and certainly not peace enforcement. However, as events unfolded, there were brief periods when Contra reluctance to disband threatened to convert ONUCA's role to one of enforcement. The scope of the operation was briefly moved up the conflict resolution spectrum (see Figure 1) from peace verification to peacekeeping for the period of Contra demobilization, but the UN continued to define ONUCA's mission as one of verification.

ONUCA's deployment began with the December 1989 arrival of the advance party in Tegucigalpa and the setting up of a provisional headquarters, under very crowded conditions, in the offices of the UN Development Program (UNDP) in Honduras.[4] For different reasons, ONUCA's operations in El Salvador, Guatemala, and Costa Rica were slower to start up and were of a lesser magnitude than those in Nicaragua and Honduras, where the Contra demobilization operation would take place.

Figure 1. A Conflict Resolution Spectrum

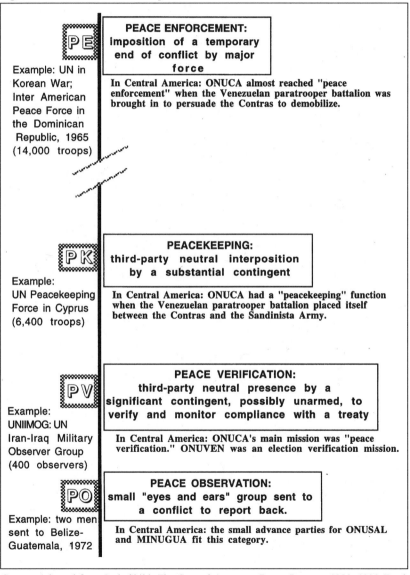

Source: Adapted from Jack Child, *The Central American Peace Process, 1983–1991* (Boulder, CO: Lynne Rienner, 1992), fig. 1.1.

Figure 2. Addressing the Basic Causes of Conflict

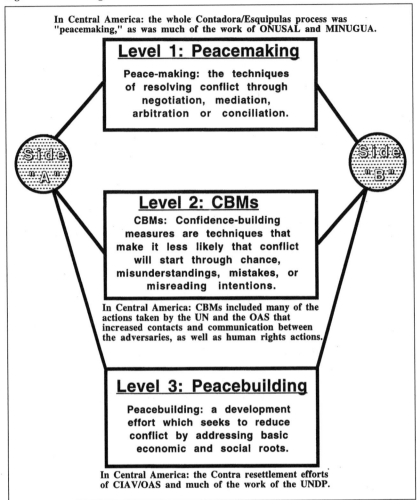

In Central America: the whole Contadora/Esquipulas process was "peacemaking," as was much of the work of ONUSAL and MINUGUA.

Level 1: Peacemaking

Peace-making: the techniques of resolving conflict through negotiation, mediation, arbitration or conciliation.

Side "A"

Side "B"

Level 2: CBMs

CBMs: Confidence-building measures are techniques that make it less likely that conflict will start through chance, misunderstandings, mistakes, or misreading intentions.

In Central America: CBMs included many of the actions taken by the UN and the OAS that increased contacts and communication between the adversaries, as well as human rights actions.

Level 3: Peacebuilding

Peacebuilding: a development effort which seeks to reduce conflict by addressing basic economic and social roots.

In Central America: the Contra resettlement efforts of CIAV/OAS and much of the work of the UNDP.

Source: Adapted from Jack Child, *The Central American Peace Process, 1983–1991* (Boulder, CO: Lynne Rienner, 1992), fig. 1.2.

Contra Demobilization and the Expansion of ONUCA's Mandate

In the weeks after the February 1990 Nicaraguan election there developed an armed standoff between the Sandinistas, weakened by their electoral loss and the numerous desertions from the Sandinista People's Army (Ejécito Popular Sandinista, EPS), and the Contras in Honduras and Nicaragua, who were also weakened by the diminishing support from the United States and widespread pressure to demobilize and return to peaceful pursuits in Nicaragua.

The effort to demobilize the Contras was initially undermined by the fact that 260 unarmed UN observers could not force the Contras to do anything. Accordingly, setting aside its historical aversion to peace enforcement, the UN Security Council decided to expand ONUCA's mandate by temporarily giving it combat power in the form of a battalion of paratroopers. Venezuela, which was already providing observers to ONUCA, volunteered this battalion. Although the secretary-general's report did not say that the demobilization would be forced, there was a clear implication that adding armed paratroopers to the unarmed UN military observers would send a powerful message to the reluctant Contras.

CIAV, ONUCA, and the Initial Repatriation of the Contras

CIAV was created as a joint approach to repatriating the Contras by the secretaries-general of the UN and the OAS on August 25, 1989, in support of the Esquipulas II Peace Plan. Its mandate was to assist in the voluntary demobilization, repatriation, or resettlement of the Nicaraguan Resistance (the Contras) in Nicaragua and third countries as well as assistance in the voluntary demobilization of all persons involved in armed actions in all countries of the region. In practice the UN involvement in CIAV was relatively short (from late 1989 through mid 1990), while the OAS participated in CIAV from the beginning and was deeply involved until 1993. In part this situation was due to the UN's emphasis on ONUCA, but it also reflected a geographic division of labor: the UN was assigned repatriation responsibilities in Honduras (where it was active only in late 1989 and early 1990), Costa Rica (where there were few Contras), and El Salvador (where there were practically none, and where the Farabundo Martí Front for National Liberation [Frente Farabundo Martí de Liberación Nacional, FMLN] was having no part in any "voluntary repatriation"). CIAV-OAS, in contrast, was assigned geographic responsibilities for Nicaragua, which meant that they were responsible for every Contra and Contra family member who crossed the border into Nicaragua and continued to be responsible for the support of most of them through 1993.

Monitoring the February 1990 Nicaraguan Elections: ONUVEN

In mid March 1989 Nicaraguan foreign minister Miguel D'Escoto asked the UN to provide observers to monitor the February 1990 elections.[5] The decision to create ONUVEN followed a study by a joint UN-OAS commission that concluded that Nicaragua's plans for the elections were basically democratic and within acceptable norms.

The February 1990 Nicaraguan elections were without a doubt the most closely observed in Latin American history. There were over 2,000 election observers, including OAS Secretary-General João Baena Soares of the OAS with 430 personnel, Elliot Richardson of ONUVEN with some 240 observers from 50 different countries, and numerous other private groups, such as those led by former president Jimmy Carter and a delegation from the Latin American Studies Association.

Assessments of ONUVEN's work have been almost unanimously positive, with laudatory comments on the observers' dedication, professionalism, and neutrality. Some friction was noted between ONUVEN, which had a short-term political mission, and existing UN entities already in Nicaragua (such as the UNDP and UNICEF), which were there for the long haul, staffed by traditional international bureaucrats, and whose institutional existence depended on not getting involved in politics. At times it seemed that the sheer numbers of observers from such a disparate set of organizations was about to overwhelm Nicaragua, and indeed the lack of coordination between the different observer groups was a problem. There was also a parallel to the ONUCA-CIAV situation, where the Sandinistas trusted the UN entity far more than they did the OAS one.[6]

ONUCA and CIAV after the Contra Demobilization

With the demobilization of the Contras completed in early July, both ONUCA and CIAV substantially changed their roles, budgets, and significance. The Venezuelan Battalion went home and the ONUCA mandate reverted to the original rather limited one of watching for violations of the Esquipulas prohibition on cross-border support of irregular forces. CIAV, however, now assumed full responsibility for supporting the former Contras in Nicaragua, as well as those (mainly dependents and the sick and wounded) who remained in Honduras. Under the geographic division of responsibility, the Honduras operation of CIAV belonged to the UN side, while that in Nicaragua was under the OAS. CIAV-UN in practice was handled by an existing UN organization, the UN High Commissioner for Refugees (UNHCR), and concentrated on repatriating the Nicaraguans out of Honduras, much to the relief of the Hondurans themselves. Because CIAV's basic mandate was to help former Contras and their families, practically anything they did inevitably got them involved in postelection Nicaraguan politics. CIAV-OAS soon found itself in a politically very difficult situation. On one hand, if they did their job poorly and failed to support the former Contras, they would be criticized by the Contras, by their OAS superiors in Washington, and by the U.S. government, which was financing the whole Contra support operation. On the other hand, if they did their job well and effectively helped the Contras, they would be criticized by the Sandinistas for going too far in keeping the Contras together, and possibly for even stimulating them to take up their arms again. While ONUCA's profile was being lowered and its personnel focused on the border areas, ONUCA could bask in the general goodwill stemming from the demobilization process that was completed in mid 1990. But at the same time, fairly or unfairly, CIAV-OAS was blamed for contributing to the unrest that characterized Nicaraguan politics from that point on.[7]

In contrast to CIAV, ONUCA was held in almost universally high regard by the Central Americans who knew of it or worked with it, an indication of its ability to stay above partisan politics. Extensive discussions with a broad range of Nicaraguans in mid 1991 confirmed this high regard for ONUCA, with no significant criticisms except for minor complaints by some former Contras (who felt ONUCA could do more for them, as CIAV was attempting), and by a few frustrated CIAV officials, who felt they were being blamed unfairly for some of ONUCA's problems. Some of the minor criticisms leveled at ONUCA inside Nicaragua were the usual ones heard in poor developing nations that resent international civil servants accustomed to a standard of living well above the norm in the host nation.

ONUCA was officially closed down on January 17, 1992, with most of the remaining 131 military observers transferred to ONUSAL the following week. A small residual staff stayed behind to clear up remaining ONUCA business over the next three months. In its two-plus years of operation ONUCA cost the United Nations $88,573,157. Its initial authorization of 260 military observers, air and naval crews, and support staff was augmented by the Venezuelan paratrooper battalion for a few months to reach the peak of 1,098 military personnel in mid 1990. Commanders included two Spanish and one Canadian general, and military personnel from ten nations, including Argentina, Brazil, Canada, Colombia, Ecuador, Spain, and Venezuela.[8]

As Jennie Lincoln and César Sereseres have noted,[9] the relations between CIAV-OAS and OAS Headquarters in Washington (especially the office of Secretary-General Baena Soares) were sometimes strained. The key people in CIAV were not traditional diplomats or international organization staffers, and they often acted in ways that were unorthodox and even audacious. Since their funding was assured by the U.S. government, they felt some independence from normal OAS constraints. This permitted them considerable latitude, even though at times they felt that OAS Headquarters was giving them the cold shoulder.

The CIAV observers were an unusual group, mainly academics, professionals, and government functionaries with few ties to the OAS itself. They were originally recruited for short-term contracts as brief as two or three months, but many of them remained in Nicaragua for periods of up to three years. Under the leadership of Santiago Murray, they did not hesitate to get aggressively involved in potentially risky situations involving confrontations between former Contras, former (and current) Sandinista security personnel, and government representatives. Their improvisation, enthusiasm, and esprit de corps—unusual in an international verification mission—gave their actions a distinctive tone. In the countryside they frequently found themselves mediating a wide range of situations involving land ownership, human rights violations, and assorted violent or disruptive actions by an impressive array of players. Lincoln and Sereseres conclude that for a time they were the "principal source of justice outside Managua."[10]

One unfortunate by-product of the conflict in Central America was the land mine. Contrary to the doctrine espoused (at least theoretically) by the military in First and Second World nations, the minefields of Central America were generally unmarked and unrecorded on maps. Once placed, mines remain active for years, waiting the pressure of an unwary foot to detonate. With an estimated one hundred thousand land mines in Central America, mainly in Nicaragua,[11] the need to locate and remove or deactivate them caused grave concern as the war began to wind down. In August 1991, Nicaragua asked the OAS for assistance, and the secretary-general forwarded the request to the IADB, which sent a group of staff officers to Nicaragua to assess the situation. A Demining Plan was developed under which the IADB, working with U.S. technical experts, would supervise the training of teams of Nicaraguan demining personnel. The Nicaraguan program operated for six months in 1993 before being suspended because of funding limitations (it was reinitiated in 1996). In those first six months the teams destroyed almost three thousand mines. Subsequently, demining operations were launched in Costa Rica and Honduras, with a pending operation in Guatemala. The primary responsibility for the program lay with the OAS Unit for the Promotion of Democracy, with the IADB providing technical support and planning assistance. The goal was to make Central America a mine-free area by 2000.[12]

The UN and the OAS in El Salvador

UN involvement in El Salvador in the late 1980s and 1990s was a complex, unprecedented, and generally successful venture in which an extraordinary set of conditions permitted a well-organized and effective international organization mission to show what peacekeeping, peace building, and confidence building could do at its best.[13] As Joaquín Villalobos, one of the key FMLN leaders, put it: "Without the United Nations, there would have been no peace process, and perhaps not even any negotiations. They managed to move both sides together, build trust between us and reach an agreement that was complex. And, because of their credibility, they were able to carry out the verification."[14]

The UN experience in El Salvador includes a series of "firsts":[15] the first time a UN peacekeeping mission was deployed before a cease-fire was in place, the first time human rights verification was included as a key element in peacekeeping, the first mission of its type headed by a civilian, the first mission in which intrusive peace-building components have so dramatically predominated, the first mission in which the UN was so actively involved in the resolution of an internal conflict from start to finish, and the first mission in which national reconciliation was such a major goal. In short, it was a truly multifaceted, multidisciplinary, and multifunctional mission.

In part the process involved mediating and negotiating the end to a long civil war, followed by verification of the peace accords. But it ultimately also came to include the setting up and verification of key elections, the promotion and protection of a fledgling democracy, establishment of a human rights verification system, restructuring of the armed forces and police, reform of the judicial system, constitutional reform, and fundamental economic and social issues such as land redistribution.

From the beginning, human rights concerns dominated ONUSAL. The first agreement was on human rights, as was the first ONUSAL presence in-country. And the enduring legacies of the Commission on the Truth and the Human Rights Ombudsman (Procuraduría General de los Derechos Humanos, PDH) will be felt for years to come.

Basically, the process worked because the two main parties, the government of El Salvador and the guerrillas of the FMLN, wanted it to work. The nation was war-weary and desperate to find an exit from the military stalemate. Other significant factors were the success of the UN and OAS efforts in Nicaragua, the end of the cold war and the eagerness of both the United States and the fast-disappearing Soviet Union to bring the conflict to closure. The UN was both lucky and able: lucky in the sense that circumstances were very favorable for its intervention, and able in that a determined Secretary-General Javier Pérez de Cuéllar (and two key assistants, Alvaro de Soto and Marrack Goulding) and a competent staff quickly grasped opportunities. In so doing they often exceeded their mandates but made the complex negotiations and verification and nation-building work to the point that El Salvador may eventually be judged the high point of UN involvement in conflict resolution, to include assisting a damaged nation to recover from a devastating and lengthy conflict.

David Holiday and William Stanley have correctly noted that the UN was in an unusually strong position in El Salvador,[16] having been involved from the beginning and having given itself strong authority to verify and mediate the peace process through the Salvadoran agreements and subsequent UN mandates. It had drafted many sections of the major agreements and knew how to interpret the language to its benefit. Further, it was backed up by an influential group of "Friends of El Salvador," including the United States, whose attempt to seek a military solution in El Salvador was fast waning in the early 1990s. The OAS, it should be noted, however, played a very marginal role in the El Salvador peace process. With no counterpart to the Nicaraguan CIAV-OAS, the OAS was limited to assisting the UN effort in relatively minor ways, and in election monitoring, especially during the 1991 legislative elections.[17]

The situation in El Salvador in 1991 was characterized by a continuing civil war and hopes for peace that culminated in intense UN-sponsored talks. These talks achieved a cease-fire agreement in the dramatic New Year's Eve Act of New York, which set up a new major UN verification and observation mission. In early 1991 there were more talks between the FMLN and the government of El Salvador. From the first stage of talks both sides had expressed an interest in having the UN (but not the OAS) involved in verifying any agreements reached. The Nicaraguan experience with ONUCA was seen as positive by almost all parties, although the FMLN was more enthusiastic about the possibility than the government, and the Far Right remained firmly opposed to UN involvement.

In late December the UN secretary-general announced that the Security Council had authorized the creation of ONUSAL, whose mission would be to supervise the accords signed between the FMLN and the Salvadoran government. Although their first task would focus on verifying respect for human rights, this would not happen until it became clear to what extent the group could function in El Salvador, especially since a cease-fire had not been agreed on. Thus, the deployment of ONUSAL was delayed until mid 1991. In the meantime, preparations were being made, including alerting ONUCA personnel that they might be detached to become the advance party of ONUSAL, as was the custom in creating new UN peacekeeping and peace-observing missions. The basic plan was to follow the successful Nicaraguan experience, first sending a small peace-observing group with a limited mandate (observing human rights and elections) that could be expanded later if warranted.

ONUSAL was formally opened in San Salvador on July 26, 1991, when Iqbal Riza signed the implementing protocol with the Salvadoran foreign minister and replaced the small preparatory office with the initial ONUSAL complement of personnel. Riza pointed out that ONUSAL's work would be in two stages. In the first two months the observer team would study El Salvador's judicial and administrative system and meet representatives from all the parties involved in the conflict. After this preliminary process, the second stage would begin, when ONUSAL would be available to receive and investigate accusations of human rights violations. Riza noted that ONUSAL was unprecedented for the UN because it had never before authorized such a mission prior to the signing of a cease-fire.[18] The unprecedented arrangement was a calculated gamble for the UN, and especially the secretary-general. It was an open secret that Pérez de Cuéllar badly wanted a signed agreement and a ceasefire between the FMLN and the Cristiani government before he stepped down as UN secretary-general at the end of 1991.

With increasing pressure from the UN, a new round of talks in September 1991 produced the New York Agreement, which established the general framework for conditions and guarantees under which the guerrillas would lay down their weapons and become integrated into the political and economic life of a post–civil war El Salvador. It also laid out the general steps for the "purging," reorganization, and reduction of the armed forces.[19] The agreement would be administered by a new National Commission for the Consolidation of Peace (Comisión de la Paz, COPAZ), which would have the support of outside parties in addition to the UN and ONUSAL. The key outside parties were the so-called Friends of El Salvador: Mexico, Colombia, Venezuela, Spain, and the United States. The UN senior official charged with peacekeeping matters, Marrack Goulding, reportedly had his staff prepare a plan for separating the Salvadoran military and the FMLN by confining them to secure areas, which would be observed by ONUSAL, backed up by peacekeeping troops.[20] This arrangement, similar to the use of the Venezuelan infantry battalion in Nicaraguan Contra demobilization, placed the UN's role somewhere between peacekeeping and peace enforcement, at least during the critical stages of reorganizing the military and demobilizing the FMLN guerrillas.

The cease-fire came with the December 31, 1991, Act of New York signed by the Salvadoran government and the FMLN in the final hours of Pérez de Cuéllar's tenure. The gamble had paid off and ONUSAL's time had come. The December 1991 New York Agreement was formalized in the signature of the Peace Agreement in Mexico City's Chapultepec Castle on January 16, 1992. Almost immediately afterward the secretary-general moved to implement ONUSAL's expanded mandate by adding the Military and a Police Division to the mission's existing Human Rights Division. The addition of these new divisions reflected the fact that the Salvadorans (with ONUSAL's help) were about to tackle the thorniest issues on the agenda: how to restructure the armed forces, reduce their size, and get them out of the business of internal policing by eliminating the old military-controlled police institutions and para-military groups such as the Treasury Police and the National Guard and creating new ones under civilian control, most notably the National Civil Police (Policía Nacional Civil, PNC). This process also involved "purifying" the armed forces and forcing out officers (including senior ones) involved in human rights violations.

From the beginning it became clear that ONUSAL's goals and timetable were extremely ambitious in the face of opposition and resistance from many of the Salvadoran parties and institutions involved. There was little trust between the FMLN and the military, and one of ONUSAL's basic missions was to try to create this trust through confidence-building measures. Or, to put it another way, even if they could not trust each other, they could at least trust ONUSAL and the integrity of the peace process. Although neither side violated the cease-fire in any serious way, there were numerous delays and foot-draggings as both parties warily watched their basic institutional nature change. Both sides failed to fully concentrate their forces on schedule as required. Weapons inventories turned over to ONUSAL were suspect, and there were good reasons to believe that the FMLN, like the Contras before them in Nicaragua, were turning in only their old and obsolete weapons and keeping their better weapons hidden for possible future use. Indeed, the discovery in May 1993 of a major FMLN arms cache in Nicaragua was one of the more serious threats to the peace process. The military (and many of its supporters among the conservative ARENA party) was very reluctant to give up control of the police and internal intelligence functions, and there was evidence that the new police institutions being created were heavily infiltrated by carryovers from the old institutions, among them numerous human rights violators.

December 1992 saw the formal end to the civil war when the FMLN theoretically disappeared as a guerrilla force and became a legitimate political party with a strong role to play in the Salvadoran electoral and legislative milieu. Shortly afterward, ONUSAL's mandate and size were expanded yet again as the Electoral Division was created in January 1993 with a primary mission of observing the national elections (president, Legislative Assembly, and mayors and municipal councils) set for March 1994. The Electoral Division functioned with thirty-six professional staff stationed in six regional offices. Although small in number, these observers were able to lay the groundwork for a major and effective observation of the key 1994 elections. When the incompetence and political maneuvering of the Supreme Electoral Tribunal (Tribunal Supremo Electoral, TSE) threatened to cause a collapse of the voter registration process and ruin the elections, ONUSAL stepped in and in effect ran the process.

ONUSAL eventually finished its operations on April 30, 1995, turning over residual responsibilities to MINUSAL, a small liaison office of about twenty staff that symbolically represented the UN's continuing commitment to the consolidation of peace and democracy in El Salvador. A number of ONUSAL functions and programs were turned over to the permanent UN entities in San Salvador, such as the UNDP. In May 1996 the UN General Assembly terminated MINUSAL and replaced it with an even smaller liaison office.

In its almost four years of operation (July 1991–April 1995) ONUSAL had a peak deployment in 1992 of 368 military observers and 315 civilian police officers, supported by some 140 international staff and 180 local staff as well as a small medical team. The Electoral Division was augmented by about 900 international observers during the key 1994 elections. There were five fatalities among ONUSAL staff (three police and two local). The dollar cost of ONUSAL was $107,003,650.[21]

The UN and the OAS in Guatemala

The Guatemalan peace process was from the beginning much more difficult than that in Nicaragua or even El Salvador, mainly because of the very inflexible positions of the major players. Several rounds of inconclusive talks between the government and the Guatemalan National Revolutionary Unity (Unidad Revolucionaria Nacional Guatemalteca, URNG) took place in Mexico in early and mid 1991. The "Mexico Accord" that came out of this first set of talks called for agreement on a schedule for implementation, compliance, and international verification of the accords. There was also a strong interest on both sides (more prevalent in the URNG) that any agreements be verified by the United Nations, to include the presence of a preliminary UN human rights verification body similar to ONUSAL in El Salvador.[22]

The beginning of the breakthrough for Guatemala and the United Nations involvement in that conflict came in late 1993 and early 1994 when the factors that had made peace possible in Nicaragua and El Salvador (war-weariness, a realization that military victory by either side was impossible, and the end of the cold war) began to make themselves felt with greater strength in Guatemala. In addition, the Central American peace process had begun to acquire its own self-sustaining momentum, and the examples of Nicaragua and El Salvador and the success of the UN in facilitating the process were in a sense contagious.

In January 1994 representatives of the Guatemalan government (including several senior military officers) and of the URNG met in Mexico and signed the "Framework Agreement for the Resumption of the Negotiating Process."[23] Negotiations were facilitated by the presence of the special advisor to the UN secretary-general, Jean Arnault. There was no mention of the OAS, although it was known that the Guatemalan military favored some role by this organization, while the URNG clearly did not trust it.

A flurry of supportive agreements signed in 1994 set the stage for the implementation phase and the cease-fire and demobilization that were supposed to come in late 1994. These agreements paved the way for an advance element of what became the UN mission in Guatemala, MINUGUA, to travel in September 1994 to talk with President Ramiro de León Carpio and the Presidential Commission for the Coordination of Human Rights Affairs, and for the formal installation of MINUGUA in Guatemala in November 1994 as a human rights verification entity. The model for MINUGUA was to be ONUSAL: above all a human rights and nation-building UN mission staffed by civilians, with the possibility of augmentation by military observers at the critical moment of demobilization and disarmament of URNG forces, who would then be converted into a civilian political party and whose guerrillas would receive vocational training to permit their rehabilitation into civilian professions.

There were hopes that this strong emphasis on human rights would prosper because President de León Carpio had risen to prominence as a human rights ombudsman and had not been reluctant to speak out against abuses of human rights by the military.[24] But little happened in 1995 and early 1996. Real power remained in the hands of the generals, who unlike their Salvadoran counterparts felt that they had won their counterinsurgency war against the URNG, even though they recognized that the price paid by the indigenous population was high. Another factor was the relatively low influence of the United States on the military, certainly compared with El Salvador. Further, thirty-five years of brutal warfare had killed or intimidated a whole generation of possible civilian political leaders.

But even in the face of glacially slow progress MINUGUA remained in place, attempting to ferret out human rights violations despite frequent stonewalling by the military. Although the UN was showing reluctance to extend its mandate indefinitely while the military and the URNG made little progress, there was a feeling that the effort was worthwhile, and the mandate was indeed reauthorized for several six-month periods as both the Guatemalan government and the URNG appealed for it to remain.

The impatience of the UN and MINUGUA was evident in the increasingly critical human rights reports released by MINUGUA, which began to cause serious strains with the government (and especially the army) since they were perceived as being harsher on the army, the army-sponsored civil defense patrols, and the police than on the URNG. Crime and lawlessness were also emerging as serious threats to the peace, and it was often impossible for MINUGUA to separate common crime from deliberate human rights violations based on political motives.[25]

By late 1994 the critical demobilization and disarmament phase was about to begin as agreements were reached in Stockholm (December 7) on constitutional reforms and the electoral system, and in Madrid (December 12) on the reincorporation of fighters into civilian and political life. The stage was set for the basic deal where the Guatemalan army would accept a reduction in size and a redefined mission in exchange for URNG's demobilization and incorporation into the economic, social, and political life of Guatemala.

With the final formal peace agreement signed on December 29, 1996, everyone expected the early arrival of a UN military component (similar to ONUCA or ONUSAL) to supervise the concentration and demobilization of the URNG and the changes in the army. But a bizarre bit of UN politics almost derailed the whole process when the People's Republic of China cast a veto in the UN Security Council blocking the sending of 155 military observers for three months (at a cost of $3.4 million) to supplement the MINUGUA mission. The People's Republic was taking this step in retaliation for Guatemala's recognition of Taiwan as a separate China (presumably in exchange for Taiwanese economic aid). While the Guatemalan government suggested the possibility of seeking a peacekeeping mission from the OAS, this was not acceptable to the URNG. The impasse was eventually resolved ten days later after Guatemala agreed to reduce its support to Taiwan.[26]

The Military Division of the United Nations Human Rights Verification Mission in Guatemala (MINUGUA's new formal name) deployed in early February under the command of a Spanish general. In a relatively simple operation it set up eight separate detachments throughout the country and supervised the demobilization of approximately three thousand URNG guerrillas and the surrender of almost two thousand rifles and other weapons. As there had been with the ONUCA (Contra) and ONUSAL (FMLN) demobilizations, there were suspicions that what was being turned in were the older and obsolete weapons, while the better and more modern ones were kept in reserve in case of renewed fighting. It later became clear that weapons were also sold in the black market and contributed to the increase in crime that quickly followed.[27] Although MINUGUA's Military Division was also charged with assisting in the creation of a new civilian police force, their mission officially ended on May 1997, and their relatively brief stay in the country meant that they had little impact in this process.

Because MINUGUA's staff was relatively small, it worked closely with other UN agencies represented in Guatemala, such as the UNDP, UNCHR, and UNICEF.[28] In contrast with the experience in El Salvador, there appear to have been few strains with these organizations. The brief presence of the 155 military observers also minimized coordination problems, as did the inactivity of the OAS in Guatemala.

MINUGUA (and the UN) experienced continuing strains with the Guatemalan government over a series of issues that included unresolved human rights cases, the disappearance of certain key guerrilla leaders, the slow pace of police reform, and problems with the land reform program. Common crime rose dramatically, as the easy availability of weapons and the lack of jobs for unemployed guerrillas and soldiers inevitably led many of them to become involved with kidnappings, burglaries, and thefts. MINUGUA repeatedly warned that the peace process was being endangered when civilians took the law into their own hands. Public lynchings and beatings of suspected criminals were becoming more common, as were "extrajudicial executions."[29] In the countryside landowners began to establish private mini-armies to defend themselves against the activities of criminals and land-squatters. The rehabilitation programs sponsored by MINUGUA and UNDP seemed to be having only a marginal impact.[30]

Events in 1998 suggested that the Guatemalan peace process was progressing very slowly, despite a comprehensive set of signed agreements and a continually extended UN presence. The human cost of the UN involvement was brought home in February when a helicopter crash took the lives of five UN staffers from four different countries. In April the brutal murder of Bishop Juan Gerardi just days after he released a blistering human rights report ("Guatemala: Never Again?") raised political tensions; MINUGUA was asked to assist in the investigation of his murder.

Conclusion: Successes and Failures

The decade and a half that followed the birth of the Contadora process saw the creation of two major UN peacekeeping missions, ONUCA and ONUSAL. The latter has been hailed (with perhaps some excessive rhetoric) by many observers as a resounding success and indeed perhaps the high-water mark of UN peacekeeping. It certainly deserves many accolades, especially when compared with contemporary UN experiences in places such as Cambodia, Somalia, and Bosnia. The UN also mounted a very successful Nicaraguan election monitoring mission in ONUVEN. As of early 1999 the outlook for Guatemala was less clear, and it appeared that the process there would be slow and painful, and with no guarantee of success.

OAS involvement in Central America was much more limited, although there was a steady contribution in terms of election supervision and other efforts to support and promote democracy. The main involvement of OAS was in CIAV-OAS, where it undertook an unprecedented Contra resettlement effort. CIAV-OAS was not without controversy, including accusations of being a tool of the United States and being too helpful to the Contras while ignoring other segments of Nicaraguan society. As noted, these criticisms were frequently unfair and motivated by political considerations. Nonetheless, the very nature of the CIAV-OAS mandate made it a reluctant but unavoidable player in the internal Nicaraguan political game, and this inevitably brought attacks. Without CIAV-OAS, the Contras might not have demobilized and could have remained a dangerous armed nuisance. Thus, the OAS too had a successful role in the Central American peace process, although not as significant a one as that of the UN.

The failures or negative aspects of the UN and OAS involvement include the use of an international organization as the instrument of a single nation's foreign policy (an accusation made occasionally against CIAV-OAS), and the bureaucratic inability of two international organizations to cooperate more closely. This criticism can also be leveled at different entities within a given international organization, such as between ONUCA and the UNDP and between CIAV-OAS and OAS Headquarters.

A major criticism is that despite the advances, as of early 2000 Central America was still far from being at peace. Many of the provisions of the detailed peace agreements had not been complied with, despite the verification mandate given to the UN and the OAS. In both El Salvador and Guatemala, for example, there were serious delays and failures in the provisions for land reform, police restructuring, changing the roles of the military, and supporting economic and social development projects. Crime was a major problem in these two countries, as well as Nicaragua and Honduras, fueled by the easy availability of weapons and the unfulfilled promises of jobs and rehabilitation for former guerrillas and soldiers.

The UN and OAS involvement in the Central American peace process changed the approach of these two organizations and introduced the concept of "multifaceted" or "multidisciplinary" missions, such as those of ONUSAL and MINUGUA. These new ideas incorporate many of the original concepts but add new approaches such as the protection of human rights, the establishment of civilian control over the military and police, and the promotion and protection of democracy. The addition and combination of functions has not come without an increase in cost and complexity. Further, there are times when a single international organization in the field faces a conflict between being the verifier of a treaty and being the builder of institutions. This is especially true of politically delicate missions such as human rights protection, for example, in ONUSAL, which was charged with finding and publicizing human rights violations that frequently were committed by officials of the Salvadoran government, while at the same time strengthening the human rights institutions of the very government it was criticizing.

In the process of Central American conflict resolution several institutions saw their roles changed or enlarged. One in particular, the IADB, found a limited but useful role in coordinating the demining efforts in Central America in collaboration with the OAS Unit for the Promotion of Democracy.

Various countries found new roles through their involvement with UN and (to a lesser degree) OAS conflict resolution efforts in Central America, most notably Canada, Spain, and Argentina. U.S. attitudes toward a UN peacekeeping role in the hemisphere changed during the Esquipulas process. Previously such a UN presence had been discouraged and even blocked in the Western Hemisphere, where the United States showed its preference for the OAS as peacekeeper.

In conclusion, the 1980s and 1990s saw much change in Central America. Despite all the problems and unfulfilled promises and dreams, Central America became a more peaceful place, and the UN—and to a lesser degree the OAS—helped make that happen and in the process made a significant contribution to the process of transition and consolidation of democracy in the region.

Notes

1. Jack Child, *The Central American Peace Process, 1983–1991* (Boulder, CO: Lynne Rienner, 1992).

2. For details of ONUCA, see *Report of the UN Secretary-General*, October 11, 1989, Document S/20895; also United Nations, *The Blue Helmets*, 3d ed. (New York: United Nations, 1996), 393–96.

3. Francesc Vendrell, UN special assistant to the UNSG, interview by author, Ottawa, May 1989.

4. For the detailed history of ONUCA's deployment, see UN, *Blue Helmets*, and the *ONUCA Observer* (Tegucigalpa, 1990), the unofficial illustrated chronicle of the peacekeeping mission.

5. For an extensive analysis of ONUVEN and the 1990 elections, see Shelley A. McConnell [a member of ONUVEN], "ONUVEN: Toward a Model for Electoral Observation" in Tommie Sue Montgomery, ed., *Peacemaking and Democratization in Central America* (Boulder, CO: Lynne Rienner, 1999). There are several other accounts of the 1990 election, such as the Latin American Studies Association's "Electoral Democracy under International Pressure: The 1990 Nicaraguan Election" (LASA, Pittsburgh, 1990). The UN has also published an extensive report (Document A/44/642, October 17, 1989).

6. McConnell, "ONUVEN," 20–21.

7. Much of the material in this section is based on interviews conducted during a research trip to Managua in June 1991 and supplemented with other interviews in Washington and Ottawa.

8. UN, *Blue Helmets*, 735–36.

9. Jennie K. Lincoln and César D. Sereseres, "Resettling the Contras: The OAS Verification Commission in Nicaragua, 1990–1993," in Montgomery, *Peacemaking and Democratization in Central America*, 3.

10. Ibid., 23.

11. Inter-American Defense Board, *Info Paper: OAS/IADB Demining Program*, May 29, 1998.

12. Information on the demining program was provided by IADB chairmen Major General James Harding, January 24, 1994, and Major General John Thompson, August 27, 1998. Also see "Recobrando tierras condenadas," *Americas* (OAS), October 1997, 53–55; "Demining in Central America," *OAS/UPD Newsletter*, July 1997, 1, 4.

13. The official history of ONUSAL-MINUSAL and the UN involvement in El Salvador is contained in the basic UN handbook on peacekeeping, *The Blue Helmets*, 425–44. For scholarly analyses of the process, see works by Tommie Sue Montgomery and David Holiday and William Stanley, "Under the Best of Circumstances: ONUSAL and the Challenges of Verification and Institution Building in El Salvador," in Montgomery, *Peacemaking and Democratization in Central America*. Also Tricia Juhn, *Negotiating Peace in El Salvador* (New York: St. Martin's, 1998). For a Latin American perspective, see Raúl Benítez Manaut, "La ONU y el proceso de paz en el Salvador," in *Revista Mexicana de Política Exterior* (Mexico City: Primavera, 1992), 35–52. For a comparison of the relatively successful El Salvador UN effort and the unsuccessful Cambodian one, see Michael Doyle, ed., *Keeping the Peace* (Cambridge: Cambridge University Press, 1997).

14. "UN Closing Book on a Rare Success Story," *Washington Post*, April 21, 1995, A29.

15. Liisa North, "Comments on 'An Agenda for Peace,' " in Hal Klepak, ed., *Canada and Latin American Security* (Quebec: Méridien, 1993), 169; Tommie Sue Montgomery, "Getting to Peace in El Salvador," *Journal of Interamerican Studies*, Winter 1995, 146.

16. Holiday and Stanley, "Under the Best of Circumstances," 4.

17. For a detailed analysis of the OAS role in the 1991 elections, see Tommie Sue Montgomery, "Good Observers, Bad Leaders and Ugly Politics: Observing Elections in El Salvador," in her *Peacemaking and Democratization in Central America*.

18. San Salvador, Canal Doce Televisión, July 26, 1991, in Foreign Broadcast Information Service (FBIS), July 29, 1991; *Central America Report*, August 16, 1991, 247; "Leftists Charge Fraud in El Salvador," *New York Times*, August 13, 1991, A5.

19. San Salvador, Radio Cadena, September 25, 1991, in FBIS, September 26, 1991.

20. *Central America Report*, September 27, 1991, 282.

21. UN, *Blue Helmets*, 444.

22. *Times of the Americas*, August 7, 1991, 1; Commission on U.S.–Latin American Relations, "Memorandum on the Guatemala Peace Talks," June 27, 1991.

23. For text and commentary, see UN Web site http://www.un.org/Depts/minugua/paz2.htm.

24. "Guatemalan President Dashes Backers' Hopes," *Washington Post*, May 13, 1995, A6.

25. UN Press Release GA/8991, November 9, 1995. Adam Isaacson, *Altered States: Security and Demobilization in Central America* (Washington, DC: Center for International Policy, 1997), 128–35.

26. "China Vetoes Use of UN Personnel," *Washington Post*, January 11, 1997, A22; January 20, 1997, A24; "Guatemalan Rebels Exchange Weapons for Dreams," ibid., March 5, 1997, A8. UN Press Releases SC/3611 and SC6314, January 10 and 20, respectively.

27. FBIS-LAT-97-032, -063 and -166 on Web site http://wnc.fedworld.gov/cgi-bin/retrieve.

28. UN, *UN Verification Mission in Guatemala (Report)*, Document A/51/936, June 30, 1997.

29. *Jane's Defence Weekly*, July 1, 1998, on Web site http://web.lexis-nexis.com/univers.

30. "Swords to Plowshares: Guatemala's Struggle," *Washington Post*, October 8, 1997, A23, A28. FBIS-LAT-97-209 on Web site http://wnc.fedworld.gov/cgi-bin/retrieve. General Víctor M. Ventura Arellano, "The Peace Process in Guatemala," in Donald E. Schulz, ed., *The Role of the Armed Forces in the Americas, Conference Report* (Carlisle, PA: U.S. Army Strategic Studies Institute, 1998), 105–8.

9

Religion in the Central American Embroglio

Edward L. Cleary, O.P.

Since religion and politics are both heavily normative phenomena—concerned, in part, with defining what is "good," "bad," and "should be"—it is not surprising that they are often intertwined. Thus they were in Central America in the latter third of the twentieth century as clergy and lay people alike found themselves propelled by their religious values and convictions to take political and social stands or as they turned to religious explanations to justify partisan positions and activity. A sharp upsurge in religious activity and changing interpretations of the role of clergy and lay persons—Catholic and Protestant alike—simultaneously flowed out of, and fed into, the dramatic social and political embroglio of the times.

The social and political involvement of the Catholic Church, traditionally the religion with the greatest following in the region, evolved markedly during this period. Responding at first to new directions signaled by the Vatican and the Latin American Conference of Catholic Bishops in the 1960s, many clergy made a socially activist "preferential option for the poor," articulated a new "theology of liberation,"[1] and backed forces for change on the isthmus—including openly revolutionary ones. Before long, however, other religious personnel, answering the call of the more anticommunist Vatican under the leadership of Pope John Paul II from 1978 onward, began supporting different forces and policies. At the same time both sectors carried on a barrage of criticism of the socially regressive implications of neoliberal "structural adjustment" in the region.

Meanwhile, Protestantism in Central America was also dramatically involved in and transformed by the drama of the times. When the period began, Protestants represented a tiny minority of the population and were generally affiliated to the so-called mainline denominations such as Presbyterian, Episcopal, Methodist, and Lutheran. Generally, clergy in these churches came to support the movement for progressive change. However, the 1980s saw a massive upsurge in proselytism and evangelizing in the region by conservative fundamentalist and Pentecostal churches. These activities resulted in a dramatic increase in the percentage of Central Americans who, by the end of the century, would list their religious affiliation as something other than Roman Catholic or traditional Protestant.

Historical Background

The Spanish colonists established patterns of church-state relations that persisted for almost five hundred years. Catholicism was acknowledged as the religion of the state: this arrangement protected the status of the Church in civil law. More important, it meant that the state provided financial resources—in the form of royal tithes, especially of agricultural products—for the Church. This economic base enabled the Church to construct places of worship and schools and to carry out charity work. These activities, in turn, gave the Church a wide-ranging presence in the cities and the countryside. Thus, through centuries of contact and service, the Church gained the loyalty of the poor.

The Central American Church was devastated in the years following independence from Spain. While the pattern of the Church as a state religion continued, the generosity of the state did not. Nineteenth-century liberalism reinforced Latin American anticlericalism—hostility toward the Church's position of power and influence—among many national leaders. State subsidies decreased, Church properties were seized, Spanish clergy were exiled, and communications with Rome were clouded. Not until the 1930s did the Central American republics restore full diplomatic relations with the Vatican.

By the mid twentieth century the Central American churches had few priests (one for every sixteen thousand Catholics), tiny seminaries, scarce economic resources, and weak organizational structures (dioceses, parishes, and staff personnel). At this point, however, the Vatican facilitated first the rehabilitation and then the modernization of the national churches. Archbishops and bishops, often mentored by papal representatives, invited priests, nuns, and laypersons from other countries to work in their jurisdictions. By 1965 the massive missionary influx from North Atlantic countries had come to furnish between 40 and 80 percent (depending on the country) of Central America's clergy.

Events in the international Catholic Church in the 1960s were even more important in propelling change than were internal factors. Not only did central aspects of Church policy change but also Central Americans were present for the process. Pope John XXIII inaugurated profound changes in Catholic teaching and practice. Of particular significance was his convocation of the Second Vatican Council (1962–1965). Some Central American bishops and their advisors participated in the council's proceedings, having been elected as representatives of national conferences or chosen by the Holy See. They went as listeners, not protagonists, and, for them, the council was a lengthy learning experience.

Vatican II had a delayed impact on Central American Catholicism. Its theological sophistication was beyond that of most Central Americans. Since it addressed liturgical reform, lay empowerment, and religious freedom in European terms, a Latin American interpretation of the council was needed. This was provided by the Latin American Bishops Conference (Conferencia Episcopal Latinoamericana, CELAM) through a two-year process of preparation leading to the famous conference in Medellín, Colombia, in 1968.

To interpret Vatican II the Medellín participants had to undertake a systematic review of the region's social and economic context and its religious life. Three steps were employed: description, judgment, and action. First, the Church had to admit that it was a sinful institution in a socially unjust situation. Second, the conference compared this situation with biblical visions of justice and peace. Third, the Church had to plan its future with certain priorities for its limited resources. Priority was assigned to the poor, in what came to be called the "preferential option for the poor." Church policy was redirected toward human rights and social justice.

The spirit animating Medellín was that of the theology of liberation. Based largely on modern European theology and biblical exegesis, it proposed that the Church's role in society be understood especially from the perspective of the poor. In 1979, another conference of Latin American bishops at Puebla, Mexico, confirmed Medellín's orientation and gave a last strong push for changes in the Central American churches. The spirit of Medellín and Puebla was incorporated in many lay groups, especially Christian base communities (comunidades eclesiales de base, CEB). In these communities, lay men and women—typically with strong clerical support—reflected on Scripture and the social teaching of the Church. Many members sought spiritual enrichment in the groups while others saw them as instruments of social and political change.

Revolutions, Wars, and Christians

While the focus in this section will be on the three Central American countries where religion and politics had the most intense interaction, none of the processes within the countries, especially peace initiatives, can be understood without reference to other countries of the region and to transnational actors. Indeed, the drama of religion and politics has several levels of analysis. Religious actors in the Central American processes were national, regional, and transnational. They included Catholic, mainline Protestant, Pentecostal, and indigenous religious leaders and followers. Within the Catholic Church there were three levels of participants: bishops conferences and individual bishops, priests and lay activists, and grassroots Catholics.

The contexts of the dramas of Nicaragua, Guatemala, and El Salvador had both notable similarities as well as significant differences. Until the 1960s the majority of Central American Catholics suffered from lack of religious training and knew little of orthodox Catholicism. Isolation from the developing world and the presence of anticlerical governments within their countries during the earlier twentieth century had left the majority of Catholics with scant pastoral care or instruction. Given the scarcity of clergy, ordinary people in Nicaragua and El Salvador fell back on the popular Catholicism that had emerged in colonial times. They practiced many devotions such as those of the Lord of Esquipulas and the rosary and celebrated religious feast days for consolation and cheer. Many Guatemalan Indians strengthened the practice of their Mayan religion.[2] Interestingly, in many cases, this popular religiosity was combined with revolutionary ideals, invigorating the ideology of those involved in mass revolt in Nicaragua, El Salvador, and Guatemala.

Many foreign observers of the upheavals in northern Central America have commented on the widespread, sentimental, and deeply held faith of the ordinary people. In Nicaragua, Jeffrey Klaiber says, "The mystique of the revolution turned out to be a fusion of this deep popular religiosity with the new revolutionary fervor."[3] In El Salvador and Guatemala, ordinary people continued in the struggle, making sense of the plagues that they suffered by tales of martyrdom.[4]

Nicaragua

The Nicaraguan revolution was the only Latin American revolution in which religion played an essential role. Religionists were key players in the insurrectionary process, in the Sandinista experiment, in the prolonged effort to obtain a viable peace, and in the post-Sandinista 1990s. That Christians would be integral to these stages was a surprise to Fidel Castro and many other observers but not to those who had read liberation theology.[5] Participation in the Nicaraguan revolution was one interpretation of progressive Christianity.[6] Reform Catholicism began having an impact on the country in the 1970s. Catholic high schools and parishes encouraged informal study groups on the social implications of Christianity. The Central American University, a small, private, Jesuit-run university founded in 1961 with help from the Somozas, became a center for social and political criticism in the following decade. In parishes, adult Christians formed CEBs where they pondered Sunday Bible readings and critiqued the social and political environment in which they lived.

In 1972 the old system was irreparably shaken when a strong earthquake destroyed central Managua, killed at least ten thousand people, and left many more homeless. Though foreign aid poured into the country, the Somoza machine diverted a large portion to personal profit. Great numbers of Catholics and Protestants, newly sensitized to the social implications of Christianity, now found it increasingly difficult to tolerate Somoza's corruption. Many, therefore, joined the Sandinista insurgents in their armed struggle against the Somozas, thus converting a small, relatively token armed resistance into an increasingly formidable guerrilla army. Christians were especially, though not exclusively, attracted to the Third Way or Insurrectionalist (Tercerista/Insurrecional) faction of the Sandinista National Liberation Front (Frente Sandinista de Liberación Nacional, FSLN) that emerged in the mid 1970s with a flexible strategy advocating a multiclass alliance and combined rural and urban insurgency.

As the "Final Insurrection" was beginning the Nicaraguan bishops wrote a pastoral letter on June 2, 1979, proclaiming that, since all peaceful means for removing the tyrant had been exhausted, violent struggle was justified. While their backing for the overthrow of Somoza was clear, the bishops' support for the revolutionary government that took power the following month was strongly conditioned by fear of the presence of hard-line Marxists among Sandinista leaders. Though moderate bishops attempted to find common ground with the Sandinista government, Miguel Obando y Bravo, the Archbishop of Managua who essentially dominated the leadership of the national institutional church, became increasingly intransigent in his relations with the Sandinistas.

Nevertheless, many of the Christians who had been essential in the 1979 insurrectionary victory would continue to make contributions during the creative process that followed. Progressive priests joined with lay persons in the effort to build a more just nation. Some took posts in the government or cooperated with its projects. For instance, Fernando Cardenal, a Jesuit priest, ran the massive 1980 Literacy Crusade, a first payment to peasants and other illiterates who had supported the insurrection. Under him, three hundred priests, brothers, and sisters joined tens of thousands of teachers and students who took months out of their lives to substantially reduce illiteracy in the country.

Meanwhile, basic questions about the political direction of the country were intensifying and sectors of the Church were becoming increasingly worried. In April 1980, the Sandinistas created a legislative body, the Council of State, which—though it gave corporative representation to most parties and groups in the country (including the Catholic and Protestant churches)—awarded greater participation than originally envisioned to pro-Sandinista interests. What Sandinistas saw as a broader platform for the poor was interpreted by opposition political leaders as a move toward one-party control. In addition, though the new government promised to hold free elections in 1985 (and actually held them in 1984), opposition groups were worried initially that it would not keep its promise.

Quite simply, many Catholics feared that, if a communist regime were eventually established in Nicaragua, religion would be suppressed. It is true that FSLN leaders repeatedly stated that they would respect freedom of religion, stressing that "the Christians have been an integral part of our revolutionary history to a degree not found in any other revolutionary movement in Latin America, and, possibly, in the world."[7] Nevertheless, many did not believe them.

The participation of priests at high levels of government also became a major point of contention. In May 1980 and mid 1981 the bishops strongly urged four priests—Foreign Minister Miguel D'Escoto, Culture Minister Ernesto Cardenal, Literacy Crusade Director Fernando Cardenal, and Social Welfare Minister Edgardo Parrales—to resign their posts. The priests argued that, since the country was in a state of emergency, the services of people with their training and talents were required. Eventually, an agreement was worked out by which the priests could continue in their secular positions while temporarily suspending their roles as priests. Nevertheless, during a visit to Nicaragua in March 1983, Pope John Paul II expressed his strong views on priests in politics, shaking his finger at Ernesto Cardenal and telling him to normalize his position (abandon his ministerial post).

Later in 1983 church-state tensions increased when the government—responding to the expanding U.S.-sponsored Contra war and leaked disinformation from the CIA, Pentagon, and State Department concerning a supposed plan for the imminent U.S. invasion of Nicaragua[8]—enacted an obligatory national military draft. The bishops objected to the law on the grounds that it obliged citizens to become members of the military—and perhaps die—even when they did not agree with the ideology of the party running the government. Some lay Catholics responded that the bishops were inciting to disobedience. Undeterred by that charge, after becoming cardinal in April 1983 in a ceremony in Rome, Obando underlined his opposition to the Sandinistas on his way home by saying Mass in Miami for a largely exiled Nicaraguan congregation including Contra leaders.

The U.S. bishops conference did not support Obando. They also denounced the U.S. policy of fostering civil war in Nicaragua that was taking thousands of lives. In the United States some 40,000 North Americans joined 850 national and local groups opposed to U.S. policy in Nicaragua, many of them with strong ties to churches.[9] Catholic bishops and Protestant church leaders were among the first to respond to the administration's assault on Nicaragua.[10] Groups associated with the Central American peace movement effectively lobbied Congress and seem to have had some role in blocking possible U.S. invasion plans in the early 1980s.

In 1986, representing the Vatican's desire for a negotiated peace, a new papal nuncio, Paulo Giglio, was sent to Nicaragua. Giglio shepherded a dialogue on two fronts. Through the early months of 1987, he sponsored a series of talks between the government and the Catholic Church. At the same time, he also helped to persuade the Sandinista government to hold peace talks with the Contras.

The major initiative for peace, however, came from Oscar Arias, president of Costa Rica, who proposed meetings of the five Central American presidents. In August 1987 these summits, Esquipulas I and Esquipulas II, culminated in a set of accords that would be implemented over the next several years. Nicaragua took the lead among Central American nations in dialoguing with the enemy. The Sandinistas invited Cardinal Obando to act as president of the National Commission of Reconciliation. He agreed. Gustavo Parajón, Protestant pastor and director of the Ecumenical Committee for Development (CEPAD), also joined the five-member commission.

In 1990 ironically the second internationally observed national elections held by the Sandinistas removed them from power and installed conservative Violeta Barrios de Chamorro as president. Nevertheless, the violence did not end. Though the Contras formally laid down their arms in mid 1990, the government's failure to honor promises to both demobilized Contras and discharged members of the Sandinista army soon produced a situation in which some twenty-two thousand troops from both sides remobilized.[11] Once again, Cardinal Obando was asked to mediate in returning ex-combatants to civilian life. By the end of the decade, most—though not all—of the reinsurgents (*rearmados*) had once again demobilized.

During the nineties, church-state conflicts continued but the issues shifted. While the Sandinista government had made public education secular, it had allowed religion as an additional class in private schools. The bishops, however, saw this period as "years of atheistic education and a systematic and persistent campaign against Catholic morality."[12] Conservative Catholics, especially from the "City of God" charismatic group, filled a number of cabinet and advisory posts in President Chamorro's administration.[13] They acted in cooperation with the bishops who took increasingly strong stands about sex education, abortion, divorce, and other aspects of public morality. Nonetheless, while strongly conservative in these respects, the bishops conference repeatedly attacked neoliberalism and criticized the Nicaraguan government for insufficient attention to the poor, as the standard of living for the vast majority grew steadily worse throughout the decade.

Guatemala

The most populous of the Central American countries, Guatemala attracted many missionaries in the twentieth century. In the two decades from 1952 to 1972 the clergy quadrupled in number and foreigners now made up 80 percent of the total. While this influx dramatically expanded the reach of the Catholic Church, it also threatened to overwhelm Guatemalan Catholics who wished to maintain the traditional church or to control pastoral theory and practice.

Faced with tremendous repression from the late 1960s onward—some of which was directed against them for being foreign—missionaries increasingly chose to work through Catholic Action and catechists. In time, these two theologically distinct programs were conflated by foe and friend alike into the single designation of catechists. Lay men and women resident in numerous villages in the Guatemalan highlands were trained in orthodox Catholicism. These native Guatemalans were vested with delegated authority to educate, to lead discussions about courses of action in the face of danger, and to interpret political events through prayer and liturgy. They typically represented a social and reformed Christianity. Maryknoll, Sacred Heart, and other missionaries trained them by the thousands, especially in the 1960s and 1970s. Catholic Action and the catechist movement changed the basic character of Guatemalan Catholicism. As Bruce Calder observed, these programs, whose collective impact was extensive, "gradually [displaced] local religious practices with more orthodox European style Catholicism."[14]

Thousands of students who would never have found a place in Guatemalan schools received a primary education from schools started by missionaries. For the majority indigenous population the result was stunning to them and to outsiders. Teachers, lawyers, linguists, agronomists, priests, nuns, and politicians flowed from these efforts. Within Indian communities and towns, community activists and organizers emerged to challenge the traditional white or Ladino hierarchies. The catechists conflicted sharply with the prevailing civic-religious leaders of traditional religion and credit-union and cooperative leaders replaced Ladino middlemen. Economic losses to displaced elites were keenly felt and blamed on foreign influences.

The Guatemalan military and ruling elite resisted the activists' challenge to their power. Catholic Action leaders and catechists became targets of death squads and of more than six hundred military massacres beginning in 1967. Frustrated by these atrocities and by military and right-wing interference in politics, a small number of Christians joined the small irregular forces to oppose military rule. The vast majority of Christians, however, attempted nonviolently to weather the state-sponsored terrorism that took the lives of over two hundred thousand civilians (Chapter 1). To make sense of this terror and upheaval in which more than a million persons were driven from their villages into internal or international exile, Christians sought consolation in the church as community, now substituted for their lost native community.

Gradually, during the late seventies and throughout the eighties, the Catholic Church became increasingly Guatemalan. For a variety of reasons, seminaries began to expand. Women entered religious life, replacing foreigners. Lay people flocked to churches in numbers never before seen.[15] New lay spiritual groups sprang up in many locations.

Another largely Catholic and more obviously political import was the Christian Democratic movement. Based on Catholic social principles, Christian Democracy—with ties to sister parties throughout Europe and Latin America—emerged in the mid 1950s from student groups at the University of San Carlos and received encouragement from Guatemala's bishops. Before long, the party had won support from indigenous communities throughout the country. Despite the party's moderate character, dozens of its leaders were murdered by death squads in the 1980s. Even so, it continued to find new leaders and, in 1986, produced the first elected civilian president in twenty years, Vinicio Cerezo.

The flood of new ideas that flowed from Vatican II from the 1960s onward and the massive problems of Guatemalan society during its bloody civil war affected the younger Guatemalan clergy and laity. Guatemalan bishops eventually replaced foreigners as bishops and gained favorable recognition internationally. This new esteem would be useful for the dangerous journey to peace and for establishing a collective memory of what had occurred.

The peace process dominated Guatemalan political life in the first half of the 1990s (Chapter 1). Catholics and Protestants were prominent in two aspects—the peace process itself and the peace movement. The movement undergirded the process of laying down arms and, more important, of taking up fundamental societal issues, such as human rights. Catholic and other religious participants—international and national, elite and grassroots—took part in the process and the movement.

When the Esquipulas II Peace Accords of 1987 did not bring immediate progress, Catholics and Lutherans formed an international ecumenical peace delegation. The group persuaded an influential sector of the army to allow the National Commission of Reconciliation (Comisión Nacional de Reconciliación, CNR) to hold talks with the Guatemalan National Revolutionary Unity (Unidad Revolucionaria Nacional Guatemalteca, URNG) in Oslo in March 1990. In the next step the URNG dialogued with five sectors of Guatemalan society in separate meetings. It also met with the religious sector of Guatemalan society in Quito, Ecuador, in September 1990, and out of that meeting an agenda of political and other issues to be resolved within a peace settlement was established.

The Oslo initiative also marked a major step in ecumenical relations, unusual in the generally tense relations between churches in Central America. Lutheran pastors in the United States and Scandinavia persuaded the Lutheran World Federation to form a peace team and to sponsor a variety of mostly behind-the-scenes efforts. The formal connections of these state churches with the governments of Norway and Sweden helped bring the latter into the process. The Vatican's Pontifical Council for Promoting Christian Unity, the Guatemalan Catholic bishops, the Catholic Episcopal Secretariat for

Central America, and the U.S. Conference of Catholic Bishops joined in the cooperative effort.

After Próspero Penados del Barrio replaced Mario Casariego as archbishop of Guatemala City in 1983, the Guatemalan Church quickly established a strong record of speaking out for peace and against both state and guerrilla violence. Archbishop Penados offered strong leadership at crucial times when society was fragmented by terror in the mid eighties. But the strength of the national church was its diffuse and united leadership. Bishop Rodolfo Quezada Toruño of Zacapa became chief delegate of the Church to the National Reconciliation Commission. He also became the commission's president. Bishop Juan Gerardi Conedara, auxiliary of Guatemala City, became Quezada's backup. The prominent neo-Pentecostal layman, Jorge Serrano Elías, also served on the CNR.

In 1989, the CNR promoted an unusual initiative, sponsoring the National Dialogue (Diálogo Nacional). It opened the way for civil society to enter the national discussion. Some sixty organizations took part, with many participants coming from six church groups. The federation of Pentecostal churches and the Jewish community, which previously had avoided involvement in national issues, joined the effort—although submitting separate programs for Guatemala's political future.

Though the National Dialogue collapsed after two years, the now vibrant civil sector stepped forward with a new initiative for peace in 1994. Religious groups and popular organizations, now in the hundreds, formed the Assembly of the Civil Society (Asamblea de la Sociedad Civil, ASC). It proposed consensus positions on peace issues and ratified or rejected agreements made in high-level negotiations.

The religious sector provided many leaders and participants for the peace movement. Movement members struggled to create a national constituency for peace, one that would be actively aware of the peace negotiations. In a society whose media had no experience in open reporting, they pressured press and radio directors to report peace negotiations and marched in demonstrations, held ecumenical services, and discussed refugee concerns, resettlement, and human rights.

Once armed conflict between the URNG and the Guatemalan army had ceased, some members of the peace movement were adamant that the gross human rights violations of the previous thirty-some years be publicly investigated and documented. The Catholic Church seized the initiative by establishing the Interdiocesan Project for the Recuperation of Historical Memory (Recuperación de Memoria Histórica Interdiocesana, REMHI). The effort to compile the report—titled "Guatemala: Never Again?"—was enormous and painstaking. Two days after it was issued, on April 26, 1998, the chief spokesman for the project, Bishop Juan Gerardi, was beaten to death.[16] Intimidation of other project leaders also occurred. However, the internationally sponsored Commission for Historical Clarification's *Guatemala: Memory of Silence* (1999) confirmed the Church's report.

El Salvador

The Salvadoran Church stood out from sister institutions in the rest of Central America in that important segments of the former had been prepared for the reforms of Vatican II. Indeed, Luis Chávez y González had used his almost forty years as archbishop of San Salvador to attempt a transformation of his archdiocese. He had encouraged native vocations and had seen that they were well trained at his new seminary or in Canada or Europe. In addition, there were intellectual resources for renewal within the Church in the form of a small but growing sector of involved lay persons. A group of Catholic intellectuals founded the Christian Democrat Party in 1960 and the latter helped create a key peasant association, Christian Federation of Peasants of El Salvador (Federación Cristiana de Campesinos Salvadoreños, FECCAS). Members of these and other organizations studied the social teaching of the church.

With Vatican II and with additional clergy coming from other countries, the pace of Church reform quickened and spread to pockets beyond San Salvador. Eventually, it became clear that bishops in other parts of El Salvador, rather than being reform-minded, had set themselves against the archbishop and auxiliary bishops of San Salvador. However, in the 1970s, priests and lay persons in the now numerous Catholic organizations turned to studying liberation theology in Christian base communities.[17] A sharpened political consciousness flowed from discussions in these groups.

The mentors of the new groups that carried the doctrines did not begin with a social revolution in mind. They and their followers simply analyzed the social and economic situation against what they read in the Old and New Testaments, often reading the Bible for the first time in their lives. John Hammond argues that "the new church doctrine, brought from abroad, found its greatest influence in El Salvador among the rural poor, and . . . its tenets implied that education and organizing are inseparable and essential."[18]

Priests and religious women in rural areas taught courses to train catechists and "delegates of the word" (leaders of Christian base communities). In the seventies, Salvadorans flowed from these religious groups to popular peasant movements and unions. As these groups became politically active, landowners with paramilitary forces linked to the police and army began the slaughter of priests and lay persons connected with them.

The short tenure of Oscar Romero as archbishop of San Salvador, 1977–1980, provides the next defining moment in Salvadoran history. Though seen as a conservative when first appointed to that position, Romero was soon moved by the brutality of the reality around him—particularly by the assassination of one of his priests, Father Rutilio Grande—to issue increasingly sharp criticisms of both the Salvadoran government and military and U.S. aid to the latter.[19] Romero was murdered at Mass in March 1980. Within months, four priests, a seminarian, and four North American churchwomen, not to mention hundreds of other civilians, were also killed.

These deaths, especially that of Romero, marked the course of the next years. They forced many Salvadorans to reconsider what political path they were taking. Some heroically renewed their efforts at protecting human rights in a murderous climate. Roberto Cuéllar began carrying a fragment of Romero's bloody T-shirt in his wallet as he continued his work as a human rights lawyer.[20]

Like Cuéllar, grassroots Salvadorans had to make sense for themselves of the political situation engulfing them. Anna Peterson traced the sources and evolution of Catholic religious beliefs in El Salvador's civil war.[21] She found that ordinary Salvadorans, like other religious people, often used narratives to place their lives within religious tradition. In contrast to the progressive Catholics in Nicaragua who used building the kingdom of God as their useful symbol, Salvadoran Catholics found the concept of martyrdom most relevant for them. Still, this was not a grim idea: thousands of Salvadorans painted small crosses with flowers and hung them on their walls.

Other Salvadorans chose violence. The five revolutionary movements pulled together at this time to form a united Farabundo Martí National Liberation Front (Frente Farabundo Martí de Liberación Nacional, FMLN) with a political wing, the Democratic Revolutionary Front (Frente Democrático Revolucionario, FDR). With the deaths of Romero and others, many Christians from the base communities and other groups joined FMLN fighters or FDR politicians. A number of them, such as Guillermo Ungo and Rubén Zamora, identified their political commitment with their Christianity.

While students at the National University of El Salvador in the late 1960s and early 1970s, guerrilla leaders had debated national politics. They were aware of international political events, including middle-class guerrilla movements in Uruguay and Argentina. However, some were especially influenced to take action when they witnessed the repression of the Catholic Church and university students and the annulling of the Christian Democratic electoral victory in 1972.[22] Some middle-level leaders attributed their enlistment in the FMLN to their experiences of working with grassroots church organizations and finding that the government's reaction was repression. In interviews with Salvadorans, Cynthia McClintock found that "the abuses against Catholic priests were pivotal in the decision of many mid-level leaders and urban professionals to join the guerrillas. For many, the assassination of Archbishop Romero in 1980 was the galvanizing atrocity."[23]

Arturo Rivera y Damas succeeded Romero, first as apostolic administrator of San Salvador (1980–1983) and then as archbishop (1983–1994). One month after taking over in 1980, Rivera accepted advice of his counselors to seek dialogue rather than confrontation (and probable martyrdom) with the forces of state-sponsored terrorism.[24] Progressives and conservatives criticized Rivera y Damas, either for losing a strong measure of leadership to conservatives within the bishops conference or for allowing the popular church to exist. However, Rivera founded Legal Defense (Tutela Legal), a secure refuge for victims or relatives of victims of the civil war and an instrument for denouncing human-rights violations. He also reinforced the work of the Social Secretariat in alleviating the suffering of the war victims. But Rivera's principal strategy was to pursue peace through dialogue.

Rivera's calls for peace fell on deaf ears until the 1984 election of the first civilian president in fifty years, José Napoleón Duarte. In October of that year, Duarte (viewed as an exemplary Christian Democrat) accepted the invitation of the FMLN-FDR—on the table since 1982—to dialogue. Archbishop Rivera was designated by the Church as mediator. Negotiations at La Palma intensified but then stalled. Almost a year later, when FMLN commandos kidnapped the president's daughter, Inés Guadalupe, Rivera y Damas managed to work out a complicated exchange. In this and other negotiations he was credited with humanizing the war.

In 1987, Esquipulas II caused a flurry of meetings between warring elements. Though both sides agreed to Rivera y Damas's presidency of two commissions, no basic agreements were reached. Rivera also sponsored the National Debate for Peace in 1988. Sixty groups, including four non-Catholic churches, took part. The landed and business classes and fundamentalist Christian churches did not.

The war, however, continued through 1991. The murderous violence reached a new level when the U.S.-trained Atlacatl Battalion, under orders from the army High Command, killed six Jesuit priests and two women helpers at the Central American University in November 1989. The principal target was believed to have been Father Ignacio Ellacuría, rector of the university. He had favored a negotiated settlement to the war and disapproved of violence—including that of the FMLN.[25]

After that dramatic atrocity, international pressures for dialogue and peace welled up from many quarters. Rivera y Damas and others had, by then, exhausted all conceivable ways to act as mediators within El Salvador. However, both fighting forces were also exhausted and, with the cold war over, the United States was willing to accept a negotiated settlement. At the invitation of all the Central American governments, the UN, through the UN Observer Mission in El Salvador (Misión de Observadores de las Naciones Unidas en El Salvador, ONUSAL), became the chief mediator. The Catholic and Lutheran Churches served on the National Commission for the Consolidation of Peace (Comisión Nacional para la Consolidación de la Paz, COPAZ) through the participation of Rivera and Lutheran bishop Medardo Gómez. Parallel to the United Nations, COPAZ became the national mechanism for overseeing and facilitating the execution of the accords. In Ian Johnstone's evaluation, COPAZ was a "critical feature of the peace process."[26]

Final vindication came to Rivera in January 1992 when his fellow bishops—though mostly conservative—elected him president of the bishops conference. Later that year he was invited to witness guerrilla commanders take the oath to convert their army into a political party—something he had sought for years. Two years later Rivera died of natural causes.

As we have seen, sharp differences in style marked the principal leaders of the Nicaraguan, Guatemalan, and Salvadoran Churches. These styles strongly affected Church unity. Though Archbishop Arturo Rivera y Damas did not approve of the more radical elements within the FMLN, he remained open to dialogue. The more diffuse national leadership of the Guatemalan Church was remarkably disposed to reaching out to divergent groups. Archbishop Obando generally avoided dialogue with the Sandinistas and became a symbol of resistance to the revolutionary government. In the long run, however, he helped in peace negotiations in both the 1980s and 1990s. The Salvadoran and Guatemalan Churches maintained internal Church unity while the Nicaraguan Church was strongly divided.

Costa Rica, Honduras, and Panama

Though not as deeply involved in the Central American drama as were the other three republics, Costa Rica, Honduras, and Panama also witnessed change and turmoil during the last third of the century. And there, too, religion and politics were deeply intermingled.

Costa Rica is somewhat different from other Central American countries in that it has no standing army and no recent tradition of repressive governments and guerrilla movements nor as great a distance between rich and poor. In the late twentieth century, its church was also different from other national churches in the region. There, the Church, through its outstanding archbishop of the 1930s and 1940s, Víctor Sanabria, supported socially progressive movements.[27] The achievements of these movements are credited with helping ameliorate social problems, thus allowing the Church to be less directly involved in politics.[28]

The government through the years established a wide spectrum of social assistance programs. Priests took positions in government agencies and institutes. Thus clergy were incorporated into the government's social assistance programs. The Church itself, through its Cáritas aid agency, came more directly to look after persons outside the state's welfare umbrella.

The Catholic Church also established a greater moral presence. Newly elected presidents were expected to meet with the archbishop of San José and to ask his blessing for their new administrations. Few politicians publicly opposed Church stands on abortion, birth control, and family law.

However, in general, the Church avoided public discourse and maintained itself above politics[29]—as it does in Chile, the other Latin American country where the political party system appears strongest.[30]

The Costa Rican Church's social moderation matched that of most of Costa Rica's citizenry. Gradual change was seen as preferable to rapid and structural change. The presence of Nicaraguan revolutionaries within Costa Rican borders reinforced Costa Ricans' disdain of radical social change. A handful of Catholic activists did attempt to move the Church to speak on social questions and applauded the bishops' pastoral letters during deep economic crises. But most Costa Ricans expected both the crises and the bishops' statements to be exceptional.

Thus attempts to change the Costa Rican Church to a more political activist stance failed to penetrate profoundly either the structures of the Church or attitudes of Church leaders. The Costa Rican Church offered little room within it for debate about national issues. Instead, the few Catholic public intellectuals found space in the National University. Pablo Richard wrote for a wide Latin American audience from the University's Department of Ecumenical Investigations. Jorge Arturo Chávez Ortiz, a Dominican priest, used the Víctor Sanabria Chair at the National University to stimulate a wide dialogue about national social questions.[31]

In Honduras in the mid 1950s the Church was in disarray and, for many Hondurans, irrelevant to their lives. No church in Latin America seemed more moribund. However, subsequent decades of pastoral work partly rehabilitated the Church at the grassroots level. In the Choluteca area, priests formed Christian base communities to bolster the extremely low level of religious instruction and lay participation in the Church. French Canadian missionaries devoted themselves especially to training many of the ten thousand Delegates of the Word. These lay leaders instructed thousands of adult Catholics while the missionaries used radio instruction to reinforce their work.

By the 1990s the Honduran Church had rebounded and was having a much greater influence on society. Symbolizing this change, Tegucigalpa archbishop Oscar Rodríguez, now president of the Latin American Bishops Conference (CELAM), became a leading voice in criticizing the social devastation Latin America was suffering by incorporating economic neoliberalism without considering its impact on the poor.

In Panama, as elsewhere, the Catholic Church found itself dealing with different issues at the national and parish levels. At the local level, the Church was concerned with how to reach and make itself relevant to ordinary people. As in Honduras, the Church was very weak at mid century. Thus, to help revitalize it, Leo Mahon and other missionaries in the 1960s created what some have called the first Christian base communities. Mahon also invented alternative parish structures to offer instruction and pastoral care to thousands in urban parishes.

At the national level, on the other hand, Panama's (and hence, to some degree, the Church's) political agenda was dominated by such issues as sovereignty over the canal—not concerns typical of the rest of Central America. A titanic effort was mounted by the Church to help the nation assert its sovereignty over the canal. For instance, as Archbishop of Panama City, Marcos McGrath, who had earlier served as a major intellectual force at Medellín, led a campaign in the 1970s to persuade U.S. legislators to vote to grant Panama full sovereignty over the canal. Issues of national domestic politics, however, were reflected in internal divisions within the Church.[32]

Conservative Reaction: What Remained

In 1994, after sixty years of progressive leadership in San Salvador, Salvadorans found themselves with a new archbishop who had, for many, a disconcerting style. Archbishop Fernando Sáenz Lacalle symbolized conservative changes that were taking place in many sectors of the Latin American Church in the last two decades of the century. Like many other bishops, he emphasized the "new evangelization." Even though this could incorporate, as many priests did, elements of progressive Catholicism including an increased role for laity and an effort to relate theology to everyday issues, Sáenz preferred an apolitical, otherworldly emphasis. The change in El Salvador was clearly reflective of a change taking place in the Church worldwide.

Elected in 1978, Pope John Paul II had introduced several changes of emphasis, three of which were of special concern to Central American Churches: he criticized and questioned liberation theology, he condemned Christian-Marxist cooperation, and he imposed rigid internal discipline on the clergy. Central American critics of John Paul II found some of his orientations antithetical to the reforms of Vatican II, Medellín, and Puebla.

The attempt to control the progressive Church was most noticeable in appointments of conservative bishops. Though by no means universal, these moves were, nonetheless, threatening to priests and lay persons involved in organizations dependent on support from above. The most evident effects of the conservative reaction were on liberation theology and Christian base communities. Liberation theology was diminished in its appeal through doctrinaire attacks on certain aspects of its teaching such as class struggle and its presumptive Marxist content.

Some major aspects of the progressive Church, however, remained strong, even enhanced by John Paul II. Criticism of neoliberalism, the effects of globalization without adjustments made for unemployed and unprotected workers, was unrelenting in Latin America.[33] Advocacy of human rights was similarly emphasized. Indeed, the most consistent message of John Paul in his many journeys to Latin America and elsewhere was protection of human rights.[34]

Protestant and Indigenous Religions

More than one hundred years of pastoral activity, at first foreign and later national, made historical Protestant churches—Presbyterian, Lutheran, Episcopal, and Methodist—well established by the last third of the century. However, from the 1980s onward, these churches were eclipsed by growth in other strains of Protestantism, notably classical Pentecostal (the Assemblies of God, Church of God, and Foursquare Gospel churches) and Neopentecostal (Elim and Shaddei). Conservative fundamentalist groups in the United States, reacting to the perceived danger of "communism" in the region, poured funds, materiel, and personnel into a crusade to evangelize Central America. Their aid especially enabled the increased use of radio and television for otherworldly messages. But, as Paul Sigmund argues, "Initial theories that emphasized foreign—mainly U.S.—money and influence have been abandoned in the face of overwhelming evidence that Pentecostal growth [was] promoted and financed by the Latin American Pentecostals themselves."[35] In any case, as of this writing, Pentecostals probably accounted for one-third of all Guatemalans, one-fifth of Salvadorans, and fairly high percentages of other Central Americans.

Some churches, especially the historical Protestant ones, played a prominent role at various stages of the Nicaraguan, Guatemalan, or Salvadoran conflicts. CEPAD and Gustavo Parajón in Nicaragua as well as Lutheran Bishop Medardo Gómez in El Salvador gained national and international recognition. Both persons had strong ties to world federations. Without the Lutheran World Federation and the Oslo initiatives, the World Council of Churches, National Council of Churches in the United States, and the Vatican, the peace process would have faltered or been delayed. Thus a new level of ecumenical cooperation was achieved in Central America far beyond the mostly polite relations between churches that had existed previously.

Like Catholics, not all Protestant figures deserve praise. Jorge Serrano Elías and Efraín Ríos Montt, both Neopentecostals,[36] served highly controversial and aborted terms as Guatemala's presidents (with widespread Catholic support). However, in contrast to the Neopentecostalist activism of Serrano and Ríos Montt, most Pentecostals were criticized as otherworldly and apolitical. Their uncritical obedience to civil rulers made them appear supporters of corrupt rulers and state terrorism.[37] In Guatemala, as noted, the mostly Pentecostal Alianza Evangélica stayed out of the peace movement.

But noninvolvement of Pentecostals was by no means doctrinaire, nor was their characterization as apolitical entirely justified.[38] First, one may say that Pentecostals were pragmatic: they entered politics when it seemed necessary and when they had enough numbers to be counted, as was true late in the century.[39] Second, Pentecostals made contributions in three crucial areas toward building democracy: civil society, elections, and sensitivity to social justice. They added to civil society through infrastructures—effective schools, literacy programs, medical and dental programs—and through inculcating a strong sense of building community.[40] Pentecostals also took deep interest in elections in Central America. To the amazement of some, almost a quarter of Church of God members voted for the Sandinistas in the Nicaraguan election of 1990.[41] Others gave Guillermo Osorno, the "Christian Road" candidate, a surprising third place in that same contest. Analysis of Salvadoran voters in a 1989 survey designed by the martyred Jesuit Ignacio Martín Baró shows a profile of Pentecostal voters as more discriminating and sensitive to social injustice than previously assumed.[42]

By the 1990s Pentecostals were no longer the "newest" religion in Guatemala. They had ceded that distinction to Maya practitioners, both Christian and non-Christian. Maya indigenous religion spread among the young—and older practitioners emerged from the shadows to practice openly. Their numerical presence had been well known since the eighties to specialists in grassroots religious practices.[43] But their cohesion into unified indigenous movements was new. This fact helps to account for lack of indigenous religious presence in the Guatemalan peace movement.

The years from 1890 to 1940 when no priests resided in many areas of the Guatemalan countryside left an opening for three generations of Maya priests and healers. The war and the peace processes served as further catalysts for indigenous religious expressions. Maya political demands were extensive. They included respect for places of Maya worship, with guaranteed access to and restricted development around Maya ceremonial sites.[44] Simultaneously, sophisticated Catholic and Protestant pastoral specialists nurtured a Maya spirituality that is Christian and not based on a Eurocentric cosmology.[45] Maya Christian movements, such as the Catholic Pastoral Indígena, also grew even though their political demands had yet to be fully expressed.[46]

Conclusion

Religion and politics were intricately intertwined in Central America during the final third of the twentieth century. Religion both affected and was affected by the unfolding political drama as the region—especially Guatemala, El Salvador, and Nicaragua—went from extreme repression to revolutionary resistance to democratic transition. At first, Vatican II, Medellín, and Puebla sensitized and motivated Christians to speak out and act in behalf of social justice and human rights. Some even felt compelled by their religious beliefs to endorse (as did Archbishop Obando y Bravo in Nicaragua in 1979), or participate in, violent guerrilla or insurrectionary efforts as a last resort in bringing an end to repressive dictatorships. Christian revolutionaries were crucial to the victory of the Sandinistas in 1979 and important in the uprisings in both Guatemala and El Salvador that, in the 1990s, would force negotiated transitions to democracy. Catholic priests also played a central role in the revolutionary government and programs in Nicaragua from 1979 to 1990. At the same time, other Christians chose a nonviolent approach in their struggle for social justice and human rights. Some—such as Archbishop Oscar Romero and the six Jesuits at the Central American University in El Salvador or Bishop Juan Gerardi in Guatemala—were dramatically martyred despite their nonviolent approaches. These, and the other many dozens of killings of priests and nuns that took place throughout the region, underlined the moral bankruptcy of the ruling systems and hastened their disarticulation.

Starting in the early 1980s, more cautious or conservative religious forces also began to make themselves felt. John Paul II—a deeply concerned, socially conscious, but strongly anticommunist pope—worked to dampen enthusiasm for liberation theology and violent insurgency. Following his lead, Archbishop and later Cardinal Obando y Bravo in Nicaragua first took a strongly anti-Sandinista position but eventually accepted the revolutionary government's invitation to play a lead role in the process of peace negotiation. Similarly, Archbishop Rivera y Damas in El Salvador chose not to confront the dictatorship in his country—as had his martyred predecessor—but instead to advocate and facilitate peace negotiations. Guatemalan bishops did the same. In the long run, this less revolutionary approach, too, made a valuable contribution to democratic transition in that the Church hierarchy in all three countries played a very important role in successful peace negotiations.

Another more conservative influence in Central America from the early 1980s onward was that of the Pentecostals. They emphasized salvation in the next world and pragmatic survival in this one rather than the need to struggle for social justice. The Pentecostals were phenomenally successful in winning converts and, before long, their variety of Protestantism could boast far more adherents than could mainline Protestantism. However, even this initially conservative thrust would have very positive implications for democratization in the region in that, as noted, the Pentecostal movement—eventually staffed primarily by native Central Americans—would play an important role in helping develop grassroots civil society organizations. Like the rich variety of civil society organizations created by faith-motivated revolutionary or socially progressive forces in these countries in the 1970s and 1980s, the latter would encourage electoral and other forms of democratic participation in the 1990s.

A final contribution of religion to the process of democratic transition and consolidation was the stubborn tendency of clergy to speak out on moral issues. In 1998, Bishop Gerardi of Guatemala lost his life attempting to establish a "historical memory" of the Guatemalan holocaust in order that it might never be repeated. And throughout the 1990s, the Central American bishops repeatedly condemned the socially and economically regressive and undemocratic nature of neoliberal structural "reforms" being implemented in the region.

The relationship between religion and politics in Central America in this period, however, was not unidirectional. Religion had affected political outcomes, but so, too, the political struggle had shaped religion. First, the upsurge in fundamental Protestantism was originally driven, in part, by politics as U.S. conservative fundamentalists gave an initial burst of support to evangelize Central America. That, and the even more important contribution of the Latin Americans themselves, caused the number of people calling themselves Protestant to rise dramatically in one decade. In addition, indigenous peoples in the Guatemalan highlands, under siege by their military and temporarily deprived of services of a similarly besieged Catholic clergy, turned for solace, community, and solidarity to native religious expression.

Finally, the Catholic Church had changed dramatically in the latter part of the century. While it had lost formal adherents to the evangelizing efforts of the fundamentalist Protestants, there is no question that it had been energized in important ways through its involvement in the social and political drama of the late twentieth century. Indeed, it had been strengthened internally in ways inconceivable thirty years earlier. A moderately strong renewal had taken place. Native priests had replaced many of the missionaries. The number of young men entering seminaries had grown between 300 and 800 percent after 1972.[47] In decade after decade, new lay organizations flourished. Thus, in a little over a third of a century, religion had confronted and challenged politics, and politics had affected religion in ways that had left both dramatically altered. In all, it would be hard to imagine the changes either had undergone without considering the impact of the other.

Notes

1. The most famous early articulation of this theology is Gustavo Gutiérrez, *A Theology of Liberation: History, Politics, and Salvation* (Maryknoll, NY: Orbis, 1973).

2. See Douglas Sullivan-González, *Piety, Power, and Politics: Religion and Nation-Formation in Guatemala, 1821–1871* (Pittsburgh: University of Pittsburgh Press, 1998).

3. Jeffrey Klaiber, *The Church, Dictatorships, and Democracy in Latin America* (Maryknoll, NY: Orbis, 1998), 196.

4. See Anna L. Peterson, *Martyrdom and the Politics of Religion: Progressive Catholicism in El Salvador's Civil War* (Albany: State University of New York Press, 1997).

5. John Kirk, *Between God and the Party: Religion and Politics in Revolutionary Cuba* (Tampa: University of South Florida Press, 1989), 162–64.

6. Ideological statements clashed with scholarship over interpretations of both liberation theology and Nicaraguan religion and revolutionary politics. See what

may be the strongest statement of this conflict: Daniel H. Levine, "How Not To Understand Liberation Theology, Nicaragua, or Both," *Journal of Interamerican Studies and World Affairs* 32, no. 3 (Fall 1990): 229–45.

7. Angel Arnaiz, *Historia del pueblo de Dios en Nicaragua* (Managua: Centro Ecuménico Antonio Valdivieso, 1990), 123–24.

8. Thomas W. Walker, "The Armed Forces," in Walker, ed., *Revolution and Counterrevolution in Nicaragua* (Boulder, CO: Westview Press, 1991), 85.

9. See esp. Edward T. Brett, "The Attempts of Grassroots Religious Groups to Change U.S. Policy towards Central America," *Journal of Church and State* 36, no. 4 (Autumn 1994): 773–94; Christian Smith, *Resisting Reagan: The U.S. Central American Peace Movement* (Chicago: University of Chicago Press, 1996).

10. Edward L. Cleary, *The Struggle for Human Rights in Latin America* (Westport, CT: Praeger, 1997), 152.

11. Rose J. Spalding, "From Low-Intensity to Low-Intensity Peace: The Nicaraguan Peace Process," in Cynthia J. Arnson, ed., *Comparative Peace Processes in Latin America* (Washington, DC: Woodrow Wilson Center, 1999), 43.

12. Conferencia Episcopal de Nicaragua, "Para vivir la esperanza del Pueblo de Dios" (Managua: CEN, 1994), 4.

13. The main Charismatic group is Ciudad de Dios (City of God). See Kent Norsworthy, *Nicaragua: A Country Guide* (Albuquerque, NM: Interhemispheric Education Resource Center, 1990), 124–25.

14. Bruce Calder, "Historical Patterns of Foreign Influence in the Guatemalan Catholic Church," manuscript prepared for *Historia General de Guatemala*, vol. 5 (Guatemala City: Fundación de la Cultura y el Desarrollo, 1992), 25, 27.

15. *La Hora*, July 18, 1990.

16. An English summary was scheduled for publication by Orbis.

17. See, for example, María Teresa Tula, *Hear My Testimony: María Teresa Tula, Human Rights Activist of El Salvador* (Boston: South End Press, 1994), 203–5.

18. John L. Hammond, *Fighting to Learn: Popular Education and the Guerrilla War in El Salvador* (New Brunswick, NJ: Rutgers University Press, 1998), 25.

19. For more details about the role of the Salvadoran church in this period, see Tommie Sue Montgomery, "The Church," in *Revolution in El Salvador: Origins and Evolution* (Boulder, CO: Westview Press, 1982), 97–117.

20. Roberto Cuéllar, interview by author, San José, Costa Rica, June 12, 1996.

21. Peterson, *Martyrdom and the Politics of Religion*.

22. Cynthia McClintock, *Revolutionary Movements in Latin America: El Salvador's FMLN and Peru's Shining Path* (Washington, DC: United States Institute of Peace Press, 1998), 251–60.

23. Ibid., 268.

24. Jaime Barnett, parish priest of Iglesia del Rosario (San Salvador), interview by author, Chicago, May 31, 1999.

25. Details of lives and deaths can be found in Teresa Whitfield's *Paying the Price: Ignacio Ellacuría and the Murdered Jesuits of El Salvador* (Philadelphia: Temple University Press, 1995).

26. Ian Johnstone, *Rights and Reconciliation: UN Strategies in El Salvador* (Boulder, CO: Lynne Rienner, 1995), 55.

27. Philip J. Williams, *The Catholic Church in Nicaragua and Costa Rica* (Pittsburgh: University of Pittsburgh Press, 1989), and Manuel Picado, various works, including *La iglesia costaricense entre Dios y el César*, 2d ed. (San José: Editorial DEI, 1989), provide histories and analyses of the Catholic Church in Costa Rica.

28. Charles D. Ameringer, *Democracy in Costa Rica* (New York: Praeger, 1982), 73.

29. Assessments of the church's influence on policy issues can be found in Cynthia Chalker, "Elections and Democracy in Costa Rica," in Mitchell A. Seligson and John A. Booth, eds., *Elections and Democracy in Central America, Revisited* (Chapel Hill: University of North Carolina Press, 1995), 105–6.

30. For Chile, see Hannah Stewart-Gambino, "Redefining the Changes and Politics in Chile," in Edward L. Cleary and Hannah Stewart-Gambino, eds., *Conflict and Competition: The Latin American Church in a Changing Environment* (Boulder, CO: Lynne Rienner, 1992), 21–44.

31. See, for example, *Cristianos y neoliberales: Teólogos y economistas debaten sobre el ajuste estructural* (Heredia, Costa Rica: Editorial Fundación UNA, 1993).

32. Stanley M. Muschett Ibarra, "Church and Politics in Time of Crisis: Noriega's Panama" (Ph.D. diss., University of Notre Dame, 1992).

33. See, for example, Guatemalan Episcopal Conference, "Mensaje" (February 26, 1999) in *Voces del Tiempo* 29 (January–March 1999): 71–73.

34. David Hollenbach, "Both Bread and Freedom: The Interconnection of Economic and Political Rights in Recent Catholic Thought," in Arthur J. Dyck, ed., *Human Rights and the Global Mission of the Church* (Cambridge, MA: Boston Theological Institute, 1985), 31.

35. Paul Sigmund, ed., *Religious Freedom and Evangelization in Latin America: The Challenge of Religious Pluralism* (Maryknoll, NY: Orbis, 1999), 3.

36. Neopentecostalism in Central America referred to a second wave of Pentecostalism, also called the Charismatic movement, that began largely in the 1960s among members of mainline Protestant churches and the Catholic Church who expressed Pentecostal beliefs and practices, such as healing.

37. The sensitive question of Protestant/Pentecostal churches as havens from the war and the cooperation of Pentecostals with repressive governments is taken up at length by Virginia Garrard-Burnett in her *Protestantism in Guatemala: Living in a New Jerusalem* (Austin: University of Texas Press, 1998), esp. 148–61.

38. See Timothy Steigenga's valuable analysis of Guatemala's religious and political situation in his "Guatemala," in Paul E. Sigmund, ed., *Religious Freedom and Evangelization in Latin America: The Challenge of Religious Pluralism* (Maryknoll, NY: Orbis, 1999), 150–74.

39. For further explanation, see Edward L. Cleary, "Introduction: Pentecostals, Prominence, and Power," in Cleary and Hannah Stewart-Gambino, eds., *Power, Pentecostals, and Politics in Latin America* (Boulder, CO: Westview Press, 1997), 11–14.

40. Douglas Peterson indicates the extent of projects in "The Formation of Popular National Autonomous Churches in Central America," in *Conference Papers on the Theme "To the Ends of the Earth"* (Gaithersburg, MD: Society for Pentecostal Studies, 1994), 2–13.

41. Robert Zub, "The Growth of Protestantism: From Religion to Politics," *Envío*, December 1992, 24.

42. Edwin Eloy Aguilar et al., "Protestantism in El Salvador: Conventional Wisdom versus Survey Evidence," *Latin American Research Review* 28, no. 2 (1993): 130, 134–35.

43. Jesús Tapuerca Ceballos, Carlos Berganza, and Fernando Zuazo, interviews by author, Alta Verapaz and Guatemala City, 1992 and 1993.

44. See the demands expressed by Demetrio Cotjí Cuxil, *Políticas para la reivindicación de los Mayas de hoy* (Guatemala City: Editorial Cholsamaj, 1994).

45. Facundo Ku Canché et al., "Toward an Indigenous Theology: A Reformed Protestant Approach," Edward L. Cleary, "Birth of Latin American Indigenous Theology," and Moisés Colop, "Is Christ Being Resurrected among the Indigenous

People?" in Guillermo Cook, ed., *Crosscurrents in Indigenous Spirituality: Interface of Maya, Catholic, and Protestant Worldviews* (Leiden: E. J. Brill, 1997), 189–97, 171–88, and 199–203, respectively.

46. Jesús Tapuerca Caballos, Carlos Berganza, and Jesús Espeja, interviews by author, Centro Akkatán, Cobán, 1992–1999; Diane M. Nelson, *A Finger in the Wound: Body Politics in Quincentennial Guatemala* (Berkeley: University of California Press, 1999), 140–41.

47. *Statistical Yearbook of the Church 1996* (Vatican City: Typis Polyglottis Vaticanis, 1997) (last year for which statistics are available) and *Catholic Almanac 1975* (Huntington, IN: Our Sunday Visitor, 1975) (for 1972 statistics).

10

Neoliberalism in Central America

Carlos M. Vilas*

Neoliberalism arrived in Central America later than it did in other parts of the hemisphere. The dynamics of revolution and counterrevolution in the region created a political setting unsuitable for an economic model that involved imposing heavy burdens upon large numbers of people. When economic crisis hit Central America in the 1980s, the population was already mobilized in support of or was suffering from the effects of revolution and counterrevolution. Thus, more than elsewhere, these political factors limited the possibilities for launching neoliberal policies to manage the economic and social turmoil. They also constrained the way in which such policies were drafted and implemented.

Neoliberalism

Neoliberalism was originally promoted by the U.S. Agency for International Development (USAID). Throughout the 1980s, USAID was an important supplier of economic, financial, and technical assistance to friendly governments—that is, governments accepting the U.S. administration's interpretation of revolution in the Isthmus as simply an extension of Cuban and Soviet plans to subvert capitalism and Western values. Even so, it would be a mistake to see neoliberalism in the region merely as a conspiracy by the U.S. government, international financial agencies, and the Central American elites. Not all elites were enthusiastic about neoliberal reforms, nor did every progressive political organization categorically reject the neoliberal agenda in its entirety. Even some members of Central America's entrepreneurial and political elites manipulated neoliberal policies in such a way that they reinforced rent-seeking behavior—an outcome severely condemned

*The author holds exclusive responsibility for the content of this chapter, which does not involve the institutions he is related to: Universidad Nacional Autónoma de México, Mexico City, and Instituto Nacional de la Administración Pública, Buenos Aires, Argentina.

by neoliberal economists and international financial institutions. Domestic elites used neoliberal policies to strengthen their own position in power relations as well.

"Neoliberalism" is a generic term for both an ideology and a set of economic policies that find their main source of inspiration in neoclassical economic theory. Neoliberalism involves a return to the classical school of political economy of the eighteenth and nineteenth centuries, strongly disparaging the influence of government and politics at large in economic affairs.[1] Neoliberalism states that only a free market is able to ensure an efficient and rational allocation of economic resources. Actions oriented to or influenced by noneconomic considerations—such as politics, ideology, or religion—can only distort efficiency and lead to economic crises. Through self-regulation, free markets naturally tend to equilibrium, neoliberalism argues. Nineteenth-century liberal political economists accepted the premise that, in order to ensure full market rationality, governments must restrict their actions to public security and national defense, issuing and enforcing national currencies, and the judicial mediation of conflicts among individuals or corporations. Twentieth-century neoliberals, however, reject almost all government intervention, advocating even the privatization of the above-mentioned activities—often advocating private policing and security, nonjudicial arbitration, profit-oriented military corporations, and the abolition of "official" currencies.[2]

When confronted with evidence, the assertion that market forces naturally produce equilibrium proves false. The history of capitalism is a long series of imbalances and crises disrupting periods of stability. What we witness is nothing like a "self-regulating market." Markets, when left to their own dynamics, encourage highly speculative behavior culminating in devastating crises. Self-regulating markets are self-defeating markets as well. When crises occur, panic substitutes for supposed market-driven rationality as economic actors clamor for political intervention to "save" the economy. Asserting equilibrium when what we see is the evidence of instability and celebrating self-regulating markets while demanding government intervention are examples of the ideological nature of neoliberal propositions.

Despite their rigidity—which is the reason they are referred to as "recipes"—neoliberal policies must be adjusted to the particular political setting in which they are to be implemented. Features such as clientelism and patronage, as well as weak and fragmented markets, have to be taken into account when such policies are implemented. It is one thing to apply neoliberal recipes to an industrial economy—endowed with a well-educated and trained labor force and a diversified export sector—and quite another to implement these policies in backward economies where market relations are fragile, economic agents lack a capitalistic mentality, and particularistic orientations are a persistent ingredient of human behavior at both the upper and the lower levels of society.[3]

While the neoliberal creed is not a novelty in Latin America, its conversion into government policies is a response to the economic crisis experienced throughout the region in the 1980s. Following the implementation of neoliberal policies by British Prime Minister Margaret Thatcher, neoliberalism was enthusiastically adopted by a number of multilateral financial agencies with heavy influence in Latin America, most notably the International Monetary Fund (IMF), the World Bank, and the Inter-American Development Bank (IDB).[4]

Neoliberal recipes normally contain three general and interrelated ingredients: stabilization, structural adjustment, and export-led growth. Stabilization is achieved through drastic reduction in the money supply. Tightening credit, devaluing currency, freezing wages and pensions, and reducing the fiscal deficit by means of severe cuts in government spending, as well as laying off workers and employees in the public sector, are all ways to cut the money supply. In combination, these measures have an initial recessionary impact due to higher import prices and shrinking domestic demand. By the same token, they are intended to improve the trade balance as devaluation propels exports and cuts imports. In fact, however, heavy dependence on imported inputs in the production of exports frequently leads to recessionary stability, making recovery a far more difficult objective. Stabilization is aimed at producing outcomes in the short term in order to set the ground for subsequent adjustment. The initial impact of stabilizing measures is a dramatic increase in domestic prices, which tend to rise to international levels. Conspicuously, wages (that is, the price paid for hiring labor) are the only exception to this trend.

Structural adjustment refers to efforts to adapt the domestic economy to the prevailing conditions in the world market. These include policies aimed at producing results in the middle term. Of considerable interest is the reduction of government involvement in entrepreneurial activities such as the production and distribution of goods, provision of services, and price-regulation for privately produced and distributed goods and services. Privatization and the broad deregulation of trade, banking, and finance are central concerns of structural adjustment. Privatization also involves a number of basic services such as health care and education, which traditionally in most of Latin America have been considered public, tax-funded activities. Normally, the privatization of government-owned firms involves a reduction in employment, which, in turn, is justified as a way to improve productivity and efficiency as well as to promote monetary stability.

Governments are expected to promote foreign trade by reducing tariffs and other trade barriers. Neoliberals are harsh critics of import-substitution industrialization and all other government-active policies. These, they argue, distort rational resource allocation by the market. Foreign rather than domestic markets are seen as the key to economic growth—much as they were in the period leading up to the 1929 crisis. The lifting of trade barriers on both imports and exports is expected to lead to more efficient resource allocation, as well as adequate price levels for goods and services in the domestic market. It is also expected to ensure both capital and technology inflows to the country, thus promoting economic modernization and overall competitiveness. Combined with stabilization and privatization, these changes are expected to attract foreign investment.

Neoliberal agendas involve a transfer of income from the middle and lower to the upper classes. While, in principle, reducing inflation benefits the poor, the policy tools used to attain this goal usually neutralize the positive impact of price stability as real wages and employment decrease, informal labor grows, and prices for foodstuffs and basic services escalate. Policies implemented to attain macroeconomic gains in fiscal and trade balances, as well as in the resumption of growth, have a high cost as they result in un- and underemployment, lower real wages, and increased social polarization. Therefore, a number of short-term targeted social policies are usually added to neoliberal reforms. Though neoliberals are not very concerned about the long-term social or political impact of their economic policies, they are interested in preventing immediate social tensions that could evolve into electoral predicaments. Thus, policy makers turn to makeshift measures of compensatory assistance to the most vulnerable victims of neoliberal therapy.

Small, Price-Taker Economies

Throughout the twentieth century, growth in the Central American economies was related to two basic conditions: rising export prices and significant inflows of foreign funds. In the long run, exports were the most important source of foreign currency with which the Central American economies could afford a great variety of imports— from fuel and other basic or intermediary inputs for production to consumer goods for the upper and middle urban classes. Most foreign investment was linked to production for export. It is thus easy to understand the strategic role played by exchange-rate policies. The central objective of governments consisted in building the most friendly institutional conditions for incoming foreign funds, as export earnings, liquid funds, or direct investment. Exchange rates work as the monetary expression of a country's articulation to international markets.

The Central American economies have additional common traits. They are small, with a combined population of around thirty million—less than 0.6 percent of the world population—and an equivalent portion of the world's gross domestic product (GDP). Central America's articulation to the world economy depends on a limited number of primary export products such as coffee, bananas, sugar, cotton, and beef. In the golden years of Central America's agro-exports (from the 1950s to the 1970s), these five products accounted for about two-thirds of all exports (77 percent in 1960–1964 and 62 percent in 1975–1979). In the 1990s, agribusiness added some new items such as flowers and vegetables. Assembly plants also made a minor contribution to exports.

The export-oriented production in Central America has only a slight effect on domestic consumption in societies whose "national" diet is mostly maize (white corn), rice, and beans. The disjunction between production for exports and production for domestic markets, however, has clear implications for the whole economy. Productivity gains in the export sector do not affect production for domestic consumption perceptibly. The contrast between advanced technologies in the former, which go hand in hand with backward, low-productivity technologies in the latter, is reflected in the starkly different living conditions for producers in the export sector (mostly capitalist firms) and producers in the domestic sector (mostly poor peasants). Industrialization, promoted since the 1960s by the Central American Common Market, did not significantly alter strategic reliance on foreign investments. Industrial production, consisting mainly of light consumer goods, relied heavily on inputs from outside Central America (primarily from the United States), while industrial exports were confined to the Central American market, thus putting additional pressure on the region's external accounts.[5]

These features lay at the core of Central America's marginal and receding involvement in the international economy. While in the 1970s the isthmus accounted for just 1.9 percent of all world exports, by the mid 1990s it had fallen to less than 0.2 percent.[6] The marginal participation of the Central American economies in export markets forced them to behave as "price-takers"—to buy and sell at prices set by others. There was no alternative but to accept prices set by larger participants in the market.[7] Besides, the international markets for most Central American commodities suffered erratic ups and downs, which increased the vulnerability of producers and placed serious constraints on the ability of governments to plan mid-term spending as they could not plan fiscal incomes from foreign trade.[8]

It is clear that one basic assumption of neoliberalism—the freedom of market players—does not apply to the Central American economies. Moreover, the export sector's high reliance on imported inputs—including oil, machinery, agrochemicals, and technologies—created a second profound disjunction between the export sector and the domestic market, the latter being relatively unimportant to the activity of the former. As noted, this disjunction reduces the validity of one conventional recommendation of the neoliberal creed: currency devaluation. Though devaluation is expected to increase export earnings, it actually increases import spending. When shifts in the exchange rate cause imports to fall below the minimum level demanded to maintain export production, the possibility of improving export earnings by devaluation is neutralized by its negative effects on more expensive imported inputs for production.

Thus, because of their structural characteristics, the Central American economies enjoy fewer development options than larger, more diversified ones. In order to grow, any economy can choose one or more of the following actions: (1) increasing export earnings, (2) reducing export expenses, (3) reducing production costs. By definition, price-taker economies have little, if any, access to 1 or 2. Action 3 remains, although only as it relates to domestic production costs. Given the high reliance on imported inputs, the only costs in which there remains some room for maneuver are domestic, mainly the cost of labor. Herein lies one of the reasons for persistent authoritarianism in most of the Central American republics. If export producers are to remain competitive in the global economy, they must keep worker salaries and prices paid to peasants at the lowest level compatible with the reproduction of an abundant, unskilled labor force. Herein lies also the basic incompatibility of progressive social change—be it revolutionary or reformist—with this particular economic setting. Unless profound organizational and technical changes are introduced in both production and distribution patterns,[9] improving working and living conditions for most of the population would involve increased domestic production costs, thus reducing international competitiveness and profitability.

Neoliberalism in War-Torn Central America: The 1980s

The 1980s were a time of great conflict in Central America. Political distress aggravated economic tensions. International prices for exports declined, capital flew from the region, and trade within Central America went down. Capital flight was the product of both the economic crisis that affected all of Latin America and the deterioration of the institutional environment for traditional private investment in the wake of revolutionary changes in Nicaragua, guerrilla and counterinsurgency operations in El Salvador and Guatemala, and the rapid involvement of the entire isthmus in the so-called low-intensity warfare promoted by the U.S. government. The dynamics of revolution, counterrevolution, and war overtook all of Central America.

Central America's economic crisis predated the one that shocked all of Latin America in 1982. Growth slowed in 1977 and stagnated in 1979. The years 1981 and 1982 were characterized by recession and growing fiscal and current account deficits, increasing money oversupply, and rapidly rising domestic prices. By 1983, income per capita in Costa Rica, Guatemala, and Honduras had declined to 1972 levels, while in Nicaragua and El Salvador it had dropped to those of the early 1960s.[10]

The international crisis of 1982 thus hit a Central America already reeling from its own crisis. Throughout the 1980s, Central America's GDP per capita would shrink twice as fast as that of Latin America as a whole. Foreign trade remained stagnant throughout the decade. In Nicaragua and El Salvador, war added to the impact of both the regional and the international crises. However, since El Salvador was a recipient of important funds from the U.S. government and international agencies, it suffered less than Nicaragua, which not only lacked such support but also came to face trade and financial sanctions imposed by the United States. Combined foreign debt of the five Central American republics more than doubled and in Nicaragua almost quadrupled. Yet, regional political turmoil and poor public policy prevented the most needy countries from turning foreign inflows into developmental inputs.[11]

Central America became ever more dependent on foreign funding, at both the macro and the micro levels. International aid was strategic in sustaining the region's economic performance—if at very low levels—and in countervailing their more urgent vulnerabilities. In 1984 the report submitted to the U.S. government by a bipartisan commission chaired by former U.S. secretary of state Henry Kissinger estimated that in order to attain GDP levels equivalent to those of 1979 by 1990, Central America would need foreign funding of no less than $24 billion.[12] In fact, as it turned out, foreign aid from all donors and lenders reached only about half that figure. Throughout the 1980s the U.S. government gave El Salvador $3.9 billion in economic and military aid. Honduras received $1.4 billion and Guatemala around $570 million. Costa Rica received $1.2 billion for economic and security purposes. Nicaragua, which from 1982 onward was denied virtually any funding from multilateral financial agencies, received bilateral official development aid from a variety of countries that totaled about $660 million per year during the 1980s.[13]

Remittances of dollars from exiles in the United States and elsewhere to families in Central America played a strategic role at the microeconomic level, enabling recipients partially to bypass the impact of crisis. By the end of the 1980s, more than 1.3 million Central Americans (mostly Nicaraguans, Salvadorans, and Guatemalans) had gone into exile, found a job, and begun to send money back to relatives. Remittances to El Salvador amounted to $3.3 billion in the 1980s and continued even after the Chapultepec Peace Accords were signed. By the end of the 1980s, remittances represented around 15 percent of that country's GDP or 97 percent of its exports. Family remittances to Guatemala and Nicaragua were smaller: $1.7 billion and nearly $295 million, respectively.[14]

Social services such as health care, social security, and education, which, with the exception of Costa Rica, had never been impressive in either reach or quality, fell into complete disarray under the combined burden of fiscal crisis, political violence, and bureaucratic incompetence. In El Salvador, Guatemala, and Nicaragua, people fleeing violence in the countryside crowded cities already unable to cope with demands for basic services.

The number of Central Americans living in poverty grew from 20.9 million in 1980 to 27.6 million in 1990 as a combined outcome of economic crisis and political violence. Regional poverty became increasingly urban—though at a slower pace than in other Latin American republics. More than 50 percent of the regional increase in poverty took place in cities, the result of migrations from the violence-ridden countryside.[15] Only in Costa Rica, which was free of political violence, did poverty recede, even in rural areas. Contributing to the reduction of poverty there was an improvement in income distribution and the implementation of welfare policies.

In El Salvador, however, income polarization between the richest and the poorest strata of the population almost doubled from the mid 1970s to the early 1990s. In Guatemala, it tripled from the early 1980s to 1989. There, and in Honduras, socioeconomic inequities were the most extreme in Latin America—with the lone exception of Brazil. Despite overwhelming social tensions, Nicaragua was able to maintain comparatively high levels of social equality in the early 1990s. Indeed, in this respect, Nicaragua was similar to Costa Rica, even though levels of per capita income were significantly lower. This fact suggests that, in all, the Sandinista regime had promoted a more even social distribution of losses, while its northern neighbors were promoting a socially regressive appropriation of gains.[16]

Starting in 1979, Central America's governments—with the exception of Nicaragua's—appealed to stabilization policies, which produced some reduction in macroeconomic disequilibrium. Yet, the balance of payments continued to deteriorate because of falling trade balances and the effect of both regional and international markets. By the mid 1980s all governments realized that they were not just experiencing a traditional balance of payments crisis. Consequently, they began implementing structural adjustment programs—in some cases, such as those of Costa Rica and Honduras, through institutional agreements and financial support from the World Bank. Structural adjustment programs shared a number of common ingredients, such as implementing financial deregulation, restructuring the government sector (later known as "state reform"), easing legal restrictions on foreign investment, and removing distortions in the price system—among domestic prices as well as between domestic and external ones. In all, adjustment aimed at ending the anti-export biases of the Central American economies, considered to be an important cause of economic dysfunction. Policy decisions involved exchange rate adjustments, that is, currency devaluations, the dismantling of trade barriers and quantitative restrictions on imports, and reform of the tax and subsidy system in order to promote production of export goods.

USAID played a central role in the decision of some Central American governments to implement structural adjustment programs. Early in 1982, for instance, after the first disbursement to Costa Rica from the Economic Support Fund (ESF), USAID announced that all subsequent disbursements would be tied to legal reforms the Costa Rican legislature was expected to pass, thus allowing the free repatriation of foreign funds and private corporate funding with no intervention of the state-owned national banking system. In 1983, the U.S. government delayed the issuance of an already approved credit to Costa Rica because of the legislature's reluctance to reform the banking system to give more room to private banking institutions. The same year USAID delayed an already approved credit line for $20 million, while the IMF delayed a $609 million loan until the Costa Rican government accepted reforming the tax system as recommended by both agencies. In 1984, USAID conditioned issuing $140 million from its ESF in order to block a law about to be passed in Costa Rica's legislature that would have given priority to cooperatives in the acquisition of state-owned firms that were being privatized. Threatened with financial strangulation, Costa Rica finally accepted the conditions imposed by lenders. Later, the World Bank joined this strategy of financial pressures, thus creating a system of cross-conditionality imposed by all institutional lenders. In 1985, Costa Rica signed an agreement with the World Bank explicitly accepting the principle of cross-conditionality between the World Bank, the IMF, and USAID.

Interestingly, the central role that Honduras played in the U.S. counterinsurgency strategy triggered abundant flows of U.S. funds. In 1985–1987, Honduras received about $550 million in both economic and military aid. However, as the Contras and their Honduran military bases receded in importance as tools of the U.S. Central American foreign policy, Washington's direct funding went rapidly down and financial aggressiveness replaced generosity. In 1989, USAID froze $70 million until Honduras signed an agreement with the IMF calling for a harsh devaluation of the Honduran currency, increased taxes to expand fiscal income, drastic cuts in government spending and bureaucracy, and greater economic deregulation.

In contrast, El Salvador enjoyed open tolerance from both USAID and multilateral financial institutions throughout these years. Apparently it was feared that the social impact of adjustment would neutralize efforts by the Salvadoran government—supported by U.S. military, diplomatic, and economic policy—to defeat the Farabundo Martí National Liberation Front (Frente Farabundo Martí de Liberación Nacional, FMLN). Despite obvious economic mismanagement and massive government and military corruption, funds continued flowing to El Salvador without any conditionality short of the political one: to defeat the revolutionaries.

In addition to imposing severe conditions for funding some governments and awarding them abundant aid if they cooperated, USAID devoted considerable effort and resources to developing a new breed of Central American entrepreneur, politician, and intellectual to promote economic adjustment in the isthmus. Think tanks were given USAID funding and training. In 1982, as an integral part of its involvement in efforts to prevent a revolutionary triumph in El Salvador, USAID helped launch the Salvadoran Foundation for Development (Fundación Salvadoreña de Desarrollo, FUSADES), which would henceforth enjoy open-handed U.S. funding. It has been estimated that in the following ten years USAID funneled about $200 million through FUSADES.[17] Drawing its membership from a cross section of the Salvadoran business community willing to join the Reagan strategy for Central America, FUSADES rapidly turned into a committed sponsor of neoliberal reforms. Ironically, however, under the Bush administration, FUSADES became a severe critic of the U.S. strategy of low-intensity warfare that, to FUSADES, was both incapable of defeating the FMLN and conducive to government and military corruption. In Guatemala, USAID sponsored the birth of the Business Chamber (Cámara Empresarial) in 1985, a nongovernmental organization devoted to policy analysis and recommendations, with emphasis on economic modernization relying heavily on abundant, cheap labor. Appealing to funds from the Caribbean Basin Initiative, USAID also joined in the creation of the Coalition and Initiatives for Development (Coalición e Iniciativas para el Desarrollo, CINDE) in Costa Rica. Through it, USAID channeled funds for agro-export development and foreign trade diversification in general. CINDE was active in pressuring Costa Rica's government to privatize government-owned firms and open up the economy to international markets.[18]

Reforms had uneven results all over Central America. Nontraditional exports to markets outside Central America experienced remarkable growth—though (with the possible exception of handicrafts) most of the commodities exported (including tropical plants, fresh flowers, pineapples, canned fruits, and *maquila* garments) involved very low value added. Yet, success in export growth and diversification was linked to currency devaluation, preferential stimuli, and foreign funding under special terms, rather than to trade and financial deregulation or fiscal reforms.[19]

Costa Rica's success was not matched in the other republics. Foreign funding to adjustment reforms had played an important role. According to one analyst, it was only the high level of aid from the U.S. government—more than $1.2 billion throughout the 1980s—that prevented the collapse of the Costa Rican economy.[20] In fact, once its government accepted cross conditionalities from U.S. and multilateral financial agencies, Costa Rica became the second largest per capita recipient of U.S. foreign aid (after Israel). Indeed, it has been argued that the country's immediate economic recovery owed more to this massive influx of funds than to the reactivation of foreign trade.[21] It should be noted also that Washington's relative generosity toward Costa Rica was in no small way related both to the latter's role as a rearguard for the anti-Sandinista Contras and the Reagan administration's focus on it as a showcase for democracy in apparent contrast to "pro-Communist" Nicaragua.

Yet, Costa Rica's relative economic success was also linked to its unique institutional development. First was the nonorthodox character of the country's structural adjustment. Despite external political pressures, the government was able to keep the basic dimensions of its incipient welfare state untouched by structural adjustment. Social security, health care, and universal education are among the most evident "comparative advantages" of Costa Rica in Central America. In addition, the country has a strong social network of cooperatives, unions, and civic organizations comprising an active civil society and a relatively accountable and efficient civil service. Finally, while military budgets grew steadily throughout the decade in the rest of the region, Costa Rica, with no formal army, did not have to devote government funds to military expenses. In all, this combination of political, institutional, and social characteristics made possible a unique type of developing capitalist system cum welfare state. It also made possible stable civilian rule and strong institutional emphasis on broad-based consensus building, which allowed the government to manage efficiently both the need for adjustment and foreign pressures for neoliberal economic policies.

In the short run, adjustment programs reduced fiscal deficits and curtailed inflation. However, external account deficits, together with military spending in countries such as El Salvador, Nicaragua, and to a lesser extent Guatemala, continued to feed inflation and neutralize efforts at stabilization. Traditional entrepreneurial opposition to tax reforms prevented significant improvement in tax collection. An illustration of this opposition was the confrontation against the Christian Democratic government of Vinicio Cerezo mounted by the Chamber of Agricultural, Commercial, Industrial, and Financial Associations (Comité Coordinador de Asociaciones Agrícolas, Comerciales, Industriales y Financieras, CACIF) as a response to a proposed mild tax reform that would have raised Guatemala's extremely low (even by Central American standards) tax coefficient. The reform was eventually defeated and the government was forced to give up on financial reforms.[22] In El Salvador, business associations had systematically opposed economic and social changes—such as agrarian reform and the nationalization of foreign trade—implemented in the early 1980s by both the progressive military juntas and the Christian Democratic government of José Napoleón Duarte to build popular support and contain revolutionary appeal.

In countries involved in revolutionary or counterrevolutionary conflict, political and institutional obstacles to efficient tax collection and to significant cuts in government spending and the import of inputs to sustain an export economy combined to reduce the sustainability of adjustment. Nicaragua was the only Central American country to raise taxes significantly in the 1980s.[23]

As in the rest of Latin America, structural adjustment in Central America was carried out with little concern for its impact on the social distribution of gains and losses. Although much of the social dislocation and suffering in the region flowed from political conflicts, which interrupted agricultural cycles and disrupted labor markets because of guerrilla and counterinsurgency operations, and internal and international migration, structural adjustment accelerated income concentration in the upper segments of society, thus increasing the combined cost for millions of Central Americans.[24]

Even the Sandinista government of Nicaragua implemented a version of macroeconomic adjustment in 1988–89. This adjustment came after an initial, shy attempt in 1985—which had been rapidly swamped by the impact of the counterrevolutionary war.[25] Though lacking any support from multilateral financial agencies—not to mention the U.S. government—Nicaragua was moderately successful in controlling some economic variables such as investment and domestic price levels. Yet, the country's fiscal deficit remained high—almost 20 percent in 1988–1990—as compared with 2.8 percent in Guatemala or 3.6 percent in El Salvador. The circulation of paper money and deposits in Nicaraguan banks was almost half of the country's GDP.[26] In the absence of any consistent policy program, Nicaragua's adjustment was successful only in the short term. After a few months, inflationary and recessionary tendencies returned with renewed strength. Hyperinflation, which had climbed to an incredible 33,547 percent in 1988, had dropped after the adjustment to "only" 1,689 percent but soared again to 13,490 percent in 1990, the first year of the administration of Violeta Barrios de Chamorro.[27]

Neoliberalism in the 1990s

In sharp contrast to the previous decade, the 1990s brought political stability and relative conservative homogeneity to the region. Representative democracy reigned across the isthmus even though social distress remained pervasive. In 1989, elections propelled El Salvador's Nationalist Republican Alliance (Alianza Republicana Nacionalista, ARENA) and Honduras's National Party (Partido Nacional) to power, both under the leadership of vocal supporters of neoliberal economics. The following year, the National Opposition Union (Unión Nacional Opositora, UNO) defeated the Sandinistas in Nicaragua and the Party of Social Christian Unity (Partido de Unidad Social Cristiana) triumphed in Costa Rica. In 1991 the Movement for Solidarity Action (Movimiento de Acción Solidaria) did the same in Guatemala. In El Salvador, Nicaragua, and Guatemala, right-wing rule was confirmed through subsequent elections from 1994 to 1996, and opposition victories in Honduras (1993, 1997) and Costa Rica (1994, 1998) involved little significant changes in economic or social policies. Peace talks between government and guerrillas eventually succeeded in El Salvador (1991) and Guatemala (1996).

Conservative rule and massive demobilization cleared the political ground for a new wave of neoliberal reforms. In public opinion surveys conducted in several Central American republics, order and stability (along with a very low trust in political institutions and leaders) ranked high in people's preferences.[28] After more than a decade of political violence, economic crisis, frustrated sacrifices, and broken promises, this was hardly surprising. Consequently, abstentionism grew by one-third in Costa Rican presidential elections from 1990 to 1994. In El Salvador's 1994 general election—the much vaunted "election of the century"—it stood at 40 percent. The figure was 49 percent in Guatemala the following year. Abstentionism also grew steadily in Honduras after 1985.[29] Only in Nicaragua, where election day procedures had been relatively clean from 1984 onward and where the stunning defeat of the incumbent Sandinistas in 1990 had convinced voters that their vote really did count, did abstentionism remain low (around 14 percent in both 1990 and 1996).[30]

In all of Central America, neoliberalism was implemented most religiously in El Salvador. ARENA approached neoliberal fundamentals as a complement to the party's never-abandoned anticommunism. For ARENA, as well as for FUSADES, neoliberalism—with its simple appeal to economic "truths"—appeared to have been a nonmilitary way to discipline workers and the poor. While people's mobilizations in the 1980s had been confronted under the banner of Western values and anticommunism, they could be opposed in the name of a free market and globalization in the 1990s. Simply, neoliberal reforms were used to reinforce the traditional power relationship between classes and other social groupings. What once had been legitimated through political ideology now was grounded on market rationale.

The initial concentration of income, resources, and assets, typical of any stabilization program, was then reinforced and celebrated in El Salvador as a dimension of traditional class politics. Furthermore, privatization was carried out not just to overcome fiscal constraints or to improve economic performance but to benefit political cronies. The privatization of banks during the Cristiani administration is a good example of the ability of Central American elites to preserve traditional privileges through formal modernization—a creole version of Asian "crony capitalism." Most of the privatized banks ended up in the hands of the Cristiani clique (the "golden ring"), which had also been benefiting from other government policies. Not surprisingly, some observers saw privatization implemented by the subsequent Calderón Sol administration as essentially the placating of the Calderón Sol clique, which had been prevented from benefiting from Cristiani's policies.[31]

Political retaliation was present in Nicaragua's version of neoliberal reforms. Privatization—including the dismantling of both agrarian and housing reforms—was approached by the elites as a means to recover what the Sandinista revolution had taken from them. The UNO government took advantage of the fact that the Sandinista regime had neglected to give legal title for most of the land distributed to either individual peasants or cooperatives. Despite explicit pre-electoral promises that land reform would be honored, the new administration quickly accepted dubious claims from former absentee owners—many of them intimately related to Somoza's dictatorship. In addition, a policy of selective credit shortages was implemented, affecting small peasants and cooperatives.[32]

Opposition to neoliberal reforms mobilized a broad scope of actors. Unions, student movements, peasant organizations, and other grassroots organizations reacted aggressively to the initial recessive and regressive impact of stabilization and privatization. In both Nicaragua and El Salvador, violent grassroots responses were intensified by political frustration in the wake of the Sandinistas' electoral defeat and ARENA's unwillingness to implement the social and economic aspects of the peace accords. A broad array of middle- and lower-class citizens and groups began organizing and protesting the inequitable impact of neoliberal reforms. Students and the urban poor staged street rallies in opposition to privatization of government-owned public services such as communications and transportation. Peasants and former combatants seized land and government buildings demanding access to land and opposing the undoing of agrarian reform. Middle-class professionals such as doctors and teachers protested budget cuts and demanded decent working conditions.

Though not as vocal, opposition to neoliberal policies also emerged from segments of the business community, particularly from those oriented toward the tiny domestic market, which, in the recent past, had enjoyed the protection of interventionist government policies and favorable exchange rates. Neoliberal criticism of import-substitution industrialization had been addressed to these segments of the Central American bourgeoisie—not just to their institutional sponsors. Currency devaluation, credit stringency, trade liberalization, tax reform, shrinking domestic consumption, and competition from imports had all dealt heavy blows to locally oriented entrepreneurs.

In both El Salvador and Guatemala, the economic chapters of peace accords were contradicted and undermined by government-sponsored economic policies. The Chapultepec accords accepted the continuity of previous economic policy definitions, making it very difficult to observe several economic provisions in the agreement, including land distribution to former insurgents and financial support to small businesses. Financial commitments to monetary stability and structural adjustment—stemming from previous deals between the ARENA government and the World Bank—made it impossible for the government to provide any substantial funding to implement the accords, thus forcing it to rely on foreign cooperation and incurring further delays in achieving such goals as the resettlement of displaced populations. The incapacity and lack of interest of the ARENA government to carry out social and economic reforms were reinforced by the most conservative representatives of the business community, who rejected any attempt at a tax reform to provide much-needed funding. The country's most influential business organization, the National Association of Private Enterprise (Asociación Nacional de la Empresa Privada, ANEP), actually refused to participate in the Forum on Economic and Social Concord (Foro de Concertación Económico-Social), thus significantly reducing the latter's representativeness. Elite foot-dragging fed social unrest and stimulated sporadic outbursts of political violence. Eventually, international lending agencies pressured government agencies to resolve the most irritating issues of the accords, for instance, the transfer of land to former FMLN guerrillas.[33]

In Guatemala, a number of sensitive issues included in the peace accords also faced opposition from the most entrenched segments of the traditional elites. Among them were land distribution, the enactment of a progressive tax reform, and institutional modernization. In contrast to El Salvador and Guatemala, in both Honduras and Costa Rica neoliberalism was consolidated in a less conflictive way—despite reluctance on the part of the Liberal government in Honduras and the National Liberation Party (Partido de Liberación Nacional) administration in Costa Rica.

Multilateral lending agencies, however, did see some need to reduce the initial negative impact of stabilization and adjustment policies on the most vulnerable segments of the Central American societies and, hence, in part to neutralize their opposition. Accordingly, they recommended the implementation of targeted social policies through soft funding—loans or donations—or through semi-autonomous government agencies. Social Investment Funds (SIF) were implemented in Guatemala (1989, 1991), Honduras (1990), El Salvador (1990), and Nicaragua (1990). The SIF were intended to provide short-term responses to critical social problems with destabilizing potential. They involved a variety of programs ranging from the short-term employment of the unskilled in public works or community services to job training and food assistance. Nicaragua's SIF were funded entirely through foreign donations. Guatemala's government contributed just 10 percent of such funds, while El Salvador's provided 22 percent of the funding for both the National Reconstruction Plan (Plan de Reconstrucción Nacional) and for programs to fight extreme poverty.[34]

Economic statistics show that almost two decades of experimentation with neoliberal fiscal policies yielded uneven results (see table). Though GDP growth returned, it was meager when compared to population growth. Despite reduced inflationary pressures, fiscal balance has still not been achieved; and, over all, despite the disappearance of most of the noneconomic factors feeding the government deficit, neoliberal reforms have been surprisingly unsuccessful.

The Macroeconomic Effects of Central America's Neoliberal Reforms

	GDP[a]		GDP per Capita[a]	
	1981–1990	*1991–1997*	*1981–1990*	*1991–1997*
Costa Rica	2.2	3.4	-0.6	1.0
El Salvador	-0.4	5.3	-1.4	2.9
Guatemala	0.9	4.1	-1.6	1.4
Honduras	2.4	3.7	-0.8	0.7
Nicaragua	-1.5	2.8	-3.9	-0.1

	Consumer Price Index[b]		
	1987–1990	*1991–1994*	*1995–1997*
Costa Rica	19.7	17.8	16.0
El Salvador	20.1	12.7	7.0
Guatemala	25.3	11.9	9.5
Honduras	14.3	17.4	22.4
Nicaragua	1,258.5	202.7	10.6

	Fiscal Deficit[c]	
	1991–1994	*1995–1997*
Costa Rica	-3.3	-4.7
El Salvador	-1.9	-1.4
Guatemala	-0.8	-0.4
Honduras	-5.7	-3.0
Nicaragua	-1.1	-1.1

	Trade Balance[d]	
	1991–1994	*1995–1997*
Costa Rica	-1,091.7	-380
El Salvador	-3,873.9	-4,238
Guatemala	-3,249.9	-2,450
Honduras	-597.0	-435
Nicaragua	-2,048.8	-1,565

	Current Account[d]	
	1991–1994	*1995–1997*
Costa Rica	-1,673.9	-566
El Salvador	-1,033.7	-577
Guatemala	-2,355.5	-1,519
Honduras	-1,377.1	-337
Nicaragua	-3,736.5	-1,588

Source: CEPAL, *Statistical Yearbook of Latin America and the Caribbean*. Santiago: CEPAL, several years.
[a]Real average annual rate of growth over the period.
[b]Average annual rate of growth over the period.
[c]As percentage of GDP, annual average.
[d]U.S. $ million accumulated in each period.

The inability of neoliberalism to match its own goals and promises was apparent in both the lack of sustained growth and the persistence of external accounts deficits. Although both trade and current account balances improved throughout the 1990s, at decade's end deficit was still a persistent feature of Central American economies, which suggests that trade liberalization, export promotion, and institutional modernization had not reduced the external vulnerability of these economies, which, in turn, relates to several of their shared structural traits.

Neoliberal reforms had not delivered meaningful results in terms of the alleviation of poverty. And it was not at all clear that they ever would. According to the World Bank, by the mid 1990s, 75 percent of Guatemalans were living below the poverty line, while two-thirds of them were below the line of *extreme* poverty. In El Salvador, 48 percent of households were in poverty—one-fourth of them in extreme poverty. Half the Nicaraguan population was also under the poverty line. These figures represent an increase in poverty since the early 1980s.[35] It can be argued, then, that increasing poverty was more than just an initial or ad interim effect of neoliberal reform. Rather, neoliberal reforms were apparently reinforcing historical tendencies toward profound social inequality in the isthmus.

By distributing food aid and small subsidies to households and to children attending school, SIF and related short-term social policies might have ameliorated extreme poverty somewhat, but structural poverty—stemming from low wages, un- or underemployment, environmental degradation, extreme social polarization, and declining prices for peasant crops—calls for a different set of economic policies. Most of these policies, however, including creating better-paid jobs, implementing alternative technologies, enacting and enforcing a progressive tax reform, and providing small producers more access to productive assets and credit, are either beyond the scope of neoliberal reforms or do not promise to deliver short-term benefits.

Institutional reforms strongly recommended by foreign lenders produced meager results. Health care reform illustrates the tensions and ambiguities associated with neoliberal reforms in poverty-ridden societies. Although Central American governments began discussing the need to reform the health care sector in the late 1980s, not until the 1990s were reforms triggered by loans from both the World Bank and IDB. Loans were granted on the condition that governments implement broad public sector reforms, reflecting lender interest in macroeconomic adjustment and state deregulation. Health care reform was approached as an integral part of government efforts to balance fiscal accounts. In Nicaragua, public spending on health services and infrastructure dropped from 5 percent to 4 percent of the country's GDP from 1990 to 1995. By mid 1996, the Nicaraguan government was spending an average of $19 per person per year on health services, or $1.50 per person per month. In Guatemala, reform increased government spending on health care from a symbolic 0.9 percent in 1990 to a still trivial 1.3 percent in 1995. Costa Rica, a country whose decision making was always more independent from multilateral lending agencies, devoted more than 7 percent of its government's budget—or $60 per person per year—to health.[36] Efficiency, cost cutting, and better managerial skills—all of which were urgently needed in Central America—were emphasized. However, efficiency was undermined by budget cuts, reducing the scope and outreach of policies and actions, and cost cutting was urged on countries already devoting meager resources to health and other social services.

Conclusion

Was neoliberalism inevitable in Central America? Were there alternatives to it? How much of the poverty and social inequality in the isthmus was it responsible for?

To avoid falling into the realm of mere ideology, we must acknowledge that, with the exception of Costa Rica, poverty and social polarization had long been characteristic of Central America. Costa Rica had become an exception through political and social reforms implemented in the late 1940s and early 1950s. In the 1980s macroeconomic accounts in all five republics had been thrown into disarray by a combination of economic and political factors at the domestic, regional, and international levels. Therefore, the need to re-introduce macroeconomic balance and to adjust these small, backward, price-taker economies to the new international setting had, for some time, been obvious to everyone, regardless of politics or ideology. However, what was inevitable was the need, not necessarily the strategy.

Revolutionary Nicaragua's relatively heterodox response to economic crisis in the mid 1980s showed that there was no inevitability in neoliberal recipes. The experiment did fail, but it is not at all clear how much of that failure was due to "technical" economic or managerial factors and how much was the product of a combination of insufficient external financial support and foreign political and military pressures. Clearly, there is a sharp contrast between the financial isolation of Nicaragua when it made its reforms and the heavy foreign funding of reform in Costa Rica, Honduras, and El Salvador in the same period. By the same token, we should remember that the Salvadoran and Guatemalan peace accords in the following decade included several socioeconomic aspects that, if implemented, would have forced a different approach to economic adjustment. The Costa Rican case, too, shows a certain room for maneuver even under persistent foreign pressures for neoliberalism. In all, these alternative approaches suggest that there are different roads to stability, adjustment, and resumption of growth, as well as to a different, more progressive distribution of gains and losses among social actors.

Politics, not just economic inevitability, made neoliberalism the dominant school of economic policy making in the region. Pressure from external lenders such as USAID (which played a pioneering role at the level of both the state and civil society), the World Bank, and the IDB was critical in the establishment of neoliberalism in Central America. The conservative reconfiguration of Central American politics added leverage to neoliberal policy making. The neoliberal insistence on the primacy of capital investment over labor was easily translated into the primacy of the landed, trade, industrial, or financial elites over working people, peasants, and indigenous groups. The ideology of the "free market" replaced anticommunism as an instrument for dealing with the economic demands of the poor and the oppressed. Neoliberalism's emphasis on the preeminence of the economic order was congenial to a ruling class accustomed to imposing its own rule at all costs.

It is then legitimate to conclude that a different power alignment of political and social actors could have devised a different strategy to confront macroeconomic chaos and to reactivate growth. Or, to put it in a not-so-speculative way, it might be concluded that the victory of neoliberalism is more indebted to the political victory of its Central American middlemen than to the accuracy of its theoretical foundations or to the soundness of its policy recommendations.

Notes

1. Adam Smith's *An Inquiry into the Nature and Causes of the Wealth of Nations* (1776) is considered to be the founding work of the classical school. However, David Ricardo (1772–1823) was the first true economist to systematize it. Thomas Malthus (1766–1834) and John Stuart Mill (1806–1873) made subsequent contributions to this school. With respect to neoliberal economics, Friedrich Hayek, Ludwig von Misses, and Milton Friedman are acknowledged as the most important names in the second half of the twentieth century.

2. Simon Sheppard, "Foot Soldiers of the New World Order: The Rise of the Corporate Military," *New Left Review* 228 (March–April 1998): 128–38; Friedrich Hayek, "Choice and Currency," Occasional Paper 48, London Institute of Economic Affairs, 1976, and *Denationalization of Money: An Analysis of the Theory of Concurrent Currencies* (1978), translated as *La desnacionalización del dinero* (Madrid: Instituto de Economía de Mercado, 1983).

3. On the importance of taking account of cultural and anthropological variables when recommending economic policies, see Emmanuel Todd, *L'illusion économique* (Paris: Gallimard, 1998).

4. On neoliberalism in Latin America, see Duncan Green, *Silent Revolution: The Rise of Market Economies in Latin America* (London: Cassell, 1995).

5. Carlos M. Vilas, *Between Earthquakes and Volcanoes: Market, States, and the Central American Revolutions* (New York: Monthly Review Press, 1995), chap. 2.

6. United Nations, *International Trade Statistics Yearbook* (New York: United Nations, various years).

7. Large coffee growers and exporters such as Brazil and Colombia can influence market prices both actively (for example, by selling smaller or larger quantities) and passively (for example, because of either adverse or very good weather

conditions). This is not true for small producers such as the Central American republics. See John Weeks, *The Economies of Central America* (New York: Holmes & Meier, 1985); Carlos M. Vilas, *Transición desde el subdesarrollo* (Caracas: Nueva Sociedad, 1989).

8. The fact that the United States had been the most important market for a number of Central American exports—such as cotton, bananas, beef, and sugar—did not reduce the impact of the international markets' ups and downs. This phenomenon could be explained by the U.S. market's sensitivity to the international markets and domestic political issues, and by the marginal impact of Central American exports, even in the U.S. market.

9. On the relative exceptionality of Costa Rica's democratic reformism, see Anthony Winson, *Coffee and Democracy in Modern Costa Rica* (London: MacMillan, 1989).

10. Vilas, *Between Earthquakes and Volcanoes*, chap. 4.

11. For figures and further development, see Vilas, *Between Earthquakes and Volcanoes*, 125–69.

12. Quoted in Ricardo Córdova Macías and Raúl Benítez Manaut, eds., *La paz en Centroamérica: Expediente de documentos fundamentales, 1979–1989* (Mexico City: UNAM, 1989).

13. Carlos M. Vilas, "Prospects for Democratization in a Post-Revolutionary Setting: Central America," *Journal of Latin American Studies* 28, no. 2 (May 1996): 461–503.

14. Vilas, "Prospects for Democratization."

15. CEPAL, *Bases para la transformación productiva y generación de ingresos de la población pobre de los países del istmo centroamericano*, LC/MEX/G3/Rec. 2, 1992.

16. World Bank, *World Development Report* (Washington, DC: World Bank, various years); Vilas, "Prospects for Democratization."

17. Gabriel Gaspar Tapia, "La modernización de las clases dominantes centroamericanas," in C. M. Vilas, ed., *Democracia emergente en Centroamérica* (Mexico City: UNAM, 1993), 51–63.

18. Carlos Sojo, *La mano visible del mercado* (San José: CRIES, 1992); Tapia, "La modernización."

19. Ian Walker, "El ajuste estructural y el futuro desarrollo de la región centroamericana," Working Paper 2, Posgrado Centroamericano en Economía y Planificación del Desarrollo, Universidad Nacional Autónoma de Honduras, 1991.

20. Gregg L. Vunderink, "Peasant Participation and Mobilization during Economic Crisis: The Case of Costa Rica," *Studies in Comparative International Development* 25, no. 4 (Winter 1990): 3–34.

21. Edgar Fürst, "Costa Rica 1982–1987: ¿Una aplicación heterodoxa 'sui generis' de políticas de ajuste estructural?" in Mats Lundhall and Wim Pelupessy, eds., *Crisis económica en Centroamérica y el Caribe* (San José: DEI, 1989), 179–204.

22. Vilas, *Between Earthquakes and Volcanoes*, chap. 4. The peace accords signed in 1996 between Guatemala's government and the URNG insurgency established that the government had to raise the overall tax coefficient to 12 percent of the GDP—which would have resulted in a 100 percent increase in tax funds.

23. Yet, by the end of the decade, tax coefficients in Nicaragua—which had reached an unparalleled 26.9 percent in 1985–1987—experienced a slight reduction.

24. Rómulo Caballeros, "Centroamérica: El recuento de una década perdida," in Marta Casaus Arzú and Rolando Castillo Quintana, eds., *Centroamérica: Bal-*

ance de la década de los 80: Una perspectiva regional (Madrid: CEDEAL, 1993), 37–71.

25. Carlos M. Vilas, "Troubles Everywhere: An Economic Perspective on the Sandinista Revolution," in Rose Spalding, ed., *The Political Economy of Revolutionary Nicaragua* (Boston: Allen & Unwin, 1987), 233–46.

26. Lance Taylor et al., *Nicaragua: The Transition from Economic Chaos to Sustainable Growth* (Stockholm: Swedish International Development Agency, 1989); Carlos M. Vilas, "A Revolution That Fell from the Grace of the People," in Ralph Miliband, ed., *The Socialist Register 1991* (London: Merlin Press, 1991), 300–19.

27. CEPAL, *Balance preliminar de la economía de América Latina y el Caribe* (Santiago, Chile: ECLAC, December 18, 1992).

28. Vilas, "Prospects for Democratization."

29. Jack Spence et al., *Chapultepec: Five Years Later—El Salvador Political Reality and Uncertain Future* (Boston, MA: Hemispheric Initiatives, 1997); Mitchell A. Seligson, *Political Culture in Nicaragua: Transitions, 1991–95* (Washington, DC: USAID, 1995); Vilas, "Prospects for Democratization"; and newspaper information on subsequent elections.

30. The official results from the Supreme Electoral Council (CSE) do show an increase in abstentionism from 14 percent in 1990 to 23 percent in 1996. However, in 1996, the CSE had been forced to throw out the badly handled vote tallies in hundreds of polling places. Oddly, it then treated actual voters in those places as having abstained. When those voters are counted as having voted, we see no increase in abstentionism from 1990 to 1996. See UCA-Nitlapan-*Envío* Team, "How Nicaraguans Voted," *Envío* 15, no. 185–86 (December 1996–January 1997): 38.

31. Fernando Sarto and Alexander Segovia, "¿Hacia dónde se dirige la privatización de la banca?" *Revista de Política Económica* 12 (1992): 3–25; Alexander Segovia, "La experiencia política del ajuste en El Salvador," in Gerónimo de Sierra, ed., *Los pequeños países de América Latina en la hora del neoliberalismo* (Caracas: Nueva Sociedad, 1994), 69–87; Carlos M. Vilas, "Un balance de la ejecución de los acuerdos de paz en El Salvador," *Papers, Revista de Sociología* 49 (1996): 77–94.

32. Richard Stahler-Sholk, "Structural Adjustment and Resistance: The Political Economy of Nicaragua under Chamorro," in Gary Prevost and Harry E. Vanden, eds., *The Undermining of the Sandinista Revolution* (New York: St. Martin's, 1997), 74–113; Laura J. Enríquez, "La reforma agraria en Nicaragua: Pasado y futuro," in Vilas, *Democracia emergente*, 133–57.

33. Michael W. Foley et al., *Land, Peace, and Participation: The Development of Post-War Agricultural Policy in El Salvador and the Role of the World Bank* (Washington, DC: Washington Office on Latin America, June 1997).

34. Carlos M. Vilas, "De ambulancias, bomberos y policías: La política social del neoliberalismo," *Desarrollo Económico* 144 (January–March 1997): 931–52.

35. CEPAL, *Bases para la transformación productiva*; World Bank, *Guatemala: An Assessment of Poverty* (Washington, DC: World Bank, April 1995); World Bank, *El Salvador: The Challenge of Poverty Alleviation* (Washington, DC: World Bank, June 1994); World Bank, *Republic of Nicaragua Poverty Assessment* (Washington, DC: World Bank, June 1995). Those living below the poverty line are unable to purchase even a very limited quantity of goods and services. Extreme poverty, in turn, implies starvation.

36. Carlos M. Vilas, "Neoliberal Social Policy: Managing Poverty (Somehow)," *NACLA Report on the Americas* 29, no. 6 (1996): 16–25.

11

Civil Society and Democratic Transition

Patricia Bayer Richard and John A. Booth

Organized groups of citizens played major roles in Central America's political turmoil from the 1970s through the 1990s, and in the eventual emergence of democracy in the region. Groups both led the long struggles for democracy and supported authoritarian efforts to resist it. Students of Central American politics have explored how associations in general or particular groups mobilized political demands and protested and fought authoritarian rule, and how others such as paramilitaries and right-wing movements helped repress popular demands for change. Most of this research on groups investigated processes and politics at the national level, rather than their impacts on individuals. In contrast, recent scholarship on "civil society" has explored how organizations shape their members' attitudes and behaviors as a means by which they affect the larger society. This focus on how civil society affects individuals—largely missing from prior research on Central America—can provide valuable insights into the process of democratization in the region.

While the concept of civil society—citizen activity in organizations—has a rich and complex history,[1] the recent writings of Robert Putnam precipitated a spate of popular, theoretical, and empirical writing. Putnam argues that civil society contributes to successful governance and to democracy and that it does so because membership in groups causes citizens to develop socially and politically beneficial "social capital"—knowledge, skills, expectations, social networks, and behaviors that enhance civility within the polity.[2] Putnam, however, fails to specify how civil society and the resulting social capital shape government performance. Nor does he address the implications of confrontational, conflictive, and even violent forms of associational activity that have been widespread in Central America.[3]

To address these gaps in Putnam's theory this chapter explores how, to what extent, and in what contexts civil society contributes to democratic attitudes, political participation, and democratic governance by examining citizens' organizational activity in Central America and how citizens' participation in groups impinges on the state through both political participation and democratic norms. The new concept of "political capital" is added to Putnam's category of social capital, and the influences of both on levels of democracy are examined. This chapter concludes that political capital more strongly links involvement in groups and democracy than does social capital and that the level and recency of political repression shape citizens' choices of group activity and participation. Participation in different kinds of groups is found to produce different sorts of social and political capital, for instance, that involvement in formal groups has different effects than involvement in communal activity. Finally, an examination of whether associational activity inevitably supports democracy reveals that it can, in some instances, reduce rather than increase civility and democratic norms.

Theory

Numerous scholars have argued that civil society contributes to democratization.[4] In such views, citizen participation in organizations operates to further democracy through a number of mechanisms. First, associational life generates social capital—trust, habits of cooperation and participation, and dense social networks.[5] Additionally, civil society groups mediate between citizen and state and mobilize citizens' interests, thereby influencing government action[6] and inculcating democratic values.[7]

Seen through Putnam's rose-colored lenses, all associational activity produces undisputed social goods; indeed, Putnam argues in his famous "Bowling Alone" article that its decline might jeopardize democracy in the United States. Other conceptions, in contrast, view civil society's contributions more neutrally,[8] or question this optimistic view of civil society.[9]

A central issue here is whether all associational activity promotes democracy. As Michael Foley and Bob Edwards put it, Which kinds of associations have democracy-enhancing effects, under what circumstances, and with what effects for the polity?[10]

This chapter seeks to answer three basic questions suggested by this discussion. First, How and to what extent do social and political capital link group membership to regimes? It has been argued elsewhere[11] that Putnam does not explain clearly how civil society impinges on government, relying instead upon vague notions of social capital: "networks, norms, and social trust."[12] He holds that citizens' participation in groups gives rise to networks of civic interaction. These networks "pervasively influence public life" insofar as they "facilitate coordination and communication," reduce incentives for opportunism, and enhance "the participants' taste for collective benefits."[13] Not only are the theoretical links advanced in these arguments obscure, but none of the social capital phenomena mentioned directly affect governmental institutions or their decisions. Putnam never elucidates how group involvement affects citizen behavior or attitudes so as to influence government performance or enhance democratization. Because this seemed a serious shortcoming, the authors of this chapter proposed and confirmed that "political capital," or behaviors and norms that impinge on government, offers greater promise than social capital for constraining regime type and performance.[14]

A second question is, How does political context affect civil society? While civil society may be important to developing and sustaining a well-functioning democracy, it is not independent of the context in which it occurs. The sociopolitical setting affects people's resources, risks, and responses. Political repression and violence, economic turbulence, and international conflict influence individuals' and groups' behaviors in society. As an example of the impact of political context on civil society, the research for this chapter revealed that political repression by regimes depresses citizens' political participation and their support for civil liberties.[15] The authors view political repression as a critical influence on individuals' political attitudes and behaviors and employ a measure of its impact here.

The third question is, Does civil society have a "dark side"? The extent to which associational activity promotes civility and democratic engagement differs among kinds of organizations. Some may encourage uncivil norms and generate violent, confrontational, and antidemocratic political participation. Examples abound, including the Ku Klux Klan and contemporary militias in the United States and right-wing extremist movements in Europe.[16] During the 1970s and 1980s a plethora of extremist groups and paramilitaries wreaked havoc in Central American nations, some acting independently of governments and others conspiring with repressive elements in the armed forces and authoritarian regimes to intimidate citizens seeking reforms. Some groups subverted or violently challenged elected governments and constitutional rule. After the 1992 peace accord in El Salvador, for instance, rightist extremist groups claimed credit for the assassination of leftist party members legally engaged in national politics.

While the data for this study do not permit examination of participation in such extremist or conspiratorial groups, they do include involvement in a broad array of groups. Indeed, even without such obvious extremist associations, the data revealed that participation in some rather ordinary local organizations had unexpected effects. One form of associational activism in particular, participation in communal activities, correlated negatively with democratic norms and campaign activism.[17] Thus there may be a darker side to some civil society activity.

Setting: Central America

Contemporary Central America provides a nearly ideal setting to explore the connections among civil society, political capital, and democratization.

The region experienced dramatic economic growth in the 1960s, faltered with the oil price shock of the 1970s, and reversed into more than a decade of severe recession in the 1980s. In response, myriad organizations mobilized citizens into politics to protest these problems and the governments under which they occurred. This action generated considerable political turbulence, especially when governments and pro-regime groups began acting to repress such protests and demands. Central America thus moved through the late 1970s and 1980s with turmoil that escalated into civil war in three countries, and with great political stress and strain in the others. Central to this ferment was the mobilization of citizens into and by diverse organizations.[18] Central Americans formed and joined all sorts of groups—unions, peasant leagues, cooperatives, church-related organizations, community and neighborhood development and self-help associations, business and economic sector groups, professional colleges, civic organizations, parent-teacher associations, ideological groups and political action groups, and myriad others. Some groups made direct political demands on government or other citizens, while others pursued narrower interests. Although violence and political upheaval subsided in the 1990s as all the region's nations implemented formal democracy, much of the organizational life previously mobilized remained. Many new groups formed because of peace negotiations, democratization, and economic recovery efforts.

This protracted political tumult, the region's recent return to political stability, and the appearance of new civilian, constitutional regimes make Central America a particularly appropriate place for the exploration of links between civil society and democratization. Formal democracy came to each Central American nation at different dates and by different paths: Costa Rica in 1948–49 by civil war (Chapter 5); Nicaragua from 1979 to 1990 by revolution and election (Chapter 4); Panama by imposition from outside in 1989 (Chapter 6); Honduras by military devolution to civilians in 1982 and later by reform of the military in 1996 (Chapter 3); and El Salvador and Guatemala by protracted civil wars followed by negotiated settlements in 1992 and 1996, respectively (Chapters 1 and 2). While the Central American nations have much in common, they varied in their levels of turmoil, repression, democracy, and processes of political change.[19]

Data

This study employs contemporary survey data from urban samples of six Central American countries—Costa Rica, El Salvador, Guatemala, Honduras, Nicaragua, and Panama—to test connections between and among civil society, social capital, political capital, demographic characteristics, political context, and levels of democracy.[20] Survey items measured citizens' reported group activity, political participation, and political attitudes and values including democratic and antidemocratic norms. The participation and democratic value items have been widely validated and field-tested in various cultural settings.[21] The key variables employed are spelled out below and national means for most of them appear in Tables 1 and 2. (For more details on the items measured, see footnotes to the tables.)

Civil Society Measures. Responses to questions concerning activity in several types of formal organizations and in communal activities provided the basis for the indices of civil society. Statistical analysis of correlations among these organizational activities suggested that there were two distinctive types of civil society in urban Central America—involvement in formal organizations (civic associations, professional groups, unions, and cooperatives) and involvement in community-based organizations such as local betterment associations and school- and church-related groups. The analysis begins with measures of both types of civil society (see notes to Table 1).

Social Capital Measures. Multiple measures from the surveys operationalize two important indicators of social capital among those mentioned by Putnam—political information and interpersonal trust (see notes to Table 1).

Political Capital Measures. Political capital—attitudes and behaviors that actually affect government—can be conceptualized as potentially having either positive or negative effects. Positive effects include norms and behaviors that tend to strengthen democracy or civility, while negative effects include those that tend to undermine or reduce democracy or civility. A substantial list of political capital variables was divided into two categories: democracy-enhancing/civility-enhancing (positive) political capital, and democracy-reducing/civility-reducing (negative) political capital. The first employs support for democratic norms and three types of political participation that take place within officially sanctioned and legal channels—voting, campaigning, and contacting political officials. The second employs measures of authoritarianism and antidemocratic norms, holding radical attitudes toward political change, alienation from democratic institutions, and ideological extremism. These variables are presented in Table 2.[22]

Demographic and Contextual Measures. Because certain demographic traits of citizens are known to influence their behavior and attitudes and thus affect the relationships examined in the study, measures of respondents' living standard, education, and sex were sometimes employed as control variables. Two additional measures were used to assess the impact of sociopolitical context. The first is the nation's level of economic development as captured by gross domestic product (GDP) per capita. The second measure taps repression at the political system level, which is assumed to affect virtually all citizens. This measure includes two equally weighted components: one assessing repression at the time of the survey and the other the history of repression in the decade prior to the survey.[23]

Table 1. Civil Society, Social Capital, and Positive Political Capital Scores, by Country

Variables	Costa Rica	El Salvador	Guatemala	Honduras	Nicaragua	Panama
Civil Society						
Formal group activism[a]	.47	.33	.66	1.05	.43	.84
Communal activism[b]	1.01	1.24	1.31	1.04	1.17	1.03
Social Capital						
Information level[c]	.83	1.25	.62	1.43	1.03	1.37
Interpersonal trust[d]	.82	.78	.74	.87	.74	1.12
Democracy/Civility-Enhancing (Positive) Political Capital						
Democratic norms[e]	6.77	5.57	5.51	6.98	6.42	7.33
Voting behavior[f]	1.91	1.39	1.51	1.86	1.62	1.72
Contacting public officials[g]	.56	.32	.41	.77	.17	.56
Campaign activism[h]	.87	.17	.25	1.08	.47	.84

Note: All country means are significantly different at the .0001 level (analysis of variance); sample Ns +/- 700 for each country.

[a]At least sometimes attend union, civic association, cooperative, or professional association; yes = 1, no = 0 for each; range = 0–4.

[b]Involvement in five community group activities; 1 = yes, 0 = no for each; range = 0–5. The groups are community development/improvement, school-parent, and church-affiliated; respondents also received a point each for working with and for contributing labor or funds in efforts to better the community.

[c]Index of political information based on correctly naming the U.S. secretary of state, the Russian president, and the number of seats in the national legislature; range = 0–3 (John A. Booth and Patricia Bayer Richard, "Repression, Participation, and Democratic Norms in Urban Central America," *American Journal of Political Science* 40 [1996]: 1205–32).

[d]Index of interpersonal trust (based on three trust orientation items); range = 0–3; higher value = greater trust in others. The trust items were: (a) "In general people are trustworthy," (b) "Most of the time people worry mostly about themselves instead of trying to help their neighbors," and (c) "Most people will try to take advantage of you if given a chance." One point was awarded for a trusting response on each item.

[e]Overall support for democratic liberties (mean of fourteen items expressing support for participatory rights); range = 1–10 (Booth and Richard, "Repression, Participation," 1205–32).

[f]Registered to vote and voted in last election; 1 = yes, 0 = no for each; range = 0–2.

[g]Ever contacted president, legislative deputy, city council member, or national government agency; 1 = yes, 0 = no; range = 0–4.

[h]Attempted to persuade others how to vote or worked on campaign in last or prior election; 1 = yes, 0 = no for each; range = 0–3.

Table 2. Democracy-/Civility-Reducing Negative Political Capital (Authoritarian, Confrontational, and Alienated Political Attitudes), by Country (item and index means)

	Costa Rica	El Salvador	Guatemala	Honduras	Nicaragua	Panama
Something might justify a coup[a]	1.31	1.20	1.24	1.06	1.16	1.25
Support suppressing democratic liberties (index)[b]	2.96	4.75	3.75	4.18	3.55	3.22
Support civil disobedience (index)[c]	1.99	2.14	2.05	4.07	2.55	1.97
Support violent challenge to elected government[d]	1.77	2.08	1.88	1.44	2.02	1.94
Favor revolutionary change[e]	.02	.03	.03	.01	.11	.08
Staunchly oppose revolutionary change[f]	.20	.14	.20	.14	.18	.27
Think nonvoters disbelieve in elections[g]	.45	.60	.52	.28	.43	.35
Leftist extremism[h]	.50	.72	.75	.19	1.22	.56
Rightist extremism[i]	1.88	1.01	1.24	1.74	1.34	2.41

Note: All country means are significantly different at the .0001 level (analysis of variance); sample Ns +/- 700 for each country.

[a]"Is there any justification for a coup d'etat?" 1 = no, 2 = yes.

[b]Index measuring intensity of approval of the suppression of three democratic liberties (prohibiting public meetings, prohibiting demonstrations, and censorship of the media); 1 = strongly disapprove . . . 10 = strongly approve.

[c]Index measuring intensity of approval of three confrontational political tactics (invasion of property, occupation of offices or factories, blockading streets); 1 = strongly disapprove . . . 10 = strongly approve.

[d]Item measuring intensity of approval of violent challenge to elected government; 1 = strongly disapprove . . . 10 = strongly approve.

[e]"Which of the following statements best describes your own opinion? This society needs radical, revolutionary change" (= 1); other responses (prefer reform or staunchly oppose revolution) = 0.

[f]"Which of the following statements best describes your own opinion? This society should be staunchly defended against revolution" (= 1); other responses (prefer reform or prefer revolutionary change) = 0.

[g]"Why do you believe others did not vote [in the last election]?" Replies of "Don't believe in" or "Disillusioned with elections," and "Didn't want to vote" = 1; all other responses = 0.

[h]Index of left-wing ideological extremism based on item tapping intensity of self-identified leftist orientation. Scale values for highest leftist self-identification = 5, next highest leftist self-identification = 4, . . . no leftist orientation = 0.

[i]Index of right-wing ideological extremism based on item tapping intensity of self-identified rightist orientation. Scale values for highest rightist self-identification = 5, next highest rightist self-identification = 4, . . . no rightist orientation = 0.

Findings

The investigation into civil society and democratization in Central America produced a range of findings that illuminate several ways citizen participation in organizations influences the political space. Cumulatively, they provide convincing evidence that not all organizational involvement is alike.

Civil Society and the Formation of Social Capital and Positive Political Capital

A comparison of national means for civil society, social capital, and positive political capital reveals significant differences among the six Central American countries on all these variables (see Table 1). Honduras and Panama have the highest levels of formal group activism, El Salvador and Nicaragua the lowest. El Salvador and Guatemala have the most communal activism, Honduras, Costa Rica, and Panama the least. Interpersonal trust is highest in Panama, lowest in Nicaragua and Guatemala. Though all countries' urban citizens are on average pro-democratic, democratic norms scores are highest in Panama and Honduras and lowest in Guatemala and El Salvador. Campaign activism is lowest in Guatemala and El Salvador, highest in Honduras and Costa Rica.

These data were analyzed to determine whether and how civil society might affect social and political capital formation, taking into account the effects of demographic and contextual variables. Based on the regression analysis reported in Table 3,[24] the study found that involvement in formal groups affects the social capital variables differently than does communal activism. Participation in formal groups increases political information but does not increase interpersonal trust. In contrast, involvement in communal activities has no impact on information but enhances interpersonal trust. Formal groups tend to engage their members in politics and provide communication links, making political information more accessible to participants. Working at the local level with others builds a confidence in those others involved. Thus we see that the type of civil society organization affects which type of social capital is enhanced.[25] Beyond that, analysis reveals that civil society activism explains little of the variation in interpersonal trust in Central America. This observation calls into question Putnam's claim that trust forms a crucial link among citizens that can influence the performance of the state.

The study found that associational activism increases positive political capital more robustly and consistently than it does social capital but, again, that formal group and communal activism make varying contributions to political capital. Formal group activism independently elevates all positive political capital variables, whereas communal activism increases only two of them, voting and contacting.

The Effect of Sex

When it comes to political and social capital, there are a few areas where sex matters. Compared with men, women have significantly less political information and less positive political capital, even controlling for their organizational involvement, education, and living standard (Table 3). That is, even after the effects of group behavior and such background factors as wealth and education are statistically filtered out, women evidence less political information and less engagement in political activities. As for negative political capital, sex matters in only two cases: women are more likely to justify coups and to oppose radical political change than are men (Table 5).

These findings cannot be understood simply through the lens of civil society theory. Rather, they require a "gender-sensitive lens."[26] In Central America, as in the rest of the world, women have less political status, access, and influence than men.[27] Although they are in flux, gender-role expectations and socialization and the political institutions that mold both the expectations and activities of those who would participate in them continue to depress women's political involvement relative to men's. The data do not directly capture such attitudinal or situational constraints, brought on by the demands of family responsibilities, that may constitute impediments to women's development of social and political capital and influence attitudes toward change.[28]

Carol Christy proposes that growing egalitarian norms and the widening scope of governmental activity, especially into arenas formerly reserved for women or the family, diminish sex differences in participatory attitudes and behavior.[29] The rapid growth of women's voting, illegal only fifty years ago in Central America, suggests that sex differences in political attitudes and participation need to be investigated longitudinally. The surveys at multiple time points apprehend the effects of sex differences at a particular moment; surveys at multiple times would allow sorting out the dynamic interaction of gender, civil society, and democratization.

Links to Level of Democracy

Using Tatu Vanhanen's index of democracy to group the Central American countries yields scores that indicate three distinct levels of democracy among the six nations.[30] Based on this result, El Salvador and Guatemala are assigned to the lower level, Panama and Nicaragua to the intermediate level, and Costa Rica and Honduras to the higher level of the democracy groups (see notes to Table 4 for details on the systemic level of democracy measure and the grouping done here).

The analysis reveals a strong link between political capital and democracy (see Table 4). Progressively higher levels of all three participation variables associate significantly with successively higher democracy levels.[31]

Table 3. Impact of Civil Society Activism on Social Capital and Positive Political Capital, with Demographic and Contextual Controls

	Social Capital			Positive Political Capital		
	Political Information	Interpersonal Trust	Hold Democratic Norms	Vote	Campaign	Contact Officials
Group activism	.080****	.022	.095****	.051**	.118****	.158****
Communal activism	-.009	.077****	-.013	.048**	.013	.192****
Standard of living[a]	.202****	.082***	.072***	.031	-.059**	-.018
Educational attainment[b]	.307****	.034	.126****	.034	.084****	.043*
Sex (M = 1, F = 2)	-.200****	.026	-.035*	-.069****	-.121****	-.058***
Repression level[c]	-.037*	-.054**	-.289****	-.240****	-.350****	-.112****
GDP per capita[d]	-.232****	-.016	-.095****	-.016	-.057**	.007
R²	.284	.023	.146	.079	.152	.094
Standard error	.896	.929	1.831	.591	.862	.823
F	219.09	13.12	90.89	45.54	95.82	55.16
Probability of F	.0000	.0000	.0000	.0000	.0000	.0000
(N)	(3867)			(3738)		

Note: Significance levels: $* = \leq.05$; $** = \leq.01$; $*** = \leq.001$; $**** = \leq.0001$; (NS) = not significant.

[a]Living standard measures family wealth based on owning color televisions, refrigerators, washing machines, telephones, and automobiles; range 0–15.

[b]Years of formal education completed.

[c]Index of systemic repression level for decade prior to and time of survey; range = 1–5; higher score = greater repression (Booth and Richard, "Repression, Participation," 1205–32).

[d]Gross domestic product per capita, 1990 (United Nations Development Program, *Human Development Report* [New York: Oxford University Press, 1993], table 1).

Table 4. Links between Civil Society, Social Capital, and Political Capital and Levels of Democracy, with Controls for Repression and Demographic Factors

Variable	Level of Democracy*		
	Low	Medium	High
Civil Society			
Group activism	.50	.60	.76
Communal activism	1.27	1.10	1.02
Social Capital			
Political information	.94	1.20	1.13
Interpersonal trust	.76	.94	.85
Positive Political Capital			
Democratic norms	5.62	6.89	6.87
Voting	1.45	1.67	1.89
Campaigning	.21	.66	.97
Contacting public officials	.36	.37	.66

Note: Significance of main effects for analysis of variance, with controls to remove intervening effects of respondents' sex, education, and living standard, and of repression. Significance level is ≤.0001 for all except communal activism, which is not significant.

*Level of democracy obtained by grouping countries based on mean national democracy scores in Tatu Vanhanen, "Social Constraints of Democratization," in Tatu Vanhanen, ed., *Strategies of Democratization* (Washington, DC: Crane Russak, 1992). Mean score for lower democracy group (Guatemala and El Salvador) = 7.65, for the intermediate group (Nicaragua and Panama) = 13.90, and for the highest democracy group (Costa Rica and Honduras) = 20.25.

Democratic norms are sharply lower in the lower-level democracies than in the intermediate- and higher-level ones. Political capital variables thus directly relate to levels of democracy in Central America.

As with the development of political and social capital, differences are discerned again between the effects of formal group and communal activism. Greater citizen activity in formal associations is found to contribute directly to higher levels of democracy in Central America, even controlling for political repression and individual characteristics. However, no similar direct effect occurs through citizens' engagement in community level groups.

Civil Society and Negative Political Capital

Table 2 presents national-level average scores for nine potentially negative political capital (civility/democracy-reducing) attitudes. Considerable, sometimes intriguing, national differences are evident there. For example, in Honduras, the region's most coup-prone country, the justification of coups is lowest, while in the region's most stable country, Costa Rica, the justification of coups is the highest.[32] In contrast, Costa Ricans are the least likely to support the suppression of democratic liberties by the government, while Salvadorans are the most likely to do so. Citizens of Costa Rica and Honduras are the least favorable toward revolutionary change (their countries had the region's lowest revolutionary upheaval in the 1980s), while Nicaraguans are the most favorable toward revolutionary change (not surprising given that Nicaragua actually experienced a revolution, many of whose supporters were among those surveyed).

Tests for connections between types of civil society participation and such negative or civility/democracy-reducing political capital reveal a now familiar pattern of differential contributions between formal group and communal activism. Table 5 presents the results of a regression analysis of the negative political capital variables, civil society and demographic variables, and two political attitudes (diffuse support for the political system and evaluation of presidential performance) likely to be related to negative political capital norms (see the footnotes to Table 5 for explanations of these variables).[33] We see that only involvement in communal activities significantly contributes to negative political capital. Yet, factors other than civil society variables have greater influence on democracy-reducing attitudes. For instance, poor evaluations of presidential performance are more strongly linked to coup justification, favoring radical change and alienation from elections.

Communal civil society activism correlates with holding leftist political views, alienation from elections, supporting revolutionary change, and justifying coups. In contrast, formal group activists manifest more confidence in elections and less support for using violence against an elected government. Both types of civil society activists supported civil disobedience.

Table 5. Impact of Civil Society Activism on Negative Political Capital, with Demographic, Contextual, and Attitudinal Controls

	Justify Coup d'Etat	Support Suppressing Democratic Liberties	Support Civil Dis-obedience	Support Violence Against Elected Government	Favor Radical Revolutionary Change	Oppose Revolutionary Change	Nonvoters' Disbelief in Elections	Leftist Radicalism	Rightist Radicalism
Group activism	.000(ns)	-.030(ns)	.093****	-.038*	.008(ns)	-.000(ns)	-.067****	.006(ns)	-.011(ns)
Communal activism	.067****	-.047**	.038*	.057**	.067***	.000(ns)	.048**	.098*****	-.065***
Diffuse support[a]	-.105****	.075****	-.159****	-.168****	-.086****	.084****	-.053**	-.082****	.073****
Evaluation of presi-dent's performance[b]	-.072**	-.042*	-.020(ns)	-.056**	-.078****	.025(ns)	-.087**	-.068****	.044*
Standard of living	-.061**	-.035(ns)	-.037(ns)	-.050*	-.038(ns)	.110****	-.011(ns)	-.075**	.102****
Education (years)	-.040*	-.055**	-.043*	-.033(ns)	-.027(ns)	-.165****	.007(ns)	.006(ns)	-.070****
Sex (M = 1, F = 2)	.073****	-.010(ns)	-.008(ns)	.011(ns)	-.013(ns)	.081****	.023(ns)	.025(ns)	.011(ns)
Repression level	.116****	-.089****	-.228****	.086***	.010(ns)	-.032(ns)	.249****	.151****	-.226****
GDP per capita	.259****	-.113****	-.302****	.091***	.003(ns)	.005(ns)	.134****	.044(ns)	.002(ns)
R²	.078	.049	.135	.054	.027	.049	.062	.049	.087
Standard error	.386	2.60	2.05	1.91	.203	.379	.480	1.05	1.59
F	30.15	18.20	55.66	20.34	9.79	18.24	23.75	18.51	33.73
Probability of F	.0000	.0000	.0000	.0000	.0000	.0000	.0000	.0000	.0000
(N)					(3213)				

Note: Significance: * $\leq$.05; ** $\leq$.01; *** $\leq$.001; **** $\leq$.0001; NS = not significant.

[a]Index based on evaluation of nine national institutions (courts, political institutions, legislature, political system, etc.); e.g., "How much confidence do you have in the National Election Office?" from scores of 1 = none to 7 = very much; range 1–7.

[b]"How good a job would you say President ———— is doing?" (1 = very bad . . . 5 = very good).

A Closer Look at Negative Political Capital

As noted above, in the initial investigation the seven types of groups covered in the surveys were collapsed into two civil society categories—formal groups and communalism. However, it seemed likely that these categories might be obscuring some important differences among specific groups. For instance, formal group civil society included civic associations and professional organizations together with unions and cooperatives. The former and latter pairs, however, are quite distinctive types of groups that mobilize people from different economic classes. Civic and professional groups draw more members from the upper and middle classes, while unions and cooperatives draw more from the working class.

To address this problem, the two civil society variables were disaggregated into their constituent groups in order to examine more closely the linkages between specific organizations and political attitudes. This would allow exploration of whether belonging to community organizations and unions, for instance, might shape the attitudes of their members differently from belonging to civic or professional associations. The premise was that socioeconomic status, which clearly affects the sorts of organizations individuals join and the resources they have to participate in politics, might correspondingly shape the way these groups mold their members' attitudes.

Thus, the analysis of civil society activism and negative political capital was extended by using the reported level of participation in each of the following: community improvement, professional, church, and school groups, and labor unions, civic associations, and cooperatives. A simple correlation analysis (not presented here, to conserve space) revealed significantly higher levels of support for confrontational tactics among communal, labor, and cooperative activists; more left-wing sympathies among labor union and communal activists; and greater likelihood of justifying coups among communal activists. These patterns suggest that groups of working-class and poorer Central Americans are willing to use confrontational or disruptive political tactics in pursuit of their goals. In contrast, civic and professional association activists showed higher levels of right-wing extremism, civic association and church group members more support for suppressing democratic liberties and opposing revolutionary change, and church group activists more support for believing that nonvoters are alienated from elections.[34] Here we found citizens in groups with more resources and better access to the political system apparently expressing a willingness to employ state power to resist change.

It is quite logical that high levels of participation in class-based organizations promote the kinds of political capital that work to the tactical advantage of the economic strata they represent and that involvement in such class-based groups promotes congruent political attitudes. Involvement in specific types of civil society organizations contributes to holding attitudes conducive to preserving or improving the position of the group and its members. As shown in findings in other settings, people adopt stands consistent with their location in the social environment, especially when associational involvement provides social support.[35]

Political Context: System-Level Repression and Political and Social Capital

The analysis reveals the power of one of the contextual variables—repression. Repression significantly lowers social capital (information and trust) and even more sharply reduces positive political capital (holding democratic values, voting, campaigning, contacting officials) (Table 3). In addition, repression appears to drive Central Americans into communal activity and away from other formal group participation. This seems to occur because local-level activism of the sort included in communalism, neighbors working together to solve common problems, does not appear to threaten authoritarian regimes and therefore prompts little effort to curtail it. Those engaging in communal civil society can work to improve their lives without attracting regime hostility and thus enjoy some political space not available to citizens in groups acting on a national scale. This, in turn, as we have seen, influences what kinds of political and social capital develop. For instance, repression also has significant effects on negative (democracy/civility-reducing) political capital, as revealed in Table 5. System-level repression significantly increases citizens' willingness to justify a coup, approval of violence against an elected government, alienation from elections, and leftist radicalism. Repression significantly decreases rightist radicalism and tolerance of civil disobedience.

This study therefore finds compelling evidence that governmental repression dramatically constrains the ability of group activism to construct the behaviors, attitudes, and networks critical to civil society theory. Repression thus has profound implications for civil society's impact on the state. This finding underlines the importance of considering relevant political contextual factors when evaluating civil society comparatively, especially in situations of rapid change.

Repression was investigated because its purpose is to curtail citizen activity, organization, and demands on government. This examination demonstrates that repression has its intended effects, diminishing the likelihood that citizens will develop or join formal associations, limiting the further development of political and social capital, and pushing citizens toward safer, less formally organized communal activism. Thus, both indirectly, by influencing groups, and directly, by shaping other political behaviors and democratic norms, repression impedes the development of social capital and lowers positive political capital while increasing negative political capital.

Discussion and Conclusions

This study began by noting inadequacies in theory about civil society and its contributions to democracy. As a remedy, the concept of political capital was introduced. The positive political capital variables registered as more robust products of civil society than the two social capital variables based on Putnam's writings. This strongly argues that scholars seeking to assess the importance of civil society, whether for democratization or other aspects of regime performance, should incorporate into their analyses what this study calls political capital—citizen attitudes and behaviors that can affect the state.

This study also shows that civil society matters among urban Central Americans. Citizen involvement in organized activities contributes to social capital, to positive political capital, and to the level of democracy. Levels of democracy were of particular interest in this investigation of how civil society might matter. More intense formal group activism and higher levels of positive political capital among urban Central Americans were found to be associated with higher levels of political system democracy. This finding supports the argument that civil society can influence the state but considerably refines Putnam's notion of how that influence is actually exercised. The attitudes and behaviors stimulated by organizational membership that most clearly shape government performance—in this case, level of democracy—are those with an explicit political referent or impact. The organizationally active are more likely to have strong democratic norms, to vote, to campaign, and to contact public officials. In contrast, participation in civil society contributes to urban Central Americans' political information only somewhat and increases their interpersonal trust not at all. Moreover, the analysis revealed that citizens' interpersonal trust and political information bear less clearly and less directly upon levels of democracy than does their political capital.

Not all organizational behavior is alike. Communal-level participation, of the sort suggested by Putnam's bowling alone metaphor, augments political and social capital less than formal group activity. Indeed, communal activism appears to constitute a special case of civil society and to perform somewhat contrary to expectations. For instance, despite positive links to interpersonal trust, voting, and contacting public officials, communal group activism in urban Central America does not enhance system-level democracy—perhaps because communal organization in poorer communities and neighborhoods is often mobilized by governments, charitable organizations, and interest groups. Its success in promoting contacting suggests that, while locally based communal civil society has people "bowling together," and trusting each other more, it may nevertheless spawn a fairly narrow exchange with the regime. Specifically, the government, at least in the short run, may co-opt such local groups on a demand-by-demand basis. This and other findings suggest that, contrary to the expectations of the developmentalists who promote communal organizations and the theorists who laud them as fonts of democracy, communalism may not generate systemic democratization because it allows Central American regimes—especially repressive ones—to buy off local activists and does not create political capital as effectively as other civil society activism.

The complex impacts of civil society upon negative political capital spurred a refinement of the analysis by disaggregating types of group involvement. Members of some groups endorse the established order, while members of others challenge it. This disparity arises from the status and resource differences of both the citizens who hold them and the types of groups to which they belong. Extreme conservatism, opposition to political change, and willingness to suppress civil liberties are the negative political capital forms of the relatively well-off members of certain civil society groups. Not surprisingly, confrontational tactics and leftist politics constitute the political capital of the organized poor.

The findings also demonstrate how powerfully the political context, in particular political repression, affects the formation and nature of civil society in Central America. They support Sidney Tarrow's contention, and that of the authors, that the causal or, at least, sequential, connection may move from state behavior to civil society deployment, not the reverse.[36] Sociopolitical context constructs and constrains civil society activities and social capital formation. The freedom to participate affects citizens' propensity and willingness to organize, and the behavior of the government itself stimulates organizations and various attitudes. The analyses here and elsewhere confirm that repression affects associational activism, various kinds of political participation, and attitudes about democratic values, while regime actions can contribute to erasing some sex differences in participation.[37] The causal sequence, while not definitively established, appears interactional, not linear and unidirectional. That is, there may be reciprocal effects between regime type on one hand and civil society and political capital on the other. Low levels of repression facilitate group development and political capital formation, which in turn may contribute to increased democracy. Repression, by discouraging civil society and generating negative political capital, may impede democratization and thus facilitate more intense repression.

Government repression in Central America discourages formal group activity but also encourages citizens to engage in community-level activity by making this forum more accessible and less dangerous than others. Repressive states probably view the local venues and the narrowly specific demands and, indeed, the self-help orientation typical of community activism as less threatening than the objectives and actions of higher order formal groups. For citizens in repressive nations, working with neighbors to repair a bridge or to collect funds to buy books for a village school's library, for instance, seems much less likely to attract the wrath of security forces than would joining a labor union. Most likely, repressive states, whether wittingly or unwittingly, make the local community a relatively safer place for participation by making formal organizations seem more dangerous, causing citizens to adjust their activities accordingly. In fact, the findings suggest that the national climate of freedom or repression may well have greater impact than civil society on the formation of political and social capital.[38]

This conclusion may be illustrated by looking at the nations that were studied. The three countries with the most intense communal civil society fall into the lowest (El Salvador and Guatemala) and intermediate (Nicaragua) democracy groups. All three experienced destructive civil wars that created great poverty and infrastructure damage of the kind that generates a need for communal activism. They also had the intense repression levels that discouraged other forms of political participation and formal group activism, as discussed above.

Just as repression dampens citizen involvement, system-level democracy promotes civil society activism. Thus, system-level democracy and participation in formal groups might have reciprocal effects. Since such reciprocal causation involves political processes that unfold over time, testing these presumptions requires more cases and different types of data than were available for this study. Yet for these Central American nations, five of which have fairly recently passed from authoritarian rule into formal democracy, and four of which have suffered violent civil conflicts, the most interesting questions of all may be how context and civil society interact.

This exploration of the presence and development of democracy-reducing or negative political capital contains reassurance for those who value political stability and democracy in Central America. Among the survey respondents, the balance between political capital types tilts strongly in favor of civility-enhancement rather than civility-reduction. Central American urban dwellers support democratic liberties.[39] Consistent with this general embrace of democracy, they also manifest low levels of antidemocratic and confrontational political norms. However, as noted above, the authors recognize the evolutionary nature of political culture and anticipate interactional effects among political context, the actions of government and other political actors, and the development of political capital and democratization. One recent study reported increases in both civil society and some positive political capital variables in Guatemala between 1993 and 1997, suggesting that peace and stability may augment positive political capital.[40] Again, a careful longitudinal study of the evolution of political capital in young democracies in Central America and elsewhere would be very beneficial.

In sum, this study of civil society in Central America has made several important contributions to understanding how organizations and organizational behavior are connected to democracy. These findings demonstrate, first, that the concept of political capital is useful in understanding civil society and its contributions to democracy. Second, civil society contributes to the formation of political capital and to democratization in Central America. Third, not all organizational involvement is alike in its effects—some enhances civility and some reduces it. Fourth, political context, especially level of repression, has a powerful influence on the formation and nature of civil society. Finally, despite the region's great strife of the 1970s and 1980s and civil society's contribution to it, and despite the correlation of some kinds of associational activism to certain antidemocratic norms, these empirical results suggest a relatively positive prognosis for democracy in Central America.

Notes

1. Michael W. Foley and Bob Edwards, "Beyond Tocqueville: Civil Society and Social Capital in Comparative Perspective, Editors' Introduction," *American Behavioral Scientist* 42 (September 1998): 5–20.

2. Robert B. Putnam, *Making Democracy Work: Civic Traditions in Modern Italy* (Princeton: Princeton University Press, 1993); and idem, "Bowling Alone: America's Declining Social Capital," *Journal of Democracy* 6 (1995): 65–78.

3. We employ the terms "participation in organizations," "associational activity," and "group activity" (or "activism") as synonyms for civil society.

4. Leonardo Avritzer, "Introduction: The Meaning and Employment of 'Civil Society' in Latin America," *Constellations* 4 (1997): 88–93; Harry Blair, *Civil Society and Democratic Development* (Washington, DC: U.S. Agency for International Development—Center for Development Information and Evaluation, February 24, 1994); David L. Blaney and Mustapha K. Pasha, "Civil Society and Democracy in the Third World: Ambiguities and Historical Possibilities," *Studies in Comparative International Development* 28 (1993): 3–24; Joshua Cohen and Joel Rogers, "Secondary Associations and Democratic Governance," *Politics and Society* 20 (1995): 393–472; Jean Cohen and Andrew Arato, *Associations and Democracy* (London: Verso, 1992); Larry Diamond, "Introduction: Civil Society and the Struggle for Democracy," in Larry Diamond, ed., *The Democratic Revolution: Struggles for Freedom and Democracy in the Developing World* (New York: Freedom House, 1992); Nicolas Lynch, "New Citizens and Old Politics in Peru," *Constellations* 4 (1997): 124–40; Alberto J. Olvera, "Civil Society and Political Transition in Mexico," *Constellations* 4 (1997): 105–23; Enrique Peruzzotti, "Civil Society and the Modern Constitutional Complex: The Argentine Experience," *Constellations* 4 (1997): 94–104.

5. Putnam, *Making Democracy Work* and "Bowling Alone"; Alexis de Tocqueville, *Democracy in America* (Garden City, NY: Doubleday, 1969); Michael Walzer, "The Civil Society Argument," in Chantal Mouffe, ed., *Dimensions of Radical Democracy: Pluralism, Citizenship, Community* (New York: Verso, 1992), 89–107.

6. Margaret M. Conway, *Political Participation in the United States* (Washington, DC: Congressional Quarterly Press, 1991); Jack H. Nagel, *Participation* (Englewood Cliffs, NJ: Prentice-Hall, 1987); Steven J. Rosenstone and John M. Hansen, *Mobilization, Participation, and Democracy in America* (New York:

Macmillan, 1993); Sidney Verba and Norman H. Nie, *Participation in America* (New York: Harper and Row, 1972); Sidney Verba, Norman H. Nie, and Jae-On Kim, *The Modes of Democratic Participation* (Beverly Hills: Sage, 1978).

7. John A. Booth and Patricia Bayer Richard, "Repression, Participation, and Democratic Norms in Urban Central America," *American Journal of Political Science* 40 (1996): 1205–32.

8. For instance, James S. Coleman, "Social Capital in the Creation of Human Capital," *American Journal of Sociology* 94 (1988): S95–S120.

9. Cohen and Rogers, "Secondary Associations"; Michael W. Foley and Bob Edwards, "The Paradox of Civil Society," *Journal of Democracy* 7 (1996): 38–52; Foley and Edwards, "Beyond Tocqueville"; Sidney Tarrow, "Making Social Science Work across Space and Time: A Critical Reflection on Robert Putnam's *Making Democracy Work*," *American Political Science Review* 90 (1996): 389–97.

10. Foley and Edwards, "Beyond Tocqueville," 15.

11. John A. Booth and Patricia Bayer Richard, "Civil Society and Political Context in Central America," *American Behavioral Scientist* 42 (September 1998): 33–46.

12. Putnam, "Bowling Alone," 67.

13. Ibid.

14. John A. Booth and Patricia Bayer Richard, "Civil Society, Political Capital, and Democratization in Central America," *Journal of Politics* 60 (August 1998): 780–800.

15. Booth and Richard, "Repression, Participation."

16. See, for instance, Jeffrey Ian Ross, "A Model of the Psychological Causes of Oppositional Political Terrorism," *Journal of Peace Psychology* 2, no. 2 (1996): 129–41; Herbert Kitschelt, *The Radical Right in Western Europe: A Comparative Analysis* (Ann Arbor: University of Michigan Press, 1995).

17. Booth and Richard, "Civil Society and Political Context," table 2.

18. John A. Booth and Thomas W. Walker, *Understanding Central America* (Boulder, CO: Westview Press, 1993); Victor Bulmer-Thomas, *The Political Economy of Central America since 1920* (Cambridge: Cambridge University Press, 1987); Mitchell A. Seligson and John A. Booth, eds., *Elections and Democracy in Central America, Revisited* (Chapel Hill: University of North Carolina Press, 1995); Phillip J. Williams, "Dual Transitions from Authoritarian Rule: Popular and Electoral Democracy in Nicaragua," *Comparative Politics* 27 (1994): 169–85.

19. See, for instance, John A. Booth and Thomas W. Walker, *Understanding Central America*, 3d ed. (Boulder, CO: Westview Press, 1999), chaps. 5–9; Seligson and Booth, *Elections and Democracy in Central America, Revisited*; Philip J. Williams and Knut Walter, *Militarization and Demilitarization in El Salvador's Transition to Democracy* (Pittsburgh: University of Pittsburgh Press, 1997); Susanne Jonas, "The Democratization of Guatemala through the Peace Process" (paper presented to the Seminar on Guatemalan Development and Democratization: Proactive Responses to Globalization, Universidad del Valle de Guatemala, Guatemala City, March 27, 1998); J. Mark Ruhl, "Honduras: Militarism and Democratization in Troubled Waters" (paper presented at the Twenty-first Congress of the Latin American Studies Association, Chicago (September 25, 1998).

20. For a full explanation of the data collection details, research support, and survey methodology, see Booth and Richard, "Civil Society, Political Capital," 784, n. 5. Collaborators on the data collection project were Mitchell A. Seligson, Ricardo Córdova, Andrew Stein, Annabelle Conroy, Orlando Pérez, and Cynthia Chalker. Survey dates ranged from mid 1991 through mid 1992 for most countries, and 1995 for Costa Rica. Respondents are urban, voting-age citizens. Though sample sizes

varied from country to country, each sample has been weighted equally at N = 700 here for national comparison purposes; overall N = 4198.

21. See, for instance, John A. Booth and Mitchell A. Seligson, "The Political Culture of Authoritarianism in Mexico: A Reexamination," *Latin American Research Review* 19 (1984): 106–24; Mitchell A. Seligson and John A. Booth, "Political Culture and Regime Type," *Journal of Politics* 55 (1993): 777–92; Mitchell A. Seligson and Miguel Gómez B., "Ordinary Elections in Extraordinary Times," in John A. Booth and Mitchell A. Seligson, eds., *Elections and Democracy in Central America* (Chapel Hill: University of North Carolina, 1989); Edward N. Muller, Mitchell A. Seligson, and Ilter Turan, "Education, Participation, and Support for Democratic Norms," *Comparative Politics* 20 (1987): 19–33.

22. We recognize that not all of the negative political capital items listed in Table 2 necessarily or always have negative implications for democracy or civility. Not all left- or right-wing partisan radicals, for instance, are opposed to democracy, although the probability of holding antidemocratic or intolerant norms tends to increase with greater partisan radicalism. Similarly, supporting revolutionary change or opposing any political change at all need not imply radical intolerance of other views, but one may argue that a rejection of the acceptability of moderate sociopolitical change implies a certain extremism. Recognizing these limitations of some of the negative political capital measures, we nevertheless believe that in formally constitutional, civilian, elected regimes (as were all of our survey countries in the early 1990s), the lack of willingness to compromise inherent in ideological extremism or holding intolerant positions regarding change connotes a potentially civility- and democracy-reducing intolerance.

23. We include the historical component on the assumption that the effect of repression on citizens will decay only gradually even after actual repression has subsided (see Booth and Richard, "Repression, Participation"). We average the two to obtain a score for each country that we assign to respondents based on their nation of residence.

24. Multiple regression analysis determines the independent effect of several variables upon another, holding constant the effect of each of the other independent variables; cell entries in Table 3 are beta weights, coefficients that indicate the relative strength and direction of influence.

25. See also Carla M. Eastis, "Organizational Diversity and the Production of Social Capital: One of These Groups Is Not Like the Other," *American Behavioral Scientist* 42 (September 1998): 66–77.

26. V. Spike Peterson and Anne Sisson Runyan, *Global Gender Issues* (Boulder, CO: Westview Press, 1993).

27. Najma Chowdhury and Barbara J. Nelson, "Redefining Politics: Patterns of Women's Political Engagement from a Global Perspective," in Barbara J. Nelson and Najma Chowdhury, eds., *Women and Politics Worldwide* (New Haven: Yale University Press, 1994), 3–24.

28. See also Virginia Sapiro, *The Political Integration of Women: Roles, Socialization, and Politics* (Urbana: University of Illinois Press, 1983); Cal Clark and Janet Clark, "Models of Gender and Political Participation in the United States," *Women and Politics* 6 (Spring 1986): 5–25; Sue Tolleson-Rinehart, *Gender Consciousness and Politics* (New York: Routledge, 1992); M. Margaret Conway, Gertrude A. Steuernagel, and David W. Ahern, *Women and Political Participation: Cultural Change in the Political Arena* (Washington, DC: Congressional Quarterly Press, 1997).

29. Carol Christy, *Sex Differences in Political Participation: Processes of Change in Fourteen Nations* (New York: Praeger, 1987), 118–20.

30. Tatu Vanhanen, "Social Constraints of Democratization," in *Strategies of Democratization* (Washington, DC: Crane Russak, 1992), 32–35.

31. The analysis of the data in Table 4 is an analysis of variance. The values in the table are simple means on the indicators for citizens at each level of democracy. The statistical analysis (analysis of variance) used in Table 4 measures the significance of the association between the individual traits and the country level of democracy, with controls designed to remove the confounding effects of several intervening variables.

32. Accounting for this striking difference is an interesting speculative exercise. Perhaps Hondurans have learned to dislike coups from bitter experience with them, while Costa Ricans may find contemplating them a purely hypothetical exercise that holds little in the way of expected consequence.

33. Diffuse support taps into a respondent's general allegiance to the political system or regime. Evaluation of presidential performance attempts to assess how well or poorly a respondent believes the president of the moment is doing in office. Either, we surmise, could influence one's predisposition toward negative political capital, for example, the willingness to justify a coup or to employ civil disobedience.

34. Only activism in school-related groups had no links with forms of negative political capital.

35. See, for instance, Eastis, "Organizational Diversity"; Dietlind Stolle and Thomas R. Rochon, "Are All Associations Alike? Member Diversity, Associational Type, and the Creation of Social Capital," *American Behavioral Scientist* 42 (September 1998): 47–65; John A. Booth and Patricia Bayer Richard, "Civil Society in Central America: The Dark Side?" (paper presented at the annual meeting of the Midwest Political Science Association, Chicago, April 23, 1998).

36. Sidney Tarrow, "Making Social Science Work"; Booth and Richard, "Repression, Participation"; Patricia Bayer Richard and John A. Booth, "Sex and Repression Effects on Political Participation and Support for Democratic Norms in Urban Central America" (paper presented at the annual meeting of the Midwest Political Science Association, Chicago, April 6–8, 1995).

37. Booth and Richard, "Repression, Participation"; Booth and Richard, "Civil Society and Political Context"; Richard and Booth, "Sex and Repression Effects."

38. This holds true even when controlling for sex, education, and standard of living (Tables 3 and 5).

39. Booth and Richard, "Civil Society and Political Context"; Booth and Richard, "Civil Society and Political Capital."

40. Development Associates, Inc., University of Pittsburgh, Asociación de Investigación y Estudios Sociales, *La cultura democrática de los guatemaltecos* (Guatemala City, January 1998).

Conclusion
Conceptual Issues on Democratization in Central America

Ariel C. Armony

Undoubtedly, there was real progress if we compare the stable and relatively peaceful political situation in Central America[1] at the end of the twentieth century with the violent conflicts that inflamed most of the region in the 1980s. Seen in the context of the most recent wave of democratization in Latin America, the unprecedented scope of political transformations in Central America in the 1990s suggested that a new type of political regime emerged in the region. There appeared to have been a fundamental shift toward forms of competitive rule that bear no precedent in countries such as Guatemala, El Salvador, Honduras, and Nicaragua: significant levels of political moderation and consensus among elites, widespread mass support for democratic institutions, and unparalleled (for the region) political inclusiveness of various social sectors.[2] In Guatemala and El Salvador, for instance, the peace accords between the government and the guerrillas represented a major advancement toward the creation of democracy, particularly because they showed that formidable political enemies were able to make concessions and compromise on fundamental issues, an outcome that would have been unthinkable in the 1980s (Chapters 1 and 2).

Political democracy in Central America in the late 1990s, however, as several of the chapters in this volume show, appeared much less nurturing of conditions such as economic prosperity and democratic behavior—which would likely contribute to the durability of this type of rule—than its advocates had prophesied. Therefore, even if we accept that the new Central American regimes were profoundly different from their predecessors, we would still have to face the question whether their novel features would last long enough to warrant the claim that the current wave of democratization inaugurated a distinct phase of nonviolent, competitive politics in the history of this region.[3]

It is clear that the spread of democracy throughout Central America— at least understood in its minimalist definition of electoral competition between elites (see the Introduction to this volume)—did not mean "the end of history" for this region's peoples and governments. However, from a U.S. perspective, the apparent "triumph of democracy" in Central America meant that the region could safely return to its traditional position of geopolitical obscurity. Central America had been a top strategic priority for U.S. foreign policy in the 1980s. U.S. aid to the region skyrocketed from 1981 to 1991, then dropped dramatically in the 1990s. This shift in levels of U.S. aid involved not only military assistance but economic as well.[4] The geopolitical preeminence of Central America thus dwindled with the "pacification" of the region. As of 2000, in the post–cold war era, Central America was no longer relevant to U.S. national security.[5]

Interestingly, Central America's return to obscurity from the point of view of U.S. policy makers was paralleled by a similar disinterest in the region among students of Latin America in the United States. Amidst a vast literature dissecting the process of transition to democracy in Latin America and the problems of consolidation, relatively few scholars devoted their attention to Central America.[6] Such disinterest was particularly significant given the astounding number of academic publications that focused on this region in the 1980s. It seemed as though Central America could not contribute much to the theoretical debate on democratization. As the authors in this book demonstrate, however, the recent processes of political transformation in the region offer a fertile soil for conceptual analysis of democratization processes.

In this conclusion it is useful to consider four issues that are not only meaningful for Central America but also carry significant potential for comparative analysis: the international context, economic development and equity, regime experience, and legacies of authoritarianism and radical popular mobilization. Obviously, these issues do not cover the multiple dimensions of democratization in Central America—and, in addition, each of them raises questions that cannot be addressed here—but they are useful to lay out a conceptual map that comprises some of the most relevant problems in the study of democracy in this region.

The International Context

Regime transitions in Central America were profoundly shaped by international forces. Two global processes initiated in the late 1970s—democratization and market-oriented reform—set up the climate in which political transformations occurred in Central America a decade later.[7] These processes of political and economic liberalization created opportunities and obstacles for domestic actors, affected their interests, and shaped the democratic regimes that emerged in Guatemala, El Salvador, Honduras, Nicaragua, and Panama (and also shaped democracy in Costa Rica). Therefore, changes in Central America's political systems cannot be properly understood without placing them in a broader international framework. To do so we need to examine the conflicting processes of democratization and market-oriented reform, particularly in countries devastated by civil war. An analysis of these global processes demands attention to two levels of analysis. First, we need to look at the impact of international developments, expressed as global or regional forces, on state institutions,[8] recognizing that institutional choices by domestic actors are contingent upon forces that operate beyond the nation-state. The role and resources of major global powers, transnational capital, and specific-issue coalitions, among other forces, create conditions for the development of certain forms of rule.[9] In Central America, the specific role played by the United States (defined by its relative position in the international context) was a preeminent factor in shaping the general climate in which institutional transformations took place in the region.

Second, international forces shaping concurrent political and economic liberalization call attention to the reciprocal effect between politics (institutional arrangements) and economics (economic policy and performance).[10] This effect is especially important for analyzing democratization processes under the so-called Washington consensus. Following other "third wave" democracies, Central American governments pursued strategies of "modernization via internationalization." As happened throughout most of the recently democratized world, their attempt at national development was dictated by the adoption of "the political, economic, and cultural patterns (democracy, markets, and consumerist individualism) that dominate the advanced capitalist world."[11] The impact of "modernization via internationalization" on the relationship between politics and economics leads us to consider, for instance, the effect of externally imposed neoliberal reforms upon democratic institutions. This perspective is particularly important because it shifts the debate away from the alleged "rationality" of these economic reforms and focuses it on the policy style associated with the actual implementation of these economic programs (Chapter 10).[12] Indeed, though often posed as mutually reinforcing, democratization and market-oriented reform in Central America evolved as inherently contradictory phenomena by the end of the 1990s.[13]

International Forces and State Institutions

How did international forces, and particularly U.S. foreign policy, affect state institutions in Central America in the 1990s? To what extent did democratic transitions result from forces beyond the nation-state? It has been argued that the decline of East-West tensions, and eventually the end of the cold war, played a major role in the wave of democratization of the late 1980s and early 1990s. The argument is that the pro-democratic shift in the international climate—resulting from decreased concerns with national security—had a positive impact on Central American politics because it created the appropriate conditions for the development of representative institutions. The expansion of democracy, viewed as electoral competition, was thus buttressed when the end of the cold war "undercut political forces at both ends of the political spectrum, reducing challenges to democratic stability and altering the pre-existing political dynamic in favor of moderation, pragmatism, and the construction of political consensus."[14] Even though international support for electoral democracy, particularly in the case of the United States, resulted not from enlightened democratic ideals but from U.S. perception that Central America's alleged threat to U.S. national security had subsided, the international context has been seen as a positive force in the democratization of Central America.[15]

In sharp contrast to this view, other analysts have argued that global changes, and the apparent pro-democratic shift in U.S. foreign policy preferences, did not result in a real expansion of democracy as a form of rule that disperses power, redistributes wealth, and allows for popular participation in decision making (Chapter 7).[16] This critical position assumes that there was a continuity between old-fashioned authoritarianism and the type of elite rule promoted in Central America by the United States and transnational interests under the facade of democracy. As William Robinson puts it, the main objective of this type of "polyarchical" regime was to deflect any challenge to the prevailing system of elite domination: "Under globalization the 'imperial state' still plays the same role of promoting and protecting the activity of transnational capital, but globalizing pressures have inverted the positive correlation between the investment climate and authoritarianism. Now, a country's investment climate is positively related to the maintenance of a 'democratic' order, and the 'imperial state' promotes polyarchy in place of authoritarianism."[17]

According to this view, as the cold war waned, U.S. strategy shifted to the promotion of electoral democracy in developing countries as a means of protecting transnational capital. Thus, alternatively, democratization in Central America could be seen as a process of political concurrence between transnational and domestic elites that served to legitimate a political order that reinforced the existing concentration of economic and political power in the hands of elites. Challenging the dominant views in the democratization literature of the 1980s and 1990s, this perspective claims that new "democracies" mask a traditional form of elite rule.[18]

These contrasting stances on the Central American case (which are only an example of various views on this subject) raise several comparative questions about the impact of international forces on domestic institutions. Let us mention two of them. First, was the U.S. role in Central America largely similar to that of the Soviet Union in Eastern Europe? Paralleling the idea that the threat of a Soviet intervention functioned as "a dam against pressing water" in Eastern Europe, could we argue that the United States— because of cold war demands—also played the role of a constraint against domestic forces for democratic change in Central America? Would this mean that, as happened in Eastern Europe, the barrier was external, but the impetus for democratization came from within?[19] Furthermore, did the manner in which the constraint was removed influence the nature of the emerging democratic regimes in different ways? To be sure, the Soviet Union disintegrated while the United States consolidated its hegemonic position in the Western Hemisphere. Such contrasting scenarios should be taken into consideration to draw comparative lessons from the transitions in Central America and post-Communist Europe.

Overall, these issues are analytically important because they can help us answer, in turn, two critical questions: How did internal and external factors interact in the Central American democratic transitions? Which external and internal conditions were necessary for deepening democracy in the region at the turn of the century? Regarding the first question, it is important to consider that, on one hand, the United States intervened in shaping democratic transitions in Central America through the National Endowment for Democracy and the U.S. Agency for International Development, focusing on the key areas of elections, judicial and police reforms, demilitarization, structural reform of the state, and the promotion of civil society (Chapter 7). On the other hand, the transitions to democracy were also a product of years of revolutionary struggle, particularly because the new regimes gave political representation to previously excluded sectors. The second question points to the importance of acknowledging that the structural causes of revolution in Central America (especially the highly unequal distribution of land and wealth) were still unresolved in the late 1990s. This lack of resolution meant that the end of armed conflict, the inauguration of competitive politics, and the apparent "pro-democratic" stance of the United States might not be enough to guarantee the deepening of democracy in Central America.

Thinking about the United States as a dam against democratization in Central America (rather than as a force promoting democracy) raises some interesting questions. Looking back into Central American political development during the cold war, one cannot help pondering whether U.S. policy toward the region in the early days of the cold war hindered a regional trend toward a democracy oriented in the direction of broad, inclusive participation that was most conspicuous in Guatemala in 1944–1954 but also included Honduras, Nicaragua, and El Salvador. Did the United States play a major role in preventing these countries from joining the second global wave of democratization that started at the end of World War II?[20] In 1945–46, Argentina, Colombia, Peru, and Venezuela held democratic elections.[21] Furthermore, Costa Rica, a country in the "backyard" of the United States, had a revolution in 1948 that resulted in a reformist, democratic government (which even nationalized the banking and insurance industries).[22] This regime change, however, occurred just before the United States expanded its policy of containment to Latin America. It was actually in 1950 when U.S. hemispheric policy shifted in the direction of anticommunism. Under the rationale that "the cold war is in fact a real war in which the survival of the free world is at stake," the Truman administration abandoned the doctrine of nonintervention in Latin America in favor of a new policy based on the premise that the protection of U.S. security legitimated any interventionist action to counter communist aggression in the hemisphere.[23] This new policy meant that, as events in Guatemala in the 1950s demonstrated, the United States would not tolerate any regime shift (such as the reformist administration of Jacobo Arbenz) perceived as politically appealing to the Soviet Union.[24] A strong argument could be made, then, that U.S. foreign policy in the 1950s played a major role in delaying the beginning of democratization in Central America for nearly four decades.[25]

The second question related to the impact of international forces on internal politics refers to the "distinctiveness" of the new political regimes in Central America. Are these regimes the expression of a new political pattern defined by broader competition and social inclusiveness? Or, as Robinson has argued, is their only original element their effectiveness to legitimate a "social order punctuated by sharp social inequalities and minority monopolization of society's material and cultural resources"?[26] Here an analysis of the impact of international forces on state institutions can be helpful to reconsider the conceptual usefulness of pendulum theories based on the "authoritarianism/democracy" dichotomy. In other words, what was "new" and what was "old" in Central America's political order in the late twentieth century?

Politics and Economics

The other issue that needs to be addressed in the light of current strategies of "modernization via internationalization" is the interaction between institutional arrangements and economic policy and performance. The demands imposed on national governments by global processes of market-oriented reform—neoliberalism—had a direct impact on the kind of institutions that emerged in newly democratized nations. In order to modernize, governments were forced to adopt economic programs that resulted in "a serious decline in their capacity to compensate losers and manage social tensions generally" and a process by which "decisions that were once controlled by elected national officials pass[ed] into the hands of actors who [could not] be voted in or out."[27] Externally imposed economic reforms thus undermined democratic institutions because they limited the ability of national governments to govern effectively, for example, to redistribute income, and seriously curtailed national sovereignty.

In addition, neoliberal reforms—usually deployed by "isolated technocrats in executive agencies"—required a policy style that emphasized autocratic modes of rule.[28] This style obviously collided with democratic decision making. As Kurt von Mettenheim and James Malloy put it, "The central theme that emerges from recent experiences of governance in Latin America is the profound tension between technocratic and exclusive policy-making patterns deemed imperative by 'rational' neoliberal economic restructuring and the ideals of broad-based participation of both citizens and associational groups historically implied by liberal and pluralistic conceptions of democracy."[29]

Interestingly, this tension affected not only the new political democracies in Central America but also the sole case of stable democracy in the region, Costa Rica. There, as John Booth explains (Chapter 5), the implementation of neoliberal policies—as demanded by international lenders—had concrete institutional effects that devalued democratic politics. Neoliberal economic restructuring contributed to curtail legislative power, concentrate authority in the presidency, and seriously reduce the ability of the electorate to influence economic policy. In addition, neoliberalism deprived the government of fundamental policy instruments to correct imbalances in distribution and dampen the incidence of poverty. Whether these developments could result in social unrest and, thus, political instability—as citizens' demands exceed the responsive capacity of the state—remained, as of this writing, an open question.

If economic policy had an impact on political institutions in Central America, the opposite was also true. As already noted, nascent democratic institutions were shaped by the impositions of modernization under the "Washington consensus." While, on one hand, neoliberal reform weakened representative institutions, on the other hand, it limited the options available to political groups. This development "reduced the stakes of the political game," thus improving the chances for reaching a consensus among elites.[30] Even though consensual solutions were often reached without including major social and political forces, the mere fact that there was a meaningful level of consensus helped not only to sustain democratic politics but also to craft economic policies oriented to prevent social disintegration.[31]

The relationship between politics and economics also touches on questions about agency and structure. These questions are especially relevant for Central America, where the export-oriented, "price-taker" economies of El Salvador, Guatemala, and Nicaragua had a long-standing affinity with exclusionary political arrangements that guaranteed, through coercion, an uninterrupted supply of cheap labor (Chapter 10). In these nations any attempt to alter the existing distribution of political power represented a simultaneous challenge to the prevailing economic system.[32] Following the insurrectionary attempts in El Salvador and Guatemala, and the revolutionary experience in Nicaragua, the question was whether the economic structure of these countries would prevent the creation of stable, participatory democratic regimes. Here the notion of agency gains relevance: Is it possible for democratically elected authorities to craft policies that sustain democracy under structural conditions that traditionally promoted authoritarian forms of rule? "The tight intertwining of politics and economics that characterizes most Central American countries makes democratization more difficult there than in the South," Terry Lynn Karl points out. "Whereas in Southern Europe and South America regime change and socioeconomic transformation could be dealt with sequentially, in Central America they must be addressed simultaneously."[33] Structural conditions, then, imposed significant constraints on domestic actors willing to deepen democratization processes.

As of the late 1990s the "modernization via internationalization" strategy did not produce beneficial effects on the region's economic structure (Chapter 10). Even in specific areas where growth had taken place, the results did not promote conditions for continued economic expansion. For example, the promotion (and resulting growth) of the maquiladora industries in El Salvador and Honduras constituted a double-edge sword. On one hand, the *maquilas* attracted foreign investment and created badly needed jobs; on the other hand, they offered low wages and did not create incentives to improve the educational level and skills of the labor force (Chapters 2 and 3).

Economic Development and Equity

There is compelling evidence that economic factors are as important as a favorable international environment for democracy to work and endure. Economic variables are thus a critical factor in Central America's democratization process because of the high incidence of poverty, the extreme gap between rich and poor, and the region's meager levels of economic growth.

First, by the mid 1990s over half of the population in Guatemala, El Salvador, Honduras, and Nicaragua lived in poverty (Chapter 10). Furthermore, poverty in Central America increased after the early 1980s.[34] This growth in the poverty rates was accompanied by the accelerated urbanization of poverty in the region. By the early 1990s approximately a third of Central America's population was living in urban areas without access to basic infrastructure and services.[35] Second, income polarization persisted throughout the 1990s in all six countries examined in this volume. In particular, income inequality grew markedly in Guatemala and El Salvador over the last two decades. As Guatemala entered the 1990s it, along with Honduras, was second only to Brazil in Latin America's ranking of nations with the most unequal distributions of income.[36] Finally, in terms of economic performance, Central America showed dismal progress after the mid 1970s.[37] Following negative trends in GDP per capita's average annual growth during the 1980s, these economies experienced a gradual process of recovery in the 1990s. However, when considered in relation to population growth or the increase of total debt, per capita income growth was scant (Chapter 10).[38]

What are the implications of these macroeconomic indicators for democracy? An analysis of the impact of economic factors on democratization demands attention to two issues: economic development and equity. As already noted, the performance of Central America in these areas was significantly poor. In terms of economic development, which involves wealth and growth, these low and lower-middle-income economies did not show very positive trends by the end of the 1990s. As for equity, which refers to the incidence of poverty and income distribution, these countries presented a marked trend toward further deterioration in the standard of living of their populations.[39] In the light of this scenario, we need to ask: Can democracy flourish in these poor, stagnant economies? Is it possible to deepen democratization processes in a context of broad inequalities?

Democratic Stability

A cross-national study of the conditions that support democratic rule (defined by its authors in a procedural way as "a regime in which governmental offices are filled as a consequence of contested elections") found that wealth, economic growth, and income equality play a critical role in sustaining political democracy.[40] Analyzing regime change in 135 countries over forty years, Adam Przeworski and his colleagues have concluded that affluence is a strong predictor of democratic stability.[41] But prosperity is not the only path to the endurance of this type of regime. Even in the poorest countries, democracy has a chance to survive if it produces economic growth and if it distributes the profits so as to reduce income inequality.[42]

A relatively even income distribution not only helps democracy to survive but also helps improve its quality (understood, for instance, as respect for political rights and civil liberties). A possible explanation for this causal relationship is that high levels of income inequality tend to increase distributional pressures, leading to heightened political conflict.[43] High levels of poverty and extreme concentration of wealth can also have a negative effect on the quality of democracy because, under these conditions, vast sectors of the population are excluded from effective citizenship. Deep inequality, as Guillermo O'Donnell argues, breeds "manifold patterns of authoritarian relations in various encounters between the privileged and the others."[44] Thus, poverty and inequality sustain power relations that remain largely authoritarian despite democratic changes at the institutional level. In addition, under a regime that claims to be a democracy, the relationship between citizens and the state must be based on an adequate level of personal autonomy that allows for meaningful political participation before, during, and beyond elections.[45] Such autonomy is not possible under conditions of widespread poverty and an extreme gap between rich and poor.

High levels of inequality produce large marginal classes. The migration of this population to urban areas in search of employment contributes, among other factors, to increased social tensions. The problem of crime becomes a central point of concern. Even though this is a phenomenon also found in advanced industrial democracies, such as the United States, it becomes a serious problem when democratic institutions are still very fragile. As urban poverty continued to increase in Central America in the late 1990s, a new array of social conflicts emerged, often breeding intolerance, violence, and corruption. A related development, resulting, to an important extent, from the urbanization of poverty and the state's ineffective reaction to it, was the inability of these regimes to establish an effective rule of law, a key component of democracy.[46]

Economic Performance and Distribution

If economic growth and some degree of equality are necessary for political democracy to endure, then it is important to consider the relationship between these two variables. How is it possible to escape from the trap of poverty? Can economic growth reduce poverty? Cross-national macroeconomic data from Latin America suggest that "growth is no sufficient condition to reduce poverty and that policies geared toward a more equitable growth pattern are at least as important."[47] Therefore, if income inequality accounts for extreme poverty levels, distributional policies could alleviate the problem of poverty, which, in turn, would contribute to strengthening democratic rule.[48] Conversely, some studies suggest a positive association between equality and growth while others indicate that inequality is linked to slower rates of economic growth.[49]

When considering the relevance of these findings for Central America, it is important to point out that distributive policies—even if they were politically plausible—constitute a potential solution only for some countries. In two of the six nations analyzed in this book—Honduras and Nicaragua— the degree of poverty is so extreme that "not even a radical redistribution of income would suffice to eliminate poverty."[50] "Poverty breeds poverty and dictatorship," Przeworski and colleagues argue.[51] Therefore, if democratic stability is buttressed by economic factors, the future of political democracy in Central America (with the possible exception of Costa Rica) was uncertain at the end of the 1990s. Of these countries, Honduras presented all the macroeconomic indicators associated with democratic failure: GNP per capita below $1,000, average annual growth rate lower than 1 percent, continued economic decline, and high levels of economic inequality.[52] Even though the Honduran economy showed signs of revitalization in 1997–98, the devastation caused by Hurricane Mitch brought that trend to an end (Chapter 3). War-related damage was another major factor affecting economic growth. It was critical in the cases of Nicaragua and El Salvador, where the destruction of infrastructure and production reached enormous proportions and greatly exceeded reconstruction assistance.[53]

As international forces meet domestic politics, economic development and equity emerge as major problems affecting democratization in Central America. The urgency to modernize backward, highly vulnerable economies in order to integrate them in the international markets had, at the end of the twentieth century, profound social and political implications for these countries. "The race to modernize will inevitably have its winners and losers," Przeworski points out. "Moreover, the winners and the losers will not be nation-states but regions, sectors, industries, and particular social groups."[54] Given Central America's history of political instability, its high rates of poverty and inequality, and the marginal participation of these economies in the global markets, the question of who wins and who loses as the international process of market-oriented reform unfolded in this region had, as of this writing, paramount importance for democratization.[55]

Second-Generation Reform

As the 1990s drew to a close the question of winners and losers expanded from the economic to the institutional arena. International lending organizations such as the World Bank began to promote "second generation" or "institutional" reform geared to correct the imperfections of "first generation" or stabilization reform, particularly the inability of neoliberal policies "to achieve higher sustained rates of growth and to make a more significant dent in poverty reduction."[56] Second-generation reform was perceived not only as deriving from democratization processes but also as a necessary, complementary phase of structural adjustment, in other words, "good macro policy is not enough; *good institutions are critical for macroeconomic stability in today's world of global financial integration.*"[57] Institutional reform in Latin America, World Bank economists argue, would have to overcome the resistance of potential losers, that is, "organized and vocal groups that benefit from the existing institutional setup," among them, labor unions and civil service associations.[58] This concern speaks about the role of neoliberalism as a rationale to discipline "losers," who are perceived as an obstacle to the implementation of rational policies. "While people's mobilizations in the 1980s had been confronted under the banner of Western values and anticommunism," Carlos Vilas points out (Chapter 10), "they could be opposed in the name of a free market and globalization in the 1990s." In this respect, the agenda of the international financial institutions appeared as essentially antidemocratic, notwithstanding their claims that free market and democracy are amalgamated. Political parties (for example, El Salvador's Nationalist Republican Alliance [Alianza Republicana Nacionalista, ARENA]), perceived by neoliberal advocates as key instruments for the implementation of second-generation reform, effectively turned political ideology into a set of rational "truths" to legitimate free-market policies. In brief, as this was written, struggles over institutional reform appeared as a primary sphere where such diverse forces as civil society, political parties, executive authority, and legislatures would test the capacity of the political system to incorporate different interests and deaden the high potential for conflict that still characterized Central America in the late 1990s.[59]

Regime Experience

A continuous democratic experience has been seen as an important asset in the construction of democracy, based on the hypothesis that experience with democratic rule is causally prior to the development of a democratic political culture.[60] Simply put, the more uninterrupted experience with democracy a country has, the less exposed it is to an "auto-regressive effect."[61] With the sole exception of Costa Rica, the countries studied here have a history of political instability.[62] In the period under examination, civilian authorities were first elected as a result of broad, unrestricted electoral competition in 1984 in Nicaragua, in 1993 in Honduras, in 1994 in El Salvador, and in 1995 in Guatemala. The tradition of political instability means that these countries would be building their democracies without prior experience in sustained democratic rule—though with the novel but brief experience of revolutionary democracy in the case of Nicaragua and radical mass mobilization in the cases of El Salvador and Guatemala.

Certain features of the region's political experience were important in the recent processes of institutional change and distinguished these transitions from others in South America and southern and post-Communist Europe. Military force played a central role in the transitions toward democracy in Nicaragua, El Salvador, Guatemala, and Panama, albeit in different ways. In Nicaragua a successful insurgency deposed the Somoza dictatorship in 1979, producing a first transition to "popular revolutionary democracy" and a second transition to electoral democracy in 1984 (Chapter 4).[63] In El Salvador and Guatemala, prolonged civil wars led to stalemate in a context of dramatic changes in the international system, impelling contending forces to end the state of war. In the case of Panama it was U.S. military force that imposed electoral democracy.[64]

Violence, then, contributed to democratic transitions in these four countries. However, if violence helped to bring about the end of authoritarianism, the use of violence in these countries also "increased the power of the specialists in violence in both government and the opposition."[65] Thus, the widespread availability of resources for violence, even after the installation of elected regimes, became an important characteristic of these transitions, particularly in Nicaragua, El Salvador, and Guatemala. A good illustration of this feature was the high level of postwar rural violence in Nicaragua in 1991–1994, when former Contras and demobilized Sandinista Army forces took up arms to demand land and economic assistance from the Chamorro government.[66] Different from the South American cases, where the weapons lay in the hands of the military, in countries such as Nicaragua arms were readily available for different social groups—even after the completion of the demobilization process.

Political Values and Attitudes

One could argue that political learning took place in Central America not only as a result of the political instability of the past but also as a consequence of the unparalleled level of violence generated in the region after the late 1970s. Thus, it could be said, the absence of democratic traditions could be balanced by a substantial "reorientation of political values," particularly among elites.[67] Increasingly, this change in elites' political values was manifested in concrete actions that contributed to democratization. The willingness of El Salvador's ARENA to concede an electoral defeat to the Farabundo Martí National Liberation Front (Frente Farabundo Martí de Liberación Nacional, FMLN) in the 1997 San Salvador mayoral race and the negotiations over property rights in Nicaragua in 1997 were two significant illustrations of this pattern (Chapters 2 and 4).

Notwithstanding the importance of political learning for democratization, this argument fails to take into account that often "the lessons learned by antidemocratic forces from the past subversion of democracy are more effective than the traditions that can be relied on by democrats."[68] This observation is very true in the Central American experience. The case of Guatemala exemplifies it. The overthrow of the democratically elected Arbenz regime in 1954 taught hard-liners how to subvert subsequent attempts at establishing democracy. The repression launched in the name of anticommunism in 1954 was an important precedent of the great waves of state-sponsored terrorism of the late 1960s, 1970s, and early 1980s.[69] In the 1990s one could argue that Jorge Serrano's unsuccessful, Fujimori-style "self-coup" of 1993 drew from Guatemala's antidemocratic lessons of the past.[70]

Whereas many authoritarian leaders lost their legitimacy as Central America democratized,[71] elected authorities did not fare well when it came to gaining citizens' trust. As this was being written, one of the most important problems associated with rulers in this region was government corruption. Corruption, or the abuse of public office for private benefit, emerged as a major feature defining ruling elites' attitudes in Central America in the 1990s.[72] Corruption, as well as patronage and nepotism, sustained an interest-intermediation system dominated by "particularistic" relationships, which seriously affected the transparency of government acts and the accountability of public officials.[73]

What of citizens' political attitudes in Central America's post-authoritarian settings? As these countries adopted political systems based on regular and competitive elections, it became possible to study not only the political attitudes of elites in this type of system but also those of the mass public, particularly their change over time. Experience with democratic politics is said to contribute to changing mass political culture. Even though it was still too early as of 2000 to assess definite changes, recently available data indicated suggestive trends. In Nicaragua, for instance, national surveys conducted in the mid and late 1990s showed an increase in the percentage of individuals who displayed high levels of both system support and political tolerance.[74] Based on these data, one could argue that this change could help democratization because these attitudes convey legitimacy to the system and contribute to guarantee the protection of minority rights.

As a general trend at the time of this writing, however, citizens in Central America showed increased disenchantment with political democracy, that is, they perceived that this system of rule did not fulfill their expectations. Accordingly, though citizens continued to support democracy over authoritarianism, they were not pleased with the way these new regimes worked.[75] If democracy means more than sustained electoral competition, in other words, if what really matters is the type of institutions that come to exist under democratic rule, then this trend raises serious concerns about the prospects for democratization in Central America.

Some students of Central America are skeptical of attempts to generalize about political culture on the basis of public opinion surveys conducted in a context of recent extreme repression and ongoing regime change. Therefore, it is useful to point out other ways to assess democratization in these countries. One of them is to focus on voter turnout. In a comparative study of Nicaragua and El Salvador, William Barnes argues that the levels of turnout and abstentionism, particularly in "foundational elections," are meaningful indicators of "the status of democratization, particularly where abstentionism is concentrated among the poor."[76] The absence of significant mass involvement through elections in democratic transitions, Barnes argues, means that "the breadth and quality of party competition and public debate" are lingering, thus showing scant progress in the process of democratization.[77] (See Chapter 2 for an analysis of voter behavior in El Salvador and its implications for democratization.)

Legacies of Authoritarianism

What are the legacies of national security states in Central America? When considering authoritarianism's effect on these democratizing polities, the problem of institutionalized impunity deserves immediate attention. Amnesty laws in El Salvador and Guatemala, as well as Honduras's inability to bring senior military officers to justice, cast doubts about the progress of democratization in terms of the rule of law. As Laura O'Shaughnessy and Michael Dodson ask in reference to El Salvador, "What kind of precedent was set by precluding legal prosecution for all human rights violators?"[78] Despite this important shortcoming, the work of El Salvador's Ad Hoc and Truth Commission, Guatemala's Commission for Historical Clarification (Comisión para el Esclarecimiento Histórico, CEH), and Honduras's Ad Hoc Commission for Institutional Reform (as well as the country's National Commissioner for Human Rights, Leo Valladares) constituted, to varying degrees, major steps in the direction of demilitarizing state and society in these countries and subjecting the military to civilian control (Chapters 1–3).[79]

In addition to the problems of truth and justice, the question of the historical memory of repression is central to the process of building democratic institutions.[80] Societal conflicts over the construction of historical memory have profound implications for moral accountability and the constitution of political identities.[81] As Western Europe had to face the legacy of World War II, new democracies in Latin America, southern and post-Communist Europe, and South Africa have had to confront their legacy of repression as they attempted to preserve, and deepen, their democratic present.[82] As in other democratizing polities, Central American societies have been confronted with the question "how the collective 'we' that remembers the past is constituted—who belongs, who is left out, and how to incorporate new generations."[83] There are various consequences of these societal struggles for democratization. For instance, whether or not communities recognize themselves as sharing a political identity with the perpetrators has important implications for establishing society's moral responsibility for past atrocities.[84] This point is particularly important in El Salvador and Guatemala where both the armed forces and the guerrillas bore responsibility (though heavily concentrated in the former) for human rights violations. For example, the historic memory project launched by Guatemala's Catholic bishops in 1994 (Interdiocesan Project for the Recuperation of Historical Memory [Recuperación de Memoria Histórica Interdiocesana, REMHI]) helped to link memory, identity, and moral accountability by allowing people (both victims and perpetrators) to talk about the past.[85] Even where the level of repression was comparatively moderate, as it was the case of Honduras, the question of historical memory was important at the end of the 1990s mainly because the middle classes had accepted government-sponsored repression as "a necessary evil" to combat communism. (In Chapter 3 this phenomenon was also found in Guatemala and El Salvador, where acceptance of state terror came not only from the middle class but also from other sectors of the population, both urban and rural.) Therefore, the creation of moral accountability becomes a complex problem in the efforts to democratize civil and political societies.

The dead and "disappeared" also constitute a central legacy of state-sponsored violence in Central America.[86] Guatemala offers the most tragic illustration of this inheritance. According to the CEH, over two hundred thousand people were either killed or "disappeared" during the thirty-six-year armed conflict in this country (Chapter 1).[87] Compared with other cases of state terrorism in modern Latin America, for each victim (either killed or disappeared) in Argentina's dirty war (1976–1983) there were ten victims in Guatemala; for each death or "disappearance" in Chile under the Pinochet regime (1973–1990) there were sixty Guatemalan victims. The CEH concluded that the Guatemalan state—acting primarily through the army—was responsible for 93 percent of all cases of human rights violations and acts of violence registered by the commission. Eighty-three percent of those victims were Mayans.[88] These data show that the fabric of Guatemala's society was dramatically altered by state terrorism. The far-reaching effects of repression on society resulted not only in extreme psychological trauma suffered by victims and relatives of victims but also in consequential changes in some fundamental features of Guatemala's political landscape such as voting patterns and interest group representation. The impact of state repression on the indigenous population deepened Guatemala's ethnic cleavages, making this a very complex case of democratization as the country attempted to build a multiethnic democracy in the late 1990s.[89]

Memories of Violence

As in other societies, Central America's political violence left profound psychological marks on individuals and communities.[90] In cases of protracted and highly violent insurrectionary processes, memories of political violence could have lasting effects on citizens' political attitudes. What kind of effects are these? And how long do they last? These are important questions especially for Nicaragua, El Salvador, and Guatemala. Whereas it is still too early to answer them, research on other cases can indicate possible trends in these countries. In a study of memories of the revolution in Mexico, Linda Stevenson and Mitchell Seligson argue that in cases of prolonged and extremely violent revolutions (for example, Mexico, Russia, and China) the tremendous amount of violence had such a strong imprint on masses and elites that "the fear of revisiting that violence has been a major constraint on violent political actions."[91] Thus, they conclude, political violence in Mexico contributed to sustaining long-term political stability.

If the main effect of political violence on political culture is a mass preference for stability, then one wants to know whether and when such impact fades, making a country vulnerable to revolution again—if the appropriate conditions are present. Stevenson and Seligson's argument is that "as time passes and the memories of the revolution fade, the degree of fear declines and more people become willing to take political actions that older generations would not have taken previously."[92] They view the 1994 Zapatista rebellion in Chiapas as confirmation of this hypothesis in Mexico. Did the memories of revolution in Central America at the end of the twentieth century guarantee political stability in the decades to come? To what extent did these memories provide a buffer against renewed social unrest? The variable of violence, then, could have considerable influence in processes of democratization. Cross-nationally, it could help explain variations in the nature of democracy as one contrasts democratic regimes emerged out of violent transitions with those that resulted from peaceful ones. Transnationally, the question of memories of revolution needs to be treated in the context of global trends that influence the domestic order of states, specifically the trend toward "a permanent and violent movement society" in the late twentieth century.[93]

Revolutionary Legacies

The legacy of radical popular mobilization is also a critical element in assessing the impact of the past on Central America's processes of democratization. The revolutionary legacy in this region could be found in the multiplicity of civil society organizations promoting the interests of women, peasants, indigenous peoples, students, and other social groups.[94] Despite having suffered extreme levels of state-sponsored repression, civic organizations in the 1990s built on their experience in confronting the state as they developed new forms of collective action under democratic politics. As argued in Chapter 1, this volume, in reference to Guatemala, the reemergence and gradual strengthening of social movements in this county from the mid 1980s onward showed the resilience of the popular sectors and their capacity to establish broad alliances that creatively combined a new rights-based discourse with a more traditional set of demands centered on distributional goals.

Civil society's efforts to advance democratization in Guatemala were not limited to these movements. Various sectors of civil society, including business, labor, and popular organizations, came together in response to Serrano's attempted coup in 1993 and successfully mobilized to protect the constitutional order. These groups, with fundamentally different political and ideological agendas, converged in a common attempt to preserve democratic rule in Guatemala. The role of civic organizations was also important in the peace process through their participation in the Assembly of Civil Society.[95]

Regime change in Central America involved a significant level of grassroots participation (see the Introduction to this volume). Democratization in Nicaragua, and to a lesser extent in El Salvador and Guatemala, was

brought about by "transitions from below." Compared to other revolutionary models in Latin America, insurgencies in these countries gave a central
role to mass organizations. In the case of Nicaragua, popular mobilization
and organization continued after the defeat of the Sandinistas in 1990. Moreover, grassroots organizations created during the Sandinista period evolved
into vibrant actors representing the interests of peasants, urban workers,
and other "popular sectors" in the 1990s. In contrast, the legitimacy and
representativeness of the Sandinista leadership were seriously weakened as
a result of factionalism, corruption, and personal scandals. In brief, the democratic legacy of the revolution lay not just in the formal democratic institutions created in the 1980s but also in this vital sector of Nicaragua's civil
society (Chapter 4).[96]

Transnational Movements

A key dilemma for Central America's civil society organizations in the late
1990s was to find an autonomous space where their demands could be advanced to the political arena. The expectation that civil society could provide the foundation for the creation of "participatory democracy on an
institutional framework of political democracy" had to take into consideration civil society's limited power in relation to the state.[97] On one hand, the
state monopolizes the allocation of economic resources and, thus, remains
the absolute center of decision making. On the other hand, state institutions
shape civic capacity because they affect, through legal and bureaucratic
means, the context in which associational life takes place.[98] However, at the
close of the twentieth century, state power was increasingly challenged by
social movements that became inherently transnational.[99] Therefore, an interesting question is whether the legacy of mass mobilization in Central
America can contribute to alternatives to the model of state "modernization
via internationalization." This contribution may take place as local and regional organizational efforts become part of nonterritorial movements with
the capacity to produce transnational collective action that affects both global and nation-specific policies. As Sidney Tarrow argues, "If movements
are becoming transnational, they may be freeing themselves of state structures and thence of the constraining influence of state-mediated contention."[100] This trend would help create a very different scenario for collective
action than the one that dominated the revolutionary struggles of the 1970s
and 1980s.

The recent global growth of transnational networks at the grassroots
(or "globalization from below")[101] has been a phenomenon associated with
the emergence of an interdependent world economic order, the internaliza-
tion of rich countries' social patterns (for example, consumerist individualism) by poor countries, and the recent wave of migration toward advanced

industrial nations.[102] These trends bore utmost importance for Central America in the 1990s. We have already made reference to the first two, so let us comment on the latter. The most recent wave of migration in Central America resulted in the departure of more than 1.3 million of Salvadoreans, Nicaraguans, and Guatemalans to the United States in the 1980s. This phenomenon surfaced as a central issue for these countries, as "the outflow of Central Americans engendered an inflow of family remittances equal to or even larger than exports earnings" (Chapter 10).[103] As noted in Chapter 2, this volume, more than a quarter of the Salvadoran population depended on foreign remittances in the late 1990s. The region's enormous reliance on inflows of income from migrants meant not only economic dependence on foreign funds but also an increasing political influence of a mass of migrants who remained connected to their homeland. This phenomenon was, indeed, part of one that was global. "The Filipino maid in Milan and the Tamil busdriver in Toronto," the Salvadoran storekeeper in Los Angeles and the Guatemalan nurse in Chicago belonged to a stream of migrants who " 'are only a few sky hours away' from their homeland and seconds away by satellite telephone communication."[104] In brief, any discussion of civil and political involvement at the local level in Central America would have to incorporate the impact of communities living abroad. In addition, as the case of El Salvador's dependence on foreign remittances shows, U.S. immigration policies had a tremendous bearing on that country's socioeconomic stability at the end of the 1990s (Chapter 7).

One of the most interesting developments in terms of transnational collective action in Central America was the gradual emergence of cross-border networks of peasant associations in the early 1990s. This movement advanced "a peasant political practice directed simultaneously at particular nation-states and the supranational institutions to which states now belong."[105] The stock of forms of action employed by the region's main peasant organization, the Central American Association of Peasant Organizations for Cooperation and Development (Asociación Centroamericana de Organizaciones Campesinas para la Cooperación y el Desarrollo, ASOCODE), represented a fundamental departure from the old tradition of agrarian mobilization and contestation. Not only were peasant leaders using a radically different repertoire—built upon a long-standing experience of demand making—but also they were addressing policy makers at the local and national levels as well as at the World Bank, the International Monetary Fund, and the European Union. As Marc Edelman explains, "Campesino involvement in lobbying, establishing international networks, building alliances with nonagricultural sector groups, and elaborating detailed and sophisticated development proposals marks a new stage in a social movement that is both very old and very new."[106] Thus, the influence of radical popular mobilization can take new forms as social movements adapt to new repertoires of collective action in response to structural changes in states and the global capitalist system.[107]

Civil Society

At the nation-specific level, the role of civil society in democratization is much more complex than many students of citizen participation had anticipated. In their study of civil society in Central America, Patricia Bayer Richard and John Booth (Chapter 11) found that civil society is largely dependent on the specific political context and that, in particular, state-sponsored repression discourages citizens' political participation and decreases the production of political capital, a major asset to democratization. This issue clearly is critical in post-authoritarian Central America. Even though the level of regime repression of the 1980s was nowhere to be found in the region in the late 1990s, the question was to what extent the new political democracies guaranteed an environment in which freedom from repression, that is, the implementation of the rule of law, allowed people readily to engage in civic activities. A series of disturbing events, including the assassination of Bishop Juan Gerardi in Guatemala and the increasing manipulation by governments of fears of crime to expand the state's coercive activity, did not help build a democratic rule of law that would encourage widespread civic participation.[108]

Richard and Booth also show in Chapter 11 that it is important to distinguish between different types of civil society organizations because they diverge in their actions and democratic values. For instance, they found that communal civil society activity (for example, working-class participation in grassroots development associations) was correlated with alienation from elections, support for using violence to force a change of regime, and justification for coups. At the same time they found that some middle- and upper-class groups were willing to support the curtailment of civil liberties and encourage government repression to prevent radical political change. Notably, through the study of civil society, Richard and Booth reveal that the social and attitudinal cleavages underlying the civil wars of the 1980s still permeated Central America's associational context in the late 1990s.

Concluding Remarks

"The theoretical paradigms that have dominated the study of Latin American politics for the past two decades . . . fail to provide a framework for understanding the political transformations of the region. Nearly all of them," Karen Remmer argues, "including corporatism, bureaucratic authoritarianism, political culture, and dependency, were constructed around the problem of explaining authoritarianism, not democracy."[109] The study of democracy in Central America, then, needs to be constructed around a set of concepts that can explain not only transitions from authoritarianism to democracy but, most important, how democratic institutions work and endure. It means understanding, for instance, how they procure economic growth while guaranteeing respect for the rule of law and how they manage to "absorb diversity and dampen the potential for conflict that diversity arouses" while having the capacity to formulate and sustain policies.[110] In addition to the various analytical perspectives offered by the authors in this book, two interrelated issues emerge as critical for the understanding of democracy: the questions of governance and order.

The problem of developing both effective and democratic governance is at the heart of democratization in the countries examined in this volume. In particular, we need to note that the neoliberal strategy has shown that market rationality cannot replace the political construction of democratic institutions. In other words, democratic governance cannot be reduced to economic efficiency.[111]

Effective and democratic governance requires more than the political will of domestic leaders. For instance, the enormous influence of U.S. policy in Central America seriously constrained the capacity of elected governments to formulate and sustain policies. U.S. foreign policy decisions therefore had a major impact on the ability of governments to generate the power capacity needed to weather economic crises and create wealth while remaining accountable to their electorates and democratizing state-society relations.[112]

Democratization in Central America was also, as of this writing, intimately linked to the problem of order. As in most of Latin America, the question of order in these countries has not been addressed as a *political* problem, that is, "as a collective and inherently conflictual undertaking," but has been resolved through the use of force and autocratic rule.[113] In this context the construction of order was based not on pluralism but on "the negation of the other," which implied the destruction of what was perceived as alien—indigenous peoples, peasants, "communists," urban squatters, and workers.[114]

Whether elected governments could generate and sustain sovereign policies and whether the demand for order could be reformulated as a political problem requiring pluralist institutional arrangements remained key questions for Central America. While representing a significant improvement from the past, the new "democracies" in the region approximated "hybrids" that combined democratic and authoritarian features.[115] In this sense democratic transitions in Central America followed some of the patterns found in their South American counterparts.[116] The evolution and interplay of transnational, international, and domestic forces (that is, ruling elites and civil society)—as well as the long-term impact of the legacies of authoritarianism and revolution—would determine the potential democratization of these polities in the twenty-first century.

Notes

1. For the purposes of this discussion, the term "Central America" refers to the following countries: Guatemala, El Salvador, Honduras, Nicaragua, Costa Rica, and Panama. See the discussion about this choice in the introduction to this volume.

2. Karen L. Remmer, "Democratization in Latin America," in Robert O. Slater, Barry M. Schutz, and Steven R. Dorr, eds., *Global Transformation and the Third World* (Boulder, CO: Lynne Rienner, 1993), 92–95.

3. Ibid., 95, 107.

4. U.S. economic assistance to Central America reached $1.2 billion in 1985, decreasing dramatically to less than $170 million in 1998. William M. LeoGrande, *Our Own Backyard: The United States in Central America, 1977–1992* (Chapel Hill: University of North Carolina Press, 1998), 584–85. See Center for International Policy, *http://www.us.net/cip/milexp.htm* (accessed November 4, 1998).

5. Under the Clinton administration, the United States began to promote a foreign policy toward Central America that seemed to support democratization beyond elections. However, it was still too early as of this writing to assess definite changes in U.S. policy toward this region.

6. Exceptions to this trend include, in addition to the literature cited in this chapter, Cynthia J. Arnson, ed., *Comparative Peace Processes in Latin America* (Washington, DC, and Stanford: Woodrow Wilson Center Press and Stanford University Press, 1999); Jorge I. Domínguez and Marc Lindenberg, eds., *Democratic Transitions in Central America* (Gainesville: University Press of Florida, 1997); Jorge I. Domínguez and Abraham F. Lowenthal, *Constructing Democratic Governance: Mexico, Central America, and the Caribbean in the 1990s* (Baltimore: Johns Hopkins University Press, 1996); Louis W. Goodman et al., eds., *Political Parties and Democracy in Central America* (Boulder, CO: Westview Press, 1992); Jeffery M. Paige, *Coffee and Power: Revolution and the Rise of Democracy in Central America* (Cambridge, MA: Harvard University Press, 1997); Mitchell A. Seligson and John A. Booth, eds., *Elections and Democracy in Central America, Revisited* (Chapel Hill: University of North Carolina Press, 1995); Richard Stahler-Sholk, "El Salvador's Negotiated Transition: From Low-Intensity Conflict to Low-Intensity Democracy," *Journal of Interamerican Studies and World Affairs* 36, no. 4 (Winter 1994): 1–59; Deborah J. Yashar, *Deepening Democracy: Reform and Reaction in Costa Rica and Guatemala, 1870s–1950s* (Stanford: Stanford University Press, 1997). See also the special issue of *Latin American Perspectives* 26, no. 2 (March 1999) on the legacy of Central America's revolutionary struggle.

7. Karen L. Remmer, "Theoretical Decay and Theoretical Development: The Resurgence of Institutional Analysis," *World Politics* 50, no. 1 (1997): 42.

8. Ibid., 52–55.

9. Peter H. Smith, *Talons of the Eagle: Dynamics of U.S.–Latin American Relations* (New York: Oxford University Press, 1996), 5.

10. Remmer, "Theoretical Decay and Theoretical Development," 55.

11. Adam Przeworski, "The Neoliberal Fallacy," in Larry Diamond and Marc F. Plattner, eds., *Capitalism, Socialism, and Democracy Revisited* (Baltimore: Johns Hopkins University Press, 1993), 48–49.

12. Ibid., 50.

13. See Terry Lynn Karl, "The Hybrid Regimes of Central America," *Journal of Democracy* 6, no. 3 (1995): 84.

14. Remmer, "Democratization in Latin America," 105.

15. Ibid., 104–5. It is important to point out that turmoil in Central America never posed a real threat to U.S. national security, despite the Reagan administration's claims to the contrary.

16. William I. Robinson, *Promoting Polyarchy: Globalization, US Intervention, and Hegemony* (Cambridge, England: Cambridge University Press, 1996), 49, 57–58.

17. Ibid., 68.

18. Ibid., 55. See also William I. Robinson, "Nicaragua and the World: A Globalization Perspective," in Thomas W. Walker, ed., *Nicaragua without Illusions* (Wilmington, DE: Scholarly Resources, 1997).

19. Adam Przeworski, "The 'East' Becomes the 'South'? The 'Autumn of the People' and the Future of Eastern Europe," *PS: Political Science and Politics* (March 1991): 21. See Jorge I. Domínguez, *Democratic Policies in Latin America and the Caribbean* (Baltimore: Johns Hopkins University Press, 1998), 42.

20. Samuel P. Huntington, *The Third Wave: Democratization in the Late Twentieth Century* (Norman: University of Oklahoma Press, 1991), 16–19.

21. Ibid., 18.

22. John A. Booth and Thomas W. Walker, *Understanding Central America* (Boulder, CO: Westview Press, 1999), 33.

23. National Security Council memorandum, as quoted in Smith, *Talons of the Eagle*, 126, see also 123–25.

24. The obvious exception was the case of Cuba in 1959, though the United States soon reacted against the revolutionary regime.

25. In Chapter 6, this volume, Steve Ropp argues that, throughout the twentieth century, the United States had tried, intermittently, to impose liberal democracy in Panama only to face resistance from its leadership. In his view, the United States failed to inculcate its political values to Panamanian elites and eventually needed to impose electoral democracy in Panama by force.

26. Robinson, *Promoting Polyarchy*, 57.

27. Przeworski, "The Neoliberal Fallacy," 49–50.

28. Kurt von Mettenheim and James Malloy, "Introduction," in Kurt von Mettenheim and James Malloy, eds., *Deepening Democracy in Latin America* (Pittsburgh: University of Pittsburgh Press, 1998), 11; Carlos M. Vilas, "Participation, Inequality, and the Whereabouts of Democracy," in Douglas A. Chalmers et al., eds., *The New Politics of Inequality in Latin America: Rethinking Participation and Representation* (New York: Oxford University Press, 1997), 29; Przeworski, "The Neoliberal Fallacy," 50.

29. von Mettenheim and Malloy, "Introduction," 11.

30. Remmer, "Democratization in Latin America," 106.

31. Ibid., 106–7; Przeworski, "The Neoliberal Fallacy," 50.

32. Karl, "The Hybrid Regimes of Central America," 78–79; Carlos M. Vilas, "Prospects for Democratization in a Post-Revolutionary Setting: Central America," *Journal of Latin American Studies* 28, no. 2 (May 1996): 465–67.

33. Karl, "The Hybrid Regimes of Central America," 78–79.

34. Vilas, "Prospects for Democratization," 469 (table 1); José Antonio Mejía and Rob Vos, "Poverty in Latin America and the Caribbean: An Inventory, 1980–95" (Inter-American Development Bank, INDES working paper, 1997), 44, *http://www.iadb.org/indes/english/An%20Inventory.pdf* (accessed June 21, 1999).

35. Vilas, "Prospects for Democratization," 469 (table 1).

36. World Bank, *World Development Report* (New York: Oxford University Press, 1989, 1990, 1991, 1994, 1998); Vilas, "Prospects for Democratization," 470–71 (table 2).

37. United Nations Economic Commission for Latin America and the Caribbean, *Statistical Yearbook for Latin America and the Carribbean* (Santiago, Chile: ECLAC, various years); Inter-American Development Bank, *http://www.iadb.orglint/sta/ENGLISH/paxnetlab/b2alhtm* (accessed November 4, 1998).

38. World Bank, *World Development Indicators 1998, http://www.worldbank.org/data/countrydata/aag* (accessed November 4, 1998).

39. World Bank, *World Development Report 1991*, 49.

40. Adam Przeworski, Michael Alvarez, José Antonio Cheibub, and Fernando Limongi, "What Makes Democracy Endure?" in Larry Diamond, Marc F. Plattner, Yun-han Chu, and Hung-mao Tien, eds., *Consolidating the Third Wave Democracies: Themes and Perspectives* (Baltimore: Johns Hopkins University Press, 1997), 305–6. See also Christian Welzel and Ronald Inglehart, "Analyzing Democratic Change and Stability: A Human Development Theory of Democracy" (paper presented at the annual meeting of the Midwest Political Science Association, Chicago, April 15–17, 1999).

41. Przeworski et al., "What Makes Democracy Endure?"

42. Ibid., 306; Bert A. Rockman, "Institutions, Democratic Stability, and Performance," in Metin Hopper, Ali Kazancigil, and Bert Rockman, eds., *Institutions and Democratic Statecraft* (Boulder, CO: Westview Press, 1997), 18–19.

43. Edward N. Muller and Mitchell A. Seligson, "Civic Culture and Democracy: The Question of Causal Relations," *American Political Science Review* 88, no. 3 (September 1994): 635–52.

44. Guillermo O'Donnell, "Polyarchies and the (Un)Rule of Law in Latin America: A Partial Conclusion," in Juan E. Méndez, Guillermo O'Donnell, and Paulo Sérgio Pinheiro, eds., *The (Un)Rule of Law and the Underprivileged in Latin America* (South Bend, IN: University of Notre Dame Press, 1999), 322–23.

45. Guillermo O'Donnell, *Counterpoints: Selected Essays on Authoritarianism and Democratization* (South Bend, IN: University of Notre Dame Press, 1999), 203–5; Vilas, "Participation, Inequality, and the Whereabouts of Democracy," 21–26; Vilas, "Prospects for Democratization," 468.

46. O'Donnell, *Counterpoints*, 205; Guillermo O'Donnell, "The Browning of Latin America," *New Perspectives Quarterly* 10, no. 4 (Fall 1993): 50–54.

47. Mejía and Vos, "Poverty in Latin America and the Caribbean," 42.

48. However, governments did not implement policies conducive to redistribution. To the contrary, as it happened in Honduras, recent financial reforms—such as the regressive tax reform launched by the Flores administration—would likely contribute to worsening income distribution (Chapter 3, this volume). See also Chapters 2 and 10, this volume.

49. World Bank, *World Development Report 1991*, 137 (fig. 72). See O'Donnell, *Counterpoints*, 210, n. 16.

50. Mejía and Vos, "Poverty in Latin America and the Caribbean," 41.

51. Przeworski et al., "What Makes Democracy Endure?" 305.

52. Ibid.; United Nations Economic Commission for Latin America and the Caribbean, *Statistical Yearbook for Latin America and the Caribbean*, various years; Inter-American Development Bank, *http://www.iadb.org/int/sta/ENGLISH/ipaxnet/ab/b2a/htm* (accessed November 4, 1998).

53. See, for instance, Joseph Collins, *Nicaragua: What Difference Could a Revolution Make?* (San Francisco: Food First, 1985), 264; Harry E. Vanden and

Thomas W. Walker, "The Reimposition of U.S. Hegemony over Nicaragua," in Kenneth M. Coleman and George C. Herring, eds., *Understanding the Central American Crisis: Sources of Conflict, U.S. Policy, and Options for Peace* (Wilmington DE: Scholarly Resources, 1991), 166–69; Alexander Segovia, "The War Economy in the 1980s," in James K. Boyce, ed., *Economic Policy for Building Peace: The Lessons of El Salvador* (Boulder, CO: Lynne Rienner, 1996), 31–37.

54. Przeworski, "The Neoliberal Fallacy," 49.

55. Vilas, "Prospects for Democratization," 465–66.

56. Shahid Javed Burki and Guillermo E. Perry, *Beyond the Washington Consensus: Institutions Matter* (Washington, DC: World Bank, 1998), 1–2.

57. Burki and Perry, *Beyond the Washington Consensus*, 3 (italics in original). See Manuel Pastor Jr. and Carol Wise, "The Politics of Second-Generation Reform," *Journal of Democracy* 10, no. 3 (1999): 34–48. It is important to point out that international lenders conditioned new loans to the implementation of public-sector reforms in Central America (Chapter 10, this volume).

58. Burki and Perry, *Beyond the Washington Consensus*, 5–6, 26–36.

59. Rockman, "Institutions, Democratic Stability, and Performance," 25.

60. Welzel and Inglehart, "Analyzing Democratic Change and Stability," 15–16, 22–24; Phillippe C. Schmitter and Terry Lynn Karl, "What Democracy Is . . . and Is Not," *Journal of Democracy* 2, no. 2 (Summer 1991): 82–83.

61. Rockman, "Institutions, Democratic Stability, and Performance," 21.

62. See Booth and Walker, *Understanding Central America*, 57–58.

63. See Philip J. Williams, "Dual Transitions from Authoritarian Rule: Popular and Electoral Democracy in Nicaragua," *Comparative Politics* 26, no. 2 (January 1994): 169–85.

64. See Domínguez, *Democratic Policies*, 37–39.

65. Huntington, *The Third Wave*, 207, as quoted in Domínguez, *Democratic Policies*, 39–40.

66. Ariel C. Armony, "The Former Contras," in Walker, *Nicaragua without Illusions*, 204–10.

67. Remmer, "Democratization in Latin America," 107.

68. Przeworski et al., "What Makes Democracy Endure?" 300.

69. Booth and Walker, *Understanding Central America*, 46–50. See Carlos Figueroa Ibarra, *El recurso del miedo: Ensayo sobre el Estado y el terror en Guatemala* (San José, Costa Rica: Editorial Universitaria Centroamericana, 1991); Susanne Jonas, *The Battle for Guatemala: Rebels, Death Squads, and U.S. Power* (Boulder, CO: Westview Press, 1991); Ricardo Falla, *Massacres in the Jungle: Ixcán, Guatemala, 1975–1982* (Boulder, CO: Westview Press, 1994).

70. Interestingly, Chapter 1, this volume, notes that the failed "Serranazo" contributed to reduce the legitimacy and power of the Guatemalan army and to strengthen civil society.

71. One notorious exemption was Guatemala's former dictator Efraín Ríos Montt.

72. As measured by Transparency International's 1998 Corruption Perceptions Index, the extent of corruption among public officials and politicians in Central America (with the exception of Costa Rica) was very high. Among these countries, Honduras stood out as one of the most corrupt countries in Transparency's survey of 85 countries worldwide. As of this writing, Panama was not included in this index. Transparency International, *http://www.transparency.de/documents/cpi/index.html* (accessed July 8, 1999).

73. See Guillermo O'Donnell, "Illusions about Consolidation," *Journal of Democracy* 7, no. 2 (April 1996): 34–51.

74. Mitchell A. Seligson, "Democratic Values in Nicaragua, 1991–1997," report to USAID/Nicaragua (Pittsburgh, 1997), chap. 2. See John A. Booth, *Costa Rica: Quest for Democracy* (Boulder, CO: Westview Press, 1998), 137–38.

75. Public opinion data collected in the 1990s revealed this trend. See, for instance, Marta Lagos, "Public Opinion in New Democracies: Latin America's Smiling Mask," *Journal of Democracy* 8, no. 3 (July 1997): 132–37. Based on their field experience and direct knowledge of Central America, the authors of chapters 1–6, this volume, observed a similar trend.

76. William A. Barnes, "Incomplete Democracy in Central America: Polarization and Voter Turnout in Nicaragua and El Salvador," *Journal of Interamerican Studies and World Affairs* 40, no. 3 (Fall 1998): 63–101.

77. Ibid., 69.

78. Laura Nuzzi O'Shaughnessy and Michael Dodson, "Political Bargaining and Democratic Transitions: A Comparison of Nicaragua and El Salvador," *Journal of Latin American Studies* 31 (February 1999): 107.

79. Ibid., 99–111.

80. Elizabeth Jelin, "The Minefields of Memory," *NACLA Report on the Americas* 32, no. 2 (September–October 1998): 23–29.

81. W. James Booth, "Communities of Memory: On Identity, Memory, and Debt," *American Political Science Review* 93, no. 2 (June 1999): 249.

82. Ibid., 254.

83. Jelin, "The Minefields of Memory," 25.

84. Booth, "Communities of Memory," 150.

85. Paul Jeffrey, "Guatemala Catholics Find the Path to a New Future," *National Catholic Reporter* 34, no. 15, February 13, 1998, 3–4. The deep political impact of the Guatemalan Catholic Church's effort to create a public record of state-sponsored violence was evidenced by the assassination of Bishop Juan Girardi immediately after the release of REMHI's report (see Chapter 9, this volume).

86. Armed conflict in Central America also caused the displacement or exile of vast sectors of the population. For instance, the UN High Commissioner for Refugees and the UN Development Program helped 1.9 million people in Central America, including refugees, returnees, internally displaced population, and individuals without proper documentation. See *http://www.unhcr.ch/world/amer/camerica.htm* (accessed July 1, 1999).

87. Comisión para el Esclarecimiento Histórico (CEH), *Guatemala: Memoria del Silencio, http://hrdataaaas.org/ceh/mds/spanish/* (accessed July 1, 1999). See also "Counting the Toll of State Terrorism," *Latin America Weekly Report*, June 8, 1995, 249. Other accounts estimated that the number of victims (killed or disappeared) in Guatemala's civil war was between 100,000 and 150,000.

88. CEH, *http://hrdataaaas.org/ceh/mds/spanish/*. On the continued legacy of the military project in Guatemala, see Jennifer Schirmer, "The Guatemalan Politico-Military Project: Legacies for a Violent Peace?" *Latin American Perspectives* 26, no. 2 (March 1999): 92–107.

89. The May 1999 referendum, which would have approved major constitutional reforms agreed in the peace accords, was a notable example of the difficulties involved in Guatemala's democratization process.

90. For an excellent analysis of the individual and societal effects of political violence—limited to cases of state terror—see the essays in Juan E. Corradi, Patricia Weiss Fagen, and Manuel Antonio Garretón, eds., *Fear at the Edge: State Terror and Resistance in Latin America* (Berkeley: University of California Press, 1992).

91. Linda S. Stevenson and Mitchell A. Seligson, "Fading Memories of the Revolution: Is Stability Eroding in Mexico?" in Roderic Ai Camp, ed., *Polling for*

Democracy: Public Opinion and Political Liberalization in Mexico (Wilmington, DE: Scholarly Resources, 1996), 60.

92. Ibid., 60–61.

93. Sidney Tarrow, *Power in Movement: Social Movements, Collective Action and Politics* (Cambridge, England: Cambridge University Press, 1994), 197–98.

94. Richard Stahler-Sholk, "Central America: A Few Steps Backwards, a Few Steps Forward," *Latin American Perspectives* 26, no. 2 (March 1999): 5. See, for instance, Kay B. Warren, "Indigenous Movements as a Challenge to the Unified Social Movement Paradigm for Guatemala," in Sonia E. Alvarez, Evelina Dagnino, and Arturo Escobar, eds., *Cultures of Politics, Politics of Cultures: Re-visioning Latin American Social Movements* (Boulder, CO: Westview Press, 1998); Erica Polakoff and Pierre La Remée, "Grass-Roots Organizations," in Walker, *Nicaragua without Illusions*.

95. Dinorah Azpuru, "Peace and Democratization in Guatemala: Two Parallel Processes," in Arnson, *Comparative Peace Processes*, 97–122.

96. Polakoff and La Remée, "Grass-Roots Organizations," 185–99.

97. Stahler-Sholk, "Central America: A Few Steps Backwards," 10.

98. John A. Booth and Patricia Bayer Richard, "Civil Society and Political Context in Central America," *American Behavioral Scientist* 42, no. 1 (September 1998): 33–47; Booth and Richard, "Repression, Participation, and Democratic Norms in Urban Central America," *American Journal of Political Science* 40, no. 4 (November 1996): 1205–32; Iris M. Young, "State, Civil Society, and Social Justice," in Ian Shapiro and Casiano Hacker-Cordón, eds., *Democracy's Value* (Cambridge, England: Cambridge University Press, 1999).

99. A parallel development promoted by some governments in the region was the attempt to decentralize the state's decision-making process.

100. Tarrow, *Power in Movement*, 196.

101. Marc Edelman, "Transnational Peasant Politics in Central America," *Latin American Research Review* 33, no. 3 (1998): 77. On the phenomenon of transnational "advocacy networks," see Margaret E. Keck and Kathryn Sikkink, *Activists beyond Borders: Advocacy Networks in International Politics* (Ithaca, NY: Cornell University Press, 1998).

102. Tarrow, *Power in Movement*, 195–98.

103. Vilas, "Prospects for Democratization," 472–74.

104. Benedict Anderson, "Long-Distance Nationalism: World Capitalism and the Rise of Identity Politics" (Amsterdam: Center for Asian Studies, 1992), 8, as quoted in Tarrow, *Power in Movement*, 196.

105. Edelman, "Transnational Peasant Politics," 49, 66–69, 75.

106. Ibid., 77.

107. Stahler-Sholk, "Central America: A Few Steps Backwards," 5–6; Tarrow, *Power in Movement*, chap. 2.

108. On the rule of law in Latin America, see O'Donnell, *Counterpoints*, 303–26.

109. Remmer, "Democratization in Latin America," 95.

110. Przeworski, "The Neoliberal Fallacy," 48; quotation from Rockman, "Institutions, Democratic Stability, and Performance," 25; Catherine M. Conaghan and James M. Malloy, *Unsettling Statecraft: Democracy and Neoliberalism in the Central Andes* (Pittsburgh: University of Pittsburgh Press, 1994), 215.

111. Norbert Lechner, "The Transformation of Politics," in Felipe Agüero and Jeffrey Stark, eds., *Fault Lines of Democracy in Post-Transition Latin America* (Miami: North-South Center Press at the University of Miami, 1998), 29; Conaghan

and Malloy, *Unsettling Statecraft*, 216; von Mettenheim and Malloy, "Introduction," 2–16.

112. von Mettenheim and Malloy, "Introduction," 5; Remmer, "Theoretical Decay and Theoretical Development," 57; Conaghan and Malloy, *Unsettling Statecraft*, 223–24.

113. Norbert Lechner, "Some People Die of Fear," in Corradi et al., *Fear at the Edge*, 28.

114. Ibid., 28–29.

115. Karl, "The Hybrid Regimes of Central America," 72–74, 80–81.

116. See, for instance, the following essays by Guillermo O'Donnell: "Transitions, Continuities, and Paradoxes," in Scott Mainwaring, Guillermo O'Donnell, and J. Samuel Valenzuela, eds., *Issues in Democratic Consolidation: The New South American Democracies in Comparative Perspective* (South Bend, IN: University of Notre Dame Press, 1992); "On the State, Democratization, and Some Conceptual Problems: A Latin American View with Glances at Some Postcommunist Countries," *World Development* 21, no. 8 (August 1993): 1355–69; and "Delegative Democracy," *Journal of Democracy* 5, no. 1 (January 1994): 55–69.

Index

About the Contributors

SHAWN L. BIRD is a doctoral candidate in political science at the University of Florida. His dissertation examines attempts at constructing local democratic institutions and procedures and norms in postwar El Salvador. With fellowships from the U.S. Institute of Peace and the Inter-American Foundation, Bird has done extensive research in Central America in 1994, 1996, and 1998–99. He holds an M.A. from the University of Colorado.

JOHN A. BOOTH is Regents Professor of Political Science at the University of North Texas. He is the author of *The End and the Beginning: The Nicaraguan Revolution* (1982, 1985) and *Costa Rica: Quest for Democracy* (1998), coauthor (with Thomas W. Walker) of *Understanding Central America* (1989, 1992, 1999), and coeditor (with Mitchell A. Seligson) of *Elections and Democracy in Central America* (1989, 1995). He has published articles and chapters on revolution, political participation and culture, and democratization in various journals and anthologies. He holds a B.A. from Rice University and an M.A. and Ph.D. from the University of Texas at Austin.

JACK CHILD is professor of Spanish and Latin American studies at American University, Washington, DC. Previously, he had a twenty-year career as a U.S. Army Latin American specialist. He has worked with the International Peace Academy (United Nations) and the U.S. Institute for Peace on issues dealing with conflict resolution and confidence building in Latin America and Antarctica. His publications include *The Central American Process, 1983–1991: Sheathing Swords, Building Confidence* (1992), *Antarctica and South American Geopolitics: Frozen Lebensraum* (1988), and *Quarrels among Neighbors: Geopolitics and Conflict in South America*. Child holds a B.E. from Yale and an M.A. and Ph.D. from American University.

EDWARD L. CLEARY, O.P., is professor of political science and director of Latin American studies at Providence College. A Dominican priest, he has focused his research on religion and politics in Latin America. His first field studies in Central America began in 1981 and quickly expanded from Catholic to Protestant churches and indigenous religion. He has published a number of articles and seven books, most recently *Power, Pentecostals, and Politics* and *The Struggle for Human Rights in Latin America* (both 1997). Cleary holds a Ph.D. from the University of Chicago.

SUSANNE JONAS teaches Latin American and Latino studies at the University of California, Santa Cruz. A specialist on Central America since the late 1960s, she has written numerous books on the region, including *Centaurs and Doves: Guatemala's Peace Process* (2000) and *The Battle for Guatemala: Rebels, Death Squads and U.S. Power* (1991). Her recent coedited books on Latin America include *Immigration: A Civil Rights Issue for the Americas* (1999), *Latin America Faces the Twenty-first Century* (1994), and *Democracy in Latin America* (1990). Jonas holds a B.A. from Radcliffe College/Harvard University, Master's degrees from Harvard University and the Massachusetts Institute of Technology, and a Ph.D. from the University of California, Berkeley.

PATRICIA BAYER RICHARD is dean of the University College, associate provost for undergraduate studies, and professor of political science at Ohio University. She has written extensively about reproductive rights and about democracy, elections, and campaigns. Her work has appeared in such journals as the *American Journal of Political Science*, *Journal of Politics*, *Women's Studies Quarterly*, and *Electoral Studies* as well as edited volumes. She served on electoral observation teams in both the 1990 and the 1996 Nicaraguan general elections. Her current research investigates political participation, support for democratic values, and civil society in Central America. She holds a B.A., M.A., and Ph.D. from Syracuse University.

STEVE C. ROPP is professor of political science at the University of Wyoming in Laramie. He is the author of *Panamanian Politics: From Guarded Nation to National Guard* (1982) and coeditor (with James A. Morris) of *Central America: Crisis and Adaptation* (1984). During the 1990s, Ropp's research expanded to include global human rights issues. One result is an edited book (with Thomas Risse and Kathryn Sikkink), *The Power of Human Rights: International Norms and Domestic Change* (1999). Ropp holds a Ph.D. from the University of California, Riverside.

J. MARK RUHL is Glenn and Mary Todd Professor of Political Science and director of the Latin American studies program at Dickinson College in Carlisle, Pennsylvania. He has written extensively on Latin American politics and specialized in Honduras. He is coauthor (with R. H. McDonald) of *Party Politics and Elections in Latin America* (1989), and his current research focus is on civil-military relations in the region. He holds a Ph.D. from Syracuse University.

RICHARD STAHLER-SHOLK is assistant professor of political science at Eastern Michigan University. He was a research associate at the Regional Coordinating Group for Economic and Social Research (CRIES) in Managua from 1984 to 1989 and taught at the Claremont Colleges in California from

1991 to 1997. He has published a number of articles on political economy and labor in Nicaragua, and on post-conflict transition in El Salvador. He is an associate editor of *Latin American Perspectives*. He holds a B.A. from Brandeis University, and an M.A. and Ph.D. from the University of California, Berkeley.

CARLOS M. VILAS is an Argentine political scientist currently affiliated with the National Institute for Public Administration in Buenos Aires. He lived in Nicaragua from 1980 to 1990 where he was an advisor to several agencies of the Sandinista government. He later taught at the National Autonomous University of Mexico. He is the author of several books, including *The Sandinista Revolution* (1986), which was awarded Cuba's Casa de las Americas prize; *State, Class, and Ethnicity in Nicaragua* (1989); *Socialist Options in Central America* (1993); and *Between Earthquakes and Volcanos: Market, State, and Revolution in Central America* (1995).

PHILIP J. WILLIAMS is associate professor of political science at the University of Florida. He has written extensively on religion and politics and democratic transition in Central America. He is the author of *The Catholic Church and Politics in Nicaragua and Costa Rica* (1989) and coauthor (with Knut Walter) of *Militarization and Demilitarization in El Salvador's Transition to Democracy* (1997). In 1991–92 he was a Fulbright Lecturer at the Jesuit University in San Salvador. Currently he is editing a book on religion and social change in the Americas. Williams holds a B.A. from the University of California, Los Angeles, and an M.Phil. and D.Phil. from the University of Oxford, England.

Latin American Silhouettes
Studies in History and Culture

William H. Beezley and
Judith Ewell
Editors

Volumes Published

Silvia Marina Arrom and Servando Ortoll, eds., *Riots in the Cities: Popular Politics and the Urban Poor in Latin America, 1765–1910* (1996). Cloth ISBN 0-8420-2580-4 Paper ISBN 0-8420-2581-2

Roderic Ai Camp, ed., *Polling for Democracy: Public Opinion and Political Liberalization in Mexico* (1996). ISBN 0-8420-2583-9

Brian Loveman and Thomas M. Davies, Jr., eds., *The Politics of Antipolitics: The Military in Latin America*, 3d ed., revised and updated (1996). Cloth ISBN 0-8420-2609-6 Paper ISBN 0-8420-2611-8

Joseph S. Tulchin, Andrés Serbín, and Rafael Hernández, eds., *Cuba and the Caribbean: Regional Issues and Trends in the Post-Cold War Era* (1997). ISBN 0-8420-2652-5

Thomas W. Walker, ed., *Nicaragua without Illusions: Regime Transition and Structural Adjustment in the 1990s* (1997). Cloth ISBN 0-8420-2578-2 Paper ISBN 0-8420-2579-0

Dianne Walta Hart, *Undocumented in L.A.: An Immigrant's Story* (1997). Cloth ISBN 0-8420-2648-7 Paper ISBN 0-8420-2649-5

Jaime E. Rodríguez O. and Kathryn Vincent, eds., *Myths, Misdeeds, and Misunderstandings: The Roots of Conflict in U.S.-Mexican Relations* (1997). ISBN 0-8420-2662-2

Jaime E. Rodríguez O. and Kathryn Vincent, eds., *Common Border, Uncommon Paths: Race, Culture, and National Identity in U.S.-Mexican Relations* (1997). ISBN 0-8420-2673-8

William H. Beezley and Judith Ewell, eds., *The Human Tradition in Modern Latin America* (1997). Cloth ISBN 0-8420-2612-6 Paper ISBN 0-8420-2613-4

Donald F. Stevens, ed., *Based on a True Story: Latin American History at the Movies* (1997). Cloth ISBN 0-8420-2582-0 Paper ISBN 0-8420-2781-5

Jaime E. Rodríguez O., ed., *The Origins of Mexican National Politics, 1808–1847* (1997). Paper ISBN 0-8420-2723-8

Che Guevara, *Guerrilla Warfare*, with revised and updated introduction and case studies by Brian Loveman and Thomas M. Davies, Jr., 3d ed. (1997). Cloth ISBN 0-8420-2677-0 Paper ISBN 0-8420-2678-9

Adrian A. Bantjes, *As If Jesus Walked on Earth: Cardenismo, Sonora, and the Mexican Revolution* (1998; rev. ed., 2000). Cloth ISBN 0-8420-2653-3 Paper ISBN 0-8420-2751-3

Henry A. Dietz and Gil Shidlo, eds., *Urban Elections in Democratic Latin America* (1998). Cloth ISBN 0-8420-2627-4 Paper ISBN 0-8420-2628-2

A. Kim Clark, *The Redemptive Work: Railway and Nation in Ecuador, 1895–1930* (1998). ISBN 0-8420-2674-6

Joseph S. Tulchin, ed., with Allison M. Garland, *Argentina: The Challenges of Modernization* (1998). ISBN 0-8420-2721-1

Louis A. Pérez, Jr., ed., *Impressions of Cuba in the Nineteenth Century: The Travel Diary of Joseph J. Dimock* (1998). Cloth ISBN 0-8420-2657-6 Paper ISBN 0-8420-2658-4

June E. Hahner, ed., *Women through Women's Eyes: Latin American Women in Nineteenth-Century Travel Accounts* (1998). Cloth ISBN 0-8420-2633-6 Paper ISBN 0-8420-2634-7

James P. Brennan, ed., *Peronism and Argentina* (1998). ISBN 0-8420-2706-8

John Mason Hart, ed., *Border Crossings: Mexican and Mexican-American Workers*

(1998). Cloth ISBN 0-8420-2716-5
Paper ISBN 0-8420-2717-3

Brian Loveman, *For* la Patria: *Politics and the Armed Forces in Latin America* (1999). Cloth ISBN 0-8420-2772-6
Paper ISBN 0-8420-2773-4

Guy P. C. Thomson, with David G. LaFrance, *Patriotism, Politics, and Popular Liberalism in Nineteenth-Century Mexico: Juan Francisco Lucas and the Puebla Sierra* (1999). ISBN 0-8420-2683-5

Robert Woodmansee Herr, in collaboration with Richard Herr, *An American Family in the Mexican Revolution* (1999). ISBN 0-8420-2724-6

Juan Pedro Viqueira Albán, trans. Sonya Lipsett-Rivera and Sergio Rivera Ayala, *Propriety and Permissiveness in Bourbon Mexico* (1999). Cloth ISBN 0-8420-2466-2 Paper ISBN 0-8420-2467-0

Stephen R. Niblo, *Mexico in the 1940s: Modernity, Politics, and Corruption* (1999). ISBN 0-8420-2794-7

David E. Lorey, *The U.S.-Mexican Border in the Twentieth Century* (1999). Cloth ISBN 0-8420-2755-6
Paper ISBN 0-8420-2756-4

Joanne Hershfield and David R. Maciel, eds., *Mexico's Cinema: A Century of Films and Filmmakers* (2000). Cloth ISBN 0-8420-2681-9 Paper ISBN 0-8420-2682-7

Peter V. N. Henderson, *In the Absence of Don Porfirio: Francisco León de la Barra and the Mexican Revolution* (2000). ISBN 0-8420-2774-2

Mark T. Gilderhus, *The Second Century: U.S.-Latin American Relations since 1889* (2000). Cloth ISBN 0-8420-2413-1
Paper ISBN 0-8420-2414-X

Catherine Moses, *Real Life in Castro's Cuba* (2000). Cloth ISBN 0-8420-2836-6
Paper ISBN 0-8420-2837-4

K. Lynn Stoner, ed./comp., with Luis Hipólito Serrano Pérez, *Cuban and Cuban-American Women: An Annotated Bibliography* (2000). ISBN 0-8420-2643-6

Thomas D. Schoonover, *The French in Central America: Culture and Commerce, 1820–1930* (2000). ISBN 0-8420-2792-0

Enrique C. Ochoa, *Feeding Mexico: The Political Uses of Food since 1910* (2000). ISBN 0-8420-2812-9

Thomas W. Walker and Ariel C. Armony, eds., *Repression, Resistance, and Democratic Transition in Central America* (2000). Cloth ISBN 0-8420-2766-1 Paper ISBN 0-8420-2768-8

William H. Beezley and David E. Lorey, eds., *¡Viva México! ¡Viva la Independencia! Celebrations of September 16* (2001). Cloth ISBN 0-8420-2914-1
Paper ISBN 0-8420-2915-X

Jeffrey M. Pilcher, *Cantinflas and the Chaos of Mexican Modernity* (2001). Cloth ISBN 0-8420-2769-6
Paper ISBN 0-8420-2771-8

Victor M. Uribe-Uran, ed., *State and Society in Spanish America during the Age of Revolution* (2001). Cloth ISBN 0-8420-2873-0 Paper ISBN 0-8420-2874-9

Andrew G. Wood, *The Firecracker Wars: Urban Protest in Veracruz, Mexico, 1870–1927* (2001). Cloth ISBN 0-8420-2879-X

Charles Bergquist, Ricardo Peñaranda, and Gonzalo Sánchez G., eds., *Waging War and Negotiating Peace: Violence in Colombia, 1990–2000* (2001). Cloth ISBN 0-8420-2869-2
Paper ISBN 0-8420-2870-6

William Schell, Jr., *Integral Outsiders: The American Colony in Mexico City, 1876–1911* (2001). ISBN 0-8420-2838-2